*Convicts of the Eleanor*

# Convicts of the *Eleanor*

## Protest in Rural England, New Lives in Australia

David Kent and
Norma Townsend

THE MERLIN PRESS
PLUTO PRESS AUSTRALIA

First published 2002 by The Merlin Press Ltd.
PO Box 30705, London WC2E 8QD
ISBN: 0-85036-504-X

Published in Australia by Pluto Press Australia
ISBN: 1-86403-172-7

British Library Cataloguing in Publication Data is available from the British
Library

Printed in Australia by Hyde Park Press

# CONTENTS

# ACKNOWLEDGEMENTS

I gnored by most readers, the acknowledgements page gives authors an opportunity to thank the institutions and individuals who assisted in a book's creation. We thank the University of New England for granting each of us a period of six months study leave without which the research could not have been completed. Research was carried out in the Archives of New South Wales, the Mitchell Library, the Society of Australian Genealogists library, the Hyde Park Barracks, the County Record Offices of Berkshire, Dorset, Hampshire and Wiltshire, and the local studies libraries in Reading, Dorchester, Winchester and Trowbridge. The staff of those institutions invariably provided expert, professional assistance whenever we required it and we thank them for it. Eric Acheson, Alan Atkinson, Paul Hammer, Erin Ihde, Harry Johnston, Andrew Messner and Gloria Obbens read portions of the manuscript at various times and we undoubtedly benefited from their comments and suggestions. Michael Roach, the University Cartographer prepared the maps. Several chapters were first explored as papers presented to our research seminar and we acknowledge the stimulus and interest of our colleagues and postgraduate students. To our undergraduate and postgraduate students who listened to so many of the arguments and anecdotes in this book as they took shape in the course of our teaching, thank you.

We also have debts as individuals. Linda Emery, Perry McIntyre, Alison Vincent, Beverly Zimmerman and especially Cathrine Truscett assisted Norma Townsend with her research while Joan Reece shared her unrivalled grasp of the intricacies of the Colonial Secretary's records. Many keen family historians whose forebears were transported for their involvement in the Swing disturbances responded to notices in the English and Australian press inviting them to share their knowledge and information about their ancestors with Norma Townsend. Bill Batten, Wilbur Besanko, Stella Bond, Robert Brown, Wendy Cowley, Patricia Doughty, Chris Fletcher, Norman Fox, Margaret Hall, David Hatherell, Kim Hatherly, Beryl Hutchinson, Bill Jocelyn, Paula Johnston, Patricia Jones, Kevin Millson, Enid Rees, Laurel Riddle, Tina Russell, Pamela Sheldon, Kevin Sullivan, Ray Sullivan, Hilda Symonds, Robyn White and Maurice Wood offered their help and something of their generosity shows through in Part II. David Kent's research in England, for Part I, was aided immensely by the unstinting hospitality of Nicholas and Barbara Kent who provided, at various times, accommodation, transport, and an environment in which writing was never a chore.

David Kent, Norma Townsend
University of New England, Armidale, N.S.W.

# PREFACE

This book was planned after a research seminar in the School of Classics, History and Religion at the University of New England, Armidale, New South Wales. The discussion which followed a postgraduate's presentation showed that many British historians writing about crime and punishment lost interest in the men and women who were their subjects as soon as they boarded the convict transports. Australian historians writing about the colonial era and the founding population were often as blinkered. At worst they were inclined to write about the men and women who landed in the convict colonies as if they had no previous lives, though more commonly the British and Irish experience was treated summarily and with over-simple generalisation. Driven partly by exasperation and partly by a pedagogic conviction that, at least for the period of transportation, Australian and British history cannot be sensibly separated, we resolved to write a book which reunited the lives divided by exile. How best to do this in a form which was manageable and which could eventually be confined to book length was not easily decided, but we finally settled on the idea of a cohort study using the men carried on a single vessel. We chose the *Eleanor* because its cargo of rural protesters was reasonably homogenous, both socially and geographically, and because it allowed us to ask questions about the trauma of transportation and the qualities a person needed to survive and, perhaps, succeed in New South Wales. It also had the added attraction that it allowed us to pursue our separate interests in popular protest, rural history and the convict system.

The convicts transported to Australia in the early nineteenth century were the best documented section of the British masses. The processes of indictment and trial recorded in British judicial and prison records were supplemented by the meticulously detailed information collected before they departed, on arrival in the colonies and in regular convict musters. The convict indents in particular have been a rich source for Australian historians and in recent years a number of scholars have used the mini-biographies contained in their columns to enlarge our understanding of Australia's founding workforce and the nation's founding mothers and fathers. Rich though the indents are, they have tended to imprison investigations of the convict system. For too long historians have been seduced by the volume and accessibility of the data which, with computer-aided analysis, can be sliced up to reveal the finest gradations of similarity and difference. As a result, the convict population has been carefully defined and categorised but the real challenge now facing historians of convictism and colonial Australia is to recover the lived experience of those men and women both as convicts and later as free citizens. We need to discover how convicts lived and worked under the penal system and how they reconstructed their lives after transportation and servitude. This is neither an easy nor a rapid task for after convicts had served their sentences the state lost interest in them and most assumed once more the anonymity of ordinariness. As so many enthusiastic family historians have discovered, the trails of many convicts grow fainter after their arrival and often disappear with their freedom.

History is always a product, and sometimes a prisoner, of the resources available to the historian. Because of this limitation, the historian working from below faces two problems. The first is the relative scarcity of documentary and material evidence recording the lived experience of ordinary people. The second is that the records which do shed light on their lives were usually created by those with the power to coerce and direct so that the beam is refracted through the prism of authority. Consequently, we see the men of the *Eleanor* most clearly as protesters, as prisoners on trial and as convicts under sentence but as free men they become more shadowy and their lives are less easily recovered. Some disappeared without trace into the Australian past but others are recorded in the registers of marriages, births and deaths. These apparently unpromising and, as yet, largely under-exploited materials are usually the sum total of what is known of men and women in New South Wales after they left the convict system. These are the principal sources used in the later chapters of this book as the colonial lives of the men of the *Eleanor* are recovered and reconstructed.

Some scepticism has surrounded this enterprise from its beginnings. Who, we have been asked, will be reading it? Is it intended for a British or Australian audience? The questions are indicative of the narrow historical focus which has closed around convictism. Our answer is that we hope it will be read in both countries. Parts of the first five chapters, written by David Kent, will be familiar to students of popular protest and the social history of nineteenth century rural Britain but will be largely new to students of colonial New South Wales. Similarly, in the later chapters, written by Norma Townsend, the basic outlines of the convict system and colonial life will be well understood by Australian readers, but details of its workings are not generally known in Britain. In both parts, however, some popular misconceptions are corrected, new insights are offered and a contribution is made to the social history of both countries by reuniting the histories of the men of the *Eleanor*. In his pioneering study, *Convicts and the Colonies,* published over thirty years ago, A.G.L. Shaw suggested that a full understanding of convict society demanded 'detailed investigations…of the districts from which the convicts came, and of those they were sent to'. He noted then that such studies were 'extremely rare' and they have remained so. It is our aim in this book to follow Shaw's advice and descend from the lofty overview to follow the life journey of a small group of men from their poverty-induced protest in Wessex, through the disruption of transportation and servitude to their eventual freedom in a very different but derived culture.

David Kent, Norma Townsend, Armidale, N.S.W., November 2000

# PART ONE

# RUINED LIVES

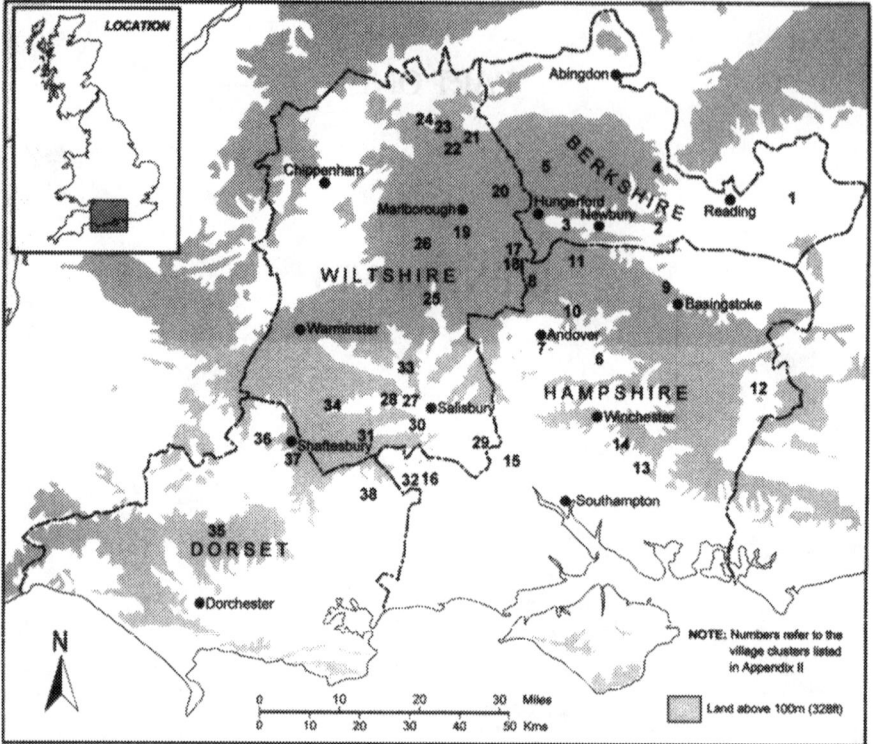

**South-Central England**

# Chapter 1

## 'MEN OF HONEST PRINCIPLE':

## THE CONVICTS OF THE *ELEANOR*

The unhappy human cargo delivered to the convict colony of New South Wales in June 1831 by the *Eleanor* did not deserve such a fate. It is doubtful if any convict transport carried a less criminal body of men nor any who were more unfairly treated. On board were 132 rural labourers and craftsmen from the counties of Wessex – Berkshire, Hampshire, Wiltshire and Dorset – exiled for taking part in protest actions which they had hoped would persuade farmers and landowners to raise wages and preserve employment.[1] In a typical incident a crowd of men visited the farms and substantial houses of their locality to destroy agricultural machines where they found them, secure agreement that wages would rise, usually to two shillings a day, and solicit donations of food, drink and money. Many of these visitations took place in daylight and the confrontations were often between men who knew each other so that the protesters were easily identified for subsequent prosecution. In protesting so openly and with such boldness, the rural protesters displayed an ingenuous self-confidence derived from their belief in the propriety and legitimacy of their behaviour. They placed their trust in direct action which had customarily been an effective means of focusing attention on social grievances and of prompting those in authority to take corrective measures. In the winter of 1830, however, this traditional course met with unusually severe treatment. The widespread nature of the disturbances in southern, central and eastern England alarmed a landowning, ruling class whose fear of revolution caused it to see any large-scale protest as a threat to its security.

The disturbances began in July 1830 in north-east Kent as a protest against Irish migrants who were competing with local men for harvest wages. The motive behind that protest, a wish to protect precious jobs, led on to the attacks on threshing machines the first of which was destroyed at Lower Hardres near Canterbury at the end of August.[2] Machine-breaking was not the only strategy of protest; incendiary attacks, public meetings to negotiate wage increases and more generous poor law allowances, and threatening letters signed by the mythical 'Captain Swing' were all employed in a very successful barrage of persuasion.[3] A special correspondent writing in *The Times* noted how readily most farmers agreed to the labourers' demands. He saw that 'they were not mad enough to refuse requests which they could not demonstrate to be unreasonable…and which were urged by three hundred or four hundred men after a barn or two had been fired and each farmer had an incendiary letter addressed to him in his pocket'.[4] For two months the disturbances appeared to be a purely local problem which the Kent magistrates dealt with very leniently at the Quarter Sessions. In early November protest erupted in Sussex whence it spread with ever-gathering momentum to engulf Berkshire, Hampshire and Wiltshire by the middle of the month and Dorset by its end. Disturbances also occurred throughout the Midlands and East Anglia and although the peak of the agitation had passed by Christmas, protest continued sporadically into the summer months of 1831.

The Swing riots swept through more than twenty counties in three months, and touched thirty-eight in all. In the most troubled counties, Berkshire, Hampshire and Wiltshire, open protest lasted for barely a week and reached a crescendo on the same day.[5] These three counties produced 40 per cent of all the recorded incidents and a similar proportion of the cases tried in the aftermath. They accounted for over 54 per cent of the agricultural machinery destroyed and 84 per cent of the recorded 'robberies' but less than 15 per cent of the cases of arson. Those statistics are a pointer to the particular form which protest took in Wessex where it was characterised by overt, collective action rather than covert, individual incendiarism.[6]

## Swing in Wessex

| Duration of disturbance | Arson & letters began | Overt protest began | Most intense period | Peak day |
|---|---|---|---|---|
| **Berkshire** | | | | |
| 10-24 Nov. | c. 10 Nov. | 15 Nov. | 18-24 Nov. | 23 Nov. |
| **Hampshire** | | | | |
| 10-30 Nov. | c. 10 Nov. | 17 Nov. | 18-24 Nov. | 23 Nov. |
| **Wiltshire** | | | | |
| 15-29 Nov. | c. 15 Nov. | 21 Nov. | 22-25 Nov. | 23 Nov. |
| **Dorset** | | | | |
| 22-1 Dec. | | 22 Nov. | 25-29 Nov. | 29 Nov. |

In Dorset, where the disturbances began slightly later, the authorities had time to prepare for action and the number of incidents was far smaller, about one fifth of those in Wiltshire and Hampshire and one quarter of those in Berkshire. The magistrates in Dorset were able to disperse some crowds before trouble began and their show of strength was a potent discouragement to open protest; as a result clandestine acts were proportionally much more significant. Arson, which accounted for less than 9 per cent of incidents in Wiltshire and 8 per cent in Berkshire and Hampshire, made up over 28 per cent of the recorded incidents in Dorset. But although arson, and more particularly the threat of arson, were powerful weapons in rural protest they were always marginal in the Swing disturbances as a whole.[7] Indeed, there were only two indictments for arson in the four counties whereas 861 men, or over 43 per cent of all those tried in England, were prosecuted for machine-breaking, robbery and riotous assembly.

The Wessex counties experienced the most intense, widespread protest and suffered the fiercest repression. Men from the four counties made up 74 per cent of those sentenced to death and 65 per cent of those transported. Of those consigned to an antipodean exile 44 per cent went to New South Wales, almost all of whom arrived on the *Eleanor*. The actions which led them to that fate, the crushing poverty which drove them to abandon their customary lethargy, the cultural context of their protest and the reasons for its savage repression are dealt with in later chapters and need no further elaboration at this point. The form that protest took in 1830, with overt, direct action and public displays of resentment, was a measure of the near universality, in southern England, of the labourers' profound sense of grievance. It was also highly unusual. After 1800 most protest action in the countryside found its expression in crime of one sort or another because the labourers, underpaid, under-employed and vulnerable, dared not risk open dissent.[8] By 1830 the processes of agrarian capitalism had made the agricultural labourer in southern England a prole-tarian pauper and it was a brave man who dared to challenge the control of the landowners, farmers, poor law overseers and clergy who dominated rural affairs. Open protest was consequently rare and the disturbances of 1830 take on a new significance when their unusual character is recognised. The labourers wanted little from life beyond a living wage and the opportunity to earn it but by 1830 even this 'fantastically minimal' expectation was denied them.[9] In a desperate, unusual and courageous attempt to obtain what was due to them they turned to open protest. However, before we can ask what sort of men the convicts of the *Eleanor* were, and test the accuracy of Joseph Mason's assessment that his involuntary shipmates were 'for the most part men of honest principle', the events of 1830 must be set in the context of popular protest in the early nineteenth century.[10]

The agricultural disturbances of 1830 displayed many of the characteristics of traditional, pre-modern forms of protest.[11] The labourers' demands were conserva-tive, defensive, essentially apolitical and founded upon a perception that they had legitimate grievances which had to be resolved and rights to be defended. Most pre-industrial protest was a response to the conviction that the proper moral, social or economic order was being undermined. Protest was usually backward-looking because labouring people relied on the security of customary practice to give meaning and structure to their lives; they worked, lived and had their being 'in grooves'.[12] A generation after Swing, Richard Jefferies noted how Wiltshire labourers were 'imbued to a great extent' with an awareness of their rights which they defended by appeals to 'the force of tradition and custom'.[13] In 1830 the moral certainty which emboldened the normally deferential labourers to confront their social superiors was founded on their conviction that they had been wronged, and their belief that they were 'not doing anything that their fathers would not have done'.[14] In seeking regular work and better wages, the labourers posed no threat to rural society; they simply wanted to assert their claim to fair treatment. Generally respectful, courteous and frequently deferential in their dealings with farmers, landowners, clergy and magistrates, the labourers sought to remind them of the responsibilities which accompanied wealth and privilege in a paternalist society.[15]

The rural protesters in 1830 were never rebels intent on systematic, organised resistance to authority; their concerns were far too localised and uncoordinated to be described as a rebellion.[16] Pre-industrial protest was usually spontaneous, lacking in organisation and always essentially a matter of 'indigenous', local issues which could only be resolved within a particular community, trade or workshop.[17] Consequently, leadership was exercised by men of influence or standing in the particular local context and their sphere of command, like the stimulus to action, was highly localised. So it was in the Swing disturbances. No matter how frequently the same complaints were raised and identical solutions sought, discontent was expressed, action taken and agreements reached at a local, parochial level in face-to-face confrontations between members of the village community. It was almost inevitable that in most pre-industrial disputes the powerless and propertyless faced their local masters who had both property and power. When the negotiative processes of meetings and petitions failed to produce results threatening letters might be employed but the ultimate weapon was always direct action against property.[18] The targets for the crowds' destructive violence were usually carefully selected for their symbolic or practical significance in a dispute and 'overturned flour carts, slit wheat sacks, broken windows, arson of hay ricks, and mangled machinery form the scenario of English pre-modern collective violence'.[19]

There was nothing anarchic about the destruction of property. Attacks on property and machine-breaking, which were far more common in the first phase of industrialisation than economic historians have acknowledged, served two separate but sometimes complementary functions.[20] Machine-breaking was an effective and long-established method for pressuring an employer during a dispute by menacing his capital and in this circumstance the workers often showed no particular resentment of the machine as such. But machine-breaking could also be an expression of the workers' hostility towards the device itself, especially when it threatened their well-being by displacing them or by cheapening their labour.[21] Although it was always of greatest significance in the textile industries, machine-breaking was part

of workplace culture in most occupations. For many years before the Swing disturbances rural labourers had used arson and sabotage as retributary and persuasive
strategies. Prosecution societies across the whole of southern England routinely
offered rewards for the detection of incendiaries and those who damaged 'any
Waggon, Cart, Plough or other Instrument of Husbandry' or stole 'any Gates,
Stiles, Rails Pales…Fences or any Iron Work belonging thereto'.[22] It is not
surprising that in 1830 rural workers attacked the labour-displacing machines which
took from them one of their few remaining sources of winter work. By destroying
threshing and other agricultural machinery the labourers employed a well understood strategy by which they could exert greater leverage in their demand for a living
wage and display their hostility to the machine itself and the socially destructive
farming practices it represented.

Labouring people in the early nineteenth century had very ambivalent attitudes
towards machinery. Machines which were essential for the conduct of a trade or
occupation and had long been used were generally accepted without question
whereas innovations which threatened the stability and security of established practice were deeply resented. Since most new machinery either replaced or cheapened
labour it can sometimes appear that workers set their face against all machinery but
that was never the case.[23] The hostility of labouring people to any machine was based
on an assessment of its social impact on the community and in the early nineteenth
century the machine was too often a symbol for 'a value system' at odds with
'community culture'.[24] This, more than anything else perhaps, helps us to understand
why the Swing protesters in Wessex not only destroyed the new agricultural
machines which most obviously threatened their well-being but also directed their
anger against textile mills, foundries and other factory-based manufacturing. When
John Jennings led a crowd into a woollen mill near Salisbury he let it be known that
his purpose was 'to break the machinery to pieces to make more work for the poor
people' and the assault on the foundry at Upper Clatford was prompted by the
conviction of local blacksmiths, wheelwrights and carpenters that it was destroying
their trades so that 'they could not live for it'.[25]

The idea that new machinery injured labouring people was widely believed. In a
contemporary pamphlet against labour-displacing machines, one labourer asserts that
if they were removed 'distress would soon disappear'. 'Yes', says another, and 'the tens
of thousands that now have no labour would soon be employed and instead of drag-
ging out a miserable existence' on parish allowances 'would be able to support
themselves and family'.[26] Machines in various forms seemed to be eroding the
economic security of the rural community in Wessex and in acting against them
labourers and craftsmen were defending the community-based values of the pre-
industrial world which were fast being eroded by the seductive philosophies of
individualism and self-interest. The Swing protesters looked to better wages and

regular work to rescue them from progressive pauperisation but their condition was a result of a major change in attitudes and social values which it was beyond their power to influence. Few, if any, are likely to have realised this fact and we must see their actions as a conservative, defensive display of outrage at developments which were eroding the harmony and order of the rural community.

Although this book is about the men who took part in 'collective bargaining by riot', it should be remembered that a great many disputes were settled without machine-breaking or menace.[27] The full extent of rural protest in 1830 was far wider than the picture derived from the incidents which were noted in the press or which gave rise to prosecutions. Farmers often voluntarily destroyed their own threshing machines to avert trouble and we are unlikely ever to know how many local settlements were agreed without any disturbance. Because the threat of direct action was very real, many farmers, overseers and magistrates were encouraged to be conciliatory. According to Frederick Page, the Select Vestry at Speen was prompted to increase the weekly wage and the bread allowance for children 'in consequence of' the machine-breaking around Aldermaston and the riot at Brimpton. The Vicar, Henry Majendie, put an offer to a delegation of labourers who agreed to the terms and met the farmers and gentry of the Vestry 'in the most peaceable and orderly manner'. 'The conduct of the labourers' was, Page noted, 'without exception marked by forbearance and civility' which led him to conclude that 'the just demands of the labourers should be peaceably acceded to'.[28] The labourers of Speen did not need to resort to direct action because the farmers' fear was a sufficient stimulus to a preemptive offer.[29] Mark Harrison is right to note that historians of popular protest have tended to reduce studies of crowd action to studies of riot in a 'slightly stagnant orthodoxy' which ignores the occasions when crowds obtained satisfaction without violence.[30] But given the patchwork of protest in Wessex in 1830 it seems likely that the success of non-violent crowds depended on the activity of those which took more robust action. In short, it is impossible to believe that labourers anywhere could have negotiated better wages and the decommissioning of threshing machines in a climate wholly free from 'collective bargaining by riot'.

Historians of pre-industrial, popular protest have consistently demonstrated that the crowds which engaged in direct action held ideas which legitimated their behaviour.[31] A fundamental belief in the need for fair treatment allowed the crowd to place the moral law of the community above the decrees of the state and a 'levelling instinct' prompted protesters to attack property, although personal violence was rare.[32] Most crowds were remarkably disciplined and purposeful and during the disturbances the labourers generally displayed a careful attention to the propriety of their actions. *The Times* observed that an 'astonishing coolness and regularity' was a feature of many confrontations and that there was 'little of the ordinary effervescence' so often displayed at moments of excitement.[33] The crowd which destroyed machines and collected largess in the villages between Kintbury and Hungerford in Berkshire was described by John Pearse MP, who confronted it in a negotiation, as a set of 'dangerous savages'. Yet this same 'mob', which contained several of the men transported on the *Eleanor*, was under a strong internal discipline and its leaders took firm steps to maintain proper behaviour and thus preserve the legitimacy of the crowd's actions. In a letter to Lord Melbourne the Deputy-Lieutenant noted that the leaders punished an individual who had stolen an umbrella from a farm by throwing him in the canal and ordered others who had taken some rabbits from a poor woman to give them back. The crowd charged each owner of a threshing machine two pounds for its destruction but when it was discovered that a local magistrate had been visited by two parties and had given a pound to the second, even though his machine was already wrecked, the leaders went to his house and endeavoured to give the money back saying 'they had taken one pound too much'. They also ensured that disturbance during this incident was kept to a minimum for they knew that the magistrate's wife was unwell and 'therefore came only in small parties'.[34]

A similar concern for propriety can be seen in many other incidents. William Cheater insisted that the wooden parts of a winnowing-machine be burnt in the open and not in a barn where the whole premises would have been put at risk. John Aldridge asked for a key to enter a building where a threshing machine was stored rather than break down the door; Solomon Allen returned a hammer he had borrowed from a farmer during a machine-breaking; Isaac Burton prevented a crowd from invading a house; Thomas Hicks led another away from a village lest its presence frighten women and children; Charles Davis helped to prevent serious injury to a farmer who had fired on protesters in his farmyard, and Robert Holdaway ensured that the old and sick were protected during an attack on a poorhouse.[35] Not only were most crowds well disciplined, but in general their confrontations with farmers, clergy, magistrates and landowners were marked by the good manners and civility of the protesters. William Stroud was the treasurer for a crowd which approached Thomas Child and asked for a donation; Child later recalled how 'they said they had called for a little money if I pleased…there was no threat…they were perfectly civil'.[36] Seven of the Dorset men on the *Eleanor* were in a crowd which approached the Rector of Buckland Newton and were 'very civil in their demeanour' while the Rector of Stour Provost maintained that the labourers who confronted him 'were not impertinent…some of the mob…pulled off their hats to me'.[37] Further discussion, in chapter two, of the incidents involving the men of the *Eleanor* and, in chapter four, of the cultural context of their actions will show the accuracy of John Stevenson's observation that the 'dominant feature' of the disturbances was their 'orderliness and ceremony'.[38] But the trial reports which form the principal source of information for these events provide only a partial picture of those 'men of honest principle' the convicts of the *Eleanor*. To put some flesh on the bones of men who appear fleetingly in the columns of *The Times* and the county newspapers we must turn to the parochial and convict records.

The men who took part in the Swing disturbances were not the socially inadequate or the criminally inclined; nor were they 'the rootless young or the desperate poor'.[39] They were, for the most part, respectable, hard-working, law-abiding labourers and craftsmen of 'almost unimpeachable character'.[40] The 'mobs' so routinely referred to in newspaper reports, trial proceedings, and some historical accounts take on a rather different character when it is realised that they were usually a genuine cross-section of the labouring portion of the village community. Most crowds consisted chiefly of agricultural labourers because they were the principally aggrieved and the most numerous portion of the rural population. Yet craftsmen and artisans figured very prominently in the protests and even more significantly in the number of those indicted and transported. Aboard the *Eleanor,* among those listing a trade or craft as their principal occupation were six carpenters, five blacksmiths, four sawyers, three bricklayers, two brickmakers, two thatchers and a tailor, shoemaker, papermaker, butcher, maltster, wheelwright, boat-builder, chimney-sweep, surveyor, brazier and whitesmith together with a good representation of the more obviously agricultural crafts.[41] There is no doubt that the authorities were both surprised and alarmed by the social consensus which the presence of so many rural artisans and craftsmen in the crowds demonstrated. As men of some standing in their local communities, often possessing modest property in their tools and materials and frequently more literate and articulate than the majority of field labourers, they were the natural leaders and were subsequently selected for prosecution to punish them for meddling in a dispute which the authorities believed was beyond their concern. The assumption that the rural community ought to have fractured along occupational lines shows how little the ruling elite understood the 'secret, opaque society' of the village in which people were bound together by economic, social and familial ties.[42]

Villages were self-contained communities; butchers, bakers, tailors, shoemakers, bricklayers, carpenters, thatchers, blacksmiths, wheelwrights and a host of other tradesmen catered to the needs of their particular locality. They occupied an important social position between the farmers and their labourers while catering to the needs of both. The more specialised among them, the blacksmith, the wheelwright, and the ploughwright, had uncommon skills but like all those who served a community they identified with the organic reality of the village rather than the abstract idea of a national industry or product. Although even quite small villages required a group of key tradesmen, in many places the less skilled crafts were often combined with agricultural labour.[43] These features show up very clearly in the indent of the *Eleanor.* Seventy-seven per cent of the convicted protesters included an agricultural activity like reaping, mowing, milking, ploughing, shearing or shepherding among their designated occupations yet 55 per cent listed a trade or some alternative to agricultural labour. In addition to the ubiquitous agricultural skills no fewer than forty-two other occupational activities were listed by the 132 men aboard.[44] Some of the more skilled men like blacksmith, John Aldridge, tailor, Isaac Burton, and carpenter, Charles Milson, declared no secondary occupation but most of the other tradesmen like papermaker, Daniel Hancock, hurdlemaker, Thomas Mackrell, thatcher, Levi Brown, sawyer, James New, and bricklayer, John Bulpitt, professed some agricultural skill and nearly all acted as reapers to take advantage of the opportunity of harvest earnings. The rural artisans and craftsmen who feature prominently in the lists of those prosecuted and transported for their part in the Swing disturbances were so intimately involved with agriculture that it is hard to imagine how they could have remained detached from the protest.

Some tradesmen, most notably blacksmiths, wheelwrights, and carpenters had good reason to make common cause with the labourers. Carpentry, the least specialised of the trades, was relatively easy to enter without a great deal of expense for the tools were comparatively inexpensive. It was, however, becoming seriously overcrowded; many who had previously practised as occasional 'hedge carpenters' moved into the open trade as their earnings from agricultural work declined.[45] All the craftsmen who served the farming sector were being squeezed by the contraction of agricultural expenditure after the war and more importantly they were facing the challenge of factory-produced implements. In the last years of the eighteenth century, as wooden implements were replaced by those made from iron, the blacksmith emerged as the most important of the rural artisans.[46] Most other trades could be tackled by a general handyman but the smith's work was too specialised. Not only was he required to make and repair the metal parts of machinery, hand tools and domestic utensils, but in his role as a shoeing smith he looked after valuable livestock.[47] After 1815, however, as rural foundries began to produce cast-iron machines with standardised parts, the blacksmith was slowly eclipsed and 'forced into the role of a maintenance man for foundry produced goods'.[48]

Declining trade, the loss of two small cottages and his forge, and the economic imperative of a very large family drove George Carter into the ranks of the agricultural labourers and machine-breakers.[49] John Aldridge clearly resented the erosion of his craft; he was seen to break the iron wheel of a threshing machine declaring 'damn him, thats a good one, I've done him now' and to a carpenter who was present he added, 'if I had my will, I should like to down with all the foundries'.[50] It is not certain if Aldridge was present at the attack on Gibbons' foundry in Hungerford but no doubt he rejoiced at the destruction of castings, machine parts and foundry equipment. In his role as one of the crowd's representatives at a meeting in the Town Hall, he demanded not only an increase in wages for tradesmen but also that 'threshing machines be got rid of'.[51] The role of blacksmiths in the assault on Tasker's foundry near Andover was noted in the press where it was alleged that 'many blacksmiths, viewing with distrust the inroads…on their trade by the improvements in cast-iron mechanism' marked down the foundry 'as the object of their vengeance and destruction'.[52] Blacksmiths, like carpenters and wheelwrights, had another practical role in rural machine-breaking for they had the tools needed to dismantle wooden casings and shatter iron parts and also the skill to use them.[53] When the crowd which wrecked machines in the Streatley and Basildon area broke its sledgehammer, the sons of the smith at Kilnbolton provided a replacement. On John Benett's estate in Wiltshire the crowd, according to an eyewitness, could not break the main bar of a large threshing machine 'till one of 'em said – here – let I try – and he smashed 'un in one blow. He were a blacksmith…and he did know just where to hit 'un'.[54]

The respectable labourers and tradesmen on the *Eleanor* and the other vessels which carried the Swing protesters to Australia were unlike most convicts. The overwhelming majority had never been in trouble before whereas other convicts transported were generally repeated offenders. Only eleven of those on board had a previous conviction and of that number only one had served a sentence in excess of six months. The others had served terms of between three days and six months. George Elkins was possibly unique among the protesters on the vessel in so far as he was the only one who had committed a crime which merited transportation. In 1829 he had taken part in a burglary at Shaftesbury and had only avoided death or transportation by confessing and turning evidence against his two associates.[55] One other petty thief, Lazarus Lawrence, was unlucky to be included among the machine-breakers since there is no evidence to connect him with any protest activity; he was a rural worker who stole a coat, a shepherd's crook and sixpence on 19 November just as the disturbances began in Hampshire and it appears that he was erroneously assumed to be a protester.[56] Given the generally high levels of crime in the countryside and the extent of poverty which fostered it, the paucity of criminal convictions among the men of the *Eleanor* is astonishing.

An abundance of evidence attests to the essential respectability, sobriety and industry of most of the men on the *Eleanor*. During the trials many farmers, landowners, and clergymen appeared as character witnesses for those accused. The cumulative impression gained from reading many accounts is that most of the men before the courts not only had unblemished characters up to the time of the disturbances but were reliable, well-respected workmen. Even more impressive are the testimonials contained in the letters and petitions for clemency which were sent to Lord Melbourne at the Home Department or to other men of influence.[57] Nine farmers of Broad Chalk and the local curate urged mercy for Levi Brown. He was, they declared, a 'hardworking, honest, industrious, and very sober man' who had served one of them for twenty years, had never been before a magistrate and was a 'steady quiet and well-behaved man' who had come 'into his present situation without having any ill design'. Several of Henry Bunce's employers noted that he always behaved 'with fidelity submission and application' and they joined with others in the parish in acknowledging his 'good character for sobriety Honesty and Industry'. They might also have added that he was loyal to his friends. Bunce appeared at the Winchester Special Commission not as one of the accused but as a witness for William Sims. He was warned by Justice Alderson not to answer any questions which might incriminate him, but in order to prove that Sims did not make the threats which were alleged Bunce chose to admit that he was present in the crowd. Alderson immediately ordered him into custody whereupon Bunce 'sprang over the bar into the dock with his former comrades, seemingly unaffected by the decision of the learned Judge', an action which almost certainly illustrates his belief in the essential innocence of the crowd's behaviour.[58] Many of those transported had shown themselves to be conscientious, diligent workmen and among others Isaac Burton, Joseph Edney, Charles Green, William Hawkins, and both George Shergolds drew encomiums from men who had employed them.

Others, in addition, had previously displayed a variety of commendable moral and social characteristics. Some mitigation of Henry Elkins' sentence was sought by the Rector, overseers and constables of Shaftesbury because he had 'hitherto supported himself by honest industry' and had not been a burden on the parish. Joseph Pope, according to the Vicar of Edmonsham, was a good man who had raised a large family 'in respectability and credit' on the scantiest means. He was 'an example' to his fellow labourers, had a good character from his former employers and even his prosecutor was distressed by the news that he was to be transported. The tradesmen of Newbury maintained that William Sims had 'always borne a good Character for Sobriety Honesty and Industry' up to the riots but, more importantly, had 'always supported an aged Mother by his labour'. Edward Harris, a 'quiet, peaceable and steady' man and a regular churchgoer was another who looked after his mother; Thomas Mackrell, who had worked as a common labourer for the same man for twenty years, was 'a most indulgent Father' to his seven surviving children; William Stroud, an 'industrious, hard working man', kept his family independent of parochial relief. Outrage at the inappropriate punishment handed out to hard-working, decent and fundamentally law-abiding men sometimes united a community in a plea for mercy. The Rector of Tangley, the principal landowner, the churchwardens, the overseers, and assorted freeholders joined with over one hundred parishioners to seek some clemency for George Carter, 'a worthy hard-working man' who had never been in trouble previously and 'would never again offend'. The parishioners of West Shefford, who had known young Jason Greenway 'from his infancy', tried to save him because he had 'an excellent character for sobriety, diligence and peaceable behaviour', had always contrived to find work, had paid his mother's rent and was well thought of by the local farmers. Some of these petitions even bear the signatures of prosecutors though few were as candid as John Brasher:

> My Lord,
>
> I was the prosecutor in the case of Henry Shergold, and I confess that I had not the slightest idea that his sentence would have been so severe, for having known the family so many years particularly the person I imagined a more slight punishment would have been inflicted on him, I candidly confess that I have not had a moments peace of mind since the passing of his sentence, I sincerely hope you will grant the prayer of the Petitioner.

It is clear that most of the men of the *Eleanor* were, by any standard, respectable and well respected members of their communities. They were truly 'for the most part men of honest principle' and the majority of them preserved that character in the colony.[59]

The Swing protesters were generally young men under thirty years of age but there is a problem with any age profile derived, as it must be, from judicial records.[60] Only a very small proportion of the total number of men who took part in protests was ever brought to trial and the decision to prosecute the leaders and those who seemed to have influence over the crowds means that our understanding of the demographics of Swing is slightly skewed. A labourer who was the 'treasurer' of a large crowd in central Hampshire maintained that the disturbances in his area were begun by the young, single labourers who were severely discriminated against in terms of wage-rates, yet the leadership of that crowd devolved on older men and it was they who were prosecuted.[61] It is, nonetheless, instructive to compare the age profile of the men on the *Eleanor* with that of the overall picture for transported convicts. Only five were under the age of twenty, less than 4 per cent of those on board, whereas in the general convict population boys and young men amounted to 19 per cent.[62] Sixty-four per cent of the men on the *Eleanor* were in their twenties while men of a similar age formed half the total of all those transported. Among the Wessex protesters, 32 per cent were over thirty but older men made up only 22 per cent of the convicts as a whole; for men over thirty-five the figures were 19 and 13 per cent respectively.

The convicts of the *Eleanor* were men of maturity and experience, men at the height of their physical powers, many of them married with families, who knew the destructive consequences of unemployment, underemployment and poverty. Marriage, with its attendant responsibilities, was a discouragement to recklessness and it is a measure of the protesters' deep conviction in the justice and necessity of their action that so many married men featured in the lists of those prosecuted. Only 19 per cent of the total population of male convicts transported was ever married but over 55 per cent of the Wessex men sent to New South Wales was either married or widowed.[63] Many of the married men felt their separation from their loved ones very bitterly. George Arlett begged the court to allow his wife and baby daughter to go with him to Australia and William Hawkins, reduced to tears by his sentence and the prospect of exile, also asked that his wife and two daughters might 'accompany him in his banishment'.[64] The files of the Home Department contain many letters and petitions from both the exiles and those they left behind requesting that the families be allowed to reunite in Australia.[65] Some of the older men left large families with several grown up children; at least four of Joseph Pope's twelve children were above the age of twenty and it may be supposed that his conviction would not have jeopardised the family economy. For men with younger families, however, and especially for those whose wives had infants to care for and were thus unable to earn much for themselves, conviction almost automatically sentenced their dependents to the tender mercies of the Poor Law. William Stroud's neighbours were certain that his transportation would force his wife and three young children to apply for parish relief.[66] The wives of Solomon Allen and Mathew Triggs assuredly faced a bleak future, each having five children under ten years of age, and the prospect was little better for those who, like Thomasine Blake, the wife of Shadrach, were pregnant when their husbands were arrested.

For many of these men parting from loved ones was the most wounding aspect of their punishment. Even at this distance in time there are sufficient clues in the convict records and parish registers for us to recover some aspects of their family life and to conclude that they prized it greatly. We should not be surprised that many of their brides were pregnant on their wedding day because working-class couples, once they had decided to marry, often enjoyed a full relationship knowing that the ceremony would generally precede any confinement. The innate respectability of the men on the *Eleanor* is confirmed by a study of the parish records which show that very few of them either fathered illegitimate children or failed to take responsibility for them when they did. Henry Bunce married Harriet Holloway three months after the birth of their son and two days before the disturbances at St. Mary Bourne which parted them. William Carter married Ann Pontin seven months after the birth of their daughter, Sarah, while Thomas Goodfellow married Ann Froom a month after their daughter was baptised. The baby was named Matilda Froom Goodfellow in an obvious strategy to use her father's name in the baptismal register and openly declare the intention of the couple to marry. It is likely that transportation prevented some marriages, but how many of the bachelors were about to wed we can never know. Only Robert Mason, an unusually literate man, commented on what may have been the experience of many single men. Writing to his mother in February 1831, he noted how Margaret, his 'dear little wandering sheep', would still 'remain destitute' and expressed the hope that one day he would 'meet her never to part again'.[67]

The protesters' attachment to their families also shows up in another rather unexpected way in the tattoos which some of them carried on their arms and hands. Sets of family initials were by far the most common form of decoration and they must be read as evidence of deep affection because tattooing, then as now, was painful and permanent. Thomas Hanson's love for his wife Mary and his subsequent story was pricked out in a series of symbols on his left arm which clearly had been added to up to the moment of exile, or had been done entirely while in gaol. 'TH heart MH 1831 Happy Return' - there in a few dark lines was a life story from which he could never be parted. George Arlett remembered his wife, Elizabeth, in their joint initials 'GA EA' while Laban Stone did likewise for Sarah and his baby son John, with a woman on his right arm and 'LS SS sun JS tree 1831 heart' on the other. Charles Davis fixed his life with Mary at a moment in time and 'CD MD GD TED 1831' was all that he could take with him of their time together. Joseph Tuck would not forget his family whose genealogy he appears to have carried on his forearms with 'JT GW and crucifixion' on his right and 'AT JT CW ET LT and heart' on his left. It was not only the married men and widowers who preserved their family connections and their sense of personal identity in this way. Some of the single men wore their initials and nothing more while others combined them with those of family members, friends, lovers and other symbols. Abraham House displayed his birth date in '1809', and several others had dates of personal significance besides '1831'. James Baker showed his trade as a miller with a windmill and Henry Toombs his affection for 'SP' whose initials he wore on his arm together with his own and the telling symbols of an archer, a heart, and the sun. The heart was by far the most popular symbol and it does not require a semiotician to divine that the message was one of love; a heart or a woman's outline, especially when combined with initials other than the prisoner's own, should probably be read as a declaration of attachment. The popularity of the sun, moon and stars might possibly be understood as a reference to eternal verities which again, in combination with initials, might be a statement of the durability of affection. Much more work needs to be done on this aspect of convict decoration using a far bigger sample but it seems evident that in their tattoos the men of the *Eleanor* betray to us their affection for their families and loved ones and a resolution that they would neither forget them nor lose their own sense of identity.[68]

Among the men who had tattoos there was an almost equal division between those who could read and write, those who could do neither and those who could only read. For the two-thirds who could not write, and perhaps more usefully for those who could not read either, there was a possible incentive to have these simple messages of affection and recollection inscribed on their skin. As a group, though, the men of the *Eleanor* were an unusually literate set of convicts. This can be seen very clearly if the figures for the men on the convict vessel are compared with a sample of an almost identical size. A total of 138 men appeared before the judges at the Reading sitting of the Berkshire Special Commission of whom only 45 per cent could read and only 18 per cent could write.[69] However, 78 per cent of the transported protesters declared at the convict muster on arrival in Sydney that they could read and 33 per cent that they could both read and write. Although a measure of uncertainty must always surround the details that convicts supplied about themselves, it seems likely that the statement of reading ability was tolerably accurate while that of writing skill might well be an understatement. Convicts who could write were generally regarded with more suspicion by the colonial authorities and some may have chosen to conceal their ability. Research into late eighteenth and early nineteenth century literacy has shown that the proportion of people able to read was generally between one-and-a-half and two times those able to write.[70] If this formula is applied to the protesters from Wessex the number who were possibly able to write rises to between 39 and 52 per cent which lends some substance to the belief that the new arrivals might have chosen to keep some things to themselves. The unusually high proportion of men on the *Eleanor* who could read, or read and write, was without doubt a direct measure of the occupational status and social characteristics of men who were the acknowledged leaders in their communities, but we should remember too that many rural workers could read.

One of the most enduring myths about rural labourers in nineteenth century England is that they were universally illiterate. This notion is entirely attributable to the demographic convention that the only effective measure of literacy is the ability to write, shown by a signature in the parish registers. Reading and writing are very different skills and for most working people there was no obvious reason why the one should necessarily be accompanied by the other. Estimates of the proportion of rural labourers who could read vary widely but perhaps half had some reading skill.[71] The writings of radical journalists like Cobbett and Carlile circulated widely in the countryside and after the disturbances the authorities endeavoured to prove that they had been caused by seditious publications.[72] This would have been a pointless exercise if the inability to read had been extensive. Furthermore, a considerable portion of the agricultural labourers must have been able to read or there would have been no point in the innumerable public notices which were posted all over the place in late 1830 to inform the men about local wage decisions.

The meticulous convict records with their measurements of height and detailed descriptions of physical appearance provide a contact with the flesh and blood existence of the protesters. They were not generally tall men: the shortest was a little under five feet (152 cms) and the tallest exactly six feet (183 cms). Only 16 per cent were taller than five feet eight inches (173 cms) while 23 per cent were shorter than five feet five inches (165cms). There is a reasonable probability that many of the men on the *Eleanor* were shorter than their fathers because few labouring men after 1800 enjoyed adequate nutrition when young.[73] Most showed signs of lives spent in hard, manual work often in inclement weather. The majority of the field labourers had the florid, wind-burned complexion of men who spent their lives in the open. George Shergold, a shepherd and fieldworker, had all his 'toes and fingers crooked from cold'. The spadesman and brickmaker, William Page, had distorted toes on both feet and William Sims' right hand was 'crooked and stiff' from using the shears of his calling. Hand injuries were common, especially among the tradesmen. Blacksmith, Maurice Pope, woodman, Henry Eldridge, farm carpenter, John Heath, wheelwright, Joseph Arney, shepherd, William Waving and ploughman, Aaron Harding all had joints missing or fingers mutilated. Seventy per cent had visible scars or injuries which were carefully noted on arrival, together with eye and hair colour, complexion and tattoos, as an aid to identification should they ever abscond. George Shergold the gardener would have been easily recognised by his sallow complexion, dark brown hair, brown eyes, the scar on the right side of his forehead near the centre, the diagonal scar at top of his nose which extended towards the right side, and the scar on his left cheek.

Convicts arriving in New South Wales were also classified by their religious affiliation but all the colonial authorities wanted to know was if a man was a Protestant or a Roman Catholic. The men of the *Eleanor* were all listed as Protestants but whether they were Anglicans or Nonconformists is unknown. It is likewise impossible to know much about the nature of their religious beliefs or if many of them were regular churchgoers. Joseph and Robert Mason were clearly religious men, regular attenders at church with an intimate knowledge of the Bible, but we do not know whether they also shared the superstitious, magical and semi-pagan beliefs common among their fellow labourers.[74] Edward Harris was reported to be 'constant' in his 'attention to the duties of the Sabbath' but did that mean he went to church or merely abstained from drinking and rough sports?[75] William and Daniel Sims castigated the Reverend William Easton of St. Mary Bourne for a sermon he preached which they said 'was against the poor' but we do not know if they heard it first-hand or by report.[76]

Although Cobbett maintained in 1823 that the labourers in southern England had 'in a great measure ceased to go' to the established church, it remained an important centre of village life.[77] The labourers were virtually compelled to use it for the essential rituals of life and death and it is likely that many were fairly regular attenders on other occasions, most notably the great festivals. Few rural workers could afford to cut themselves off entirely from the church or alienate the parish clergyman, for many charitable disbursements were administered by the parson who was also intimately involved in vetting those who sought poor relief.[78] By 1830, in many parts of southern England the Anglican parson was aligned with those who ground the labourers down and was viewed with understandable mistrust by the labouring poor. Cobbett railed against the 'Hampshire parsons' who were 'neither more nor less than another sort of landlord', whose pluralism had led to neglected churches and neglected parishioners.[79] Many also served as magistrates, much to the Duke of

Wellington's dismay, and were active in protecting the game and property of their landed neighbours; the Vicar of Kintbury, Reverend Fowle, who was notorious for prosecuting poachers, was popularly believed to receive a commission on each conviction.[80] Others, like William Cobbold, the Vicar of Selborne, treated their parishioners with contempt and fought an unremitting campaign to extract every penny of their clerical dues from the village community.[81] A farmer told Cobbett that he doubted if 'there was a more unhappy place in England' than Selborne where the litigious, tithe-grabbing Cobbold had begun so many suits against his parishioners that he had shots fired through his window.[82]

Some clergymen clearly believed that they exercised great influence on their flocks and the production of tendentious sermons for the poor, urging a passive acceptance of suffering and submission to authority, was a veritable vicarage industry.[83] In reality, however, many clergymen were severely handicapped by the social gulf which separated them from their parishioners. Augustus Hare, the Rector of Alton Barnes, a remote village under the downs in the Vale of Pewsey, was 'from education and habits of life unacquainted with the character and wants of the poor'.[84] Furthermore, wrote his daughter, he could not comprehend 'the poverty of their minds' nor 'their prejudices and superstitions'. Hare believed he was respected, even loved, by the community but during the disturbances, which eventually led Charles Davis, Gifford North and Laban Stone to New South Wales, he sided with the farmers, believing 'our tithes must fall as the price of labour rises', and he even took part in an armed attack on a protesting crowd. He was then astonished that his docile, ignorant, superstitious parishioners 'threatened vengeance' so vociferously that he was obliged to keep 'out of sight from that time'. Even before the disturbances many Anglican parsons in Wessex were losing touch with those they were supposed to serve so that the clergy, according to a former Wiltshire curate, the Reverend Sydney Smith, had 'no more influence over the people-at-large than the cheezemongers (sic) of England have'.[85]

As the Established Church became increasingly irrelevant and oppressive, many rural people turned to the 'liberating' dissenting and nonconformist churches which offered an inspiring counterpoise to the Anglican emphasis on obedience and submission.[86] Between 1801 and 1831 the number of Methodist places of worship in the four counties increased from 72 to 225 and the Baptist from 44 to 114.[87] In addition, many barns, cottages and even open spaces were certified as meeting places and the issuing of certificates is evidence of active non-conformity even where no chapel existed. No part of Wiltshire, for example, was without its meeting place and over five hundred were certified between 1815 and 1830, chiefly for the Wesleyan Methodists although the Primitive Methodists made up ground very rapidly after 1825.[88] Suddenly and dramatically rural labourers were offered a choice in the matter of religious observance. In 1830, the people of Downton could attend the parish church or either of two Wesleyan chapels in the village while in the adjacent hamlet of Redlynch were another Wesleyan and two Baptist chapels.[89] Methodist meetings were usually conducted by local lay-preachers who understood the working folk they gathered together, spoke to them in their own language and offered a message very different from that of the gentry-dominated Church of England. According to Richard Jefferies, many Wiltshire labourers were nonconformists 'not out of any decided notion…of ceremony or theological dogma' but out of 'a class feeling'. In the chapel the labourer had 'no feeling of inferiority', the service, the hymns and the preacher were his and he had 'a sense of proprietorship in them'.[90] Religious dissent was a demonstration of independence but there was often a price to be paid. Agricultural labourers George and James Loveless, long before they acquired notoriety as the Tolpuddle martyrs, were preaching regularly throughout south-east Dorset where to be a Dissenter was a sin for which there was no forgiveness and which almost guaranteed persecution.[91] The sin consisted in refusing to conform to the role cast for working folk by the Established Church.

The men of the *Eleanor* had also refused to conform to society's expectations but it is impossible to establish how many, if any, were active religious dissenters for the evidence is wholly circumstantial. In New South Wales, Joseph Mason attended the Methodist chapel in Parramatta and from 1820 there had been a Wesleyan society close to his village in Hampshire. Thomas Hanson, the moving force behind the protests around Basildon, had an uncle who was a non-conformist preacher. A Baptist minister signed a petition on William Cheater's behalf and George Durman and John Pound were part of a crowd at Ramsbury led by a Primitive Methodist.[92] The influence of nonconformity among the men of the *Eleanor* was probably greater than these tantalising fragments suggest. It has been claimed that in the areas affected by disturbance in 1830-31 there was an 'obvious correlation' between nonconformity and unrest.[93] It is likely that a significant number of those on the *Eleanor* had some contact with religious dissent in the years before 1830. This was especially likely in open parishes which were less tightly under the control of the squire and parson and in the large upland parishes where greater distances and a more scattered population made supervision difficult. Although it is unlikely that the role of religious dissenters in the protests of 1830 will ever be fully resolved it is reasonable to suggest that they had a positive influence. They provided an example of working-class independence by their refusal to worship in the official church and they may have provided leaders from among the tradesmen and craftsmen who, as men of standing in their communities, made it easier for the labourers to shrug off their mentality of deferential acceptance.[94] But in seeking a reason for the outburst of protest in 1830 we must look elsewhere.

The circumstances which shaped the lives of the rural poor in late 1830 were not new. Poverty, underemployment, and exploitation had been commonplace since

1815 and the processes which created them had been in train since the mid-eighteenth century. For more than a generation rural labourers had been 'the most depressed sector of the English working classes' yet adult men passively accepted the situation into which they had been born.[95] Why then did protest erupt on such a scale in a year which was not significantly different from any other?

The population explosion of the late eighteenth and early nineteenth century resulted in a chronic oversupply of agricultural labour in southern England at a time when opportunities for by-employment in manufacturing were diminishing and primitive economic rationalism was recasting the social relationships of master and man to the disadvantage of the latter. In 1830 fieldworkers were close to their peak numbers. The 'fields and farmyards were more densely peopled than ever before or since' and consequently more were vulnerable to every twist of fortune which affected their lives.[96] Living as they did on a largely bread-based diet, rural labourers were extremely sensitive to anything which pushed up the price of their staple food. Wet summers and poor harvests in 1828 and 1829 led to increased wheat prices. In the 'fearsome' winter of 1829-30 many faced 'exceptional cold, hunger and unemployment', and by the autumn of 1830 the prospect looked similarly bleak to men and women who knew the reality of hunger and malnutrition.[97] A Hampshire farmer noted in his diary that the year began badly, 'the winter...the severest I ever remember', with frosts and snow into the middle of February. The summer was 'also very wet being the third...in succession' and across the corn-growing region there was a mounting uncertainty about the quality and quantity of the harvest.[98] If it did nothing else, unease over the possible price of bread in the coming winter made the labourers especially resentful of their abysmally low wages and intolerant of threshing machines which reduced still further the opportunity for some to find work.

On several occasions after 1815 wheat prices were higher than they were in 1830 and the level of unemployment and underemployment was scarcely different, but with each passing year the structurally induced crisis worsened as the population rose. The agricultural labourers of southern and eastern England were in a parlous condition but it needed more than 'the shared experience of poverty and shared feelings of resentment' to provoke them into protest.[99] The stimulus would seem to have been the lenient treatment of the Kent protesters which encouraged men in adjacent East Sussex to press their own local claims very successfully. Thereafter, the movement acquired its own momentum by a 'process of emulation' as news of the events spread.[100] At the East Kent quarter sessions at Canterbury on October 22 the first Swing protesters were tried and the seven machine-breakers were given a caution and three days in prison.[101] It is significant that machine-breaking in Kent escalated after the trial and news of the disturbances filled the national and county press. Across southern England rural labourers quickly absorbed the significance of what had happened. During many confrontations claims were made that some of those present had 'come out of Kent' and that the government had somehow sanctioned the removal of the threshing machines, statements which suggest that the labourers saw the lenient sentences as a recognition of the legitimacy of their grievances.[102] The labourers learned of what was happening by a variety of means; news spread inexorably by word of mouth along local lines of communication from village to village and centrifugally from market towns while newspapers penetrated the countryside from the major highways.[103] It was along the roads from London in particular that news spread fastest and most widely and it has been suggested that they played an important role in 'radicalising' enough people in the countryside for the Swing disturbances to be seen as a political protest in which villages with a core of militants might promote and inspire action in 'more tradition-bound' communities.[104]

In some places, like the villages around Sutton Scotney where Joseph and Robert Mason belonged to an active radical society, the disturbances undoubtedly had a political dimension which was probably made more intense by the agitation for parliamentary reform, the triumph of the reformers in the elections held in July 1830 and the outbreak of revolution in France. But in Wessex as a whole the labourers' aspirations were more basic: 'a very slightly better wage, the destruction of machines, the opportunity to work while preserving their dignity'.[105] Their expectations were very modest and their demands moderate but to attain what they believed was their due these 'men of honest principle' had to throw off their customary acquiescence and become assertive.

## Notes

1    146 men were transported to New South Wales for their part in the Swing disturbances of 1830-31. Those on the *Eleanor* were joined by a further six men from Wessex who arrived on other vessels and together they form the subject of this book. The handful from other parts of England, two from Bedfordshire and one each from Kent, Cambridgeshire, Norfolk, Herefordshire, Shropshire and Derbyshire, have been excluded.

2    R. Wells, 'Social Protest, Class, Conflict and Consciousness, in the English Countryside 1700-1880', in M. Reed & R. Wells, *Class Conflict and Protest in the English Countryside, 1700-1880*, London, 1990, p. 159-60.

3    E.J. Hobsbawm & G. Rudé, *Captain Swing*, London, 1969, p. 97.

4    *The Times*, 17/11/1830.

5    The table showing the chronology of protest and the statistics used in this and the following paragraph are based on Hobsbawm & Rudé, op. cit., Appendix III, 'Table of Incidents', pp. 311-58, and on Appendices I and II, pp. 304-5, 308-9. This is still the only attempt to plot incidents across the nation but it is undoubtedly an underestimation as shown by Wells, 'Social Protest', in Reed & Wells, op. cit., p. 166.

6    Regional differences in the type of Swing disturbances are well displayed in A. Charlesworth (ed.), *An Atlas of Rural Protest in Britain 1548-1900,* London, 1983, pp. 135, 152-3.

7    Hobsbawm & Rudé, op. cit., pp. 12, 203.

8    R.A.E. Wells, 'The Development of the English Rural Proletariat and Social Protest, 1700-1850', in Reed & Wells, op. cit., pp. 29-53.

9    'A Very English Rising', *Times Literary Supplement,* 11 Sept., 1969, p. 991. Authorship of this anonymous review of Hobsbawm & Rudé, op. cit., has been attributed to both E.P. Thompson and R. Cobb.

10   An account by Joseph Mason, in the form of a letter to Charles Bastin of Wherwell, of his experiences in New South Wales following his transportation, Berkshire Record Office (hereafter BRO), D/EWd Z1, p. 8. This account is reproduced in D. Kent & N. Townsend (eds), *Joseph Mason, Assigned Convict 1831-1837: Doomed to the earth's remotest region,* Melbourne, 1996, p. 39.

11   For typologies of protest and their characteristics, see C. Tilly, 'Collective Violence in European Perspective', in H.D. Graham & T.R. Gurr, *Violence in America: Historical and Comparative Perspectives,* New York, 1969, pp. 13-27; G. Rudé, *Paris and London in the Eighteenth Century :Studies in Popular Protest,* London, 1970, pp. 17-34.

12   R. Jefferies, *The Toilers of the Field,* London,1981, p. 51.

13   Ibid., pp. 46-7.

14   'A Very English Rising', p. 991.

15   E.J. Evans, *The Forging of the Modern State: Early Industrial Britain 1783-1870,* Harlow, 1983, p. 146.

16   J. Chambers, *Rebels of the Fields: Robert Mason and the convicts of the Eleanor,* Letchworth, 1995, uses the terminology of rebellion but offers no evidence to show that the labourers' protest had any features which merit that description.

17   Rudé, op. cit., pp. 19-20, 31.

18   Charlesworth, *Atlas of Protest,* p. 5; Rudé, op. cit., pp. 19, 26-7.

19   S.H. Palmer, *Police and Protest in England and Ireland 1780-1850,* Cambridge, 1988, p. 53.

20   M. Berg, 'Workers and Machinery in Eighteenth Century England', in J. Rule (ed.), *British Trade Unionism 1750-1850,* London, 1988, p. 52.

21   E.J. Hobsbawm, *Labouring Men,* London, 1964, pp. 5-17.

22   Articles of Agreement of the Whitchurch, Streatley and Basildon Association, 1822, BRO, D/ER O5.

23   A.J. Randall, *Before the Luddites: Custom, Community and machinery in the English woollen industry 1776-1809,* Cambridge, 1991, pp. 287-88, idem, 'The Industrial Moral Economy of the Gloucestershire Weavers in the Eighteenth Century' in Rule (ed.), op. cit., pp. 29-51, idem, 'The Shearmen and the

Wiltshire Outrages of 1802: Trade Unionism and Industrial Violence', *Social History*, 8, 1982, pp. 283-304.

24 Randall, *Before the Luddites*, p. 289.

25 *The Times*, 23/12/1830, 5/1/1831

26 Fragment of a pamphlet against machinery in Benett Correspondence, WRO, 413/23.

27 Hobsbawm, op. cit., p. 7.

28 Letter of 21/11/30, Public Record Office (hereafter PRO), HO 52/6/11.

29 M. Harrison, *Crowds and History: Mass Phenomena in English Towns, 1790-1835*, Cambridge, 1988, p. 27, citing E.J. Hobsbawm.

30 Ibid., pp.13-14.

31 Hobsbawm, op. cit., p. 7; E.P. Thompson, 'The Moral Economy of the English Crowd in the Eighteenth Century', *Past and Present*, 50, 1971, pp. 76-136, 'The Moral Economy Reviewed' in *Customs in Common*, London, 1991. From an extensive literature see also J. Stevenson, *Popular Disturbances in England 1700-1870*, New York, 1979, pp. 91-135; R.W. Malcolmson, 'A set of ungovernable people': the Kingswood colliers in the eighteenth century' in J. Brewer & J. Styles (eds), *An Ungovernable People: The English and their law in the seventeenth and eighteenth centuries*, London, 1980, pp. 85-127; A. Randall, in Rule, op. cit., pp. 29-51.

32 Rudé, op. cit. p. 31; Palmer. op. cit., pp 51-3.

33 *The Times*, 17/11/1830, and see Chapters Two and Four.

34 For The Deputy-Lieutenant's letter see J.L. & B. Hammond, *The Village Labourer 1760-1832*, London, 1920 edition, p. 241.

35 *The Times*, 8/1/1831, 3/1/1831, 31/12/1830, 7/1/1831, 28/12/1830; *Reading Mercury, Oxford Gazette* (hereafter *RMOG*) 6/12/1830.

36 Ibid., 25/12/1830.

37 Ibid., 14/1/1831.

38 Stevenson, op. cit., p. 240.

39 Ibid., p. 242.

40 Rudé, op. cit., p. 29.

41 The convict indent, or muster roll, for the *Eleanor* is the source for the discussion of the protesters' occupations, criminality, age, condition, literacy and physical characteristics which form the substance of this chapter. Archives Of New South Wales (hereafter AONSW), 2/8257, Reel 2421.

42 J.F.C. Harrison, *The Common People*, London, 1984, p. 251.

43 For the discussion of tradesmen see J.H. Porter, 'The Development of Rural Society', in G.E. Mingay (ed.), *The Agrarian History of England and Wales, Vol. VI, 1750-1850*, Cambridge, 1989, pp. 855-57; D. Grace, 'The Agricultural Engineering Industry' in Mingay, op. cit., p. 521; J.A. Chartres, 'Country

Trades, Crafts and Professions', in Mingay, op. cit., pp. 416-45.

44 The occupations listed in addition to fieldwork and the numbers in each category are set out below. Note the high numbers in the trades related to horse transport which expanded greatly during the agricultural revolution, the solid representation of the major rural trades and crafts and the overall range of skills found in rural communities everywhere. [14] Ostler/groom, [11] Carter, [7] Carpenter, [6] Gardener, Sawyer, [5] Blacksmith, [4] Roadmaker, [3] Bricklayer, Brickmaker, Woodman, [2] Horsebreaker, Butcher, Wheelwright, Tanner, Bricklayers Labourer, Thatcher, Brazier/Whitesmith, Indoor Servant, [1] Maltster, Tailor, Papermaker, Hurdlemaker, Baker, Pond-maker, Ironfounder, Plasterer, Slater, Porter, Jockey, Hedger, Road Surveyor, Fencer, Miller, Farrier, Boat/barge builder, Hop-planter, Drover, Well-sinker, Barber, Chimney-sweep, Shoemaker, Carpetweaver.

45 Chartres, op. cit., pp. 423-5.

46 Grace, op. cit., pp. 523-5.

47 E. Brill, *Life and Tradition on the Cotswolds*, Gloucester, 1990, p. 59.

48 Grace, op. cit., pp. 523-5.

49 Hampshire Record Office (hereafter HRO), 42 M67/PW 14; letter of Richard Fortescue, reproduced in Chambers, op. cit., p. 144.

50 *The Times*, 3/1/1831; BRO, D/E Pg O 1/5.

51 Ibid.

52 *Salisbury and Winchester Journal*, 29/11/1830. Hereafter *SWJ*.

53 Hobsbawm & Rudé, op. cit., pp. 245-6.

54 C. Williams, *Basildon, Berkshire*, Reading, 1994, p. 106; A.G. Harfield, 'Captain William Wyndham of the Hindon Troop Royal Wiltshire Yeomanry', *Journal of the Society for Army Historical Research*, Vol. 42, 1963, pp. 27-35.

55 Chambers, op. cit., p. 168.

56 Ibid., p. 211.

57 The documents relating to the men named in the next two paragraphs are reproduced in Chambers op. cit. in the alphabetically arranged listing of rioters pp. 119-300.

58 *The Times,* 24/12/1830. See Chapter Two.

59 Hobsbawm & Rudé, op. cit., p. 248.

60 Ibid., p.247.

61 A. Somerville, *The Whistler at the Plough*, Manchester, 1852, p. 262.

62 For the convict statistics see L.L. Robson, *The Convict Settlers of Australia*, Melbourne, 1965, pp. 182.

63 Ibid., p. 183.

64 *The Times*, 5/1/1831.

65 The documents relating to family reunions are reproduced in Chambers, op.

cit., in the alphabetically arranged listing of rioters pp. 119-300.

66   Ibid., p. 177.

67   A.M. Colson, 'The Revolt of the Hampshire Agricultural Labourers and its Causes 1812-1831', M.A. thesis, University of London, 1937, pp. 152-3.

68   D. Kent, 'Decorative Bodies: The significance of convicts' tattoos', *Journal of Australian Studies*, No. 53, 1997, pp.78-88.

69   *The Times*, 28/12/1830.

70   R.S. Schofield, 'Dimensions of Illiteracy, 1750-1850', *Explorations in Economic History*, 10, 1973, p. 440.

71   Ibid., p. 62.

72   A. Kussmaul (ed.), *The Autobiography of Joseph Mayett of Quainton 1783-1839*, Aylesbury, 1986, pp. 70-1.

73   S. Nicholas & R. Steckel, 'Heights and living standards of English workers during the early years of industrialisation, 1770-1815', *Journal of Economic History*, 51, 1991, pp. 937-957.

74   Colson, op. cit., Appendix III, pp. 264-306; Mason Letters 1852-65, Mitchell Library MSS 2290.

75   Chambers, op. cit., p. 189.

76   *The Times*, 24/12/1830.

77   W. Cobbett, *Rural Rides*, Harmondsworth, 1967, p. 180.

78   Wells, 'English Rural Proletariat', in Reed & Wells, op. cit., pp. 37-8; Porter, op. cit., p. 888.

79   Cobbett, op. cit., pp. 63-4, 135.

80   HRO, 25 M 61/1/59, Wellington to Fleming, 20/12/1829. By 1832 clerical magistrates constituted about one quarter of all the justices in England and Wales. G.E. Mingay, *A Social History of the English Countryside*, London, 1990, p. 126.

81   HRO, 32 M 66/PO 10.

82   Cobbett, op. cit., p. 152, fn. p. 521.

83   See for example the work of the Curate of Hampstead Norris, C. Davy, *The Pious and Happy Labourer or The Religion of the Bible the Poor Man's Best Friend*, London, 1820, *Cottage Sermons or Short discourses Addressed to Plain People; being Principally Designed for the Use of Pious Cottagers and those in Humble Life*, 2 vols., London 1827; J.F. Moor, *The Duty of Submission to civil authority: a sermon preached in the parish church of Bradfield, Berks, on Sunday, November 28 1830 on occasion of the late disturbances in that neighbourhood*, London, 1830.

84   A.J.C. Hare, *Memorials of a Quiet Life*, 2 vols., London, 1874, pp. 287, 356, 354-5, 358, 355.

85   Cited in Porter, op. cit., p. 887.

86   Ibid., pp. 890-91.

87  Parliamentary Papers, *1851 Census of Great Britain: Religious Worship*, Vol. LXXXIX, 1852-3, Table D, pp. ccxxix, ccxli, ccxlvii, ccxlviii.

88  J.H. Chandler (ed.), *Wiltshire Dissenters' Meeting House Certificates and Registrations,* Devizes, 1985, pp. 75-126

89  E. Billinge, 'Rural Crime and Protest in Wiltshire 1830-1875', Ph.D. thesis, University of Kent, 1984, p. 190.

90  Jefferies, op. cit., pp. 77-8.

91  Dorset Record Office, NM2 C1/MS 1/1, Weymouth Circuit Plan 1830; G. Padden (ed.), *Tolpuddle: An historical account through the eyes of George Loveless,* London, 1984, p. 7.

92  Williams, op. cit., p. 106; BRO, D/EWd Z1, p. 15; Chambers, op. cit., p. 151; *Devizes and Wiltshire Gazette*, 2/12/1830.

93  Hobsbawm & Rudé, op. cit., p. 186.

94  Ibid., p. 187.

95  Wells, 'English Rural Proletariat' in Reed & Wells, op. cit., p. 34.

96  W.A. Armstrong, 'Rural Population Growth, Systems of Employment, and Incomes', in Mingay, op. cit., p. 643.

97  A. Armstrong, *Farmworkers in England and Wales: a social and economic history, 1770-1980,* London, 1988, p. 73.

98  HRO, 96 M 88/1.

99  J. Rule, *The Labouring Classes, in Early Industrial England 1750-1850*, London, 1986, p. 359.

100  Rule, *Labouring Classes*, p. 359.

101  Hobsbawm & Rudé, op. cit., p. 101.

102  Charlesworth, *Atlas of Protest*, p. 153. G.E. Mingay, ''Rural War: the life and times of Captain Swing', in Mingay (ed), *The Unquiet Countryside*, London, 1989, p. 37.

103  A. Charlesworth, *Social Protest in a Rural Society: The Spatial Diffusion of the Captain Swing Disturbances of 1830-1831*, Norwich, 1979.

104  Ibid., pp. 30-39.

105  'A Very English Rising', p. 991.

# Chapter 2

# 'WE DON'T WANT TO DO ANY MISCHIEF':
# THE VOICE OF PROTEST

This chapter is not a comprehensive account of the Swing disturbances in Wessex. Rather, it is a narrative of events involving the men transported to New South Wales. In reconstructing the incidents we have, whenever possible, isolated the dynamics of social interaction and attempted to catch the voice of protest in order to understand the behaviour of men who paid for their protest with exile.[1] In the four counties the disturbances were relatively uncomplicated by the agitation over tithes and rents found elsewhere and there was less co-operation with farmers.[2] As a result, protest in Wessex was a direct expression of the labourers' concerns; they resented labour-displacing agricultural machinery and they needed an increase in wages. The modest aspirations of one Wiltshire labourer were probably shared by the majority of his fellow labourers – 'we don't want to do any mischief, but we want the poor children when they go to bed should have a belly full of 'tatoes instead of crying with half a belly full'.[3] To secure the very limited social protection they sought, the labourers resorted to a familiar form of direct action which was shaped by custom and popular culture.

### Berkshire

The disturbances in Berkshire commenced in the eastern part of the county with the usual prelude of threatening letters and a few arson attacks. Open protest began and ended in this area with the machine-breaking activities of a single group of labourers around Waltham St. Lawrence. Solomon Allen, the leader of a small party which destroyed two threshing machines, told a farmer that 'they were 40 sworn men come out of Kent to drive the country before them'.[4] This was scarcely credible since he had worked for the farmer before and was a near neighbour. Allen's statement indicates that news of the disturbances in the south-east was percolating through the countryside and he was prepared to exploit the fear it created.[5] The labourers informed another farmer that they had been sworn in by the magistrates at Reading to break all the machines in the county; 'by virtue of their oath they were compelled to do their duty', for which they charged only five shillings. This equally incredible claim was made quite often and it seems likely that it was an attempt at self-justification combined with a degree of wishful-thinking about the behaviour of those in authority. For many labourers the destruction of machinery which threatened employment was a social imperative and as someone in this party declared, they were going 'to break all the machines and regulate the country for six months, and set it to rights'.

At one farm the party was refused food and drink even though James Simonds was waving a sword about. The threat of an all-consuming fire secured both refreshment and the farmer's invitation to destroy his machine provided his ricks and barn were spared. The machine had already been dismantled, an action which suggests that there was some truth in Allen's claim that the farmer had received notice of intent, but, as he said, 'it was easily put up again'. Allen, as 'foreman of the gang', ordered Wheeler to smash the teeth out of the iron horsewheel with his sledgehammer. This was done by the light of a candle and lantern borrowed from the farmer and held by Charles Horton. In a picaresque conclusion, Allen borrowed a hammer to repair their broken sledgehammer. It was duly returned, even though it would have been useful on a further occasion, and the party departed after consuming 'as much beer as they wished'. The speedy detention of this group probably prevented any further displays of overt protest in east Berkshire although arson attacks continued for some time.[6]

In central Berkshire a major outbreak of machine-breaking began on 18 November in the villages around Aldermaston. Thirty-five threshing machines were wrecked in the course of as many hours in the most concentrated bout of machine-breaking anywhere in the country.[7] Of all the machines broken in Berkshire nearly half were wrecked in this foray. The fictions of a link with the disturbances in Kent and official sanction for the destruction of machines were repeated in this incident. George Williams, 'Staffordshire Jack', declared 'that he had been all over Kent…that he was employed by Government to break machines' and would be paid five shillings for each. When the crowd arrived at Mr Hickman's farm at Aldermaston at ten o'clock in the morning of the 19th, having been out all night, they told him that they had already broken thirty-one machines and 'would break every machine in the county before they slept'.

The size of the crowd fluctuated as it moved from farm to farm. Many joined voluntarily and some were pressed although the level of persuasion used can never really be known. A witness told of horses being unhitched and men 'pressed from the plough'. Another alleged that George Williams 'held a stick over my head, and said he would be d-d if he would not beat my head off with it if I did not follow the mob'. The same individual claimed to have been beaten after he tried to escape and then ducked in a pig-trough because the crowd was 'ashamed to see me so bloody'. One hundred and thirteen men were counted by William Hawkins during a brief stop in the grounds of Aldermaston Park but one of those present suggested that many others had been missed.

From the moment of joining the crowd at the Hind's Head, Thomas Hicks took control and at Mount's farm he directed it away from the house lest Mrs Mount and the children be alarmed. He also led twenty or thirty men into a violent confrontation at Brimpton. Edward Cove, the vicar of Brimpton and a magistrate, assembled an armed party to 'put the rioters down'. When the two groups met head on, Cove read the Riot Act but the labourers would not disperse and a short, violent affray ensued. Hicks, Luke Brown, Daniel Hancock and Edward Harris were identified as the chief combatants among the protesters. During the struggle Hicks opened his waistcoat to a farmer and invited him to 'shoot if you like', before resuming his efforts to evade arrest by whirling his sledgehammer around. The sledgehammers, pieces of iron, parts of threshing machines, and iron balls on sticks with which the labourers were armed inflicted some nasty wounds but could not prevent the arrest of half the participants and the subsequent detention of the others. The larger crowd melted away and there were no further disturbances in these parishes. Defiance was not eliminated of course. When some of the rioters were taken into Reading Gaol one said to Hicks 'we'll set the b-y place on fire' and Daniel Hancock, who had been very active in the fight, threatened to 'mark' the constable who detained him if he was gaoled for three or four years. That comment is very revealing for it shows that although the labourers recognised that they would probably be punished for their part in a riot, they had no comprehension of the dire penalties in store for them. But on 19 November nobody could have predicted the escalation of violence and destruction which would follow across three counties in a matter of days.

The other major wave of machine-breaking in Berkshire occurred around Hungerford in the west of the county. Two separate groups were engaged in this series of disturbances. The 'Hungerford mob' consisted of labourers who lived in, and around, the town while the 'Kintbury mob' comprised men from that village on the Newbury road and other adjacent settlements. John Aldridge, Isaac Burton, Charles Green, Jason Greenway and William Waving were part of the Hungerford crowd which on 22 November destroyed machines at Welford, Avington, Boxford, Chievely and several other places. The other band, with flag and horn, had started its work on the evening of 21 November in Kintbury and had continued the following day in Inkpen, Hampstead-Marshall, and West Woodhay before entering Hungerford.

The machine-breaking and collection of largess was carried out with the usual combination of menace and restraint.[8] The Kintbury men did not use the threat of fire, preferring instead to threaten the fabric of the house. Frederick Webb refused to part with a sovereign but the cry of 'down with the house' persuaded his wife to hand over the money. William Clarkson, gamekeeper to the local Member of Parliament, Charles Dundas, was equally reluctant to provide a donation until the crowd – with William Sims, a bricklayer, and Alfred Darling, a former blacksmith, very prominent – began an assault on his cottage exclaiming 'we will have it down in three minutes'. The threat worked well for the Kintbury men collected a large sum and their treasurer had over one hundred pounds in his possession at the time of his arrest.[9] In general though, there was remarkably little damage to the fabric of farmhouses and barns, apart from a broken door and a window or two, and the level of property loss was restricted to an item of agricultural machinery. The scale of damage and loss was greatly increased, however, when the crowd entered Hungerford and attacked Richard Gibbons' foundry.

The destruction of the iron foundry was, indirectly, the result of an attempt to defuse the situation in the countryside around Hungerford. John Willes, a magistrate who was in the town on the morning of 22 November, learned of the disturbances and rode out with a small party to intercept the machine-breakers. He encountered the combined groups near Denford and promised to do whatever he could to relieve the men's grievances, provided they accompanied him to Hungerford for a meeting. This offer was well received with cries of 'Mr Willes for ever' and a round of cheers. On reaching the edge of town, however, the self-control of some of the crowd slipped and, ignoring Willes' pleas, they stopped to break some windows. Attention then shifted to Gibbons' foundry where the crowd was briefly checked by a nearby resident who offered five sovereigns if the place was left alone. But when someone shouted 'hark forward, go at it, beat the iron to pieces', the crowd of around five hundred surged through the gates and proceeded to destroy bellows equipment, a crane, a furnace, some flasks for making moulds, and many of the machinery wheels made in the foundry. The crowd then moved to the Town Hall to meet with Willes, John Pearse, the Member of Parliament for Devizes, and several other local dignitaries. When the crowd would not listen to his address from the Town Hall steps, Willes invited a deputation of five men from each contingent to continue negotiations inside.

The Hungerford deputies demanded twelve shillings a week wages, the removal of machinery and a reduction in house rents. Pearse promised that wages would be raised but he ignored the question of machinery and referred the labourers to their landlords over the matter of rents. This appeased the Hungerford deputation but the Kintbury men who then stepped up to the table were less easily satisfied. William Oakley, a wheelwright whose village foundry had been wrecked in the first flare-up at Kintbury, was the principal spokesman of this group. Pointing out that the authorities did not have 'such d-d flats to deal with now, as you had before', Oakley demanded two shillings a day for labourers until Lady Day with two shillings and sixpence thereafter, and three shillings and sixpence for tradesmen. Almost as an afterthought, and in what seems like an act of calculated defiance, he added, 'and as we are here, we will have £5 before we leave the place or we will smash it'. Another deputy, striking his sledgehammer on the floor, agreed – 'Yes, we will have it, or we will have blood, and down with the b-y place'.

The social animosity which fuelled the frustrations of labouring people is evident in this incident. Pearse, as one of the law-creating, law-enforcing elite, refused to sanction any donation. To this Oakley responded, 'you gentlemen have been living long enough on the good things; now it is our time, and we will have them. You gentlemen would not speak to us now, only you are afraid and intimidated'. When the worthy protectors of property hesitated he urged them to 'look sharp', and warned them against 'laying your heads together to commit us to prison for the sake of £2 a piece'.[10] The aggression and defiance of the Kintbury men paid off for they collected their five pounds and some villages were sufficiently impressed by their achievements to send a message inviting them to join a combined operation the next day and there was talk of a march on Newbury.[11] Willes and Pearse would have been particularly alarmed by the deputies' contempt for authority. In the confrontation with Dundas's gamekeeper, William Sims had declared that 'if Mr Dundas were in his own house and in a chair he would drag him out on the floor by the head and after that pull the house down over him'. When sentiments like that were voiced by common labourers about an elderly and liberal-minded parliamentarian, the propertied elite must have realised how uncertain was the loyalty and deference of the masses.

Although the arrest of the Kintbury men put an end to the disturbances around Hungerford there were several other outbreaks in Berkshire, two of which produced residents for New South Wales. The first began north of Thatcham and moved east to Streatley and Basildon on the Thames. The second occurred in the valley which stretches north-west from Newbury into the Downs and centred on Eastbury, East Garston and West Shefford. In many respects the former outbreak might be seen as the archetypal Swing disturbance. The labourers gathered in the churchyard at Yattendon on 21 November for a perambulation which lasted until the early hours of 24 November when soldiers from Reading dispersed them. The party was orderly and disciplined, it was 'preceded by a horn…the rear kept up by whippers in', it confined its property damage to machines and injured nobody.[12] Farmers were asked to sign a paper which promised twelve shillings a week to married labourers and nine shillings to single men. Thomas Hanson and Charles Milson were the crowd's 'fore-leaders'.[13] Hanson recruited support very actively declaring that he wanted 'to get a sight of people together to strike for wages and break machines'. Milson collected the fee for the work of destruction and there was no question of compromise. John Frome of Streatley offered four shillings but was made to pay the full amount, 'for their rule was 5s'. The payment legitimised the labourers' action and was seen as an appropriate reward for their effort. Farmers who were reluctant to sign the wage agreement or make a donation had their labourers pressed into the crowd. Joseph

Edney was identified as the man who kept the crowd together; 'he walked behind with a stick and threatened to strike any person who attempted to get away'. However, one man could not have prevented desertions from a crowd of over one hundred. Most were present because they wanted to be there and if Edney's task was to prevent desertion he was singularly unsuccessful because the crowd which reached Basildon was a mere fragment of the earlier body.

The band which made their way up the Lambourn valley breaking at least ten threshing machines was directed by Thomas Mackrell. At Palmer's farm in East Garston, Mackrell 'held up his stick to direct and encourage' the younger men in their destruction of a water-driven machine valued at £150.[14] This crowd charged £2 per machine and Mackrell, at least, saw the occasion as an opportunity for some rough social justice. At West Shefford, where a machine was wrecked and the usual largess requested, Mackrell told John Westbury that he had heard the farmer was 'the worst in the parish'. The final flurry of protest in Berkshire occurred in the northern part of the county where the labourers were more concerned with negotiating wage increases than destroying machines, and the presence of a troop of yeomanry averted more serious trouble.

### Hampshire

The disturbances in Hampshire followed the usual warning signals. Farmers in the Portsmouth area received threatening letters from 10 November and there were isolated cases of arson, including one on the Duke of Wellington's estate at Strathfield Saye. Protest 'in open day' began on the 17 November in the south-east corner of the county when labourers from West Sussex crossed into Hampshire and destroyed threshing machines in the vicinity of Fareham and Havant. Thereafter, the disturbances spread with astonishing rapidity and within two days incidents were reported from all parts of the county. One of the largest crowds was formed when the men from villages in the Dever valley, north-west of Winchester, congregated at Sutton Scotney.

The day of protest began with the collection of largess by groups of labourers in Micheldever and the other villages.[15] The labourers knew what they wanted – 'an advance of wages to 2s. a day, and to break…machinery'. At a meeting with a magistrate in Sutton Scotney, in addition to their demand for twelve shillings a week for married men and nine shillings for single, the men asked for a gallon loaf and sixpence for every child over two years. They also rather cheekily asked for wages for the two days spent in machine-breaking. William Paine, who lost a threshing machine to a polite, disciplined party thought that the wage increase was quite reasonable and he was sufficiently at ease with his visitors to offer them beer and a promise of the higher rate. The crowd charged Paine one pound for breaking his machine but the fee varied somewhat according to the status of the owner. Thomas

Dowden, the largest employer in the parish, was made to pay two pounds 'because he had most land', and at East Stratton Sir Thomas Baring's steward was asked for ten pounds. The sum thus collected was considerable and by the end of the day the treasurer was carrying almost £40. Some money was expended on food and drink but the crowd was scrupulously well-behaved. When it stopped for refreshment at a public house, the leaders stipulated that each man should have only half a pint and Joseph Mason insisted that an account be kept for the beer consumed which he then paid for. At the end of the day the crowd mustered in a meadow at Sutton Scotney where the remaining money was distributed among the participating parishes.

One ugly incident occurred when William Baring, with a posse of twenty-five men, attempted to arrest a similar number of labourers at Northington Farm near Micheldever. Baring collared someone at the front of the crowd which promptly rescued the man but during the pushing and shoving a young man aimed a blow of his hammer at him. While no real injury was done, except to the brim of Baring's hat, much was made of this incident and the young man paid for his impetuosity with his life.[16] The authorities chose not to notice how well controlled all the parties were in this area. Although they were armed with rural implements, crow-bars, sledgehammers, pump-handles, axes, bludgeons and sticks, and could have caused considerable injury to people and property there was little violence and almost no unnecessary damage. This was no frenzied rural *jacquerie*. Indeed, the protesters went to great lengths to behave honourably. Francis Callendar, Sir Thomas Baring's steward, bargained with the crowd which promised not to go up to Baring's mansion, Stratton House, if Callendar donated £10 to the fund. He did, and the crowd honoured its pledge.

Even so, individual enterprise could not be regulated, and isolated acts of intimidation could happen anywhere. After the large crowd had dispersed, small groups continued to wander the darkening countryside soliciting donations. James Annells, Jacob Turner and twenty or thirty others visited two houses in Newton Stacey where their request for largess was accompanied by the invitation to 'look at the light over the hills'. Leonard Lywood interpreted this strange request as a subtle threat, and he must have thought himself wise to part with fifteen shillings when about an hour later the sky was lit by a large fire at Barton Manor Farm.[17] Responsibility for the fire was never established – there was not one commitment for arson at the Winchester Commission – but the Attorney-General in opening the case against Annells noted that he was connected in some degree with the fires.

The disturbances which broke out in and around Andover on 19/20 November were marked by a level of disorder and destruction which made them far more menacing than the events described above. More damage was done to machinery in this episode than anywhere else in the county.[18] The troubles began on 19 November with the destruction of agricultural machinery in a village outside

Andover.[19] A prisoner taken to the gaol was subsequently freed by a 'huge multitude' which broke down the gates and carried him in triumph through the town. Shopkeepers locked their doors and put up their shutters against the crowd, which was especially large and volatile for it was the occasion of the Andover Fair. By evening, it was common knowledge that the following day an assault would be made on manufacturing establishments in the area. This awareness suggests a level of co-ordination and planning which may have been quite widespread in the Swing disturbances but which shows up very rarely in the surviving records. Forewarned, the owners of Tasker's Waterloo Foundry in Upper Clatford two miles from Andover closed down the works and extinguished the furnace fires to minimise the risk of extensive damage in the event of an attack.

On the Saturday morning labourers from surrounding villages again marched into Andover. Some carried stale bread on pitchforks, a symbol often associated with agitation arising from distress. In a further display of the labourers' attachment to the traditional protocol of protest the crowd took its complaint to those in authority. The local magistrates were meeting at the Upper Angel public house to frame a statement about wage increases and allowances in the hope of averting disturbances in the area.[20] John Gilmore and William Shepherd with three others 'came into the justice-room in rather a violent manner'. Presumably these men had been deputed to act as negotiators and present the labourers' case to the authorities. How the discussion was handled is unknown but the outcome was all that the labourers might have wished and was strikingly similar to the demands made by the Micheldever men. The magistrates and farmers agreed on the usual amounts of twelve shillings for adult men and nine shillings for youths but did not relate the wage to marital status. They also pledged three shillings a week to the aged and infirm with sixpence and a gallon loaf for children. Notices signed by seventy 'occupiers of land' in the area announcing the new wage rates and allowances were printed on 23 November and posted in the town and surrounding villages.

The foreman of Tasker's was also at the Upper Angel and recognised Gilmore and the Manns brothers. The labourers were convinced that the foundry was bad for everyone, farm labourers, smiths and carpenters. The building, James Manns declared, 'should come down' and, with his brother, Isaac, and Charles Fay as flag-bearer, he led the crowd to Upper Clatford where they were instrumental in forcing the gates. Once inside, the large crowd exchanged its bludgeons for hammers and better tools stored in the foundry, and proceeded to attack the water-wheel, the lathes, a pressing machine, and various casting moulds. However, the damage which the crowd could inflict was limited. It took three-quarters of an hour to bend and break some of the parts of the wheel and, as Robert Tasker acknowledged, the crane could not be destroyed without 'very heavy implements'. Equipped as it was, the crowd might have laboured for several hours more without a significant increase in actual damage. The windows and roof were more vulnerable, however, and the fabric of the building was extensively damaged.

The assault on Tasker's foundry had one very unusual aspect. The crowd refused to compromise in its task of destruction even when offered 'plenty of sovereigns if they would'. In many Swing incidents the victim mitigated the extent of damage by a prudent offer of money or victuals and the crowd, once symbolic destruction had occurred, accepted the donation and moved on. But at Tasker's, the crowd was adamant that the foundry should come down. John Howell, the foreman at the works, offered to pay the protesters whatever was required to halt the damage, but he later admitted that 'some of them were offended' by his gesture. When a similar proposition was put to Gilmore by one of Tasker's journeyman he spurned it saying 'd-n their eyes – no money – go to work'. The refusal to be bought off suggests that the labourers were utterly committed to the destruction of the foundry and that the public assault was an index of community displeasure.

The very openness of the incident sheds some light on the thinking of those involved. When William Stanford was asked what good might come from the destruction, he replied that 'Mr Tasker would, perhaps, prefer their doing what they had done to having his farms set on fire', a remark which might have been a threat or a calculated assessment of the most appropriate course of action. The latter seems likely for the methods of open protest had succeeded. A week after the Andover disturbances, a magistrate wrote to Lord Melbourne, the new Home Secretary, that 'the Peasantry have not only dictated a rate of wages, not only destroyed all agricultural machinery, and demolished iron foundries, but have proceeded in formidable bodies to private dwellings to extort money and provisions – in fact, have established a system of pillage'.[21]

The 'system of pillage' occurred across the county. It was very pronounced in the villages on the Hampshire Downs which stretched north-west from Basingstoke to the borders of Wiltshire and Berkshire. At Vernham's Dean a crowd visited several isolated farms breaking agricultural machines where they found them and demanding largess.[22] The men transported to New South Wales, like so many others, made no attempt to conceal their identities and their farmer-employers had no difficulty in recognising them. Jacob Wiltshire who demanded a sovereign from Darius Bull had worked for him for many years and according to the farmer 'had always borne a good character'. The crowd which solicited two sovereigns and beer from Mary Sergeant was interrupted by the arrival of Edward Holmes, the parish constable. He could not seriously hinder the crowd's behaviour but he did recognise fellow villagers. Robert Cook was armed with a hatchet and with George Hopgood made 'the most violent threats' to the constable. The reports of the trial do not indicate the particular roles played by the others who were transported but it seems reasonable to assume that the farmers and the constable named those who were prominent in the crowd's activities.

William Sclater of Tangier Park, Wootton St Lawrence, was equally able to identify the men who demanded two sovereigns from him.[23] This crowd, complete with
a horn-blower, traversed several parishes around Basingstoke impressing support,
breaking machines and collecting donations in the usual manner. The leaders, who
included Charles Pain and John Batten, ordered that there be 'no blood nor no fire'
and no robbery. A gentleman who had no money in his pocket and offered the crowd
his watch instead was told, in no uncertain terms, that they would not take it.[24] Most
of the men were equipped with nothing more menacing than the countryman's ubiquitous stick and only seven or eight had hammers. A carpenter working in a house
at Worting was pressed into the crowd largely because he had a hammer which
someone said 'would suit us very well'. When Sclater refused to contribute, Pain, who
carried a sledgehammer, threatened, 'then we must go to work'. The warning that
soldiers were on their way proved no deterrent for, as one of the labourers said, 'we
don't care for the soldiers; we can die but once; the soldiers won't fire upon us'.
Fortunately this miscalculation of class loyalty was not put to the test. The crowd
forcibly incorporated Sclater's gardeners into their number and, by posing a threat
to the house, persuaded its owner to part with his money.

The men who demanded money at the Reverend William Easton's house at St
Mary Bourne were members of his parish but they were prepared to invade his house
for they were concerned with more than the collection of largess.[25] This was an occasion where 'mob-begging' was used to register community disapproval of an
unpopular individual.[26] The crowd initially stopped at the garden gate, which was
fastened against them, where the clergyman's son asked what they wanted. 'To come
in', someone replied suggesting that they were intent on a personal confrontation
which went beyond the usual protocol. Although the crowd ultimately demanded
and obtained money the insistence on entry to the garden was significant. When this
was refused the leader, William Sims, broke open the gate with his pick-axe and the
men moved up to the house where some pushed their way inside.

The unusually aggressive display was prompted by anger at Easton's attitude to
the plight of the labourers. Sims took the cleric to task for preaching a sermon the
previous Sunday which 'was against the poor'. Daniel Sims, William's son, also castigated Easton saying, 'damn you, where will your text be next Sunday'. Given the
prevailing nature of social relationships in the countryside and the powerful position
of the parson, the resentment felt by Easton's parishioners must have been very great.
Easton, for his part, tried to calm things by informing the crowd that their request
for increased wages had been met and that a notice to that effect had been posted at
the church. He also claimed to be a friend to the poor, a claim which would have
seemed a little odd to those who knew him so well for Easton was a wealthy pluralist;
his annual income was close to £550 yet this friend to the poor paid a miserly five
shillings a year in poor rates.[27] In this incident, as in several others in Hampshire and

many more in Sussex, there was a strong element of anticlericalism and resentment at the large tithes collected by some clergy. The crowd which swept through the parishes of Burghclere, East Woodhay and Highclere showed a similar lack of respect for the clergy.[28] William Stroud led a small collecting party to the Reverend Barton's residence in Burghclere where he demanded two sovereigns and threatened 'to beat the house down' by calling up the rest of the crowd if he was refused. The clergyman was not at home but Stroud insisted on payment; Barton's servant was told that if his master had been present the sum would have been five pounds.[29]

The attack on the poorhouses at Selborne and Headley, south-east of Alton, had much in common with disturbances in adjacent West Sussex where the operation of the Poor Law and concern over tithes were major issues. In the 1820s farmers frequently claimed that the burden of tithe payments made it harder for them to increase wages.[30] The labourers on the Sussex border shared the common hostility to agricultural machinery but they also collaborated, to some extent, with the farmers to make a wage increase conditional upon a reduction in tithes. Aaron Harding informed the Reverend William Cobbold of Selborne that the farmers had agreed to raise wages to twelve shillings a week provided the labourers, in turn, secured a reduction of the tithes.[31] Cobbold thought the wage rise quite reasonable although he bridled at Harding's suggestion that 'we must have a touch at your tithes too'. However, pressure from the crowd and the farmers who were in attendance persuaded Cobbold to sign an agreement to reduce his tithes by half to £300. Someone suggested that '£4 a week is quite enough' – an extraordinarily generous sentiment when the clergyman's unearned income would still have been more than six times the sum the labourers sought for their weekly toil. The crowd insisted on having the agreement on paper and waited while Cobbold's bailiff drew it up.

Armed with the agreement, the crowd set out to secure the signatures of local farmers to the wage increase, and Robert Holdaway, a carpenter and wheelwright, was deputed to carry the paper and make the necessary approaches. A tradesman and former innkeeper, Holdaway was probably seen as someone unlikely to be overawed by the farmers. In the course of the day the crowd, with two flag-bearers and a horn-blower, visited a number of farms breaking machines, levying largess and obtaining signatures to the agreement. The following day the perambulation continued in the neighbouring parish of Headley where Holdaway met with the Reverend Dickenson, who had agreed to reduce his tithe, and the farmers in The Bush public house. The agreement was endorsed and the farmers donated some money to be spent by the crowd.[32] In the matter of wages and tithes the collective protest was a success, but the attacks on the poorhouses in both parishes jeopardised that achievement.

The assaults on the Selborne and the Headley poorhouses show the depth of popular anger and resentment towards the prevailing system of poor relief. When Cobbold first encountered the crowd he was told by Harding and others that they were going to evict 'old Harrison', one of the Guardians who lived in the workhouse. Cobbold was assured that they were not going to pull the place down and, given the limited nature of the damage, the protest at Selborne has all the marks of a symbolic gesture. The absent guardian's family was allowed to leave and then the crowd proceeded to break some windows, doors and partitions, and damage the roof by pulling off tiles. Somehow a fire started but it was put out by one of those later indicted for his part in the affair. As Justice Parke noted during the trial, the crowd stopped short of total destruction of the building 'of their own accord' and he suggested 'that they intended…to go no further than such injury'. All this points to a ritualistic expression of anger which was channelled into some relatively minor damage to a building whose very presence was a reminder of the social injustice which the labourers endured.

A similar judgement was planned for the Headley poorhouse on 23 November. At eight in the morning Matthew Triggs approached the master, James Shoesmith, to obtain the release of his uncle, who was an inmate, because he thought 'there would be a row or a piece of work at the house that day'. Later in the morning, the Headley people were joined by a crowd from Selborne, and around one thousand, with Holdaway at their head, moved on the building. Some of those present had been impressed; Triggs, armed with a 'famous large' bludgeon, compelled the workmen at Headley Rectory to join the crowd. Great care was taken to limit the risk of personal injury. Holdaway told Shoesmith, 'I mean you no harm, nor your wife, nor your goods, so get them out as soon as you can, for the house must come down'. The rooms of certain old people and some sick children were identified by marking the windows so that they could be protected. A few of the crowd tried to enter the building before all the precautions were in place but they were called back by Henry James who helped the master remove his goods and later posted a guard outside the children's quarters. The damage done to the poorhouse was more serious than had occurred at Selborne. The crowd broke the windows, doors, and partitions and tore down the ceilings and rafters in the garrets. Triggs and John Heath were busy on the roof where forty to fifty thousand tiles were ripped off. No room was left intact except those of the aged paupers and the sick children who were helped outside, 'covered over and kept from harm all the while'. At Selborne the crowd was active for about fifteen minutes while at Headley the destruction lasted for well over an hour. It seems likely that the leaders lost control because the crowd found Shoesmith's store of home-made wine. The master later gave evidence that Aaron Harding 'was doing nothing but drinking my wine' and his brother, Thomas, 'was quite drunk'. This incident was one of the few that got out of hand; symbolic damage had been over-taken by destruction valued at eight hundred pounds. Holdaway, who had tried several times to call the crowd away, complained when he saw the seriousness of the situation, 'I am sorry to see it – it is too bad – it will hang me'.[33] On the last point he was wrong, but the authorities saw the wrecking of the poorhouses as particularly threatening to the social order.

No less worrying were the occasions when the farmers gave active encouragement to the labourers and made a reduction of tithes and rents a prerequisite for any increase in wages. This collaboration, a feature of a number of incidents across the southern part of the county from the South Downs to beyond Winchester, brought the labourers into direct conflict with the pillars of rural society, the clergy and the landowners. At Upham the crowd, accompanied by several farmers, attempted to persuade the Reverend Mr Haygarth to lower his tithes so that the farmers could increase wages.[34] The Owslebury men wrote out an agreement which a sympathetic farmer, later transported to Van Diemen's Land for his involvement, carried around to his neighbours persuading them to sign. The agreement promised a wage increase to two shillings a day 'on consideration of our rents and tithes being abated in proportion'.[35] On one side of the paper the occupiers of land pledged to raise wages while on the reverse, tithe-owners and landlords confirmed they would reduce their imposts. This party was reasonably successful in obtaining signatures, but at East Wellow the Reverend Thomas Penton flatly refused to sign a similar agreement and the farmers were equally hostile as a consequence.[36]

Although wage and tithe negotiations featured prominently in these incidents, the crowds did not forsake machine-breaking and the collection of largess. In attending to their task, the labourers were both orderly and assertive. Abraham Childs, 'acting as an officer and calling out commands', led a column of over two hundred men, six abreast, on its perambulation through Upham, Corhampton and South Stonham. Childs had tied a brightly coloured handkerchief around himself like a sash, presumably as a mark of authority or so that he could be seen by the crowd. The vaguely military order of this particular party, which must have increased its menace, was not lessened by William Primer's firing of a gun as a signal for the crowd to assemble.[37] These crowds also asked for particularly large amounts, either as largess or as the fee for the destruction of machinery. At Preshaw House in Corhampton, the home of Walter Long Esq., Childs and his party demanded ten guineas. The East Wellow labourers asked the Reverend Penton for ten pounds, and William Adams, armed with an axe, sought five sovereigns from Lord Northesk's steward, and 'twelve or fourteen pounds' from another landowner, although he settled for five.

In many confrontations the crowd's menace was governed by the number of local men present. Out of their own parish the labourers were often bolder than they might otherwise have been. Many of those who were active in East Wellow were outsiders. A Romsey solicitor recalled how he and a magistrate encountered men 'just coming out of Wiltshire' who threatened to drag the magistrate off his horse because he had committed several of their fellows to gaol the previous day. One farmer endeavoured to disperse the crowd by identifying the men from the local parish but only succeeded in provoking a visit to his own farm where John Pointer, whose leadership was signified by the riband around his hat, asked for two pounds as payment for the destruction of a chaff-cutter. Although the farmer was reluctant, he was persuaded to part with a pound when Pointer was bold enough to note that 'we can work as well by night as by day'. The threat of arson was undoubtedly the most terrifying in the protesters' arsenal of menace, and on this occasion, like many others, it was sufficient to produce compliance with the crowd's wishes.

The last important disturbance in the county, at Fordingbridge near the border with Wiltshire and Dorset, realised all the authorities' worst fears. The crowd, which broke agricultural machinery, levied largess for several miles around and attacked two manufacturing establishments in the town, was commanded by a charismatic stranger mounted on a white horse, who called himself 'Captain Hunt'.[38] The labourers, addressed him bare-headed, protected him and endowed him with an extraordinary authority. The adoption of the name of a well-known radical who had recently visited the area added political overtones to a protest which was generally apolitical. 'Hunt' claimed to have come 'from 20 miles above London' with men from Kent, 'the most desperate that were out'. He identified the labourers' actions with the radical cause and was heard to call out, 'Liberty is all I want!'. In reality, 'Captain Hunt' was James Cooper, an ostler from East Grimstead in Wiltshire, but his role in the Fordingbridge affair was worthy of any 'Captain Swing' and he paid for it with his life.

William Shepherd manufactured threshing machines at Stuckton near Fordingbridge; his premises were an obvious target because the crowd was 'determined to destroy all machinery'.[39] Aaron Deadman, Charles Read and William Newman were particularly conspicuous in the machine-breaking at Shepherd's. Later in the day, after a perambulation through the countryside destroying machinery and collecting food and drink, the crowd turned its attention to Samuel Thompson's sacking manufactory. The attack on this establishment was carefully planned. Some five hours beforehand, Joseph Arney, who was doing roadwork 'scraping the dirt', warned a passing miller that 'the factory would be beat down' before he returned from market. When the attack began, Arney and Henry Eldridge 'were almost the two first who went to the factory' in a crowd armed with iron bars and bludgeons. Eldridge, who admitted being present at the destruction of sixteen threshing machines that day, helped to wreck the spinning and weaving equipment and broke some windows. George Clarke, Samuel Quinton and Charles Hayter were seen breaking machines inside the building and other equipment which was thrown into the yard. The one-armed Hayter was very active, waving his hand from an upstairs window to encourage the crowd, and wielding a bar of iron to great effect. In a public house later in the evening, someone was heard to remark that 'I'll be d-d if that old man there did not do more with his one arm in breaking the machinery than any man with his two'. The crowd was in the mill for about forty minutes and in that time managed to do damage estimated at one thousand pounds. During the early evening, they gradually dispersed although several small parties continued to forage the area for largess.

There were few disturbances in the mainland part of the county after Fordingbridge. On the Isle of Wight the protest tapered off into covert action with a few fires and threatening letters, but by 28 November the labourers' protest in Hampshire was virtually over.

## Wiltshire

Although the disturbances in Wiltshire were broadly similar to events in Berkshire and Hampshire, they were marked by an intensity which reflected the desperate condition of the labourers in the arable portion of the county. Wages in the chalk-land area of corn and sheep farming were 'notoriously low' and even in summer could be as little as seven or eight shillings a week.[40] The few days grace which the authorities had before the disturbances in Berkshire and Hampshire spread into Wiltshire alerted them to the need for placatory action but even when the magistrates met at Devizes to confirm a wage increase, the rate for six days labour was set at ten shillings and not the twelve commonly agreed in the neighbouring counties.[41] However, because the farmers and magistrates made immediate concessions there were fewer demands for increased wages than in the other two counties. In Wiltshire the labourers' anger was directed more specifically than elsewhere at agricultural machinery; in a few days they accounted for one quarter of all the threshing machines destroyed in England. But the warning which the authorities had of impending trouble allowed them to marshal their forces and the labourers met more resistance than previously. Farmers and landowners in Wiltshire were more likely to threaten the protesters with firearms than their counterparts to the east and the yeomanry was deployed more often. As a result, many of the confrontations were marked by quite fierce skirmishes.

As occurred elsewhere, overt protest began after a number of arson attacks. On Sunday 21 November a crowd destroyed a threshing machine at All Cannings near Devizes, and at Hippenscombe on the Hampshire border another began its work in a very systematic way. Farmers in these thinly populated upland parishes were visited by small parties who requested that machines be dismantled, thereby enforcing the labourers desire without direct action. When resistance was encountered the crowd returned in greater numbers. On the afternoon of 21 November about sixty men approached William Fulbrook, asked him for money, advised him to dismantle any machines in his possession, and warned that his compliance would be checked on a later visit.[42] The following afternoon Shadrach Blake was one of about a dozen men who returned to the farm. Fulbrook, who had indicated the previous day that he resented the labourers interference in his affairs refused to give the men of the inspection party the food and drink they requested. At four in the afternoon the labourers were very likely in some need of sustenance and their expectations were not great for Blake suggested that they would be satisfied with a shilling instead. When Fulbrook rejected this request for appropriate hospitality the situation deteriorated and normally suppressed tensions came to the fore.

With social relations so delicately balanced it is easy to visualise the angry slide into naked hostility. Blake warned the farmer of the crowd's potential for destruction, telling him that if he did not provide something 'we will be back with a mob before four o'clock in the morning and burn your house down'.[43] Someone threatened to break down the farmhouse doors, and Fulbrook, declaring that he would shoot anyone who tried, actually took up a gun and pointed it at the men who were now rattling the palings of his fence. According to Blake, he threatened to blow their brains out. This forced the inspection party to depart but between eight and nine o'clock that evening a crowd of around 300 returned. The labourers proceeded to smash the windows and doors of the farmhouse and destroy a threshing machine. Blake was later heard to boast that they 'had not left a whole square' of glass in Fulbrook's house and that they 'had served the old fellow out nicely'.

Once again the limited nature of the damage done to Fulbrook's farm is striking. The crowd might easily have demolished, burned or thoroughly looted it. In an equivalent Irish rural protest such behaviour would not have been unusual.[44] But this crowd, like so many others during the Swing disturbances, was content with symbolic, expensive, nuisance damage which demonstrated the depth of community disapproval, in this case almost certainly triggered by Fulbrook's aggression and his refusal to observe the protocol of hospitality. After the incident at Fulbrook's farm, Blake was overheard arranging with others to resume their activities at eight the following morning. This was evidently an organised protest and the level of community support it embodied might be gauged by the participation of Robert Baker and his brother. They were part of the crowd which re-assembled on the morning of 23 November to destroy threshing machines and collect largess in the parish of Shalbourne. At their trial it was asserted that both had excellent characters up to the time of the disturbances and that they were leaders of such influence in their community that but for them 'there would have been no riot'.[45]

The acute sense of propriety which the labourers routinely displayed reflected the influence of men who commanded respect within the community and the self-conscious maintenance of an appropriate code of conduct is a feature of many incidents. At Lockhart's farm in Buttermere, Job Waldron negotiated with the bailiff while two other parties destroyed threshing machines in separate barns. 'We have no wish to hurt you', Waldron assured the bailiff but he insisted that the men expected money and victuals. Although about thirty labourers were in the house there was no damage or theft and, as soon as money was proffered, Waldron called the men together ordering them to 'do no more mischief'.[46] Maurice Pope, a master blacksmith and noted London prize-fighter, was one of the leaders of the crowd which broke threshing machines around South Savernake. At one house in Wootton Rivers the housekeeper refused the demand for two sovereigns but handed over two half crowns. When pressed by Pope she explained how her elderly master was a pensioner 'under Lord Ailesbury' whereupon he agreed to settle for ten shillings, received the additional amount, shook hands, and called the crowd away.[47] Crowds were also very particular about who was to receive the money collected. When George Durman, the treasurer for the Aldbourne labourers, was not on hand to collect the money for breaking a threshing machine at Church's farm the crowd insisted that the money be given to a prosperous tanner who had accompanied them, saying 'give it to this gentleman on horseback, he is a good fellow and we will protect him'.[48] As a man of substance who was willing to supervise the activities of the crowd, Thomas Goddard was both a natural authority and, from the labourers' point of view, a guarantor for the legitimacy of their conduct.[49] The general discipline and order which most crowds displayed only serves to exaggerate the rare occasions when individuals behaved inappropriately. John Pound had been part of a crowd breaking machines in the vicinity of Ramsbury, but around midnight he knocked on a door in the village demanding bread, cheese and beer 'or he would have blood for his supper'.[50]

In Wiltshire protest did not gain momentum gradually; it exploded across the county. Within twenty-four hours of the first collective action at All Cannings and Hippenscombe, scarcely any part remained untouched, except for the central portion of Salisbury Plain and the area surrounding the woollen towns on the border with Gloucestershire and Somerset. In the north of the county near Swindon, many farmers from disturbed parishes like Wanborough, Liddington and Wroughton were sworn in as special constables, and in discussions with the magistrates it was agreed that higher wages would only be negotiated once the protest was suppressed.[51]

Several things in these incidents point to the greater militancy of the protesters in Wiltshire and help to explain the determined stand taken by the men of property. The Wanborough crowd was quick to threaten damage to farmhouses when making demands for largess after the destruction of agricultural machinery.[52] William Prince, for example, was informed that the crowd would break everything in his house if he did not give some money. Although the labourers assured James Spicer that they were not 'firemen' they were perhaps even more threatening than the covert incendiary. They marched behind a tricolour flag and John Reeves had a handkerchief around his hat which he said had been dipped in blood. The stiff appearance of that item certainly convinced some of the farmers who were approached for money.

The flag and hatband were potent symbols in the theatre of protest. They hinted at a degree of violence which was, in most instances, never realised but it is also possible that they indicate a real awareness among some labourers that they were engaged in a serious social conflict. The leader of the crowd which impressed labourers from their ploughs around Liddington maintained he was 'fighting for bread'.[53] In neighbouring Wroughton, Joseph Watts, identified by one of his followers as 'our captain' who 'receives the money', threatened a farmer by holding a grub-axe over his head in an uncharacteristic gesture of violence towards an individual.[54] Even though normal constraints were stretched to the limit, these crowds and their leaders still preserved a remarkable self-discipline.[55] When Reeves confronted John Langford at the door of his farmhouse the farmer ordered him away 'and he walked out of the yard immediately' to resume negotiations some distance away. The tricolour flag and a bloody handkerchief might have betrayed the labourers' sentiments but Reeves' instinctive response was to obey a reasonable instruction. This might have been the result of social conditioning or an attention to common politeness but it is also possible that it was a conciliatory gesture which acknowledged that the labourers were winning their war against threshing machines.

Many farmers attempted to avert trouble by voluntarily dismantling or destroying their threshing machines. The labourers believed that farmers who dismantled their machines or placed them in the open to await destruction were condoning and, perhaps, even welcoming their removal. At the very least, it was seen as a gesture of encouragement which made the later prosecutions for machine-breaking seem like an act of betrayal. These sentiments were clearly visible in the incidents at Enford and Netheravon.[56] The protest began when the labourers learned that the Overseers were meeting to discuss wage rates. The men gathered in the churchyard and presented a demand for two shillings a day with a gallon loaf and sixpence per week for each child 'as it was in the paper'. The latter remark deserves to be noted for it indicates that the labourers knew about the agreements reached on identical terms in Hampshire several days previously. Although the Overseers unhesitatingly accepted the proposal the labourers proceeded to destroy threshing machines on adjacent farms and in a workshop where others were being built. Several of the local farmers had put their machines out in the fields where the crowd might find them. A witness for one of those later accused maintained that 'the farmers all drawed out their machines...Farmer William Martin told me and another man that he had put his machine out and that any person might break it to pieces'. After the event the farmers maintained that fear had inspired their actions and that no-one had endorsed machine-breaking. The labourers, convinced that the farmers had reneged on an agreement, felt betrayed. As one man, later transported to Van Diemen's Land, told his trial judge 'it is a very wrong thing that I should suffer for doing what the farmers had given us consent to do'.

A similar feeling of being wronged was the reason for the violent affray and damage done at Robert Pile's farm in Alton Barnes.[57] The crowd which had been active in the All Cannings and Manningford area had been promised by Sir Edward

Poore that he would argue their claim for higher wages with the farmers and magistrates. He had donated a sovereign and agreed to meet the protesters in Pewsey the following day to discuss further the matter of wages. Reassured by this acknowledgement of the legitimacy of their cause, the labourers continued their perambulation through the parish destroying machines and soliciting largess. 'Captain' Charles Davis appears to have been the leader and he and Laban Stone received money at several farms before the crowd arrived in the village where some men stopped to solicit a donation at the Rectory and assure the Rector's wife that they meant no harm. When Reverend Hare saw the labourers moving towards Pile's farm he rang the church bell in the hope of summoning some assistance. Significantly, no labourers came to his aid but the churchyard was rapidly filled with women and children who wanted to see what was going on. The crowd arrived at the farm where about fifty men went into the yard to break the threshing machine. Davis and two others informed Hare of their conversation with Poore; they announced that they were breaking no laws by destroying machines and claimed that their action was sanctioned by a magistrate. Davis specifically denounced wanton destruction: 'if we meet with any incendiaries we will deliver them up to the magistrates, hanging is too good for them. We only wish that every man can live by his labour'. These disciplined, legally-minded protesters who had secured the support of a local magistrate and the co-operation of many farmers were diverted into a widely reported affray by the return of Robert Pile and his inappropriate response to the scene in his farmyard.

Pile expected the labourers to visit his farm for he had already dismantled his machine. He appears to have had no great fear of their coming either, since he had ridden to Marlborough Fair early in the morning leaving his mother and sisters at the farm. The men in the farmyard posed no threat to person or property, other than the threshing machine, and they were taken aback when Pile galloped into the yard 'with oaths and threats' firing a pistol. Dismounting, he took up a double-barrelled shotgun which Reverend Hare had thoughtfully fetched from the house and pursued the labourers around his rick-yard and barn. The shotgun was discharged but eventually the labourers surrounded, disarmed and attacked their assailant. Gifford North smashed the gun with his sledge-hammer, someone shouted 'kill the d-d son of a bitch', and Pile alleged that Davis said 'you tried to shoot me, and now be d-d to you, I'll do for you'. This uncorroborated statement lacks credibility for Davis and another labourer actually rescued Pile from the attentions of the crowd. Understandably enraged, some of the crowd forced their way into the house, after knocking the door off its hinges, and destroyed a considerable quantity of china and furniture. They only departed when Mary Pile handed North a ten pound note. She had initially offered five pounds but this was evidently regarded as insufficient compensation for her brother's armed assault. When the more suitable sum was received the crowd was called to order and withdrew with no further damage or theft.

Within a day rumours were circulating of Pile's murder and the destruction of his farmhouse; the event subsequently attracted much publicity but the important facts were consistently overlooked.[58] Before Pile's return the crowd was peaceable, orderly and under the control of its leaders. His assault enraged the men who were fired upon but even then he was protected by some of the protesters and the damage inside the house, while more extensive than the usual broken windows, was not structural. At the trial which resulted from this episode, a witness stressed that there was nothing which could have prevented the complete demolition of the property if the crowd which numbered between two and three hundred had been so inclined. Furthermore, Mary Pile acknowledged that the labourers 'did not offer me any violence'. The affray at Alton Barnes was entirely the result of Pile's failure to follow the script for his part in this theatre of protest. He later claimed that he fired to prevent the men setting fire to his ricks but it is clear that arson was anathema to the crowd led by 'Captain' Davis. As far as the labourers were concerned Pile had invited the destruction of his machine by previously dismantling it and their protest had been, in some way, sanctioned by legal authority. There was nothing personal in their action at his farm; as one man said, 'we've nothing to say against you, Mr Pile. We are breaking all machines, yours along with all the others'. By his unwarranted response Pile had betrayed the understanding which existed between the labourers and most other farmers in the area. He was directly the cause of his own misfortune.

The labouring people who attacked the factories along the River Nadder to the west of Salisbury believed that machinery, of any sort, was the cause of their misfortune. Young John Jennings, who was one of the first to force his way into Brasher's woollen mill in Wilton, told the owner's son that he was 'going to break the machinery to pieces to make more work for the poor people'.[59] Most of the crowd was equipped with nothing more destructive than sticks and the effective damage was accomplished by Jennings, who picked up an iron bar inside the mill, and William Francis who used an axe he found on the premises. The crowd took nearly an hour to break the equipment with the inadequate tools they carried but nonetheless caused considerable damage. Those who wrecked Nash's woollen mill in Quidhampton were better armed with hammers and bludgeons and the owner reported that some of his machines were broken beyond repair.[60] John Ford led a crowd which saw no reason to discriminate between agricultural machinery and that in the local silk and woollen mills.[61] For some individuals, of course, more private motives might have been at work. One young man who took part in the destruction of Nash's mill had been employed there, but whatever prompted his involvement must remain a matter of uncertainty. He stood silent at his trial, saying nothing in his defence and calling no character witnesses.

No ambiguity surrounds the labourers' intentions in the villages across the southern part of the county. Agricultural machinery was destroyed and largess demanded, as happened in many other incidents, but there were fewer demands for food and more for money which were unrelated to the service of machine-breaking. It was as if the labourers were beginning to lay a form of tax on the propertied. At Whiteparish the crowd, led by horn-blower Aaron Stone, demanded money from a surgeon who lived in the village.[62] He had no machinery but was a man of property and position. During his trial, Stone claimed that the crowd had been persuaded by two gentlemen who lived in the parish to go out and collect as much money as they could. John Burroughs and William Hibberd with two others visited a house in Ebbesbourne Wake where the owner was persuaded to hand over two sovereigns to his allegedly tipsy visitors by the threat that they would call up the larger mob and knock his house about.[63] An identical threat was employed by George Shergold who led a crowd through the village of Stapleford where he secured largess from a gentleman living in the village only after the front door had been splintered, the windows put at risk, and the crowd had called out 'fire and destruction to you'.[64]

Although the labourers continued to imply that the money they collected while machine-breaking was a reward for the service they had performed, the increasing reluctance of farmers to pay may indicate that the impost was seen by both sides as a form of tax. Mr Pinniger of Combe Bisset let the crowd break his threshing-machine, which he had removed to a field, but he resisted any demand for money.[65] He assembled a small force, armed himself with a pair of pistols and threatened to 'bore a hole' in anyone who attempted to enter his farmyard. Someone provoked him to fire saying 'you can only kill one' though serious injury was avoided when both pistols flashed but failed to ignite the charges. As the crowd surged into the yard, James Toomer struck the lantern from a neighbouring farmer's hand and told Pinniger 'you have had your turn long enough, but now we will have ours'. A farmer of Ebbesbourne Wake, whose chaff-cutting machine had been broken by the crowd, refused Levi Brown's demand for two sovereigns until the labourers shook their sticks and declared their intention to make him comply.[66] William Cheater, the self-confessed 'foreman' and treasurer of the crowd at Damerham, saw the money he demanded from the bailiff at Budden's farm as a form of insurance – 'we hear you have money to give us rather than have any mischief done'.[67] This crowd too was quick to raise its sticks, rattle fence palings in a threatening manner, and demand prompt payment from those it approached. Violence, while rarely released, was close to the surface of many of the incidents in Wiltshire but at Tisbury pent-up social tensions and fears erupted into a full scale battle.

The Tisbury riot was certainly the 'most sensational and the most bloody' episode in the four counties, and the trial of those involved was the first case heard at the Salisbury Commission.[68] The crowd of machine-breakers who moved through the parish impressing workmen from the fields was shadowed from around nine in the morning by John Benett, a county Member and local landowner with several large, expensive threshing machines on his estate.[69] Charles Jerrard the younger was one of the leaders and it seemed to Benett that he identified his importance by a sash worn around his body. The labourers made it clear that they wanted an end to threshing machines and a wage of two shillings a day. All Benett offered was details of the proclamation offering rewards for the detention of machine-breakers and incendiaries. The suggestion that they might have been 'firemen' was deeply offensive to the protesters who declared 'we don't burn – we have nothing to do with fires'. Benett also made it clear that he opposed any wage increase and would not tolerate the destruction of his machines. It was never likely that 'Gallon-loaf Benett' would make any concession to mere labourers who, he maintained, should be paid no more than would cover their house rent, a gallon loaf per person, and threepence over for other food and clothes.[70] At Pythouse Farm he had to watch while the crowd ignored his orders, wrecked one of his machines and started to dismantle the barn in which it was housed. To add injury to insult, Benett was hit in the face by a stone thrown from the crowd, which moved on to another of his farms to destroy more machines before being cornered by the Hindon troop of yeomanry in a plantation near Linley Farm. Even though the outcome was never in doubt, the labourers persisted in hand to hand fighting for about twenty minutes before some fled and others were rounded up, cut and bleeding, and shipped off to Salisbury.

On the day that the military regained the initiative in south-west Wiltshire another troop of yeomanry dispersed the crowds blockading Warminster and the Swindon troop started to mop up opposition in the north of the county. Although there were a handful of incidents during the next few days the labourers' protest in Wiltshire was effectively ended on 25 November. This was partly due to the deployment of the yeomanry and special constables, and partly to the evaporation of energy which overtakes any protest stimulated by local grievances. At the end of November the labourers might have believed that they had achieved considerable success; many machines had been destroyed or voluntarily dismantled, and wage increases had been agreed in many places. The latter were short-lived, however, and farmers soon began to seek wage reductions and other ways to keep their costs down. A wage cut from nine to eight shillings a week led to a strike at West Lavington at the end of May 1831, and the employment of 'outsiders' by a Dauntsey farmer in June provoked a threatening letter.

> This iz to give you notice that it iz determined that all grazz cut by outcomerz or hay made by outcomerz will be burnt to azhez let it be whozever it may az the poor of this parish are uzed very bad through that cauze zo if you employ out comerz you will zee your rick yards full of azhez inztade of hay and corn with zome of your cowz hamztringz cut.[71]

The writer of this letter clearly believed that the farmers should show their social responsibility and concern for the well-being of the community by offering the available work to local people. Job Hatherell, who was convicted for writing the above threats, allegedly told another labourer that the farmers would have something to make their 'hair curl' if they continued to employ 'outcomers' instead of 'their own native poor'.[72] Unfortunately for the labourers, most farmers had chosen to abandon the practical side of paternalism even though they continued to demand deference and obedience. With the collapse of the labourers' protest and the gradual re-imposition of the unyielding authority of the farmer, the landowner, the clerical magistrate and the overseer, covert action became the characteristic form of rural protest until the emergence of agricultural trade unionism. In his covert action, Hatherell had anticipated the form which rural protest would take for the next forty years.

### Dorset

When the 'contagion' of protest reached Dorset, the farmers and landowners were well prepared to deal with it. By promptly dismantling many threshing machines and promising higher wages and allowances they acknowledged and, to some extent, appeased the labourers' major grievances. The local authorities also took steps to prevent disorder by deploying the yeomanry and recruiting a large force of special constables.[73] Mr Berkeley Portman reported from Bryanston that 'we are all safe in our division…we can assemble 200 armed and mounted and about 2000 pedestrian special constables ready to resist any mob'. The *Sherborne and Yeovil Mercury* comforted its readers with the announcement that the gentry, farmers and leading tradesmen were prepared 'to follow the magistrates wherever they may please to lead them'.[74] Several of these large vigilante forces patrolled the countryside, assisted by smaller troops of yeomanry, breaking up crowds and taking prisoners where necessary. In conjunction, these measures effectively restricted open protest.

Although the Dorset labourers wrecked threshing machines and collected largess they did so with great civility and little rancour. When the Rector of the parish intercepted the Buckland Newton crowd on its way to a dismantled machine at Pount's farm, the men listened politely to his promise to call a vestry meeting and attend to their wishes.[75] John Young insisted that the Buckland men, who 'were not impertinent', told him 'we don't intend to hurt the farmers'; the men were clear, however, that rents and tithes had to come down so that wages could go up. Matthew Galpin was able to negotiate with this crowd and arrive at a settlement which preserved his threshing machine as long as he did not use it. Few farmers were as keen to save their machinery as Galpin. The Thorne brothers and Abraham House, who were tried for breaking William Coward's machine, maintained that it 'was brought out to the field for the purpose of being broken'. John Pount dismantled his machine and left the iron frame about 300 yards from his house and David Gillingham of Cann had taken a similar step. Under examination Gillingham agreed that he had said that he 'did not care whether the machine was destroyed or not'.[76] In Dorset there was a general acceptance that, for the time being at least, the labourers had won the battle over agricultural machinery. For this reason the authorities were inclined to concentrate their energy on the prevention of disorder rather than the prosecution of machine-breakers. As one magistrate admitted, 'had we committed for participating in and aiding the burning of machinery we might have committed two-thirds of the labouring population of the district'.[77]

The Dorset magistrates' chief concern was to isolate the county from the neighbouring upheaval and they had good reason to be alarmed given the particularly menacing character of the disturbances at Fordingbridge and Tisbury. Their anxiety was prompted by an acute understanding of the way disturbance spread through the countryside radiating outward from the villages as crowds followed local leaders, picking up men and momentum until protest became self-sustaining in a new location. On 26 November a public notice posted in Blandford announced that the purpose of the vigilante force was to 'convince the Incendiary and insubordinate that they are not at least to cross the Dorset Boundary with impunity'.[78] The authorities were particularly anxious to eliminate external influences from any protest, for the presence of outsiders in a crowd almost certainly increased risk of serious trouble. In the event, even though the force of special constables certainly limited and contained protest in Dorset, it proved impossible to stop the movement of people and ideas across such an arbitrary division as a county border. When disturbances began to occur in Cranbourne Chase a local justice maintained that 'the progress of the disorder was from Salisbury' and there is clear evidence of a link with the events at Fordingbridge.[79] Abraham House's brother maintained at his trial that he was induced to go with the crowd around Buckland after a man named 'Hunt' had ridden through his village and 'told us that Government wished the people to break the machines and that they should be paid for their trouble'.[80] Joseph Pope, it was alleged, prefaced his demands for money with a claim to be 'Colonel Hunt's serjeant' adding that 'I must have money to pay my men to go through the country'.[81] In his defence Pope claimed that he had ventured out with his neighbours to see the crowd that had come from Fordingbridge and had been forced to go along. During Pope's trial it was also proved that William Cheater, the leader of the Damerham protesters, was active in the crowd which crossed into Dorset. Cheater had made no secret of his identity or his purpose during the earlier protest, and his appearance in Dorset would suggest that he either followed, or helped to spread, the contagion of disturbance before fleeing to London. We shall never know to what extent protest was spread by especially active individuals, nor the full geographical range of their activities, for these tantalising possibilities disappear with the containment of the protest in Dorset, where Swing, as a phenomenon with an apparently constant velocity, reached its southwestern limit.

## Notes

1 Each man transported has been linked to a specific incident. In Appendix II these are identified by the parish or parishes in which they occurred and the county boundaries used are those which applied in 1830. The date of the incident and the size of the crowd, where known, are also given. The range of issues involved has been listed for most events were far more complex than the offences for which the men were indicted.

2 E.J. Hobsbawm & G. Rudé, *Captain Swing,* London, 1969, p.116.

3 *The Times,* 23/11/1830.

4 Reports in *The Times,* the county press, the files of the Home Department and, for Hampshire, the *Report of the Proceedings at the Special Commission holden at Winchester December 20th and eight following Days,* London, 1831 ( hereafter *Proceedings*), are the principal sources for most of the incidents in this chapter. To avoid unnecessary repetition the references for each incident are consolidated into a single reference at the first appropriate place. Thus for this event, *The Times,* 31/12/1830; *Reading Mercury Oxford Gazette* (hereafter *RMOG*) 3/1/1831; *Berkshire Chronicle, Windsor Herald* (hereafter *BCWH*) 27/11/1830, 1/1/1831; Public Record Office (hereafter PRO), HO 52/6/106-7.

5 G.E. Mingay, 'Rural War: the life and times of Captain Swing', in Mingay (ed), *The Unquiet Countryside,* London, 1989, p.37.

6 Hobsbawm & Rudé, op. cit., p. 135

7 *The Times,* 30/12/1830, 31/12/1830, 4/1/1831; *RMOG,* 22/11/1830, 13/12/1830, 3/1/1831, 10/1/1831; *BCWH,* 1/1/1831,8/1/1831; PRO, HO 52/6/11, 91-92.

8 *The Times,* 29/12/1830, 31/12/1830, 3/1/1831; *The Salisbury and Winchester Journal* (hereafter *SWJ*) 3/1/1831 ; *The Devizes and Wiltshire Gazette* (hereafter *DWG*) 25/11/1830, 30/12/1830; PRO, HO 52/6/16, 22, 25, 27, 45, 60-65, 111-13; Deposition of John Atherton, BRO. D/E Pg O 1/5.

9 Hobsbawm & Rudé, op. cit., p.138.

10 Oakley was, no doubt, referring to the widely held belief around Kintbury that the local vicar, Reverend Fowle, who was notorious for prosecuting poachers, did so to receive a commission on each conviction. *BCWH,* 1/1/1831.

11 PRO, HO, 52/6/62; *SWJ,* 29/11/1830; Hobsbawm & Rudé, op. cit., p. 138.

12 Ibid., p.139.

13 *The Times,* 3/1/1831; *RMOG,* 3/1/1831; *BCWH,* 8/1/1831; C. Williams, *Basildon, Berkshire: An Illustrated History of a Thameside Parish,* Reading, 1994, pp. 106-07.

14 *The Times,* 8/1/1831, 10/1/1831; *RMOG,* 10/1/1831; *BCWH,* 8/1/1831.

15 *The Times,* 22/12/1830, 23/12/1830, 25/12/1830, 30/12/1830; *Hampshire Chronicle and Southampton Courier* (hereafter *HC*) 22/11/1830, 27/12/1830,

3/1/1831; *Hampshire Advertiser and Royal Yacht Club Gazette* (hereafter *HA*) 25/12/30, 1/1/1831; *SWJ*, 27/12/1830, 3/1/1831; *Proceedings*, pp. 35-40, 70-72, 87, 89-90; PRO, HO 52/7/5, 44, 191-3.

16 Henry Cook was a nineteen years old ploughboy who had worked on farms since the age of ten. The villagers of Micheldever saw his execution as murder and collected subscriptions to correct the false impression given of him by the press reports. When he was buried the whole village escorted his body to the grave. Almost a century later the legend persisted that snow never lay upon it which, although untrue, is indicative of the villagers' wish to remember the injustice suffered by a poor boy who lay in an unmarked but not unknown grave.

17 *Proceedings*, pp. 44-45.

18 I. Anstruther, *The Scandal of the Andover Workhouse*, Gloucester, 1984, p. 70.

19 *The Times*, 23/12/1830; *HC*, 29/11/1830, 27/12/1830; *HA*, 25/12/1830; *SWJ*, 22/11/1830, 27/11/1830, 29/11/1830; *Proceedings*, 46-53, 65, 69-79; PRO, HO 52/7/43,46, 48-9, 53; L.T.C. Rolt, *Waterloo Iron Works: a History of Taskers of Andover 1809-1968*, Newton Abbot, 1969, pp. 44-46.

20 PRO, HO 52/7/106.

21 PRO, HO 52/7/116.

22 *The Times*, 23/12/1830, 28/12/1830; *HC*, 27/12/1830; *HA*, 25/12/1830, 1/1/1831; *SWJ*, 3/1/1831; *Proceedings*, p. 44.

23 Depositions of H.B. Wither & W.L. Sclater, HRO, 10 M 57/O 3; *The Times*, 23/12/1830, 24/12/1830; *HA*, 25/12/1830; *SWJ*, 27/12/1830; *Proceedings*, 54-58, 62-63.

24 Depositions of C. Warson & H.B. Wither, HRO, 10 M 57/O 3.

25 *The Times*, 24/12/1830; *HA*, 25/12/1830; *SWJ*, 27/12/1830; *Proceedings*, pp. 68-69.

26 J.L. & B. Hammond, *The Village Labourer 1760-1832*, London, 1920, p. 239.

27 Anstruther, op. cit., pp. 65, 70n.

28 *The Times*, 25/12/1830, 28/12/1830, 29/12/1830, 31/12/1830; *HC*, 13/12/1830, 3/1/1831; *HA*, 1/1/1831; *Proceedings*, p. 78; PRO, HO 52/7/70.

29 J.M. Chambers, *Hampshire Machine Breakers: The Story of the 1830 Riots*, Clifton, 1990, p. 57.

30 E.J. Evans, 'Some reasons for the growth of English rural anti-clericalism, 1750-1830', *Past and Present*, 66, 1975, pp. 84-109.

31 *The Times*, 28/12/1830, 30/12/1830; *HC*, 27/12/1830, 3/1/1831; *HA*, 25/12/1830, 1/1/1831; *SWJ*, 3/1/1831; *DWG*, 30/12/1830; *Proceedings*, 64-65, 75-78, 88-89; PRO, HO 52/7/120-24.

32 H. Budd to J. Bonham Carter, Hampshire Record Office (hereafter HRO), 94 M 72/F 15; Chambers, *Hampshire*, p. 53.

33  Ibid., p. 53.
34  *The Times*, 25/12/1830; *HC*, 29/11/1830, 3/1/1831; *HA*, 1/1/1831; *Proceedings*, p. 73.
35  *The Times*, 25/12/1830; *HA*, 1/1/1831; *SWJ*, 3/1/1831; *Proceedings*, pp. 91-93.
36  *The Times*, 28/12/1830; *HC*, 3/1/1831; *HA*, 1/1/1831; *Proceedings*, pp. 79-80.
37  *SWJ*, 27/12/1830.
38  Hobsbawm & Rudé, op. cit., p.121; Hammonds, op. cit., pp. 235-6.
39  *The Times*, 21/12/1830, 22/12/1830, 23/12/1830; *HC*, 29/11/1830, 27/12/1830, 3/1/1831; *HA*, 25/12/30; *SWJ*, 29/11/1830, 6/12/1830, 27/12/1830; *DWG*, 23/12/1830; *Proceedings*, pp. 6-35, 40-41; PRO, HO 52/7/21-4, 29-31, 132-3, 248-9.
40  Hobsbawm & Rudé, op. cit., p. 122.
41  PRO, HO 52/ 11/130.
42  J. Chambers, *Wiltshire Machine Breakers*, Vol. I, Letchworth, 1993, p. 25.
43  *The Times*, 8/1/1831; *SWJ*, 10/1/1831.
44  S.H. Palmer, *Police and Protest in England and Ireland, 1780-1850*, Cambridge, 1988, *passim*.
45  *The Times*, 10/1/1831.
46  Chambers, *Wiltshire*, I, pp. 33,144.
47  Ibid., pp. 48-9; *SWJ*, 10/1/1831.
48  *The Times*, 6/1/1831.
49  *SWJ*, 6/12/1830. For his well-intentioned gesture he was transported to Van Diemen's Land.
50  *The Times*, 10/1/1831.
51  Chambers, *Wiltshire*, I, p. 32.
52  *The Times*, 10/1/1831, 6/1/1831.
53  Ibid., 8/1/1831; Chambers, *Wiltshire*, I, p. 42.
54  *The Times*, 6/1/1831; *SWJ*, 10/1/1831.
55  Ibid.
56  Chambers, *Wiltshire*, I, pp. 28-9, 182-4; see too Wiltshire Record Office (hereafter WRO), 1553/12 for accounts of the co-operative dismantling of machines.
57  *The Times*, 7/1/1831, 8/1/1831, 10/1/1831; *SWJ*, 29/11/1830, 10/1/1831; *DWG*, 25/11/1830; A.J.C. Hare, *Memorials of a Quiet Life*, Vol. 1, London 1874, pp. 352-57; Gloucestershire Record Office, 1571/X/63, T. Scott to T. Estcourt 7/11/1830; Chambers, *Wiltshire*, I, pp. 43-6, 145-52.
58  PRO, HO 52/11/23.
59  *The Times*, 5/1/1831; *SWJ*, 10/1/1831.
60  Ibid.
61  WRO, 1553/12; Chambers, *Wiltshire*, II, p.77.
62  *The Times*, 6/1/1831; *SWJ*, 10/1/1831.

63 Ibid; *The Times*, 6/1/1831.

64 Ibid., 5/1/1831; *SWJ*, 10/1/1831.

65 *The Times*, 7/1/1831; *SWJ*, 10/1/1831; WRO, 1553/12; Chambers, *Wiltshire*, I, pp. 53, 159-60.

66 *The Times*, 8/1/1831; *SWJ*, 10/1/1831; Chambers, *Wiltshire*, I, p. 172.

67 *The Times*, 8/1/1831; Chambers, *Wiltshire*, I, p. 55.

68 Hobsbawm & Rudé, op. cit., p. 125.

69 *The Times*, 3/1/1831; *SWJ*, 29/11/1830, 6/12/1830, 3/1/1831; *DWG*, 2/12/1830; WRO, 413/23, 1553/12; PRO, HO 52/11/56-7, 52/7/284-5.

70 W. Cobbett, *Rural Rides*, Harmondsworth, 1967, pp. 296, 527n.

71 Western Circuit Indictment Book, PRO. ASSI, 25/22/12.

72 *DWG*, 21/7/1831. It was alleged that the letter was written on a half sheet of paper which Hatherell had bought at the village shop. Hatherell's poverty and presumably his inability to afford a whole sheet probably caused his conviction, for the tear line and watermark on the letter and the other half sheet matched.

73 *Dorset County Chronicle, Somersetshire Gazette and General Advertiser* (hereafter *DCC*), 1/12/1830; *The Western Flying Post, Sherborne and Yeovil Mercury and General Advertiser*, 6/12/1830; PRO, HO 52/7/221.

74 W.H. Parry Okeden, 'The agricultural riots in Dorset in 1830', *Dorset Natural History and Archaeological Society*, 52, 1930, pp. 81-2; B. Kerr, *Bound to the Soil, A Social History of Dorset 1750-1918*, London, 1968, p. 113; *SWJ*, 29/11/1830, 6/12/1830.

75 *The Times*, 13/1/1831, 14/1/1831; *SWJ*, 17/1/1831.

76 *DCC*, 13/1/1831; *The Times*, 13/1/1831.

77 PRO, HO 52/7/227.

78 Parry Okeden, op. cit., p. 88.

79 PRO, HO 52/7/226, 278.

80 *The Times*, 13/1/1831.

81 Ibid.

# Chapter 3

# 'THE WORST USED LABOURING PEOPLE UPON THE FACE OF THE EARTH': PAUPERS AND PROLETARIANS

No mystery surrounds the cause of the Swing disturbances; they stemmed from the grinding poverty which was the lot of most agricultural workers in southern England. The labourers sought better wages and regularity of employment to keep poverty and hunger at bay. In a little over a generation the agricultural labourer in southern England had become a pauper, but the men and their families who suffered this remorseless impoverishment were never wholly crushed or demoralised by the process. Protest is never the action of compliant victims but a course of action chosen by those who believe they have been wronged, who understand what is their due and sense that they are able to help themselves.[1] After the riots, the Royal Commission on the Poor Law asked its respondents to comment on what they felt were the causes of the disturbances in their parishes. The clerics, landowners, magistrates, and overseers in Wessex overwhelmingly blamed low wages and unemployment.[2] What seemed so obvious after the labourers had erupted in protest had been a feature of rural society since 1815 but had been virtually ignored as a social issue. The burden which an increasingly impoverished agricultural workforce placed on the ratepayers attracted much attention although the circumstances which created that poverty were accepted almost without comment.

The landowning, governing class was deeply shocked by Swing and was panicked into an unnecessarily savage response. The security of that class was founded upon the quiescence of the labouring population but while fears of the unruly, urban, industrial masses were often voiced, rural labourers were taken for granted. Although perceptive observers of rural society drew attention to the crisis in the countryside, their warnings were largely ignored by those in power. In January 1830 Thomas Goodlake of Letcombe Regis wrote to the Home Secretary about the large number of men who were unemployed during the winter. He warned that 'the present mode of treating them leads to distress and consequent despair'.[3] A month later Earl Stanhope drew the attention of the House of Lords to 'the deplorable state' and 'the increasing misery' of agricultural labourers which, he claimed, denied them 'even reasonable sustenance' and would lead to 'anarchy and ruin' if the situation was not speedily remedied.[4] Even the fear of revolution and the partition of the land which Stanhope conjured up was not sufficient to persuade their Lordships to address the problems of the poor. During a debate on the cause of the disturbances in early November the Duke of Richmond reminded the House that many petitions for parliamentary action to remedy distress had been received during the year, yet 'their lordships had not thought it necessary to take [them] into consideration'.[5] In November 1830 Parliament was forced to take notice.

The material circumstances of agricultural labourers in the corn-growing counties worsened after 1815 as they suffered the wage-reducing effects of surplus labour and the employment-reducing effects of new farming practices.[6] Their plight was further compounded by the decay of rural industries which had formerly provided employment for women and children, and by the diminished access to land and the erosion of customary rights which accompanied enclosure. The pauperisation of a large section of the population took place quite slowly over thirty to fifty years, but by 1830 many families knew only pinching hunger and underemployment. Low wages, high prices and a withering of all opportunities for an adequate subsistence virtually guaranteed that few labourers could expect to receive 'a fair share' of the increased food supply they produced.[7] William Cobbett believed that the maxim of Scripture was being reversed so that 'those that work shall not eat, and those that do not work shall have the food'.[8] All that stood between most families and starvation was poor relief but as costs rose with spiralling post-war unemployment so attitudes to the labouring poor changed. From 1815 to 1834 Poor Law officers sought to reduce the sum spent on relief while actively discouraging the poor from seeking it. Of all the things which drove the labourer down, none was so bitterly resented as the erosion of poor relief and the mean-mindedness which reduced the labourer to the plaything of the ratepayers. In some parishes, like Fawley, men were 'degraded to the level of beasts of burden...[and] yoked like cattle to the wain to draw loads from one place to another'.[9] The factors listed above will be examined at length in the course of this chapter but their combined effect prompted Cobbett to declare in 1826 that southern farm workers were, 'the worst used labouring people upon the face of the earth'. According to 'the labourers' friend', the landowners' and farmers' dogs and horses were treated with more civility and were considerably better fed.[10]

Cobbett was outraged by the existence of poverty in the midst of wealth. The agricultural sector was still prosperous after the end of the war, even though among farmers and landowners there was much talk of depression. In fact the agricultural crisis was exaggerated and the problems, such as they were, were confined largely to the wheat growing areas of southern and eastern England.[11] During the French wars wheat prices had risen dramatically under the stimulus of relative scarcity and increasing demand so that arable farmers enjoyed windfall profits.[12] The artificially inflated prosperity which the high prices brought to wheat producers and landlords accelerated a number of important changes. Landowners enclosed more land which could be ploughed up for arable, and in Wessex large tracts of the open chalk down-land were brought under cultivation.[13] The new farms were often very large, a tendency continued by the consolidation of small units into larger tenancies.[14] Most farm rents went up during the wars and many of the newly created farms on the most marginal lands were leased at extraordinary sums. High rents and boom prices encouraged farmers to maximise production; the wartime period saw the extensive introduction of new machinery, new methods, new crops and, most significantly, a new attitude to labour.[15] The large tenant farmers who were the chief agents of this agricultural transformation were thoroughly infected with economic rationalism and conducted their enterprises in the pursuit of high profits and in the expectation of continuing high prices.[16] By 1815 the 'superstructure of Chalkland agriculture' had come to rely on 'sky-high prices for wheat and mutton'.[17] The bubble burst with peace, a succession of good harvests, and a significant lowering of wheat prices.

The worst affected farmers were those on marginal land and those who had taken up farms at high rentals during the wars. Both quickly ceased to be competitive as prices fell after the war, and there is no doubt that for such men the agricultural crisis was real enough. Other farmers who were content to pay high rentals during the war now sought substantial reductions so that landlords, in turn, complained that they could not get an adequate return on the capital they had invested in enclosure and improvement. The nation's governors, overwhelmingly landowners living off farming rents, did all they could to protect the farmer by imposing a Corn Law, which maintained the domestic price for wheat, and by tacitly endorsing all the socially destructive cost-cutting measures which farmers were adopting. Indeed, the many Parliamentary investigations into agriculture after 1815 persuaded the ruling class that they were driven by economic imperatives as they abandoned their social responsibilities to the labouring poor.[18] The belief in a profound agricultural depression encouraged farmers to press home the twin processes of pauperisation and proletarianisation which shaped agrarian capitalism in the early industrial economy. If, however, it can be shown that the fall in prices was roughly offset by a corresponding fall in costs, it would mean that we can be properly sceptical about the severity of the depression which supposedly prevented the farmers from paying adequate wages.

Although by 1826-30 wheat prices were 35 per cent lower than the wartime peak in 1811-15, the longer term trend was less dramatic. The average price over the war years was 80.6 shillings a quarter which fell to 66.6 shillings for the period 1816-30, a reduction of 17 per cent. Even then, the post-war price was 40 per cent higher than the average price for the period 1781-92.[19] This drop in prices was to a large extent offset by rent reductions. Around Blandford rents had fallen by 20 per cent as early as 1821.[20] The farmers, land-agents and surveyors from Wessex appearing before the Select Committee on Agriculture in 1833 testified that since 1815 rents had been reduced across the board.[21] The size of the reduction depended on whether the farmer had taken up his farm before or during the war. In the former instance, decreases of 10 to 15 per cent were usual and in the latter it was commonly 20 to 25 per cent, although reductions of up to 35 and even 50 per cent occurred.

After rent, the major cost was labour, and wage rates fell dramatically in the post-war years. By the end of 1822 labourers in Dorset were paid between ten pence and one shilling a day, or five to six shillings a week; around Andover, Cobbett noted, wages had been brought down to six shillings.[22] On the Wiltshire chalklands the average weekly rate fell from twelve shillings in 1814 to a mere seven shillings in 1830, a drop of over 41 per cent.[23] Farmers after the war not only paid their men less, they also reduced their expenditure on labour by cutting back the numbers of men in constant employment, by using men whose wages were subsidised out of the poor rates and by adopting machine-threshing. Operating costs, too, fell after the war. Charles Osborn, a land-agent and tenant-farmer in Hampshire, maintained that there was 'a great saving by using cast-iron instead of wrought' for machinery and equipment, while ploughs, wagons, carts and harness were all 25 per cent cheaper. Tradesmen's bills were also smaller for instead of three shillings and sixpence a day with beer, which they charged during the war, they received 'generally 3s' by the 1830s.[24] For many farmers the drop in prices was matched by an approximately equivalent cut in costs, and for the more efficient profits were maintained by increased production. Even though the agricultural labour-force increased only minimally between 1815 and 1830, the output per man grew considerably; in the case of wheat the yield per acre went up by some 16 per cent.[25] The population of England had increased by more than a third in the twenty years before 1831 and yet the nation still met about 85 per cent of its food needs.[26] Although some small, undercapitalised farmers and those who had foolishly taken up leases at the peak of the boom were forced out of business after the war, it is hard to accept the long established view that the post-war years were 'one of the blackest periods of English farming'.[27] The arable sector was most certainly under pressure but there is no evidence that British farming was in crisis, and William Paine's account book for his farms at Micheldever shows high levels of profit in the late 1820s.[28]

Agricultural production increased dramatically during the war years partly because more land was cultivated, partly because of new farming practices, but most importantly because farmers and landowners became more entrepreneurial.[29] The rapidly expanding population encouraged farmers in the corn growing regions to maximise both production and profit. In the buoyant environment of rising demand it was not surprising that the farmers quickly adapted to the logic of market forces. After the war, when lower prices made it harder for farmers to maintain their high expectations, economic rationality dictated cost-cutting measures. This, it was argued, was perfectly natural for, as Osborn explained to a Parliamentary enquiry, farmers were 'like other men, they like to make good bargains, and when the shoe pinches they get relief where they can'.[30]

Relief was found in a variety of economies, most notably the slashing of wage rates. When the Chairman of the Berkshire Quarter Sessions observed in January 1830 that 'it was too generally the practice to beat down the labouring classes in amount of wages' he accurately recorded the post-war trend.[31] During the war labour was scarce and the labourers enjoyed a brief period of bargaining strength, but after 1815 the demobilisation of around a third of a million men and the continuing consequences of rapid population growth eroded that advantage.[32] From 1815 wage rates in the arable counties moved steadily downward as farmers took advantage of the over-supply of labour; in Wiltshire wages dropped by nearly 20 per cent in the first five years alone.[33] The parliamentary enquiry into labourers' wages in 1824 heard how in parts of Dorset the average wage was not more than six shillings a week, which was insufficient to maintain a couple with two children and meant that 'every labourer with more than two children was a pauper'.[34] For unmarried men wage rates were lower still and this was a potent source of discontent in November 1830. The treasurer of the Micheldever crowd recalled that the young, single men suffered most, for they were paid only four and five shillings a week when it was estimated that an unmarried labourer needed 8s. 2d. a week for proper food and lodging alone.[35] It was not surprising that 'the young men led the others and forced them into it' for they were the chief victims of the over-supply of labour.[36]

Surplus labour pushed wage rates down but the labourers' earnings were further eroded by unemployment and underemployment. Cereal production required large labour inputs at seedtime and harvest but much less during the remainder of the year. After 1815 few labourers ever knew the security of annual, or even half-yearly, hiring because farmers increasingly hired labour for short periods or for specific tasks and dispensed with it once the busy season was over. According to one Wiltshire farmer and land-agent with more than thirty years' experience, farmers had become 'much disposed to employ men occasionally, not all the year round...When I first commenced business it used to be customary to hire them for the whole year, and to employ them in the winter, but that is not the case now'. Another land-agent who administered over 15,000 acres in the same county maintained that the number of men in constant employment had diminished greatly because the use of casual labour was now an instrument of farm management. James Comely, a tenant farmer at Compton since 1799, told the same story: 'taking the tenantry in general, as soon as the harvest is over they reduce their hands as much as they can, in order to save the amount of outgoing'. It was, he said, simply a 'matter of economy'.[37] From April to September most labourers could find work, even if the opportunities for their wives and children shrank as a consequence, but unemployment soared soon after harvest and many remained in that state throughout the winter.[38]

Although any generalisation about the extent of unemployment in units as small and diverse as the parish is difficult, it is evident that across Wessex between 20 and 40 per cent of the labourers were out of work during the winter. In Lambourn, one third of the three hundred labourers in the parish were unemployed; at Romsey it was a little over that fraction, and in Downton as high as two fifths.[39] Surprisingly though, many farmers refused to accept that there was a serious problem of disguised unemployment; they needed a great deal of labour at certain times and it was very convenient to have it both available and willing.[40] After the war labourers were hired when they were needed and they were cheap. Haymaking and harvesting could be done more rapidly and with less loss than before. According to Comely he could now finish his reaping in a week to ten days when for many years it had taken at least three weeks. Although he maintained that there were 'never too many' hands at harvest time, he was one who rightly acknowledged that by 1830 there were probably only two months in the year when the farmer had work for all the labourers.[41] The shortening of harvest activity suited the farmer, but for labourers it meant a further contraction of family income, for there were even fewer weeks when the whole family might be employed on the highest wages.

Farmers trimmed their costs and also the potential earnings of the labourers in a variety of other ways. Farm service and 'living-in', with their built-in costs to the employer, were progressively abandoned for reasons which Cobbett was quick to point out:

> Why do not farmers now feed and lodge their work-people as they did formerly? Because they cannot keep them upon so little as they give them in wages.[42]

Farm servants had always fared better than those who 'boarded out'. In Hampshire they 'generally fed on pork and puddings the greatest part of the year' and sometimes even had a joint of meat on Sundays. The inflated prices of the war years persuaded farmers to reduce household consumption by dispensing with farm service so that they might sell a greater volume of their produce in the market. Labourers who lived out may have been paid higher money wages in compensation but 'their standard of comfort unquestionably fell'.[43] After the war the desire to keep costs down ensured that there would be no resurgence of farm service. Witnesses who appeared before the Select Committee in 1833 confirmed that farmers in Wiltshire and Hampshire had abandoned living-in 'in order to reduce their expenses as much as possible' and they noted the disappearance of annual hirings except for a few key workers like carters and shepherds.[44] Labourers, if they were lucky, were hired for six months, but for most the hirings were considerably shorter – a month, a week, and in winter, the most desperate time of all, by the day.[45] By the 1820s farm labour for many men had become a casual employment, providing at best a precarious subsistence which was instantly insufficient when winter unemployment threw many men on the parish.

The labourers resented any change in farming practice which reduced the demand for labour, and they were especially hostile to the loss of any wintertime employment. The tasks which provided most work after harvest were digging field drains and threshing; both were under threat after 1815. Spade-draining was labour intensive and had been an important source of employment on the heavier soils of the four counties. Drainage work, however, slowed in the 1820s because the landowners, who bore the expense of underdrainage, would not expend their capital, and the farmers who paid for the clearing of ditches cut back on that outlay.[46] The labourers who lost this form of work saw themselves being replaced by the mole-plough, which had been developed as a labour-saving implement during the French wars. Machines for winnowing, chaff-cutting and, most offensively, threshing also gradually whittled away their other source of winter work.[47] The labour-displacing effect of machine threshing was recognised from the start. The machine was 'a positive and great good where flail men are few', wrote William Marshall in 1818, but it was a 'parochial evil' where labour was abundant.[48] Hand threshing normally provided work for around three months after the harvest and as opportunities for winter work diminished the threshing machine became a focus for discontent.[49] The earliest machines were expensive – from perhaps £70 for one driven by a single horse to £500 for a water driven machine – and tended to be used only on the largest farms, of which there were many on the chalklands.[50] But in 1829 a mechanically-minded small farmer of Westbury invented a portable threshing machine which cost less than ten pounds and was easily constructed by village craftsmen.[51] This brought machine threshing within the capacity of the smallest farmer and signalled the potential disappearance of the labourers' last hope for regular winter work.

Although pressure of numbers and changing farm practices made the southern rural labourer a pauper by driving wage rates down and making work harder to obtain, the decline in real wages was even more damaging. Between 1815 and 1830 money wages in agriculture fell by around 25 per cent and were no higher in 1825 than in 1795.[52] In the four counties, which were 'notorious' for their low wages, the fall was often greater; wage rates in 1830 were the same as they had been in 1770.[53] Unemployment, of course, reduced actual earnings still further. For some workers in urban occupations the post-war fall in prices brought an improvement in real wages but agricultural workers experienced no such benefit.[54] Farm wages 'sagged' while those of artisans and white-collar workers 'soared', and in 1830 the labourers' real wages had only recently returned to the level of the late 1790s.[55] Labourers' earnings 'tended to lag behind' changes in the cost of living and from the late 1790s to 1830 their purchasing power was reduced.[56] There is no reason to question the contemporary belief that labourers' real wages had fallen since the 1790s, nor that they were lowest on the arable chalklands for, as Cobbett remarked, 'the more purely a corn county, the more miserable the labourers'.[57]

In 1830 a sympathetic pamphleteer suggested that a labourer with a wife and four children required 14s. 5d. per week for 'proper' food and another 8s. 3d. for soap, candles, fuel, rent and clothes; an annual expenditure of £58 18s.[58] Not long after the Swing disturbances an estimate was made of the household earnings of an identical family in Heytesbury.[59] If the husband had been in the unlikely circumstance of constant employment at eight shillings a week, the family income, including the earnings of the wife and children, would have amounted to £37 16s, falling short of the modest living standard recommended by an amount equivalent to the man's wages. Two things should be noted from this comparison. The first is the absolute impossibility of a labourer maintaining a reasonable standard of living. The second is the part women and children played in generating household income. While the employment opportunities for boys remained fairly good, those for women and girls deteriorated with adverse effects on family living standards. The oversupply of male labour saw women displaced from some tasks about the farm and by 1830 their employment was largely confined to the poorly paid activities of spring, early summer, and harvest. If they were fortunate, women might find farm work for perhaps one third of the year, but in many places they shared the experience of the Titchfield women who had lost their former cottage employment of spinning and knitting and now had only the opportunities of hay-making and harvest.[60] Many rural industries in Wessex employing women and girls contracted during the 1820s.[61] At Rodbourne, lace-making declined 'very fast'; at Sherborne, silk-throwing was 'very depressed'. The manufacture of woollens in Wiltshire and Hampshire, once a source of 'great employment' was by 1826 'wholly gone'.[62] A few rural industries employed a small number of women but the large scale employment of women and girls in remunerative cottage employment or rural industry had all but ceased by 1830. With declining opportunities for non-agricultural employment and less rewarding work on the farm, women and girls could not contribute sufficiently to household income to offset the low wages paid to their husbands and fathers.

Household income and the survival of labouring families were also adversely affected by two of the key processes of agricultural improvement, the consolidation of holdings and the enclosure of the commons and waste. One of the most significant features of post-war agriculture, especially on the chalklands, was the formation of large farms suited to sheep and corn husbandry.[63] The process of consolidation had been gaining momentum for some time. The village of Durweston, near Blandford, which contained thirty small farms in the late 1770s had only two twenty years later; Stoke Charity which once had ten farms was reduced to two by 1825.[64] In the fifty years to 1830 the number of farms in Wiltshire declined by about one eighth, but the contraction was not spread evenly across the county. It was much more pronounced on the chalklands than in the dairying region of the Somerset and Gloucestershire borders. Almost all the land enclosed in Wiltshire between 1815 and 1850 was south of the escarpment of the Downs causing considerable depopulation as Thomas Davis had predicted in 1794.[65] The creation of large farms, which was achieved by enclosing the open fields, consolidating smaller tenancies, and the purchase of small freeholds, had important social and economic consequences.

An many that wer little farmers then
Be now a-come all down to leabren men;
An leabren men, wi empty hands
Do live like drones upon the workers lands[66]

Not only were many small cultivators forced into the swelling ranks of the under-employed labourer, but the overall demand for labour was reduced. Larger farms effected economies of scale, intensified the seasonality of employment and unem-ployment, and changed the gender balance of agricultural work.[67] Consolidation accelerated the social division of the countryside into 'but two classes of men, *masters* and *abject dependants*', and was unquestionably one of the central factors in the creation of a rural proletariat.[68]

Almost every aspect of agricultural improvement was to the labourer's disadvan-tage but none was more damaging to his precarious household income or more corrosive of his fragile independence than enclosure of the commons and wastes. By 1830 most labourers in southern England had little access to cultivable land beyond their cottage garden, if they were fortunate enough to have one.[69] Enclosure, the plat-form on which all other improvements rested, progressively dispossessed the small cultivator even though the social dangers of this consequence were recognised. The vital importance of access to land for the well being of the labourer was recognised by the Board of Agriculture in 1796. The General Enclosure Bill, drafted to expe-dite the process, contained a proposal to convert some of the wastes into allotments which a labourer could hold for fifty years and thereafter occupy on a long lease provided he erected a cottage. [70] The proposal acknowledged that the wage-labourer had to supplement his earnings by growing vegetables if he was not to become a pauper. The General Enclosure Act did not make any land available for the labourers, even though previously enthusiastic advocates of enclosure like Arthur

Young urged the necessity of such a measure. The interests of the landowners and the mass of labourers were antithetical and nothing was done to arrest the latter's descent into absolute poverty.

Enclosure was a clear demonstration of the primacy of self-interest even though, as Young admitted, 'nineteen Enclosure Acts out of twenty' injured the poor.[71] The Rector of Broad Somerford published, in 1831, a pamphlet significantly entitled, *The Poor Man's Best Friend, or Land to cultivate for his own Benefit,* in which he noted how few enclosures made any allowance for 'the privileges which the poor man and his ancestors had for centuries enjoyed'.[72] Ironically, in the aftermath of Swing many landowners and farmers rediscovered the social value of allotments, which were recommended as a certain way to reduce the social resentments which poverty had stimulated.[73] But in the post-war period, as fewer and fewer smallholdings were available, the 'key factor in a labourer's fortunes' was whether or not he had access to some common or waste.[74] On those open lands the labourer might find fuel for heating and cooking, forage for a cow, sheep or some geese, bracken for bedding in the pig-sty, and other benefits dependent on custom and the locality.[75] As the Reverend David Davies of Berkshire realised, 'depriving the peasantry of all landed property' had 'beggared multitudes'. The labourers enjoyed a 'partial independence' by virtue of their access to land; once this was lost, they were 'reduced...to the precarious condition of hirelings who, when out of work, must immediately come to the parish'.[76]

Although in agricultural and economic terms the enclosure of open fields was always the most important element in the process which transformed the rural landscape, the relative importance of the enclosure of commons and wastes became greater after 1800 because of its effect on the labouring poor.[77] The price of corn encouraged landowners, whose enclosure of the open fields was largely completed by 1800, to turn their attention to those tracts over which the labourers exercised their common rights. These were not inconsiderable acreages; in 1800 the waste amounted to 9 per cent of Berkshire, 13 per cent of Dorset, 18 per cent of Hampshire and 23 per cent of Wiltshire, and in each county there were still some surviving open fields where common grazing occurred after harvest and access to these was jealously guarded.[78] A little under a third of the wartime enclosures in Dorset and over a half of those in Hampshire created consolidated holdings from the previously open common and waste.[79] By the end of the war the amount of publicly accessible land had been considerably reduced, and the commons and wastes that remained took on a special importance for those labourers who relied on them in so many ways.

The enclosure of commons and wastes was a blow to the labourer's household economy, but it had even more profound consequences for it removed his last vestige of 'partial independence'. It created that total wage dependency which made unemployment and low earnings a calamity. For farmers and landowners the loss of independence which followed the enclosure of the commons and wastes was a distinct improvement.[80] There are few better examples of the hypocrisy which shaped class relations in this period. Self-reliance and independence, those cardinal virtues of liberal political economy, were less valuable when they inhibited the formation of a subservient, docile, and dependent proletariat. And when those who had lost their partial independence were finally driven to seek the assistance of relief, their social superiors decreed that it should be denied in order to make them more independent.

It is not surprising the rural poor resented the enclosure of the open lands for they placed a high value on their sense of independence. By 1830 the economic benefit to be derived from the steadily diminishing commons and wastes was clearly limited but their psychological significance was considerable. Labourers on the borders of Berkshire and Hampshire some years after Swing were horrified by suggestions that the surviving patches of fifty and a hundred acres of common be enclosed and improved. The land might have been 'wet, sour, [and] neglected' but the labourers, who were attached to their 'little privileges', were certain that once it was improved 'the farmers and the lord of the manor would send their sheep and cattle and eat [the grass] all up even in one day'. The poor had access only while the land remained unenclosed, unimproved and unattractive; as one man put it 'touch the common with a plough and it is no longer the poor man's property'. The recorder of this interview, Alexander Somerville, noted that the common offered labourers 'an independence which, even if not worth a penny, they would still cherish, merely because it was a soil other than the bare highway, on which they could set the soles of their feet in defiance of the rich man, their landed neighbour'.[81]

Although the connection between enclosure and disturbance in 1830 is far from clear, it appears that recently enclosed parishes were more likely to be discontented than others.[82] Evidence of earlier resistance to enclosure is clear; at Mere, rioting and the destruction of fences delayed the completion of the enclosure award for fourteen years, and popular objections prevented the enclosure of Potterne Field until provisions were made to lease portions of the common to smallholders.[83] In Wiltshire, 44 per cent of those parishes which had experienced enclosure since 1800 were affected by the Swing disturbances.[84] Nowhere in the four counties was there a disturbance which was explicitly focused on the destruction of enclosure fences, but we can reasonably assume that resentments generated by enclosure and the expropriation of the commons were part of the wider protest.[85]

The example of the Dorsetshire disturbances supports this view. Most of the Dorset men transported to New South Wales were caught up in the disturbances around Buckland Newton in the Vale of Blackmoor. Although in 1830 the commons had not yet been enclosed, the grazing rights belonged to a handful of individuals and a mere twenty-seven acres were left for 'the exercise and recreation of the labouring poor'. David Gillingham, whose threshing machine was destroyed by a crowd led by George and Henry Elkins, had acquired most of the open field formerly enjoyed by the villagers of Cann before it was enclosed in 1812.[86] On the border with Wiltshire a crowd, of which Joseph Pope may have been a member, demanded money from a land-surveyor whose livelihood derived from enclosure. This act, whose symbolic significance should not be underestimated, was accompanied by a beating of the surveyor's paling fence.[87] Men from the villages around Cranbourne were particularly sensitive to enclosure of the extensive commons and wastes which made up the Chase. At least twenty parishes and townships in Dorset and eight in Wiltshire were affected by the enclosure award of 1829.[88] As the area around Cranbourne was perhaps the most troubled in the county in 1830, it seems likely that resentment at the recent enclosure award played no small part. The labourers lost much with the expropriation of the commons and wastes; it was 'a plain enough case of class robbery'.[89] They lost their corporate rights in access to the land, they lost their common rights without equivalent compensation, and they lost the last possibility of economic independence. As wage dependent proletarians their future was bleak unless they could obtain adequate wages and regular work.

William Cobbett had a simple prescription for social well being: 'the labourer must have his *belly full* and be *free from fear*, and this belly full must come out of his *wages* and not from benevolence of any description'.[90] Cobbett estimated that the '*bare eating and drinking*' of a labourer, his wife and three children required an expenditure of over £62 a year.[91] In this dietary he included meat, which few labourers had tasted with any regularity since the 1780s, but even if his allowance for mutton is subtracted the total was, at £48, still twice the typical income of such a family. The 'half-starved' men and women who passed their lives amidst flocks of sheep and who, by their labour, created great wealth, enjoyed 'not a bit of good beef, or mutton or veal, and scarcely a bit of bacon'. They were, said Cobbett, fed, clad and lodged worse than felons and West Indian slaves.[92] One of the men who took part in the protest led by the Mason brothers looked back with pleasure on the food he received as he served his sentence on a hulk at Portsmouth: 'we had plenty of victuals', bread, biscuit, oatmeal, pea soup, vegetables, and above all meat.[93]

Cobbett understood better than most of his contemporaries that a labourer measured contentment in terms of a full belly and a roof over his head. It is by such concrete measures that we can best explore the labourers' living standards. After 1815 a full belly was increasingly hard to obtain and hunger became an inescapable part of life.[94] Although wage rates and actual earnings both fell between 1815 and 1830, the price of bread remained the same.[95] Wheaten bread, purchased from a local baker, formed the most important single item in a labourer's diet and took the largest portion of the family budget.[96] White bread, which was the preferred staple of rural workers in southern England, had once been a luxury but, increasingly from the 1790s, it became a symptom of poverty. Home baking was only possible where labourers had cheap fuel.[97] The Reverend David Davies noted that in Berkshire villages 'where fuel is scarce and dear, poor people find it cheaper to buy their bread of the baker than to bake it for themselves'.[98] The progress of enclosure and the geography of the chalk uplands further reduced the opportunities for gathering wood and turf and many labourers could not afford to buy fuel for heating or cooking; if they were lucky they might manage one hot meal a week.[99] In this situation, white bread, which unlike the coarser home-produced variety could be eaten on its own, provided the cheapest form of sustenance. Bread washed down with tea, no matter how weak, re-brewed or concocted from burnt crusts, made 'many a cold supper seem like a hot meal'.[100] The importance accorded to bread did not diminish in the years up to and beyond 1830 but by that date the labourer's diet was significantly different and, from his perspective, worse.

The respondents in the four counties who replied to the Poor Law enquiry were asked what the labourers ate; from their comments it is clear that a major dietary shift had occurred and that potatoes were by 1832 almost as important as bread. According to a Hampshire clergyman, 'bread and potatoes, with a little tea and cheese' was 'the ordinary food of the labourer' and his observation was echoed by many others. At Rodbourne the labourers subsisted 'a good deal on potatoes' and where a man was less skilled, Mr Poulett Scrope believed, his food 'would be potatoes alone, with little or no bread'.[101] In 1824 the Reverend Henry Walter had reported that the labouring families in his part of Dorset lived 'almost entirely on tea and potatoes' even though they had very frugal habits.[102] Mary Hunt from Studley, who had married a labourer in 1815, declared that while she raised her family she 'often had only salt and potatoes for days together', and it was the opinion of a Wiltshire doctor that 'where there is a family, potatoes do, and must, necessarily form the principal food'.[103] It was a sign of the labourers' poverty and steadily falling living standards that by 1830 they could afford less and less bread and relied increasingly on potatoes flavoured with lard, salt, or a scrap of bacon eked out with nettles and other greens.[104] The potato may well have been an adequate nutritional substitute but it was a dietary adjustment which was made reluctantly. As the Barton Stacey protesters told the Reverend Joliffe 'we have been living on potatoes long enough, and we must now have something better'.[105]

Some who reported on diet believed that the labourers could live on their earnings 'if their food was confined to bread and potatoes'. The more thoughtful, however, recognised that every household had expenses beyond those of mere subsistence which could not be met without dietary economies and the assistance of poor relief. John Hughes and Thomas Goodlake, both Berkshire magistrates, believed that once deductions had been made for soap, candles, fuel, clothing, and footwear, the labourer could afford only the 'barest subsistence'. If he additionally paid one shilling a week house-rent his earnings were 'not enough to subsist and clothe' his family as their labour required. The Overseer of the Poor at Parkstone made an identical observation while Douglas Hodgson of East Woodhay bluntly declared that it was 'impossible' for a labourer to live on the wages of his labour, if he also paid rent and bought fuel and clothes, even though he 'lived on bread and potatoes'.[106]

Because most labourers and their families were undernourished, their health and earning capacity suffered as a result. 'The great evil', according to Dr Greenup of Calne, and the cause of most of the health problems of the labouring class was 'insufficiency of food'. He attributed over 80 per cent of the diseases he treated in women, girls and boys to 'their food being insufficient in quantity, and not good enough in quality'.[107] Poor nutrition, and a diet low in protein and fats, eroded the labourers' health and strength leading to early ageing, sickness and a diminishing capacity for hard work.[108] Some twenty years after Swing, the 'meagre diet' of the Wiltshire labourer was, according to Caird, responsible for the absence of 'that vigour and activity' which marked the 'well-fed ploughman of the northern and midland counties'.[109] A man engaged in heavy physical work needed around 3,500 calories a day; a labourer who could afford the pound and a half of bread, which had long been considered the desirable daily minimum, obtained about 1800 calories. Even with the addition of a little lard, cheese or butter, and perhaps some vegetables, his diet was unlikely to be more than 2250 calories and so, slowly and inexorably, the farm labourer literally wore himself out. In many respects the calorific intake of farm labourers in the early nineteenth century was similar to that of the underdeveloped world today and had similar economic consequences.[110] From 1815 to 1830 agricultural labourers existed on wages which were below subsistence levels and did not permit them to meet their nutritional requirements. Ultimately, the effort which a man could expend was determined by his wages and not his wages by his effort.[111] Attained adult height is a direct measure of juvenile nutrition and thus of family living standards. The adult height of rural Englishmen fell in the early nineteenth century; men born in 1813 were about an inch shorter than a cohort born in 1780.[112] The young men who took part in the Swing disturbances were likely to have been shorter than their fathers. Such evidence is telling proof of the destructive consequences of undernourishment caused by a low standard of living.

All the labourers' household expenses rose in the post-war years but none was more burdensome than the increase in house rents, which doubled between 1815 and 1830.[113] Henry Drummond, a Hampshire magistrate, was certain that the exorbitant rent demanded for cottages was 'one of the chief causes of the agricultural labourers being in a worse state now than they ever were'.[114] Rents of three to five pounds a year were commonplace but as Charles Osborn pointed out 'when a man has to pay 1s. 6d. or 2s. per week for his cottage, he has not now enough left to keep his wife and children'.[115] Cottages were expensive and very crowded because there was never sufficient rural housing to meet the demand. The 'scarcity of cottages' was 'a subject of much complaint in Dorsetshire' which, according to William Stevenson, led to inevitable and immodest overcrowding.[116] Few cottages had been built for letting before the last part of the eighteenth century because farm labourers tended to live-in while single, or occupy a farm cottage during an annual hiring once they were married. After the war, economic rationalism and the pressure of population created a rural housing crisis. Changed hiring patterns, the consolidation of tenancies, the desire of farmers to put some social distance between themselves and their labourers, and the recommendation of Poor Law reformers that farmers and landowners pull down cottages to discourage settlement, all contributed to the contraction of on-farm accommodation.[117] After 1815, labourers increasingly rented cottages built by tradesmen, shopkeepers and 'persons of small capital' who hoped 'to secure a large profit on their outlay'.[118] To provide a return to the builder, such cottages were cheaply built and inadequately maintained, and when they were concentrated, as so many were, in open villages like Ramsbury, they were a prescription for rural slums which rivalled the worst that Manchester could offer.[119]

Most of the agricultural labourers in the four counties lived in conditions that can only be described as squalid. In part these conditions were a result of the building process. The poorest dwellings might consist of little more than four posts set in the ground to support the cross beams, with walls of wattle and daub 'just a little higher than a man's head', an earth floor and a thatch of reeds or straw. While such a construction might occasionally have been warm and weatherproof, all too often the walls were thin, the thatch full of holes and the site waterlogged because, in most instances, the cottage had a ditch at the back which acted as both cesspool and sewer.[120] Slightly more substantial dwellings were normally one and a half storeys high with a room at ground level and a sleeping platform above, while the best cottages had three or four rooms on two levels. But however they were constructed, in most cottages the rooms were very small and their occupants were very numerous.

The characteristic deficiencies of rural dwellings were visible at Stourpain, near Blandford, where a row of cottages was built backing into a hill. Passages between the houses allowed the contents of pig-sties, privies and rubbish pits to flow into the open gutter of the street whenever it rained so that the cottages were 'nearly surrounded by streams of filth'. Many had stone floors which were permanently damp because they were lower than the ground outside. One two-roomed cottage was home to a family of eleven who lived on the ground floor during the day and shared the upstairs room at night. The bedroom was ten feet by ten feet, 'the roof was the thatch, the middle of the chamber being about seven feet high', and there was one window about fifteen inches square. In this space, on three beds set a few inches apart, slept the entire family. In one, the husband and wife with a baby of four months and an infant aged one and a half, in the second, twin daughters aged twenty and another girl of seven and in the third, four sons aged from seventeen down to ten. The author of this report noted that it was not an extraordinary case for 'more or less every bedroom in the village was crowded with inmates of both sexes of various ages' because there were too few cottages.[121] In such conditions the diseases of poverty and overcrowding flourished. Tuberculosis was common and there were regular outbreaks of typhus. Inadequate nutrition, poor housing and disease were symptoms of England's major social problem from the 1790s onwards: chronic rural poverty.

Although Cobbett believed that a labourer should be able to provide for his family out of his wages, this was virtually impossible after 1815; most families had to rely on the diminishing benevolence of poor relief.[122] Many labourers were thrown on the parish during the winter months and most were susceptible to the 'particular life-cycle' of rural poverty which struck families when the children were too young to be economically useful and a wife's earnings were circumscribed by domestic ties.[123] When Aaron Harding sought the assistance of poor relief at Selborne throughout 1827 he had seven children, the four youngest of whom were aged eight, six, three and one. By the time of the disturbances there was another mouth to feed and he had been left a widower.[124] Like so many married men with families, the poverty-trap had also closed around Thomas Radborn and his wife Harriet who, in 1830, had five children under the age of eight. After 1815 the principal demand on the Poor Law was for 'unemployment benefits for seasonally employed agricultural labourers'.[125] There were many parishes in south Wiltshire where over half the labourers received some relief during the year.[126] At Tolbridge, where the average wage of six shillings meant that every man with two children was a pauper, 'the great mass of labouring people [were] thrown on the parish for support' and the numbers receiving relief rose from under sixty in 1770 to over 320 in 1824.[127] By 1830, wages in the four counties were so low that some labourers, like Aaron Harding, needed assistance even when they were in employment.[128] In Hazelbury Bryan over a quarter of labouring families received 'make-up pay', even in the summer months when work was plentiful.[129] Between 1815 and 1830 the terms 'labourer' and 'pauper' became synonymous as relief, which for nearly two hundred years had provided emergency assistance, became a routine part of labouring life.

Wages and family size usually determined the level of assistance which, in theory, was to provide a basic sustenance. The principle of providing relief to the able-bodied poor had been established by Gilbert's Act in 1782, but the most influential formulation was that of the Berkshire magistrates who met at the George and Pelican Inn in Speenhamland in May 1795. The combination of rising prices and poor harvests had created such distress that the magistrates met with the intention of setting a minimum wage which would guarantee the labourers an adequate standard of living. In the event, they recoiled from that socially responsible step; instead, they invited the farmers to increase their pay scale and issued an instruction that insufficient wages should be supplemented by an allowance from the poor rates. The family income thus obtained was deemed sufficient if it allowed a labourer to purchase three loaves a week for himself and one and a half loaves for each of his dependents.[130] This system, with various modifications, was common across much of southern England; Berkshire, Dorset and Wiltshire were all classified as Speenhamland counties. In Hampshire, and in other non-Speenhamland counties, the labourers' basic income was made up to a determined minimum by a system of child allowances which were usually paid once the family had three or more children. Although the sentiments behind these measures were undoubtedly well-intentioned they had a disastrous effect because low wages were institutionalised. Farmers, knowing that the wider, rate-paying community would bridge the gap, had no incentive to pay a living wage and every incentive to keep wages down.[131] Between 1815 and 1830 what had been 'a reasonable short-term palliative' during the war turned into 'a long-term disaster'.[132]

Low wages and an over-supply of labourers meant that ever increasing numbers sought relief. Expenditure on poor relief went up in the immediate post-war years, reaching a peak in 1818, but as the cost to the rate-payers rose so attitudes to the poor and their entitlement to support changed.[133] Between 1818 and 1830 the population of the four counties increased, the nation grew richer, but expenditure on poor relief fell. In Kintbury, for example, between 1811 and 1831 the population went up by 26 per cent, expenditure on poor relief went down by 46 per cent, and the per capita expense of relief fell by 72 per cent.[134] In practical terms this meant that the poor had less to eat. At the time of the Swing disturbances the price of bread in Tilehurst was the same as in the winter of 1815, when the sum given in relief purchased over seven and a quarter loaves. In November 1830 it bought less than half that amount.[135] Similar figures can be produced for many parishes in Wessex. During the 1820s the chief concern of poor law administrators was to deter paupers from seeking relief by a variety of measures which had in common only a mean-spirited obsession with economy. According to a sympathetic magistrate writing in 1830, the poor in southern England were 'ground to the dust' by the operation of the Poor Law and the idiosyncratic harshness with which it was applied in different parishes.[136]

One manifestation of the changed attitude to the poor can be seen in the more numerous appointments of professional guardians and overseers. According to Sir Frederick Morton Eden, it was generally agreed 'that standing overseers keep down the rates more than officers annually elected'.[137] The Sturges Bourne Acts of 1818 and 1819, which increased the power of the major ratepayers relative to the rest of the community, also eased the way for the more general employment of professional officers.[138] As employees of the ratepayers, positioned between the local rich and the local poor, salaried guardians and overseers served their masters well by keeping costs down. They were paid out of the same poor rate in which they were expected to achieve economies, with obvious consequences. In successive meetings in the winter of 1826-27 the Micheldever vestry resolved to establish a poor house, appoint a guardian at a salary of thirty pounds a year and reduce 'the allowances hitherto paid'.

The number receiving outdoor relief was virtually halved as the young and old were despatched to the poor house and others like Widow Hughes had her allowance cut in half.[139]

To be effective the overseer had to be intrusive and suspicious as well as economical.

It is his duty to make himself intimately acquainted with the situation of every family or person who usually claims relief, with the amount of his wages, the person by whom employed, the number in each family, the ages of the children, their health and various wants...to give information concerning these objects to the Vestry...By these means fraud and impositions are detected, and such is the difficulty of practising them, that they are not often attempted.[140]

The power of the permanent overseer was much resented. In November 1830 a group of protesting labourers complained of the 'petty tyranny and dictation' of men who, as strangers in the community, were 'callous to the ties of nature, lost to every feeling of humanity, and deaf to the voice of reason'.[141]

The overseer controlled those on relief in various ways. He might put them on some form of parish work for which they received their pittance; he might send them from one farmer to another, on the 'roundsman' system, to work at a wage subsidised by the parish; he might deploy them by the 'labour rate' under which a ratepayer employed men according to the amount of his poor-rate assessment, or he might even put their labour up for auction.[142] His power was considerable; a Select Committee Report in 1828 noted that the wages paid for parish employment appeared 'to depend entirely on the Overseer'.[143] The parish work organised by the overseer was often demeaning and absurdly under-rewarded. Between Warminster and Westbury, Cobbett happened on thirty men digging a twelve acre field; they had been set to this parish work at ninepence a day. The tillage was '*four times as good*' as ploughing but how, asked Cobbett, were 'their miserable families to live on 4s 6d a week?'[144] In each county men were often put to work in the gravel pits and on the roads, breaking stones, filling in holes and grading the surface. Joseph Arney was engaged on roadwork, 'scraping the dirt', when he learned of the proposed attack on the Fordingbridge factory. The labourers, regarding such work as entirely without purpose, saw it as a form of punishment imposed on them 'to gratify the malice of the overseers' and ratepayers.[145] At Micheldever, shortly after the disturbances, the vestry resolved that 'such of the labourers as shall misconduct themselves' should be put to work on the roads.[146] The labourers rightly discerned a penal element in the administration of poor relief as it became an instrument of social control. The granting or withholding of relief was a powerful weapon to hold over labourers who needed that assistance for their survival.[147]

The poor were shamefully treated in ways large and small. It is no wonder that the poorhouse and the poor-law officers in Headley were a target for resentment when all the recipients of parish relief were required to wear a metal badge bearing the letters HP – Headley Poor.[148] The attack on the Selborne poorhouse almost certainly had its origins in the community's 'universal feeling of disgust' at a regime which only a few years before had seen the inmates chained to the walls.[149] Cookham and Leckhamstead were effectively 'dispauperised' by a policy which denied any relief to the able-bodied and forced recipients into a workhouse. The Leckhamstead Workhouse, erected in 1827, cut the parish expenditure by one third and allowed the vestry to abolish the system of bread-related child allowances. It was claimed of Cookham, where the parish was 'the hardest taskmaster and the worst paymaster', that 'the conversion of the able-bodied into independent labourers' was the reason for the slight nature of the disturbances in November 1830.[150] It is more likely, however, that the relative quiet reflected the cowed state of labouring people rather than the morally improving effects of malnourished independence. But of all the humiliating, mean-spirited actions the labourers were forced to endure, none was more bitterly resented than the reduction of allowances. Not only was relief harder to obtain, it was worth much less.

Throughout the 1820s, legislators, economists, and moral reformers pondered the problem of the poor and the escalating burden of relief. At the parish level, however, the rhetoric of political economy seemed to prompt only one question: how little could the labourer live on? In 1826, to show 'how the labourers are now *screwed* down', a sympathetic Hampshire farmer presented the following comparison.

Arthur Young, in 1771…allowed for a man, his wife and three children 13s 1d a week *according to the present money prices.* By the Berkshire Magistrates table, made in 1795, the allowance was for such a family, according to present money prices, 11s 4d. Now it is according to the same standard 8s.[151]

Allowances were still commonly set against the price of bread but less was allowed for the money. The Winchester magistrates, whose rates were influential in determining the county standard, reduced the allowance of bread by 20 per cent in 1822. In the autumn of 1830 the rate was cut again. At Weyhill, the male allowance was reduced to a quarter loaf per day. That was effectively half the allowance suggested by the Speenhamland magistrates.[152] At Hindon the 'minimum of weekly support' for a man, his wife, and six children, was set at 10s 9d; the price of the gallon loaf was 1s 3d so that the family was expected to survive on a little over eight and a half loaves a week. By the Speenhamland formula the family needed 14s 10d, which would have bought nearly twelve loaves. The Wiltshire labourers on this scale were thus receiving 22 per cent less than was recommended in 1795.[153]

The attack on the Poor Law, which intensified during the 1820s and gave rise to the Amendment Act of 1834, was founded on the assumption that the provision of relief actually created poverty. 'A lavish and indiscriminate charity', the chairman of the Swallowfield vestry maintained, had 'the effect of making paupers not relieving them'.[154] Malthusian political economists alleged that the availability of relief encouraged improvident marriages which contributed to population increase and the over-supply of labour. They also maintained that the law of settlement kept labour rooted to the spot, preventing men from moving in search of work, and their belief that 'the causal chain ran from outdoor relief to low wages' had become an article of faith.[155] The Poor Law Commissioners had no difficulty in demonstrating the validity of their prior assumptions nor in convincing themselves that the poor were largely to blame for their own misfortune. In recent years, historians have shown that most of the claims which underpinned the attack on the Poor Law had no substance.[156] The notion that the payment of allowances was a cause of population increase was 'fundamentally erroneous'.[157] Parishes which abolished the allowance system saw no significant reduction of the birth rate or the number of marriages contracted.[158] Labourers did not rush into unwise marriages to beget children and obtain allowances. The payment of allowances which kept people from starving was a response to underemployment and low wages. Nor was labour which was able to move prevented from doing so by the Poor Law. The large out-migration from the four counties, the spectacular expansion of towns in southern England, and the evidence of seasonal labour movements all indicate that 'the single and footloose labourer' was not tied to his parish.[159] Over 13 per cent of the Wessex transportees were born in a different county to that in which they were convicted and many had been very mobile within their native county. In the 1820s, however, the property-owning rate-payers believed the myths which had been building around the Poor Law; deterrence became an operating principle and relief was given grudgingly with the result that only a small portion of those in need actually obtained assistance.[160]

The mean-mindedness of deterrence, however it was wrapped in the rhetoric of moral improvement and political economy, eroded still further the precarious security which the poor laws provided. To force allegedly work-shy labourers to strive for their subsistence and deter them from seeking relief the Select Vestry of Swallowfield resolved:

> That no part of the labourers' wages be paid out of the poor rates.
> That men out of work be employed at hard work by those who can afford it at very low wages.
> That no pauper receive relief in money, except in special cases; of which the select vestry will judge as they arise.
> That the midwife not be paid by the parish.

That mothers of bastard children be made to contribute to their support.

That nothing be given in aid of rates or rent.

That all funerals at the parish expense be conducted as pauper funerals, in the most homely manner; and that the grave be dug in that part of the church-yard to be appropriated to paupers from the poor-house.

Beaten down in life, the poor of Swallowfield were to be humiliated and segregated in death. The able-bodied unemployed in the poor-house were also restricted to the most meagre diet of one gallon loaf and a pound of cheese each week. As the chairman noted, 'it was not our intention to provide a comfortable subsistence: we wished not to invite but to deter them'.[161] Across southern England the triumph of deterrent policies was a clear sign that the rural community was fracturing along the fault-lines of economic self-interest.

For the labourers, the whittling away of poor relief was not only an attack on their material well-being but also on their customary rights. It is important to remember that most of the men caught up in the Swing disturbances had never known a situation where wages were sufficient by themselves. Like most rural workers after about 1780 they relied on the 'safety-net' of poor relief; it was one of the certainties of life. Poor relief, said Cobbett, kept the labourer 'as secure from beggary as the king upon the throne'; it was 'no alms but his legal dues'.[162] Many labourers maintained a distinction between the allowances which enabled them to survive and the charity of the parish. A Berkshire magistrate noted how a man was not thought to be 'on the parish' if he 'only has his weekly earnings made up to the price of two gallon loaves for himself, and one for every other member of his family'. The labourers believed that 'bread money', as the allowance was often called, was 'as much their right' as the wages they received for their labour.[163] Unfortunately for rural workers, their belief in their customary entitlement to poor relief was no longer shared by those who ruled over them.

The labourers had lost almost all their common rights and customary access to land. As wage dependent proletarians they expected to have regular employment and a living wage, but these, too, were denied them. In November 1830, when they finally endeavoured to obtain social justice, they found that they had also lost their customary entitlement to protest. They had long endured exploitation, now they had to suffer betrayal.

## Notes

1    See for example G. Rudé, *The Crowd in History*, New York, 1964; J. Stevenson, *Popular Disturbances in England 1700-1870*, London, 1979; J. Knott, *Popular Opposition to the 1834 Poor Law*, London, 1986; M. Harrison, *Crowds and History: Mass Phenomena in English Towns 1790-1835*, Cambridge, 1988; E. P.

Thompson, *Customs in Common*, London, 1991, pp. 264-5.

2  Parliamentary Papers, *Report of the Royal Commission on the Poor Laws*, 1834 (hereafter *RC Poor Laws*, 1834), Vol. XXXIV, *passim*.

3  Public Record Office (hereafter PRO), HO 52, 6/2.

4  *Annual Register*, London, 1830, p. 21.

5  *The Times*, 3/11/1830.

6  D. Mills, 'The Quality of Life in Melbourn, Cambridgeshire, in the Period 1800-1850', *International Review of Social History*, 23, 1978, pp. 382-404.

7  Ibid., p. 404; D.A. Baugh, 'The cost of poor relief in south-east England 1790-1834', *Economic History Review*, 28, 1975, p.61.

8  W. Cobbett, *Rural Rides*, Harmondsworth, 1967, p. 337.

9  H. Hopkins, *The Long Affray: The Poaching Wars in Britain*, London, 1986, p. 182; *Annual Register*, p. 21.

10  Cobbett, op. cit., p. 320.

11  E.L. Jones, *The Development of English Agriculture 1815-1873*, London, 1968, pp. 11-12.

12  E.J. Hobsbawm & G. Rudé, *Captain Swing*, London, 1969, p. 30.

13  H.C. Prince, 'The Changing Rural Landscape, 1750-1850', in G.E. Mingay (ed), *The Agrarian History of England and Wales*, Vol. VI, 1750-1850, p. 51; A. Harris, 'Changes in the Early Railway Age, 1800-1850', in H.C. Darby (ed), *A New Historical Geography of England after 1600*, Cambridge, 1976, p. 181.

14  T. Davis, *General View of the Agriculture of Wiltshire*, London, 1794, p. 8; W. Pearce, *General View of the Agriculture in Berkshire*, London, 1794, p. 19; W.F. Mavor, *General View of the Agriculture of Berkshire*, London, 1813, p. 88; E. Little, 'Farming of Wiltshire', *Journal of the Royal Agricultural Society*, 1844, p. 162; J. Caird, *English Agriculture in 1850-51*, London, 1852, pp. 81, 89.

15  J.H. Bettey, *Wessex from AD 1000*, London, 1986, pp. 253-58.

16  Hobsbawm & Rudé, op. cit., pp. 31-33.

17  E.L. Jones, 'Eighteenth century changes in Hampshire chalkland farming', *Agricultural History Review*, 8, 1960, p. 19.

18  H. Perkin, *The Origins of Modern English Society*, London, 1969, pp. 183-95; P. Mandler, 'Tories and Paupers: Christian Political Economy and the Making of the New Poor Law', *Historical Journal*, 33, 1990, p. 83.

19  B.R. Mitchell, *British Historical Statistics*, Cambridge, 1988, p. 756.

20  Parliamentary Papers, *Select Committee Report on the Depressed State of Agriculture*, 1821, p. 150. (Hereafter *SC Depressed Agriculture* 1821)

21  Parliamentary Papers, *Select Committee Report on Agriculture*, 1833 (hereafter *SC Agriculture*, 1833), pp. 49, 55, 57-8, 191, 465, 514.

22  Parliamentary Papers, *Select Committee Report on Labourers Wages*, 1824 (hereafter *SC Wages*, 1824), p. 46; Cobbett, op. cit., p. 58.

23  *Victoria County History of Wiltshire* (hereafter *VCH, Wiltshire*), Vol. IV, London,

1959, p. 81.

24 *SC Agriculture*, 1833, p. 466.

25 E.L. Jones, 'The agricultural labour market in England, 1793-1872', *Economic History Review*, 17, 1965, p. 325.

26 E.A. Wrigley, 'Men on the Land and Men in the Countryside: employment in agriculture in early nineteenth-century England', in L. Bonfield, R. Smith & K. Wrightson, *The World We Have Gained*, Cambridge, 1986, p. 334.

27 Lord Ernle, cited in A. Armstrong, *Farmworkers in England and Wales: a social and economic history 1770-1980*, London, 1988, p. 61.

28 HRO, 5 M 68/4; Hobsbawm & Rudé, op. cit., p. 30.

29 Ibid., pp 30-34; P. Deane, *The First Industrial Revolution*, Cambridge, 1976 edition, pp. 45-50.

30 W.A. Armstrong, 'Rural Population Growth, Systems of Employment and Incomes', in G.E. Mingay (ed), *The Agrarian History of England and Wales, Vol. VI, 1750-1850*, Cambridge, 1989, p. 701; *SC Agriculture*, 1833, p. 474.

31 *The Times*, 4/1/1831. D.O.P. Okeden, *A Letter to the Members in Parliament for Dorsetshire on the Subject of Poor Relief and Labourers' Wages*, Blandford, 1830, p. 9.

32 Jones, 'Agricultural labour', p. 323; G.E. Mingay, 'Rural war: the life and times of Captain Swing', in Mingay (ed), *The Unquiet Countryside*, London, 1989, p. 38.

33 *SC Depressed Agriculture*, 1821, Vol. IX, p. 80.

34 *SC Wages*, 1824, p. 32.

35 *A Plain Statement of the Case of the Labourer for the Consideration of the Yeomen and Gentlemen of the Southern Districts of England*, London, 1830, p. 21; A. Somerville, *The Whistler at the Plough*, Manchester, 1852, p. 262.

36 Ibid.

37 *SC Agriculture*, 1833, pp. 48, 56, 187.

38 K. Snell, *Annals of the Labouring Poor: social change and agrarian England 1660-1900*, Cambridge, 1985, pp. 22, 155-8; *SC Agriculture*, 1833, pp. 55-6.

39 *RC Poor Laws*, 1834, Vol. XXX, pp. 17, 427, 572; E. Billinge, 'Rural Crime and Protest in Wiltshire 1830-1875', Ph.D. thesis, University of Kent, 1984, pp. 158-60, 365-70; D.S. Stafford, 'A Gilbert Act Parish: the Relief and Treatment of the Poor in…Hungerford, Berks. 1783-1834', M.Phil. thesis, Reading University, 1983, p. 246.

40 A. Charlesworth (ed), *An Atlas of Rural Protest in Britain 1548-1900*, London, 1983, p. 142. For 'disguised unemployment' see M. Blaug, 'The Poor Law Report Re-examined', *Journal of Economic History*, 24, 1964, pp. 236-39.

41 *SC Agriculture*, 1833, p. 187.

42 Cobbett, op. cit., p.227.

43 J. Burnett, *Plenty and Want: A social history of diet in England from 1815 to the*

*present day*, London, 1979, pp. 31-33.

44 *SC Agriculture*, 1833, pp. 64, 196; A. Kussmaul, *Servants in Husbandry in Early Modern England*, Cambridge, 1981, pp. 120-34.

45 For a full discussion of the end of farm service, Snell, op. cit., pp. 67-103.

46 *SC Agriculture*, 1833, pp. 47-8, 54.

47 For the wartime boom in the manufacture and use of agricultural machinery see D. Grace, 'The Agricultural Engineering Industry', in Mingay (ed), *Agrarian History, Vol. VI*, pp. 525-28; P. Horn, *The Rural world 1780-1850: Social Change in the English Countryside*, London, 1980, p. 88; M.D. Neuman, *The Speenhamland County; poverty and the poor laws in Berkshire, 1782-1834*, New York, 1982, pp. 33-35; Jones, 'Agricultural labour', p. 324; Billinge, op. cit., p. 51.

48 Cited in Armstrong, *Farmworkers*, p. 62.

49 Protest against threshing machines was an important element in the East Anglian disturbances of 1815, 1816, 1822. Horn, op. cit., pp. 88-9; Charlesworth, op. cit., p. 144; S. Macdonald, 'Further progress with the Early Threshing Machines: A Rejoinder', *Agricultural History Review*, 26, 1978, p. 29.

50 Ibid., p. 31; Mavor, op. cit., pp. 129-36; W. Stevenson, *General View of the Agriculture of the County of Dorset*, London, 1812, pp. 144-63.

51 N.E. Fox, 'The spread of the threshing machine in central southern England', *Agricultural History Review*, 26, 1978, p. 28.

52 Armstrong, *Farmworkers*, p. 65; M. Blaug, 'The myth of the Old Poor Law and the making of the New', *Journal of Economic History*, 23, 1963, pp. 162; S. Horrell & J. Humphries, 'Old questions, new data': Families living standards in the Industrial Revolution', *Journal of Economic History*, 52, 1992, p. 860; P.H. Lindert & J.G. Williamson, 'English Workers living standards during the Industrial Revolution: A New Look', *Economic History Review*, 36, 1983, Table 2, p.4, Table 5, p. 13.

53 Caird, op. cit., p. 513; Bettey, op. cit., p. 262; Armstrong, 'Rural Population', pp. 706-711.

54 S.G. Checkland, *The rise of industrial society in England*, London, 1964, pp. 227-28; G.J. Barnsby, *The Standard of Living in England 1700-1900*, Wolverhampton, 1985, pp. 30-1.

55 Lindert & Williamson, op. cit., p. 7, Fig. 1 p. 12.

56 T.L. Richardson, 'Agricultural labourers' standards of living in Kent 1790-1840', in D. Oddy & D. Miller (eds), *The Making of the Modern British Diet*, 1976, p. 107, and Richardson, 'Agricultural labourers' wages and the Cost of Living in Essex, 1790-1840: A Contribution to the Standard of Living Debate' in B.A. Holderness & M. Turner, *Land, Labour and Agriculture, 1700-1920: Essays for Gordon Mingay*, London, 1991, p. 89; Blaugh, Myth, p. 168.

57 Snell, op. cit., pp. 25n, 38; Cobbett, op. cit., pp. 206, 258.

58 *Plain Statement*, p. 23.

59 *RC Poor Laws*, 1834, Vol. XXX, p. 575. In late 1830 a Berkshire landlord calculated that the minimum living costs of a husband, wife and two children were over 30 per cent higher than the prevailing wage of eight shillings a week. *Reading Mercury Oxford Gazette* (hereafter *RMOG*), 13/12/1830.

60 *RC Poor Laws*, 1834, Vol. XXX, p. 431.

61 M. Berg, *The Age of Manufactures*, London, 1985, pp. 108-28.

62 *RC Poor Laws*, 1834, Vol. XXX, pp. 578, 145; J. De L. Mann, *The cloth industry of the West of England*, Oxford, 1971, pp. 157-93; Cobbett, op. cit., p. 317.

63 *Victoria County History of Berkshire*, Vol. II, London, 1907, reprinted 1972, p. 221; *VCH, Wiltshire*, Vol. IV, p. 69.

64 F.M. Eden, *The State of the Poor*, London, 1797, facsimile edition 1966, Vol. II, p. 148; Cobbett, op. cit., p. 266. William Barnes also noted the process of consolidation among dairy farms in Dorset:

>Then ten good dairies were a-ved,
>
>Along that water's winden bed,
>
>An, in the lewth o' hills and wood,
>
>A half a score farm-housen stood:
>
>But now, - count all o'm how you would,
>
>So many less do hold the land, -
>
>You'd vind but vive that still do stand,
>
>A-comen down vrom gramfer's. B. Jones (ed.), *The Poems of William Barnes*, Vol. I, London, 1962, p. 105.

65 Davis, op. cit., p. 87; *VCH, Wiltshire*, Vol. IV, p. 68-9; Harris, op. cit., pp. 176-7.

66 B. Jones (ed.), op. cit., p. 161.

67 Pearce, op. cit., p. 42; Mavor, op. cit., p. 78; Stevenson, op. cit., p. 90; Snell, op. cit., pp. 147-58.

68 Cobbett, cited in Horn, op. cit., p. 53.

69 G.E. Mingay, *A Social History of the English Countryside*, London, 1990, p. 90; Mavor, op. cit., p. 75.

70 J.L. & B. Hammond, *The Village Labourer 1760-1832*, London, 1920, p. 51.

71 Cited in Armstrong, 'Rural Population', p. 723

72 Hammonds, op. cit., pp. 61-2.

73 *RC Poor laws*, 1834, Vol. XXXI, pp. 10, 15-17, 137-9, 141,144-5, 411-16, 422, 424-8, 430-7, 565-74,576-80; B. Jones (ed.), op. cit., pp. 93-95.

74 Mingay, *Social History*, p. 91.

75 The poor also suffered as other customary rights of real economic significance for a labouring family, such as gleaning and wood-gathering, were redefined as crimes against property in the late eighteenth and early nineteenth centuries.

76 D. Davies, *The Case of the Labourers in Husbandry*, London, 1795, pp. 56-57.

77 M.E. Turner, *English Parliamentary Enclosure: Its Historical Geography and*

*Economic History*, Folkestone, 1980, p. 71.

78 H.C. Darby, 'The Age of the Improver 1600-1800', in Darby, op. cit., p.50. In 1842 the townsfolk of Newbury tore down the fences which a landowner had erected in the open fields where the 'Freeholders and Inhabitant Householders' had pastured cattle after harvest from time immemorial (Berkshire Record Office (hereafter BRO) D/EX 241 Z3) and at Portland there were complaints that 'tenents rights be don away with' when Portland common was enclosed in 1846 (Dorset Record Office (hereafter DRO), D1/OM 28).

79 Turner, op. cit., pp. 192-95; *Victoria County History of Dorset*, Vol. II, London, 1908, reprinted 1975, p. 256; *Victoria County History of Hampshire*, Vol. V, London, 1911, reprinted 1973, p. 431, Eighteenth Century Changes, pp. 10-11.

80 J. Barrell, *The dark side of the landscape: The rural poor in English painting 1730-1840*, Cambridge, 1980, p. 4; Snell, op. cit., pp. 170-74; Hammonds, op. cit., p. 76.

81 Somerville, op. cit., pp. 101-04.

82 Hobsbawm & Rudé, op. cit., p. 180; A.M. Colson, 'The Revolt of the Hampshire Agricultural Labourers and its Causes 1812-1831', University of London M.A thesis, 1937, p. 29.

83 *VCH, Wiltshire*, Vol. IV, p. 68.

84 Hobsbawm & Rudé, op. cit., p. 180.

85 Machine-breakers from Berkshire were involved in an anti-enclosure incident across the Thames at Basington in Oxfordshire. After destroying a threshing machine they forced the landowner to declare aloud 'No Inclosure', thereby publicly renouncing his long-declared but unpopular intention to enclose lands in the parish. *Berkshire Chronicle, Windsor Herald* (hereafter *BCWH*), 27/11/1830.

86 B. Kerr, *Bound to the soil: A Social History of Dorset 1750-1918*, London, 1968, pp. 104, 107. Gillingham was also a prominent figure in the Cann Vestry which decided in the hard winter of 1817-18 that no poor relief would be given to any able-bodied man.

87 Ibid., p. 102; *The Times*, 13/1/1831; *The Salisbury and Winchester Journal* (hereafter *SWJ*), 17/1/1831.

88 Summary of enclosure awards in A.C. Cox, *Index to the County Records*, Dorchester, 1938, p. 77.

89 E.P. Thompson, *The Making of the English Working Class*, Harmondsworth, 1968, p. 237.

90 Cobbett, op. cit., p. 45.

91 Ibid., p. 308-09.

92 Ibid., pp. 261, 279-80, 337. Cobbett, *The Poor Man's Friend*, London, 1829, Letter IV, paras. 100-101.

93 Somerville, op. cit., pp. 39, 264-65.

94 Burnett, op. cit., p. 47.

95   Mingay, *Social History*, p. 39; Mitchell, *British Historical Statistics*, p. 770

96   Eden, op. cit., Vol. II, p. 15; Cobbett, *Rural Rides*, p. 306; see Richardson, op. cit., for a more detailed reconstruction of a household budget.

97   Cobbett, *Rural Rides*, p. 259.

98   Cited in Burnett, op. cit., pp. 16-20.

99   Davis, op. cit., pp. 154-5; Cobbett, *Rural Rides*, p. 258; Burnett, op. cit., p. 19, Mingay, *Social History*, p. 116.

100  Davies, op. cit., p. 118; E.G. Hayden, *Travels Round My Village: a Berkshire book*, London, 1901, p. 24.

101  *RC Poor Laws*, 1834, Vol. XXXI, pp. 569, 579.

102  *SC Wages*, 1824, p. 45.

103  Parliamentary Papers, *Report of the Special Assistant Poor Law Commissioners on the Employment of Women and Children in Agriculture*, 1843 (hereafter *Report, Women & Children*, 1843), pp. 59, 68.

104  In some parts of Wiltshire farmers grew 'immense quantities' of coarse cabbage which they offered to their harvest labourers as a wage supplement; R. Jefferies, *The Toilers of the Field*, London, 1981, p. 21, 79, 90; Somerville, op. cit., pp. 119-20, 142-43; G.E. Fussell, *The English Rural Labourer*, London, 1949, pp. 90, 127-36.

105  Burnett, op. cit., p. 41; *The Times*, 30/12/1830.

106  *RC Poor Laws*, 1834, Vol. XXXI, 18, 25, 144, 437.

107  *Report, Women and Children*, 1843, pp.58-9.

108  J.D. Marshall, *The Old Poor Law 1795-1834: Second Edition*, Basingstoke, 1985, p. 39; Mingay, *Social History*, p. 86; Armstrong, *Farmworkers*, p. 42.

109  Caird, op. cit., p. 85.

110  Armstrong, *Farmworkers*, p. 42.

111  Caird, op. cit., p. 85, noted the farmer's practice of paying labourers 'a lower rate of wages than is sufficient to give that amount of physical power which is necessary for the performance of a fair day's work'; Blaug, 'Poor Law Re-examined', p. 242.

112  S. Nicholas & R. Steckel, 'Heights and living standards of English workers during the early years of industrialisation, 1770-1815', *Journal of Economic History*, 51, 1991, p. 955.

113  B. Kerr, 'The Dorset Agricultural Labourer 1750-1850', *Proceedings of the Dorset Natural History and Archaeological Society*, Vol. 84, 1962, p. 166; Armstrong, *Farmworkers*, p. 65.

114  *SC Wages*, 1824, p. 47.

115  *RC Poor Laws*, 1834, Vol. XXXI, p. 10-29, 137-45, 410-38, 565-80; *SC Agriculture*, 1833, p. 466.

116  Stevenson, op. cit., p. 456.

117  Parliamentary Papers, *Select Committee on Emigration*, 1826-7, Vol. V, p. 537;

E. Gauldie, 'Country Homes' in G.E. Mingay (ed), *The Victorian Countryside*, Vol. II, London, 1981, p. 536; Caird, op. cit., p. 95; Fussell, op. cit., p. 54.

118   *RC Poor Laws*, 1834, Vol. XXXI, p. 10, 14, 16, 23, 137, 139, 410, 412, 419-24, 431,436-7, 565, 571, 579.

119   Mingay, *Social History*, pp. 111-12. Many cottages were built from whatever material was at hand. Peartree Cottage in Milton Lilborne was built in the early nineteenth century; 'it was almost square in plan and had a main… living room on the ground floor with two small additional rooms behind the stack in a lean-to. A lath and plaster partition divided the upper floor. The construction combined late timber-framing…limestone red bricks and yellow bricks…chalk rubble and cob. Many of the building materials were re-used'. P.M. Slocombe, *Wiltshire Farmhouses and Cottages 1500-1850*, Devizes, 1988, p. 24.

120   Jefferies, op. cit., p. 57-8. Cobbett, *The Poor Man's Friend*, Letter IV, para. 110, described cottages he visited at Uphusband in 1826; 'Never did my eyes before alight on such scenes of wretchedness! There was one place, about 18 feet long and 10 wide, in which…when all were at home, had to contain *nineteen persons*; and into which, I solemnly declare, I would not put 19 pigs; even if well bedded with straw. Another place was shown me…The *bare ground*, and that in holes too, was the floor in both these places. The windows broken, and the holes stuffed with rags, or covered with rotten bits of board. Great openings in the walls, parts of which were fallen down, sand the places stopped with hurdles and straw. The thatch rotten, the chimneys leaning, the doors but bits of doors, the sleeping holes shocking both to sight and smell; and, indeed, every thing seeming to say: 'these are the abodes of wretchedness''.

121   *Report, Women and Children*, 1843, pp. 20-1.

122   In 1813 Mavor noted that it was 'wholly impossible' for Berkshire labourers to support a family even on 'fair and reasonable wages', Mavor op. cit., pp. 474-77.

123   Snell, op. cit., p. 28; N. Gash, 'Rural Unemployment 1815-34', *Economic History Review*, 6, 1935, p. 92.

124   Hampshire Record Office (hereafter HRO), 32 M 66/ PR7, PO 6.

125   G.R. Boyer, 'The Old Poor Law and the Agricultural Labour Market in Southern England: An Empirical Analysis', *Journal of Economic History*, 46, 1986, p. 118.

126   Marshall, op. cit., p. 38; P. Dunkley, 'Paternalism, the Magistracy and Poor Relief in England 1795-1834', *International Review of Social History*, 24, 1979, p. 375.

127   *SC Wages*, 1824, p. 32.

128   His payments varied from a maximum of twelve shillings on a single occasion, through twelve weeks at ten shillings and eightpence during the late winter falling to two shillings and sixpence and three shillings during the harvest season. HRO, 32 M 66/PO 6.

129   J. Campbell-Kease, *A History of Hazelbury Bryan*, Hazelbury Bryan, 1983, p. 163.

130   BRO, Q/SO 7, Order Books, May 1795; W.E. Tate, *The Parish Chest: A Study of the Records of Parochial Administration in England*, Cambridge, third edition, 1969, 231-32; M.D. Neumann, 'A Suggestion Regarding the Origins of the Speenhamland Plan', *English Historical Review*, 84, 1969, pp. 317-22. In all the variants of the bread scale the unit was the 'gallon' loaf weighing 8 lbs. 11 oz.

131   Reverend H. Wake, *Abuse of Poor Rate!! A Statement of Facts submitted to The Candid and Unprejudiced*, Andover, 1818, pp. 7, 11-12, 14-15; Address of the Guardians of the Poor, Headley Parish, 1822, HRO, 44 M 69/J8/1; Okeden, op. cit., p. 12.

132   H. Newby, *Country Life: A Social History of Rural England*, London, 1987, p. 36.

133   Marshall, op. cit., p.28.

134   *RC Poor Laws*, 1834, p. 16.

135   J.L. Gayler, 'The Relief of the Poor in Tilehurst 1770-1850', Oxford Certificate in Local History Thesis, 1983, Appendix 3.

136   Hammonds, op. cit., pp. 229-31; Charles Dundas, addressing the Berkshire Grand Jury in January 1830, noted that 'it was too generally the practice to beat down' parish allowances. *The Times*, 4/1/1831.

137   Eden, op. cit., p.13.

138   Marshall, op. cit., p. 30; Neuman, op. cit., p. 181; Cobbett, *The Poor Man's Friend*, Letter IV, para. 105.

139   Vestry Meeting, 28/12/1826, January 1827. HRO, 7 M 80/PV 1.

140   Cited in B. Bushaway, *By Rite: Custom, Ceremony and Community in England, 1700-1880*, London, 1982, p. 198.

141   *The Times*, 25/11/1830.

142   See in Berkshire, for example, BRO, DP 78 18/4, DP 139/8/1, DP 34/18/5; Horn, op. cit., pp104-5; S.G. & E.O.A. Checkland (eds), *The Poor Law Report of 1834*, Harmondsworth, 1974, pp106, 327.

143   Parliamentary Papers, *Select Committee Report on that Part of the Poor Laws Relating to the Employment or Relief of able-bodied Persons from the Poor Rate*, 1828, Vol. IV, p. 4. (Hereafter *SC Employment or Relief*, 1828)

144   Cobbett, *Rural Rides*, p. 351.

145   *VCH, Berkshire*, Vol. II, p. 227; Checklands, *Poor Law*, p. 320.

146   Vestry meeting 29/1/1833, HRO, 7 M 80/PV 1

147   R.A.E. Wells, 'The development of the English rural proletariat and social protest 1700-1850', *Journal of Peasant Studies*, 6, 1979, pp.115-39. The Vestry at Manston withheld relief from those who did not attend church, DRO, PE/MAN/VE 1, meeting of June 8, 1819. At Speen it was noted in the 1820s that 'the information constantly registered in the books of the Select Vestry' made it easier to use poor relief with discrimination, N. Fox, *Berkshire to Botany*

*Bay*, Newbury, 1996, p. 22.

148  J.O. Smith, *One Monday in November: The Story of the Selborne and Headley Workhouse Riots of 1830*, Bordon, 1993, p. 6.

149  Letter from E.J. White pleading the cause of Robert Holdaway, Jan. 1831, HRO, Photocopy 378.

150  Checklands, *Poor Law*, pp. 337,339, 341-42, 355; see too the diary of William Gibbons, Constable of Cookham Dean 1800-39, BRO, D/P 43/10/1.

151  Cobbett, *Rural Rides*, p. 419.

152  Anstruther, op. cit., pp. 58-9.

153  *SC Employment or Relief*, 1828, p. 62; Tate, op. cit., p. 231; see Billinge, op. cit., for various allowance scales in Wiltshire and BRO D/P 34/18/5 for a 'Speen Table' used at Chieveley (B) in the 1820s.

154  Henry Russell in Neuman, op. cit., p. 199. The Duke of Wellington was convinced that distress was a product of poor relief, Wellington to Fleming, HRO, 25 M 61/1/60.

155  Blaug, 'Poor Law Re-examined', p. 242.

156  Blaug, 'Myth of Old Poor Law', 'Poor Law Re-examined'; Baugh, 'The cost of poor relief'; J.P. Huzel, 'Malthus, the Poor Law and Population in Early Nineteenth Century England', *Economic History Review*, 22, 1969, pp. 430-452, 'The Demographic Impact of the Old Poor Law: More Reflections on Malthus', *Economic History Review*, 33, 1980, pp. 367-81, 'The Labourer and the Poor Law 1750-1850', in Mingay (ed), *Agrarian History Vol VI*, pp. 755-792.

157  Huzel, 'Malthus',p. 451.

158  Huzel, 'Demographic'.

159  Marshall, op. cit., pp. 41-3.

160  P. Mandler, 'The Making of the New poor Law *Redivivus*', *Past and Present*, 117, 1987, p. 146; Mingay, *Social History*, p. 108.

161  Cited in Neuman, op. cit., pp. 196, 198-9.

162  Cited in S.H. Palmer, *Police and Protest in England and Ireland 1780-1850*, Cambridge, 1988, p. 39.

163  Checklands, *Poor Law*, pp. 97-8, 361.

# Chapter 4

# 'MONEY OR BLOOD':

# PROTEST AND CUSTOMARY BEHAVIOUR

In November 1830 the labourers and craftsmen displayed their anger in a manner shaped by custom and popular culture. All human action occurs within social and cultural contexts which give meaning to behaviour; if those contexts are not recognised we are unlikely to receive the message the action is intended to communicate.[1] When the activities of the Swing protesters are placed in their proper social and cultural setting we will understand why so many took part in riotous behaviour, often by day, in local communities where they were well known to the farmers, landlords and manufacturers they confronted and thus bound to be identified. The disturbances and the labourers' ingenuous confidence in the propriety and legitimacy of their actions were rooted in a plebeian culture which recognised a right to protest and had established modes of expression.[2] The labourers' behaviour was conditioned by the expectation that their protest would be tolerated because it conformed to custom.

Custom had several guises. First and foremost it offered a 'rhetoric of legitimation' which equipped labouring people in the early nineteenth century to defend their interests against encroachment.[3] It provided a psychological and practical justification for dissent which frequently involved the assertion of a popularly recognised right or privilege. Custom, with its sanction of tradition, also offered a protection against innovation and anything which appeared to threaten some aspect of a community's well-being or interest. The appeal to custom was central to the moral economy of food rioters and it underpinned the resistance to enclosure; it was equally significant in the manufacturing sector where it was enlisted to defend long-established work-practices and rates of pay.[4] In towns and villages where popular festivities and recreations were threatened by the improving moral earnestness of reformers, custom always provided the first line of defence.[5] Custom was central to a value-system which placed reciprocity and mutual obligation above self-interest.[6] In great things and in small, custom shaped the labourers' lives and the Swing disturbances are incomprehensible without an acknowledgement that the legitimation of custom fostered a sense of right and entitlement.

Custom was deeply embedded in social and economic relationships and formed the principal bulwark of those without political power.[7] The 'rhetoric of legitimation' can be seen in the following account of a dispute between a farmer and the villagers of Purton around 1820. The farmer, whose orchard abutted the village green, decided to enlarge it and he 'accordingly set to work, pulled down the original wall, and built a new one not forgetting to take in several feet of the green'. The green was the site of the annual fair and was thought to belong to the unmarried men of the village who often assembled there in the evening to amuse themselves in singlestick and boxing matches. At this threat to their common possession

> The villagers *felt great indignity...*[and] *resolved to reclaim their rights.* They waited till the new wall should be complete, and in evening of the same day a party of about forty marched to the spot armed with great sticks, pickaxes etc., and very deliberately commenced breaking down the wall. The owner on being apprised of what was passing, assembled all his domestics and proceeded to the spot, when a furious scuffle ensued, and several serious accidents happened. At last, however, the *aggressor* finding he could not succeed, proposed a settlement; he entirely removed the new wall on the following day, and returned it to the place where the old wall stood.[8]

Several things are noteworthy in this account. The villagers clearly believed that a customary right had been transgressed, even though a few feet off the green would have made little difference to its use. Although they might have prevented its construction at any time, the villagers waited until the wall was complete, a strategy which guaranteed the maximum loss to the farmer. They were prepared to assert the primacy of custom and community interest over individual self-interest even though the defence of their right involved the destruction of property and physical conflict. Similar sentiments were at work in November 1830 when threshing machines caused the same sort of offence as the orchard wall.

Custom also determined the occasions when community opinion was expressed, and the manner in which various rights and entitlements were claimed or defended. The agrarian calendar was organised around the feasts, fairs and festivals which marked the progress of the seasons. These events, in addition to their social attractions, provided an opportunity for the community to assert its collective identity in customary forms of behaviour.[9] The holidays and celebrations which dotted the year from Plough Monday in January to mumming and wassailing around Christmas and New Year were occasions when labouring people were temporarily released from the normal social constraints which regulated their lives and work.[10] They were opportunities for the common folk to be assertive, to demand respect and acknowledge-ment from their social superiors, and to be indulged in the public rituals and performances, the 'raucous and vivid street theatre', which the occasion demanded.[11]

Popular culture, in its recreational and celebratory forms, was always tinged with disorder and menace. The protest which began in Andover in November 1830 started on the first day of the annual fair when the town was full of labourers.[12] Fairs and feasts often led to more serious social disturbances, for the people recognised that on such occasions they enjoyed a licence to insult the local authorities, damage property and generally reverse normal social proprieties.[13] Indeed, it was widely believed that the processes of law were suspended for these periods.[14] The labourers of Hannington who broke agricultural machinery and collected largess during the Swing disturbances were alleged to have declared 'that there was no law for that night'.[15] Popular festivities were an outlet for sentiments which were ordinarily suppressed. They served as a social safety valve by allowing the common people to subject their local hierarchies to deri-sion and, sometimes, a degree of rough-handling.[16]

To survive, such customary practices needed more than the involvement of labouring people; they had to be tolerated by those in authority. In this period the governing classes were rarely surprised by the 'unruly habits of their fellow-coun-trymen'.[17] Rioting and protest had a customary protocol which was recognised by protesters and authorities alike.[18] Part of that protocol – an important part which gave rioting in England 'a certain historical legitimacy' – was the understanding, shared by patricians and plebs, that disorder and indiscipline were part of popular culture.[19] The recognition that the common people would occasionally give vent to their frustrations in a disruptive and sometimes violent manner was partly a matter of pragmatism, for local authorities rarely had the means at hand to contain or control social disturbance. It was also an acknowledgement that most protest was very localised and would resolve itself with the satisfaction of a particular grievance. Furthermore, while the people's assertion of their customary rights in a rowdy and threatening manner might have appeared to challenge authority, in fact it served to reinforce it.

Social anthropologists have shown how many customs involving confrontation between rulers and ruled employ rituals of status reversal which, paradoxically, re-affirm the hierarchical relationship.[20] According to Turner, the liminal people, who are normally passive and powerless, assert themselves in rituals of confrontation which have at their core a view of society as an organic whole, or *communitas*. 'Liminality', he says, 'implies that the high could not be high unless the low existed', and by using rituals of status reversal the powerless and lowly insist that the 'high must experience what it is like to be low'.[21] During these rituals the people who 'habitually occupy low status positions in the social structure are positively enjoined to exercise ritual authority over their superiors, and they, in their turn, must accept with good will their ritual degradation'. These events are seen most commonly in calendrical rites at those well-defined points in the seasonal cycle which mark the passage from scarcity to plenty and back to scarcity, though they also occur when 'calamity threatens the whole community'.[22] These actions do not in any way undermine the social order. Rather they endorse it, for the common people seek only to remind those who govern their lives that they are essential to their well-being and deserve respect.

Historians of popular culture have used these anthropological insights to explain the menacing challenge to authority and order which was a feature of so many customs in pre-industrial society.[23] Carnival, charivari and the array of customs which turned the world upside down by inverting normality take on new meaning in the context of liminality and *communitas*. Many English popular customs drew their vitality and durability from the opportunity they presented for a demonstration of strength by the customarily powerless, and for the confidence they bred which allowed the labouring folk to set aside their normal habits of deference.[24] With these ideas in mind, the form and manner of the Swing disturbances provide clear evidence that the behaviour of the men involved was shaped by custom and popular culture.[25]

Although much stress is placed on the 'multiformity' of Swing protests across southern and eastern England, one type of incident was predominant.[26] Typically, a crowd of men marched around the farms and villages of their locality breaking agricultural machines where they found them and levying donations of food, drink and money. Levies of this sort were a long-established feature of rural life. The calendar contained numerous occasions when largess was demanded from the wealthier section of the community, and the menace of personal humiliation or damage to property routinely accompanied such proceedings. On Shrove Tuesday, a day famous for the 'liberty of servants', young men in the four counties went 'lent-crocking' around the farms and villages.[27] At each house they would demand a donation and if it was not forthcoming the householder's front door was pelted with broken crockery, stones and other rubble. William Barnes, the dialect poet, recorded the rhyme used in Dorset in the 1830s:

> I be come a shrovin,
> Vor a little pankiak,
> A bit o' bread o' your biakin,
> Or a little truckle cheese o' your own miakin,
> If you'll gi' me a little, I'll ax no more,
> If you don't gi' me nothin, I'll rottle your door. [28]

While lent-crocking offered some indulgence to rowdy behaviour, it was underscored by the notion that the prosperous should aid the less fortunate, an idea which was central to this Wiltshire shroving chant.

Is the best barrel tap't?
Is the bread and cheese cut?
Please ma'am I'm come shroving here.
Eggs and lard and butter is dear,
That's what makes me come shroving here.[29]

Plough Monday and Guy Fawkes Day were also occasions when the demand for largess was accompanied by menace. In those places where Plough Monday was celebrated, the householder risked some damage to house or property if the demands of the plough-bullocks were not met, and the miserly or overbearing often found themselves burned in effigy on Guy Fawkes night.[30] An account from Purton in 1827 noted how the young men of the village went around the houses begging faggots for the bonfire. If they met with a refusal they would chant

If you don't give us one
We'll take two,
The better for us, sir,
And worse for you.

A farmer who denied them and stood watch over his woodheap had a new pump stolen which was consigned to the flames 'amidst loud acclamations'.[31] Guy Fawkes night also provided an opportunity to solicit largess. Late in the century the following chant was used by young men in Berkshire.

Ladies and gentlemen sitting by the fire,
Please put hands in pockets and give us our desire;
While you can drink one glass, we can drink two
The better for we, and none the worse for you. [32]

Over Christmas and New Year carolling, mumming and wassailing were thinly disguised opportunities for 'collective begging' in which, even if menace was less obvious, the householder's reputation was at stake.[33] The message in this speech at the conclusion of many Berkshire mummings was unambiguous.

I be poor old Happy Jack.
With wife and family at my back;
Out of nine I have but five
And half of them be starved alive.
Roast-beef, plum pudding and mince pie,
Who likes them here better than I?

The roads be dirty my shoes be bad
So please put something in my bag. [34]

The prompt to generosity in the last lines of every mumming play reminded the listeners of their obligation to assist the less fortunate. An individual's standing in the local community could be jeopardised by a lack of generosity to those who bestowed their wishes for future prosperity and good health in return for a small gift of food, drink or money. By far the most important of these rituals of charity, however, were the widely celebrated 'doleing days' in November and December and especially the feasts of All Souls, St Clement, St Catherine, St Andrew and St Thomas.[35] On these occasions a labouring family could expect, as a customary right, a valuable supplement to its fragile household economy in the form of cash or produce garnered in the previous harvest.[36] These 'doleing days' were an aspect of liminality which not only empowered the labouring population but also brought useful material gains during the winter months.

The labourers' requests for largesse and their celebrations in the public house provide further evidence of the way the disturbances were shaped by customary behaviour. Commensality, 'the sharing of food and drink in a harmonious relationship', was a central feature of social relationships in the countryside.[37] By asserting the importance of friendship and neighbourliness, commensality gave a visible form to *communitas*. The sharing of food and drink was the customary way of celebrating the completion of any task or cycle in the agricultural calendar. In the corn lands, the harvest suppers provided by farmers for their labourers were simply the most widely celebrated and most lavish examples of commensality.[38] They bound the farmers and labourers together in a recognition of their joint interest in the harvest and were a reward for the intense labour of harvest-time. They were also occasions when the normal social constraints were relaxed. The harvest supper

...brought the masters level with their men
Who pushed the beer about and smok'd and drank
With freedom's plenty never shewn till then
Nor labourers dar'd but now so free and frank
To laugh and joke and play so many a harmless prank. [39]

The harvest supper, the parish wake and the club feast at Whitsun were the most important displays of commensality but the same principle underscored many popular customs and ceremonies.[40] Plough Bullocks, shrovers, mummers and wassailers all expected their efforts to be rewarded. So did the Swing protesters.

The labourers who demanded food, drink and money reproduced behaviour which was part of their normal social relationships. The levy was their fee or reward for the service they had performed in destroying the machines which were a threat to the community's well-being. It was part of the customary protocol that donations were a payment for a service rendered. On 'Tolling Day' at Sherborne the local bell-ringers collected their tribute from Lord Digby whose house they visited

> with two large stone jars, which are there filled with some of
> his lordship's strong beer, and, with a quantity of bread and
> cheese, taken to the church by the tollers and equally divided
> amongst them, together with a small remuneration in money
> ... *as a compensation for their labour.*[41]

The recipients of rural charity did not see themselves as beggars and this protocol preserved their sense of pride.[42] The customary service could be a performance by mummers, carollers or wassailers, the bestowing of good wishes or blessings on doleing days, or it could be the destruction of a threshing-machine. And just as customary, charitable largess reinforced the prevailing social relationships and provided an opportunity for the expression of *communitas*, so the levies demanded and received by the crowds of Swing protesters assured them of the propriety of their actions; the donation endorsed the deed.

In other ways too the behaviour of the crowds in 1830 displayed the influence of custom. The labourers rarely strayed far beyond the boundaries of their own or an adjacent parish. The leader of the crowd at Ashton-Tirrold who insisted that 'we won't go out of our own parish', was governed by the practicalities and proprieties of custom.[43] Charitable relief was always sought within the community where recipients and donors knew each other, just as local grievances were solved in the local setting. Indeed, the concept of *communitas* could only work in face-to-face relationships; a social code of mutual responsibility had no meaning among strangers. In their perambulations around the farms of their parishes, the Swing protesters followed another long-established practice. Processioning was an important element in village life during Rogation week and in most other ceremonies and rituals for it 'represented a public affirmation of the physical and social bounds of the community'.[44] When the crowds of Swing protesters organised themselves to air their grievances and voice their expectations, the parochial perambulation was the natural course of action.

Parish processions and perambulations to collect largess may have been tinged with menace and rowdy behaviour but they could not have survived had they been seriously disruptive. A basic level of order and discipline had to be maintained. In accounts of the marches of the Swing protesters there are frequent references to the orderliness, the discipline and even the courtesy of the labourers and there is abundant evidence of careful crowd control. The crowd that marched 'three abreast' around Aldermaston, Brimpton and Wasing was kept together for over twenty-four hours without any undue violence or disorder. It was described by a witness as 'well marshalled'.[45] There were similar accounts of the orderly formation of marchers in Newton Tracey, Upper Clatford, and many other places.[46] Even when the crowd did not process in strict formation, the perambulations were almost invariably well disciplined. The Attorney-General was surprised by the degree of control and one of the Home Office's correspondents, writing from Boxford, drew attention to the fact that there had been 'hitherto no violence, no outrage, but on the contrary a singular degree of peaceable, respectful demeanour'.[47]

Most crowds responded promptly to the commands of their acknowledged leaders. George Shergold led those who surrounded Christopher Ingram's house in Stapleford at three in the morning demanding bread, cheese, and cider. Faced with the farmer's initial refusal, Shergold turned to his fellows and said 'now for the windows boys', which prompted further noise and threats but no actual damage. As soon as Ingram agreed to donate five shillings, Shergold beat his stick on the ground three times shouting 'silence, silence, I am your captain', and when the money was received he repeated his action and led the crowd away.[48] William Cheater was at the head of sixty to seventy men who demanded money at Mr Budden's farm in Damerham. He boldly declared his identity and role saying, 'my name is William Cheater; I am foreman of the mob, and I don't care who knows it'. His control was not in question either, for at another farm he was credited with saving the farmer's premises when he prevented the crowd from burning a winnowing-machine inside a barn.[49] During the attack on the workhouse at Headley, Henry James and Robert Holdaway were able to call the crowd back outside the gates, protect the master's wife and children and shield the inmates from accidental injury. And when the work was done, Holdaway could command, 'come away we have done enough'.[50]

In charitable and festive customary activities, civility and menace went hand in hand, for labouring people had 'alternating identities'. Depending on the occasion, they were deferential or rebellious and frequently both at the same time.[51] This paradox was an aspect of liminality which was very evident during the Swing disturbances. William Paine of Borough Farm in Micheldever commented on the civil behaviour of the labourers he conversed with as they walked to his barn to destroy his threshing machine.[52] At Northington, a labourer 'broke…[a] machine with a crow-bar but otherwise behaved in a civil and respectful manner'.[53] The striking labourers who confronted Lady Cavan at Fawley met with little sympathy and received only a homily on the evils of idleness but as her Ladyship noted, 'they were very civil'.[54] At Winfrith, the crowd which assembled to demand a wage increase approached the authorities 'respectfully and with their hats in their hands'.[55] Many of the gentry, clergy and magistrates who confronted the protesters during their perambulations and gave evidence at the trials, admitted that they generally received a respectful hearing even if their advice was ignored. The crowd which traversed

Micheldever, Sutton Scotney and East Stratton listened to the Reverend Cockerton and even tried to enlist him as their spokesman in negotiations with the farmers. Cockerton, though apparently sympathetic, refused to assist or contribute to the fund but was given a cheer for his efforts nonetheless.[56] Custom, and the social relationships it shaped, created the 'alternating identities' displayed by labouring people during the Swing protest; it also regulated the rituals of performance which expressed disapproval and suggested menace.

The perambulating crowds had a vocabulary of symbolic action derived from customary practice and frequently employed commonplace forms of ritualised public behaviour in times of protest.[57] In rural communities throughout England 'rough music' was a traditional means of focusing attention on individuals who had offended community standards in some way or another.[58] In the 1890s it was still regarded as 'the strongest expression of outraged opinion that a country district is capable of conveying'.[59] Rough music was an essential part of charivari, skimmingtons, hoosets and ridings, and on these occasions 'two social contexts merged, the penal and the festive'.[60] The publicly humiliating punishment was carried out by a crowd which blew horns, beat drums, rattled pots and pans, yelled, hissed and shouted abuse usually outside the offender's house. It has been suggested that such practices 'rested on a folk-loric tradition that the populace had the right to supplement the legal system' so that community censure could be used when the judicial system failed or the event fell outside the scope of the law.[61] These rituals of condemnation were well entrenched in the four counties. In Wiltshire, charivaris had a long history and were both common and elaborate.[62] Around 1820, a woman at Cleeve, accused of 'going wrong' with a married man, was subjected to a skimmington in which 'she was carried on a hurdle with rough music from her home…through the village'. In 1830 a 'church and king' mob greeted a Primitive Methodist preacher with a cacophony of sheep-bells, horns, old tins and a 'very tornado of shouting and screaming'.[63] Thomas Hardy was familiar with such customs in Dorset and set a 'skimmety', with accompanying rough music, in the Dorchester of *The Mayor of Casterbridge*.[64] As recently as 1920 the labourers of Shinfield, Swallowfield and Risely used rough music to defeat an attempt to fence off a traditional right of way which the men used on their way to work.[65] Rough music was also often part of the festivities of fairs and holidays. In Sherborne it was noted in 1827 that

> To the present time Pack Monday fair is annually announced three or four weeks previous by all the little urchins who can procure and blow a cow's horn, parading the streets in the evening, and sending forth the different tones of their horny bugles, sometimes beating on an old saucepan for a drum, to render the sweet sound more delicious, and not unfrequently a whistle-pipe or fife is added to the band.[66]

Satiric noise, as 'a ritualised expression of hostility' and as a symptom of exuberant spirits, was part of popular culture.[67] It appeared in both forms during the Swing disturbances.

The labourers who visited Mr Pount's farm at Buckland Newton 'came with a great noise and a blowing of horns', and these characteristics were repeated almost everywhere.[68] Many farmers were first alerted to an imminent visitation by the noise of the perambulating crowd and the drone of the ubiquitous cow horn. Elizabeth Randall of Hampstead Marshall was awakened at five in the morning by 'a great noise and the sounding of a horn'.[69] The narrator of a fictionalised account of the disturbances published in 1830 'heard a good deal of uproar and tumult' in the distance 'intermingled at times with the heavy monotonous sound produced by blowing a cow's horn' which, significantly, he took to be rough music of a domestic origin.[70] Most crowds made a great deal of noise on their approach, on receipt of a donation, and on their departure. Derisory hooting and hollowing, occasionally incorporating bloodcurdling slogans, was usually a feature of the crowd's arrival. The racket, which continued while the crowd was denied satisfaction, usually changed to triumphant huzzaing once the objective was achieved and the festive context replaced the penal. 'It was customary', according to a carpenter with a crowd near Basingstoke, that at each house visited the sum received was loudly announced 'and a Hurrah was raised on leaving'.[71]

The sounding of cow horns served a purpose beyond the noise of rough music; it was a means of summoning, controlling and directing the noisy throng. The movements of the crowd which traversed the parishes of Aldermaston, Brimpton and Wasing seemed to an observer to be orchestrated by a horn or bugle. The man with the horn blew it 'going to or quitting any place' and it was 'as if by blowing the horn he was calling them together after the machine was broken'.[72] A Hampshire crowd listened to a magistrate read them the Riot Act, but when their leader called 'on, boys on,' 'they set up a yell, blew a horn, and moved on'.[73] The horn-blower in a crowd, if identified, was automatically cast as a leader which indicates the responsibility the authorities accorded to the role. According to a witness at their trial, Thomas Hanson and Edmund Viccus 'blew the horn in turn' during the wrecking of Mr Austin's threshing-machine at Basildon. On trial with them were Charles Milson, Joseph Edney, James West and two others. Hanson was the moving force in the organisation of the local protest, and all except Viccus seem to have played an active part in the destruction of the machine. Apparently he did nothing but sound the horn but was still transported.[74] One of the men charged with riotous assembly and the robbery of William Sclater of Tangier Park in Wootton St Lawrence admitted that 'the horn was to give the signal'. Forty to fifty men confronted Sclater while another hundred or so waited outside his gates. Sclater declared that he resisted the demand for two sovereigns until the man with the instrument 'looked first at me and then at the gang, and said 'Shall I blow?'. The menace was obvious and Sclater, faced with a choice of parting with two guineas or risking an attack on his house, was guided by prudence.[75]

The threat to Sclater's house was part of the vocabulary of symbolic action and customary ritual. The damage to property which was visited on the ungenerous during Plough Monday, Shrove Tuesday and Guy Fawkes celebrations, although condemned by the enemies of custom, was implicitly licensed by community endorsement. The threat to gateposts, hedges, lawns, windows and doors was part of the ritual, and the penalty for meanness was understood. It was, however, a penalty which was strictly limited to nuisance damage. The same protocol applied in the Swing disturbances. The Reverend Penton of East Wellow was confronted by a crowd which insisted he sign a pledge to reduce his tithes. He refused, but when asked politely for two sovereigns he complied 'not on account of any force they displayed to him, but to prevent his windows from being broken'.[76] It is not surprising that the Swing crowds used a rhetoric which was familiar nor that the sanction of damage was strictly limited.

Although, given the size of many crowds, the total destruction of farmhouses and barns could have been achieved with ease, the damage to buildings was almost entirely restricted to doors, windows and window frames. These items were described by the Attorney-General during the trial of Charles Davis, Gifford North and others, as the 'most vulnerable parts' of a dwelling.[77] Doors and windows were an obvious target for they were easily broken, expensive to repair, and a serious discomfort in late November. Such damage, however, did not threaten the structural integrity of the house; the crowd restricted its persuasive violence to the exterior of the property. The first damage was likely to be to the door if the owner was unwise enough to remain inside instead of meeting the crowd's leaders at the threshold. Many reports mention the thunderous knocking by which crowds summoned the householders. Doors of inch-thick oak or elm were very durable but many were damaged if the owner stayed locked inside. Mr. Taplin of Worting refused to part with any money until John Batten held up his sledgehammer 'and appeared as if he would strike the door'.[78] Christopher Ingram watched the crowd beat on his door until one of the panels was split, but it was the threat to his windows which prompted him to throw down some money wrapped in paper.[79]

Normally, a threat to break the windows was sufficient to produce compliance. At Damerham the crowd which demanded ten shillings from James Scammell said 'they would beat the windows in if they did not get it, and began to beat the window-shutters with their sticks'.[80] On Sir Thomas Baring's estate at East Stratton the sum demanded of his steward was proportionately greater but the threat was the same, 'we'll smash the windows of the house if we don't get £10'.[81] Occasionally, the threat to the windows was supplemented by more serious menace to the fabric as at Eastwoodhay and Wickfield where the crowd threatened to unroof houses, but it is important to stress that such instances were very rare. [82] The threat to 'beat the house in' which appears in many of the trial accounts must be interpreted as a symbolic utterance, the first step in the ritual of intimidation which might progress, in due course, to actual damage and, sometimes, to forced entry. Generally, the threat was sufficient but where the owner was unusually obdurate or attacked the crowd the confrontation was likely to progress to property damage.

Joseph Randall of Hampstead Marshall suffered damage to his farmhouse because he endeavoured to resist the demands of the crowd at every stage. He would not deliver the key to the barn where his threshing machine was stored, so the men had to break in; he also refused to pay them the fee they were collecting from all the farms in the area or to give them food or drink. Faced with this defiance Alfred Darling, who carried a sledgehammer, raised it as if to strike the door while another man who was equipped with two pieces of iron belaboured the brickwork of the surround. Joseph Nicholas, according to Elizabeth Randall, 'then got over a low wall opposite the kitchen window, and began breaking the window, and knocked the whole of it, sash, glass, shutters, frame, and everything, into the room'. At this juncture, Elizabeth urged her brother to negotiate saying 'now they have broken into the house, we had better give them something or we shall have them all in'. Through the hole in the kitchen wall Randall offered half the sum demanded which the crowd accepted in acknowledgement of the fact that, as one of the labourers said, 'he has stood like a man'. [83] At Hippenscombe, a farmer's son, when approached by a small collecting party, pointed his gun at them and threatened to shoot any man who tried to enter his house. Later in the day, around suppertime, a much larger crowd of between two and three hundred returned and about twenty of them forced their way into the house after breaking in the doors and windows. No damage was done inside the house but someone swept up the tablecloth and all the supper things upon it, including a tea-caddy. For the theft of that item Shadrach Blake was transported. [84]

On the rare occasions when forced entry took place, houses were not wrecked by a trampling throng. Intimidation was usually achieved when the house was breached and a token body entered to enforce the crowd's will. A notable exception, however, was the damage inflicted to Robert Pile's house at Alton Farm. Pile had fired a pistol and a shotgun at the crowd in his farmyard in his efforts to stop the destruction of his threshing-machine. Enraged by this inappropriate and idiosyncratic response, the crowd smashed a solid elm door, broke eleven sash and casement windows and frames, a looking glass, sets of china, a clock, and destroyed some furniture. The damage was carefully controlled for Mary Pile, who was in the house, gave evidence that someone said they would not leave until they had some money from Pile and spoke of breaking the house as well as the furniture. She also noted that the men 'offered me no violence'. The crowd had responded with a degree of violence to property which was unusual, but which matched the violence it had experienced. It stopped a long way short of the total destruction of the house which another witness admitted was entirely within its capacity.[85]

House invasion was not entirely outside the realm of customary behaviour. Mummers generally made their way unceremoniously into the kitchens and hallways of the houses they visited, rarely waiting to be invited, and this social presumption was one of the reasons why their presence was less welcome as the century wore on. A visit from the Christmas Bull was even less likely to have been appreciated in the Wiltshire and Dorset villages where the custom was established. A man wearing, or carrying, a hollowed out bull's head, complete with horns and eyes made of bottle-glass, was led around the parish by his keeper accompanied by a crowd of men and boys. The Bull would visit substantial householders unannounced at dusk and 'was given the freedom of every house and allowed to penetrate into any room'. Moved as much by prudent self-preservation as by the dictates of custom, the inhabitants would 'flee before his formidable horns' especially since by the end of the evening 'neither the Bull nor his keeper could be certified as strictly sober'.[86] Like most customary visitations a donation was accepted at each house visited but on no other occasion did the visitors enjoy such a remarkable degree of licence. The Christmas Bull invaded the private parts of the house, whose residents were subjected to a ritual of terror and implicit status-reversal and although only the Bull and his keeper were allowed in the entire crowd probably shared the vicarious pleasure of the moment.

The theatre of confrontation played out during the Swing disturbances involved carefully choreographed rituals of challenge and response. Rough music and the threat of property damage were familiar features but crowd actions were also often made more menacing by slogans. Two phrases were repeated time after time. The first was redolent of Old Testament vengeance. 'We will have blood for blood', 'blood or money', 'money or blood', 'blood for breakfast', and 'blood for supper' is a selection of the slogans heard in each county. They are notable for their similarity and the emptiness of the threat. Whatever rhetoric the drama might demand, injury to persons was alien to customary forms of protest. No landowner, farmer, clergyman or poor-law officer was killed during the Swing riots. In the four counties, the most serious injury inflicted by the protesters was the broken arm sustained by Robert Pile; otherwise the injuries were mainly cuts and bruises. Calls for blood or money were intended to shock and intimidate but never to be implemented; they were simply a dramatic chorus. The second message, in shouts of 'one and all' stressed the solidarity of the participants and implied a community consensus familiar to exponents of rough music. The leaders of skimmingtons and other rituals of humiliation and condemnation recognised that those events lost their power if they did not express the opinion of the majority of the community. To this end they compelled the reluctant to join in and even punished those who tried to opt out as did the leaders of crowds in November 1830.[87]

Close study of many incidents suggests that no-one who was confronted by a noisy, machine-breaking, window-smashing crowd was seriously alarmed by it. Mary Pile and Elizabeth Randall knew they were in no personal danger, irrespective of the damage done to their houses. At the trial of William and Daniel Sims and Henry Bunce, William Easton alleged that during the invasion of his vicarage at St Mary Bourne his wife was 'too frightened to speak'. The good cleric conveniently forgot that his wife had negotiated with the invaders while he languished upstairs and that his daughter who was present all the time expressed no particular fear.[88] Many witnesses who appeared before the Special Commissions in the four counties acknowledged that they were not terrorised by the protesters. Some prosecutors insisted that they were frightened, but since a sense of fear had to be proven for a successful prosecution this was to be expected. It seems as though the 'terror' experienced was generally in inverse proportion to the individual's familiarity with the popular culture of the labourers. Maria Hare, Mary Frampton and Mary Russell Mitford show a *frisson* of fear in their journals, but most farmers' wives, like their husbands, the country clergy and the local magistrates, displayed a resignation born of their familiarity with rural custom.[89]

Bread, cheese, beer and cider were demanded and received in most confrontations. These were the basic fare of rural hospitality and all that the labourers could expect, although George Williams drew attention to himself by declaring that he 'must have a glass of punch'.[90] While it would stretch credibility to claim that the farmers made their donations happily, there were few occasions when the labourers' requests were denied, and little evidence to suggest that they were particularly resented. The request and the gift were, after all, part of that customary commensality which cemented relations in the countryside. The labourers probably believed that the conjunction of commensality with protest added a measure of legitimacy to their actions so that the food and drink were their just reward. At Draycot Foliat three men 'begged in a civil manner for some victuals' which were given to them; then, after receiving the gift, they broke a threshing-machine.[91] Commensality sometimes provided a striking endorsement of the labourers' actions. The crowd which broke a threshing-machine at Whiteparish was advised by Squire Wynne, 'a gentleman…staying at Squire Bristowe's', of the best way to shatter cast iron by heating and pouring on cold water, and was then treated to 'three or four buckets of Squire Bristowe's strong beer' which Wynne sent for.[92]

Sharing food and drink was also a customary way of sealing an agreement; it reinforced the contract between the parties. A successful negotiation with a local landlady at Owslebury and her signature on a pledge to reduce rents and raise wages, prompted a call for 'some meat and drink'.[93] The Rev William Cobbold's signature on an agreement to reduce his tithes so that the farmers could increase wages, led the crowd to call for money or beer to endorse the settlement. Five pounds worth of beer was sought but the miserly Cobbold authorised only a pint per man paid out of the poor fund.[94] Gifts of food and drink could even defuse a confrontation as occurred at Baulking where a farmer wanted to fire on the small crowd which approached his farm. His more prudent wife averted trouble by giving the men 'two loaves and nearly a whole cheese'.[95] The labourers in requesting and receiving food and drink used a ritual which was deeply embedded in rural custom and understood as conduct which affirmed the stability and common purpose of the community.

The collection and distribution of money during the disturbances was supervised by men the crowd chose as the 'treasurer' in accordance with the practice of many other 'ceremonial visitations'.[96] Those selected were clearly men who could be trusted; they were men of good reputation in their communities and their respectability gave weight to the request for largess. The treasurer of the crowd which Joseph and Robert Mason led around Barton Stacey, East Stratton and Micheldever noted how 'they said I wor honest, and they gave it me to carry. I had £40 at one time – £40 every shilling'.[97] Of one Wiltshire labourer the Attorney-General observed, it was the 'respectability of his character which led the prisoner into his present situation'. He was chosen by the crowd to receive the money, 'he being considered the most honest and trustworthy of the whole'.[98] Robert Baker and his brother were, according to a prosecution witness, men of excellent character; they were leaders in their parish 'but for whom there would have been no riot'. One can surmise that their good character made the collection and disposition of £22 much safer.[99]

At the end of a perambulation, and sometimes after a treat of food and drink in a public-house, the money which had been collected was distributed, as it was on other occasions of customary charity. After a day spent in machine-breaking and exacting levies, the labourers of Owslebury marched onto the Downs where they 'were drawn up in line four deep, and were ranked off by scores to receive their respective shares'. Each man received about two shillings from a collection of £16 or £17, an amount equal to the daily wage the labourers were demanding.[100] A labourer, who was with the East Stratton men mentioned above, claimed that their treasurer bought each man a half-pint of beer in the public house before adjourning to a meadow to divide the rest of the money between the participating parishes.[101]

In soliciting largess the labourers followed the practices of customary 'collective begging'. Firstly, in many places they demanded a standard fee for the destruction of a machine, or fixed the donation at a set amount. The sum varied greatly between localities; in Berkshire it was as low as five shillings in some places and as high as two pounds in others, and some individuals were required to pay more. The amount, however, is less important than the notion which underlay the labourers' demand. They decided that a proper figure should be set for their service; in doing this they adhered to the framework of custom, for calendrical ceremonies always had a standard form of response considered appropriate to the occasion. The labourers also believed that their actions were legitimate if a donation was given and not actually taken by force. They seem to have believed that robbery required a degree of force. A Micheldever machine-breaker defended himself against a charge of robbery by insisting that he asked 'civilly for the money,...and the prosecutor gave it to him and that he thanked him very kindly for it'.[102] Levi Brown, a Wiltshire thatcher, led a crowd to Mr Rebbeck's farm where they broke a chaff-cutter and collected money in consequence. Brown insisted in his defence that 'he took the money but had not demanded it'.[103] The men who confronted William Sclater at Tangier Park, Wootton St Lawrence, adamantly refused to take two sovereigns from his pocket, which was the only way he said they would get it, declaring, 'no, you shall give it to us'. When Sclater had the money in his hand he was jostled by John Batten and it fell to the ground where it was retrieved by Charles Pain whose defence was that 'I did not take the money out of Mr Sclater's hand'. The judge in Pain's case noted that 'the prisoners had laid great stress upon the fact of their not having taken the money by force, but having it given to them'. The law, Mr Justice Alderson declared, 'recognised no such evasion'; if money was demanded in a menacing manner it was immaterial if it was given, taken from the person, picked up from the ground or sent on afterwards, the act was still a capital felony.[104] Justice Parke was equally certain that for robbery to be proved 'it was immaterial whether the party...took the property with his own hand, or...induced the other party...to part with it'. Furthermore, 'it was of no importance whether the transaction was coloured by any pretence of taking it as a gift'.[105]

The law was thus clearly at odds with the customary practices of doleing and other ceremonial visitations. During the trial of Robert and Joseph Mason and others for robbery, the Crown prosecutor suggested that their guilt would be proved

> by showing that they were in a body before they went to Mr Callendar's house – that they went to it together – that they all participated more or less by their threats, their gestures, and other demonstrations in the extortion of money – that they retired from the place in a body, and that they were after- wards discovered sharing among themselves a sum of money, which they had somehow or other obtained.[106]

In other words, behaviour which was customarily associated with collective begging in its various forms was seen as evidence of criminal conduct. On Plough Monday, Shrove Tuesday, Guy Fawkes night, doleing days and many other occa- sions, similar behaviour was tolerated, even if it was also increasingly resented; in November 1830 it was prosecuted. The traditional practice of demanding largess and the manner of its collection were thus effectively criminalised and the role of the trea- surer in a ceremonial visitation, which usually fell to men of some standing in the community, was now extremely risky.

Treasurers, like horn-blowers, were easily identified and, not unreasonably, they were seen by the authorities as leaders in the protests. The crowd at Basildon and Streatley acknowleged Charles Milson as one of its 'foreleaders'; he asked for money at the houses the crowd visited 'and took it when any was given'.[107] A witness to the disturbances at Selborne and Headley identified Robert Holdaway as 'leading the mob and counting out money to the people'.[108] When Thomas Langford's farm in Wroughton was visited, Joseph Watts demanded money for breaking the threshing-machine and Langford swore that several voices cried out 'give it to Watts, he is our captain, and receives the money'.[109] Edward Harris 'was the person who demanded and received the money' during the perambulation of Aldermaston, Brimpton and Wasing and he later paid for eighteen gallons of beer, and seventeen shillings worth of bread and cheese at the Hind's Head.[110]

It was natural for the labourers to end their perambulations in a public house. Drink was central to the traditions of 'popular sociability' in the countryside.[111] The public house was the focal point of village social activity and most customary visitations culminated in the consumption of food and drink purchased with a portion of the collected fund. Charles Milson and Thomas Hanson, the organisers of the Basildon and Streatley crowd, led one hundred and fifty men to The Compasses where they had beer and bread.[112] William Cheater, the leader and treasurer of the Damerham men, led his fellows to the Compass Inn, and at Buckland Newton the protesters adjourned to the King's Arms.[113] The men who traversed Easton, Martyr Worthy and Avington ended their march in two public houses. At the Bat and Ball in Avington the treasurer for that portion of the crowd put a pile of money on the table and asked for someone to count it. The sum amounted to £19 3s 6d which, after paying for some beer, was then divided among the fifty-two people present. The men got seven shillings each and the boys two shillings and sixpence or three shillings.[114] The East Stratton men who had collected £40 in their progress, including £10 from Francis Callendar, Sir Thomas Baring's steward, were followed to the public house by Callendar's clerk. What followed gives an insight into the desire for propriety so characteristic of the Swing protesters. The men were treated to half a pint of beer each; there was no orgy of drunkenness. The clerk, who had positioned himself by the cellar door, was instructed by the treasurer 'to keep count of the beer that was drawn'. Later, Joseph Mason directed him to make out a bill for the beer and gave him £5 to pay for it. The men were then drawn up in an adjoining meadow where Mason distributed the balance of the money between the three parishes.[115] The sharing of food, drink and money was also a means of preserving solidarity among the labourers. During the trial of Charles Davis, a witness alleged that he had been forced to go with a crowd which refreshed itself at the Rose and Crown at Woodbury. When he tried to absent himself from the next machine-breaking foray, Davis insisted he continue because he 'had partaken of their bread, cheese and beer'.[116]

## ROBBERY AND MACHINE-BREAKING INCIDENTS[117]

| Nov. | BERKS | | HANTS | | WILTS | |
|---|---|---|---|---|---|---|
| | Robbery | Machine-breaking | Robbery | Machine-breaking | Robbery | Machine-breaking |
| 18 | 4 | 5 | 2 | 9 | | |
| 19 | 4 | 6 | 7 | 5 | | |
| 20 | 1 | 1 | 5 | 2 | | |
| 21 | 1 | 2 | 9 | 2 | | 2 |
| 22 | 8 | 8 | 17 | 11 | 8 | 25 |
| 23 | 23 | 20 | 27 | 16 | 38 | 43 |
| 24 | 6 | 8 | 6 | 4 | 12 | 12 |
| 25 | | | | | 2 | 13 |
| 26 | | | 1 | | | 4 |
| % of Robbery on St Clement's | 49 | | 37 | | 63 | |
| % of Machine-br. on St Clement's | 40 | | 33 | | 43 | |
| % of Robber & Mach-br. on St Clems | 44 | | 40 | | 51 | |

It also seems that customary practice affected the chronology of events in the three most affected counties. In Berkshire, Hampshire and Wiltshire the disturbances reached a crescendo on the same day – St Clement's Day, 23 November. This was one of the important doleing days before Christmas, a day when it was customary for rural labourers to solicit gifts of food and money. Liminality and commensality were an integral part of all doleing customs and we have seen how they influenced the Swing disturbances. St Clement's and St Catherine's, two days later, were widely celebrated throughout England although it is unclear how generally they were observed in Wessex. The uncertainty is the result of a gap in the folkloric record but there is enough circumstantial evidence to sustain the belief that doleing occurred. The survival of St Clement's doleing was recorded in Sussex in the late nineteenth century, in Berkshire the day was traditionally associated with the solicitation and consumption of small spiced cakes and in Hampshire it was a feast day for blacksmiths. Even if southern England had not been wracked by turmoil, it is likely that the St Clement's doleing would have taken place according to custom, and rural labourers would have approached the more prosperous members of their communities for assistance.[118]

Although the progress of disturbance from Kent, through Sussex and Surrey, to Hampshire and Berkshire was a matter of chance, the coincidence of a doleing day is very evident in the escalation of activity on St Clement's Day and is too striking to ignore. In Hampshire, 28 per cent of all the recorded events occurred on 23 November, in Berkshire it was 40 per cent and in Wiltshire 42 per cent. The labourers, it would seem, took advantage of the licence customarily extended on days reserved for the collection of charity to pursue their demands. It is possible that many were more inclined to become involved in events on that day because of its function in the customary calendar.

The significance of St Clement's Day is revealed by an analysis of the incidence of 'robbery' and machine-breaking during the seven days of most intense disturbance. The escalation of activity on 23 November is hard to explain without reference to the popular custom of doleing on St Clement's Day. It is probable that the labourers were utterly unselfconscious about their involvement in the protest, and confidently assertive in their demands for donations, because their actions were associated with an important event in the customary calendar.

Another St Clement's Day custom may also have influenced the course of the Swing disturbances. St Clement was the patron saint of blacksmiths and 23 November was traditionally celebrated by a shortening of the working day, the collection of donations during a perambulation, plenty of drinking, and sometimes a supper in the evening. A rhyme for St. Clement's Day, recorded in 1827, shows how the blacksmiths' celebration involved the demand for largess.

> Come all you Vulcans stout and strong,
> Unto St. Clem we do belong,
> I know this house is well prepared
> With plenty of money and good strong beer,
> And we must drink before we part,
> All for to cheer each merry heart.
> Come all you Vulcans, strong and stout,
> Unto St Clem I pray turn out [119]

The day of most intense disturbance in the four counties was the very day when blacksmiths were most likely to be *en fete*. The role of blacksmiths in machine wrecking was noted in an earlier chapter, and it must be remembered that they were often community leaders and the tradesmen who were best equipped with the tools for breaking cast iron. The scale of machine breaking and the effectiveness with which it was carried out on St Clement's Day was quite possibly linked to the fact that it was a day for customary festivity among blacksmiths.

When the behaviour of the Swing protesters is placed in the context of custom and popular culture, their innocent self-confidence and ingenuousness is more readily understood. Custom offered a rhetoric of legitimation which allowed them to act against a perceived threat to their well-being and assert their claim to fair treatment in their local environment. Custom also afforded them a vocabulary of action and fostered the belief that their behaviour was proper because it conformed to customary ways. For these reasons they were both unprepared for and deeply shocked by the reaction of local and national authorities and the punishment which sent men to New South Wales for no crime of which they were conscious.

## Notes

1    J. Philipp, 'Traditional Historical Narrative and Action-oriented (or Ethnographic) History', *Historical Studies*, Vol. 20, 1983, pp. 349-50.

2    For the most comprehensive treatment of the features of plebeian culture see P. Burke, *Popular Culture in Early Modern Europe*, London, 1978, and E.P. Thompson, *Customs in Common*, London, 1991.

3    Ibid. p. 6.

4    E.P. Thompson, 'The Moral Economy of the English Crowd in the Eighteenth Century', *Past and Present*, 50, 1971; J.M. Neeson, 'The Opponents of Enclosure in Eighteenth-Century Northamptonshire', *Past and Present*, 105, 1984; J. Rule, *The Experience of Labour in Eighteenth Century Industry*, London, 1981, pp. 194-216; A. Randall, 'The Industrial Moral Economy of the Gloucestershire Weavers in the Eighteenth Century', in J. Rule (ed), *British Trade Unionism 1750-1850: The Formative Years*, Harlow, 1988; A. Randall, *Before the Luddites: Custom, community and machinery in the English woollen industry 1776-1809*, Cambridge, 1991. As late as 1842 the townsfolk of Newbury endeavoured to maintain their rights of access to two open fields after the harvest by an appeal to custom. The pasturage enjoyed by the householders did not, in their eyes, depend on 'the concession and good will' of the landowner but was a 'legally established custom' enjoyed 'for so long as time'. Berkshire Record Office (hereafter BRO), D/EX 241 Z3.

5    R.W. Malcomson, *Popular Recreations in English Society 1700-1850*, Cambridge, 1973, *passim;* A. Delves, 'Popular Recreation and Social Conflict in Derby', in E. Yeo & S. Yeo (eds.), *Popular Culture and Class Conflict 1590-1914*, London, 1983, pp. 89-127.

6    Malcomson, op. cit., pp.110-11.

7    C. Fisher, *Custom, Work and Market Capitalism: The Forest of Dean Colliers, 1788-1888*, London, 1981, p. vii.

8    W. Hone, *The Every Day Book or Everlasting Calendar of Popular Amusements, Sports, Pastimes, Ceremonies, Manners, Customs and Events*, London 1827, Vol. II, p. 1207, emphasis added.

9    Y-M. Berce, ( Trans. A. Whitmore), *History of Peasant Revolts: The Social Origins of Rebellion in Early Modern France*, Oxford, 1990, pp.20-22.

10   R.W. Malcolmson, 'Leisure', in G.E. Mingay (ed), *The Victorian Countryside*, Vol., II, London, 1981, p.603; D.A. Reid, 'Interpreting the Festival Calendar: Wakes and Fairs as Carnivals', in R.D. Storch (ed), *Popular Culture and Custom in Nineteenth Century England*, London, 1982, pp. 71-99.

11   R.D. Storch. 'Persistence and Change in Nineteenth Century Popular Culture', in Storch (ed), op. cit., p. 6.

12   I. Anstruther, *The Scandal of the Andover Workhouse*, Gloucester, 1984, p.60. The imminent market day at Devizes was a cause of concern to an anonymous correspondent who wrote to Melbourne on 22 November. Gloucestershire Record Office, 1571/X/63.

13   J.M. Golby & A.W. Purdue, *The Civilisation of the Crowd: Popular Culture in England 1750-1900*, New York, 1985, p. 23.

14   Malcolmson, *Popular Recreations*, p.82-3. As late as the 1930s the young people of Pitton believed that some laws were in abeyance on Guy Fawkes night. They ignored the presence of police, stole besoms to use as torches, built barriers of faggots across roads and set fires in unauthorised places; R. Whitlock, *The Folklore of Wiltshire*, London, 1976, p. 64.

15   J.M. Chambers, *Wiltshire Machine Breakers*, Vol. I, Letchworth, 1993, p.197.

16   L. Coser in Malcolmson, op. cit., pp.76,79.

17   N. Gash, *Aristocracy and People 1815-1865*, London, 1979, p. 37.

18   R. Porter, *English Society in the Eighteenth Century*, Harmondsworth, 1982, pp119-20.

19   S.H. Palmer, *Police and Protest in England and Ireland 1780-1850*, Cambridge, 1988, pp. 47, 52.

20   M. Gluckman, 'Rituals of Rebellion in South-East Africa', in Gluckman, *Order and Rebellion in Tribal Africa*, London, 1963; V. Turner, *The Ritual Process; Structure and Anti-Structure*, London, 1969, Cornell edition, 1977.

21   Ibid., pp.95-7.

22   Ibid., pp. 167-9,177.

23   Burke, op. cit., pp. 199-204; B. Bushaway, *By Rite: Custom, Ceremony and Community in England 1700-1880*, London, 1982, pp. 167-68; Berce, op. cit., pp. 26-34.

24   Malcolmson, *Popular Recreations*, p. 80.

25   Bushaway, op. cit., p. 167.

26   E.J. Hobsbawm & G. Rudé, *Captain Swing*, London, 1969, p. 195.

27   Burke, op. cit., p. 190; Bushaway, op. cit., pp. 170-72. A.R. Wright & T.E. Lones, *British Calendar Customs, Vol. I Movable Feasts*, London, 1936, p. 4.

28   W. Hone, *The Year Book of Daily Recreation and Information*, London, 1839, pp. 1599-60; for similar shroving rhymes from Berkshire and Hampshire see Wright & Lones, op. cit., Vol. I, pp. 16, 19, and for Wiltshire Whitlock, op.

cit., pp. 48-51.

29 Bushaway, op. cit., p. 190. At Purley the following shroving chant was recorded in the 1890s.

Knick-knock, pan's hot.

I'm come a shroving;

Bit of bread and a bit of cheese,

That's better than nothing.

Last year's flour's dear

That's what makes poor Purley children come shroving here.

The chanters showed their displeasure if no gift was forthcoming by throwing things at the door. P.H. Ditchfield, *Old English Customs*, London, 1896, pp.60-61.

30 Malcolmson, *Popular Recreations*, p. 165-6; R.D. Storch, ''Please to Remember the Fifth of November': Conflict, Solidarity and Public Order in Southern England 1815-1900', in Storch (ed), op. cit.

31 Hone, *Every Day Book*, Vol. II, pp. 1379-80. Similar menace can be seen in a Guy Fawkes chant from Berkshire.

A stick and a stake for our good king's sake.

If you won't give one, I'll take two

The better for me, the worse for you. Ditchfield, op. cit.,p. 161.

32 Ibid., pp.161-62.

33 Bushaway, op. cit. p. 193.

34 Ditchfield op. cit., p. 314. Two Wiltshire mummings closed with the following variants:

'Christmas ale makes us dance and sing;

Money in purse is a very fine thing

Ladies and gentlemen give us what you please' F.A. Carrington, 'On Certain Wiltshire Customs', *Wiltshire Archaeological and Natural History Magazine*, Vol. I, 1854, p. 81.

'Now all you ladies and gentlemen who's got a crown or a pound to spare

Shave Old Dad and cut his hair

His hair so long and his beard so grey

He want a passol of money to send him away'. F. Gilmour, 'A Mummers' Play from Limpley Stoke', *Wiltshire Archaeological and Natural History Magazine*, Vol. 83, 1990, pp. 155-62.

35 Ditchfield, op. cit., pp. 27, 166-72.

36 Bushaway, op. cit. p. 183. A wassail song from Wootton Basset reminded the listener of the practical value of wintertime largess which was sought in return for blessings called down by grateful recipients, Wright & Lones, op. cit., Vol. III, p. 224.

'Wassail, wassail! all over the town
Our bread is so musty, our cheese is so brown,
God send our Master a good crop of corn
With the wassailing bowl we drink to thee'.

37 Bushaway, op. cit., p. 37; A. Williams, *A Wiltshire Village*, London, 1912, p. 240. E.G. Hayden, *Travels Round My Village: a Berkshire book*, London, 1901, pp. 134-5.

38 On September 4 1830 about seventy people sat down to a harvest supper at Lower Farm near Purley and consumed two and a half sheep weighing 124 lbs. twelve mutton pies and fourteen plum pies. Farm Diary, BRO, D/EWi E 17.

39 Cited in Malcolmson, *Popular Recreations*, p. 81.

40 Bushaway, op. cit., p. 200. W. Howitt, *The Rural Life of England*, London, 1838, p. 445.

41 Hone, *Every Day Book*, Vol. II, pp. 1255-56, emphasis added.

42 Bushaway, op. cit., p., 190.

43 *The Times*, 10/1/1831.

44 Bushaway, op. cit., p., 82; for fuller details of Rogation week processions see pp. 81-88.

45 *The Times*, 4/1/1831.

46 Ibid., 6/1/1831; 23/12/1830.

47 G.E. Mingay, 'Rural War: the life and times of Captain Swing', in Mingay (ed), *The Unquiet Countryside*, London, 1989, p. 48. Bushaway, op. cit., p. 191.

48 *The Times*, 5/1/1831.

49 Ibid., 8/1/1831.

50 Ibid., 28/12/1830.

51 Thompson, op. cit., p., 10.

52 *The Times*, 22/12/1830.

53 Ibid., 28/12./1830.

54 Ibid., 29/12/1830.

55 Ibid., 14/1/1831; H.G. Mundy (ed), *The Journal of Mary Frampton*, London, 1885, p. 361.

56 *The Times*, 25/12/1830.

57 Berce, op. cit., p. 40, *passim*.

58 Thompson, op. cit., pp.,467-533.

59 Ditchfield, op. cit., p. 179.

60 M. Ingram, 'Ridings, rough music and the reform of popular culture in early modern England', *Past and Present*, 105, 1984, p. 92; Ditchfield, op. cit., pp. 178-79.

61 Ingram, op. cit., p.,93.

62 Ibid., p. 81. P. Robinson, 'Royal Justice and Folk Justice: Conflict Arising Over

A Skimmington at Potterne in 1857', *Wiltshire Archaeological and Natural History Magazine*, Vol. 83, 1990, pp. 147-54, notes thirteen recorded skimmingtons inWiltshire between 1835 and the early twentieth century.

63   E. Bradby, *Seend: A Wiltshire Village Past and Present*, Gloucester, 1981, pp. 227-9; B. Croucher, *The Village in the Valley: A History of Ramsbury*, Ramsbury, 1986, p. 175; *The Introduction of Primitive Methodism in Berkshire 1829-30: A Jubilee Memorial*, Newbury, 1880, pp.8-9.

64   A recent skimmington at Whitechurch Canonicorum was noted in Ditchfield, *op. cit.*, pp. 180-81 and the activities of a 'rough band' by Williams, op. cit., p. 242. See too, Dorset Record Office, D/FIL/F 59.

65   Personal communication from Mr Guy Stiff (b. 1910) of Swallowfield who witnessed the incident. For three successive nights, between six o'clock and midnight, over one hundred labourers raised a cacophony with bells, tins, buckets, pots and pans and horns, after which the path was re-opened and the customary access restored.

66   Hone, op. cit., Vol. II, p. 1308.

67   Thompson, op. cit., p. 469.

68   *The Times*, 14/1/1831.

69   Ibid., 1/1/1831.

70   *Machine-Breaking, and the changes occasioned by it in the Village of Turvey Down. A Tale of the Times, November, 1830*, Oxford, 1830, p. 20.

71   Deposition of W. Lawes, Hampshire Record Office (hereafter HRO), 10 M 57/O 3.

72   *The Times*, 30/12/1830; Williams, op. cit., p. 296.

73   Loc. cit.

74   *The Times*, 3/1/1831. For Aaron Stone's role as a horn-blower at Whiteparish, *The Salisbury and Winchester Journal*, 10/1/1831.

75   *The Times*, 23/12/1830; 25/12/1830

76   Ibid., 28/12/1830.

77   Ibid., 7/1/1831.

78   Deposition of W. Lawes, HRO, 10 M 57/O 3.

79   *The Times*, 5/1/1831.

80   Ibid., 8/1/1831.

81   Ibid., 22/12/1830.

82   Ibid., 29/12/1830, 3/1/1831.

83   Ibid., 1/1/1831.

84   Ibid., 8/1/1831.

85   Ibid., 7/1/1831.

86   Report from a Women's Institute publication *Dorset Up Along and Down Along*, cited in C. Hole, *British Folk Customs*, London, 1976, p. 47.

87   Ingram, op. cit., p. 97.

88   *The Times*, 24/12/1830.

89   A.J.C. Hare, *Memorials of a Quiet Life*, Vol. 1, London, 1874, pp. 353-62; M.R. Mitford, *Our Village: Sketches of Rural Character and Scenery*, Vol. V, London, 1832, pp. 5-13; Mary Frampton in E.A. Smith (ed), *Reform or Revolution: A Diary of Reform in England 1830-32*, Stroud, 1992, pp. 42-44.

90   *The Times*, 30/12/1830.

91   Ibid., 8/1/1831.

92   Ibid., 6/1/1831.

93   Ibid., 30/12/1830.

94   Loc. cit.

95   *The Times*, 8/1/1831.

96   Bushaway, op. cit., p. 193.

97   A. Somerville, *The Whistler at the Plough*, Manchester, 1852, p. 263.

98   *The Times*, 10/1/1831.

99   Loc. cit.

100  *The Times*, 30/12/1830.

101  Ibid., 22/12/1830.

102  J.L. & B. Hammond, *The Village Labourer 1760-1832*, London, 1920 edition, p. 252.

103  *The Times*, 8/1/1831.

104  Ibid., 24/12/1830. H.B. Wither of Manydown House had used the same tactic and his coachman who followed the crowd to Tangier Park had informed Sclater of events there. Depositions of H.B. Wither & W.L. Sclater, HRO, 10 M 57/O 3.

105  *The Times*, 22/12/1830.

106  Loc. Cit.

107  Ibid. 3/1/1831.

108  Ibid., 28/12/1830.

109  Ibid., 6/1/1831.

110  Ibid., 30/12/1830.

111  D. Underdown, *Fire from Heaven: Life in an English Town in the Seventeenth Century*, London, 1992, p. 63.

112  *The Times*, 3/1/1831.

113  Ibid., 8/1/1831,14/1/1831.

114  Ibid., 23/12/1830.

115  Ibid., 22/12/1830.

116  Ibid., 7/1/1831.

117  Hobsbawm & Rudé, op. cit., Appendix III, Table of Incidents, pp. 311-58.

118  This dole chant recorded in Sussex was characteristic of many others.

Cattern' and Clemen' be here, here, here,
Give us your apples and give us your beer,
One for Peter, two for Paul,
Three for Him who made us all;
Clemen' was a good man,
Cattern' was his mother;
Give us your best,
And not your worst,
And God will give your soul good rest. Bushaway, op. cit., p. 185.

119 Hone, *Every Day Book*, Vol., I, p. 1502. Around Winchester the blacksmiths also added to the festivities by exploding gunpowder on their anvils, Wright & Lones, op. cit., Vol. III, pp. 173-4.

## Chapter 5

# 'THE MACHINE-BURNING WAS LIKE A CIVIL WAR IN THE COUNTRY': REACTION AND REPRESSION

'We do not come here to inquire into grievances', declared Mr Justice Alderson at the first Special Commission sitting at Winchester, 'we come here to decide law'.[1] A few of the more politically aware prisoners, like Robert and Joseph Mason, might have detected in Alderson's remark a sign that their fate was settled. As the landowning and governing elite re-established its authority in the countryside, questions of social justice were set aside and the legitimacy of the labourers' complaints ignored. Alderson's comment had but one meaning; in the winter of 1830-31 the men who appeared before a court because of their involvement in the protests could expect no sympathy. The governments of the Duke of Wellington and Earl Grey – the latter having replaced the Iron Duke at the peak of the disturbances – differed fundamentally on the question of parliamentary reform but on the treatment to be meted out to the Swing protesters they were of one mind. The disturbances had to be suppressed, ruthlessly and efficiently. In the aftermath of Swing, the aristocratic state exacted a terrible and terrifying retribution.

The protesters were tried in ninety courts sitting in thirty-four counties. Of the 1976 prisoners, 252 were sentenced to death of whom nineteen were executed, 505 sentenced to transportation and 644 imprisoned.[2] No other social protest had ever been treated so savagely. More were transported for their part in the Swing disturbances than for all the other protests which troubled the English authorities between 1790 and 1848 put together.[3] Transportation had a profound effect on the families and communities of those exiled and the authorities relied on its terrifying example. The punishments handed down to working men in 1830 and 1831 were long remembered; on the eve of the First World War the story was still told in Wiltshire villages of their unjust exile.[4] For an equivalent use of the terror of transportation one must look to the aftermath of the Irish revolt in 1798 and Culloden in 1745. England had seen nothing to rival the punishments handed down in 1830 and 1831 since Monmouth's rebellion almost one hundred and fifty years previously.[5] Those events involved a challenge to the nation's political establishment and the prospect of civil war; the Swing disturbances posed no such threat, yet they were crushed with a comparable degree of savagery. The reaction was an indication of the deep shock felt by the landed, ruling class.

In 1830 England's aristocratic governors were under attack on several fronts and when the rural protests began they were already on the defensive. Many of those who made up the propertied, political nation believed that revolution and civil war were a distinct possibility. Their feeling of vulnerability, however, had little to do with the poverty and distress of the labourers in Wessex villages. It was more the product of industrial and political discontent in the north of England and frustration among parliamentary reformers across the country. It is against the background of mounting discontent in the textile towns and ever more strident calls for parliamentary reform that the response of the authorities to the upheaval in the countryside must be considered.

Most governments after 1815 expected trouble from the rapidly growing industrial towns which had been infected with political radicalism in the 1790s and had supported the working-class radical movement until it was forced into submissiveness after Peterloo. In 1830 the menace of a discontented, politicised and unionised industrial labour force was very real. The cotton industry in Lancashire and Cheshire experienced a severe slump in 1829-30 following an earlier depression in 1825-26 which had prompted the worst episode of machine-breaking since the Luddites in 1812. Rumours of arming and incipient revolution and the familiar language of menace prompted the government to reinforce the garrisons of some northern towns.[6] Labouring men once more adopted the language of 'rights'. A speaker assured a large crowd at a Manchester meeting that 'no military force could withstand them if they would only assert their rights like men'.[7] Spinners were told by their union leaders that working men might 'yet save themselves from all the horrid consequences of poverty, pauperism, ignorance and crime' by combining together to fight 'unprincipled and greedy' tyrants.[8] In 1830 'the old links between industrial and political agitation were being reforged' for the first time since Peterloo.[9]

During the strike in 1829 the cotton industry of the north-west was virtually closed down and in the bitter aftermath over 80,000 spinners joined the General Union. The following year John Doherty endeavoured to bring a broad cross-section of the labour-force into his National Association for the Protection of Labour. The Association's main strength lay in the north-west but it quickly spread into Yorkshire, the Midlands and South Wales.[10] In late 1830 the employers' attempt to enforce a wage cut led to a revival of the acrimonious dispute; weavers paraded the streets of Manchester armed with pistols and clubs. Doherty, understanding that violence would probably lead to the deployment of troops, displayed the authority of the union when he insisted on a disciplined general strike which lasted until March

1831. If anything this probably increased the alarm of the landed rulers for, although they always expected trouble from the industrial towns and knew how to deal with violence, the spectre of an organised working class terrified them.[11] Industrial discontent, fuelled by the severe economic crisis, was certainly a cause for concern in 1830, but the coincidental revival of demands for parliamentary reform and the anti-aristocratic sentiment of the electorate made any protest far more menacing.

The reform movement contributed to the mounting state of panic which overwhelmed both Tory and Whig governments during the Swing disturbances. Central to the arguments of reformers like Attwood, Hunt, Cobbett and Carlile was the conviction that the country was seriously mismanaged because of the narrow distribution of the franchise and the extent of aristocratic control. The degree to which many others in the unreformed electorate shared that view, was revealed during the general election called after the death of George IV at the end of June. Throughout the country there was such a clear demonstration of dissatisfaction with Parliament and its domination by aristocratic, landed magnates that 'the men of the establishment found themselves naked to the world'.[12] The struggle was most obvious in the borough constituencies where corrupt corporations often sustained aristocratic control. At Marlborough the corporation duly elected the Marquess of Ailesbury's nominee but the angry townsfolk tore their gowns from their backs. At Shaftesbury, although Lord Grosvenor's wealth secured the return of his candidate, the electoral charade provoked a riot and the promise of another challenge at the next election.[13] Lady Georgina Stuart-Wortley noted how in the counties, where an electoral contest occurred, 'the old established county interest has been defeated'. At Winchester, one of the county members was 'obliged to leave the place of election in disguise for fear of the just-enraged people who had assembled'.[14] 'The aristocracy', as Henry Brougham astutely observed, had 'been taught a lesson', but had it learned anything? The short answer is that the Whigs under Grey had, but the government of Wellington evidently had not.

Wellington believed that 'beginning reform is beginning revolution' and he was not alone in that opinion.[15] Some of the grandees were convinced that their fate hung in the balance and that a revolution was the likely consequence of the people's loss of faith in the aristocracy. The symbolism and language of revolution was very apparent during 1830. At Preston in Lancashire, where Henry Hunt was elected on what virtually amounted to universal male suffrage, the campaign was enlivened with tricolour flags and banners with slogans like 'Bread or Blood' and 'Liberty or Death'. Urban riots, which continental experience had shown were often precursors of revolution, occurred in a number of cities during the election, including Preston, Northampton, Bristol, Norwich and Banbury.[16] The French revolutionary flag was waved at the Prime Minister and members of the cabinet during their inaugural journey to celebrate the opening of the Liverpool to Manchester railway in

September.[17] Audiences at the radical meeting place, the Rotunda, who gathered to hear the latest denunciation of the system by Cobbett, Carlile or some other critic wore tricolour cockades in their hats to demonstrate their commitment to French principles of liberty and equality. The revolution in Paris in July 1830 had little or no effect on voting behaviour during the general election but was a very significant inspiration for those who saw in the abdication of Charles X and the eviction of the conservative, royalist Ultras a lesson for the British ruling class.[18] It was in that spirit, perhaps, that the event was praised by labouring men in Kent and Sussex as the rural disturbances gained momentum.[19]

In 1830 a revolution seemed increasingly likely. When Earl Stanhope warned the House of Lords in February that 'the land-owners were not safe for a single year' and that continuing neglect would lead the poor, 'by their superior numbers', to enforce 'a partition of the land', few were inclined to take his doom-laden jeremiad seriously.[20] By mid-September, however, talk of revolution was heard everywhere in London and by the middle of the following month even Wellington was forced to admit that 'everybody is frightened'.[21] By the first week of November London was in a panic. The funds dropped three per cent as speculators, those most sensitive weathercocks of stability, showed their lack of confidence in the government after Wellington declared himself opposed to all reform. Hostile crowds forced the cancellation of the royal visit to the Mansion House on Lord Mayor's Day. The Prime Minister was hissed and booed at public appearances and fearing an attack on Apsley House he drew up a plan for its defence. In expectation of impending upheaval, shopkeepers talked of arming themselves to protect their property from 'the unpleasant feeling…rising among the working classes', troops rumoured to number 10,000 were quartered around the capital and the newly established Metropolitan Police was on full alert.[22] On 9 November, when the Swing disturbances were still confined to incidents in Kent and East Sussex and ten days before the tidal wave of protest broke upon Hampshire and Berkshire, Princess Lieven wrote to her brother Alexander to tell him that 'we too in England…are just on the brink of a revolution'. Wellington had told her, she added, that 'as far as the disorders of the mob' were concerned 'he knew how to repress them'.[23] The government was on the defensive, besieged by events largely beyond its control, fearful that the cancer of revolution might reach Britain as it had so many other parts of Europe. To preserve the political power of the aristocracy, the Prime Minister was resolved to resist reform and ready to meet upheaval with musket, sabre and grape-shot. When large-scale disorder began it scarcely mattered that it came from such an unlikely and largely unexpected quarter as the agricultural labourers nor that it was far from being the revolutionary event that was expected. The rural disturbances were put down as efficiently and ruthlessly as circumstances would allow.

Swing alarmed a vulnerable ruling establishment but it also demonstrated that the social order of the countryside, which the rulers largely took for granted, was fast being eroded. In many respects this came as a profound shock because the social and political pre-eminence of the landed elite was founded on the notion of the fundamental, paternalistic harmony of rural society. The propertied classes expected the rural poor to be deferential and subservient; when that expectation was shattered in 1830 there was outrage at the labourers' base ingratitude and betrayal.[24] A gentleman who made a journey into Hampshire towards the end of November 1830 believed that 'it was all over with landed property'. 'Not from fear of the disturbances', he stressed, 'but from...the disaffected state of feeling among the lower orders'.[25] Swing uncovered the 'subterranean rifts' which were normally concealed by the almost congenital passivity of agricultural labourers but which were a recurrent feature of post-war rural life.[26] The heightened social tension was largely attributable to the re-ordering of relationships which seemed to be a necessary part of the modern agrarian economy.[27] When landowners and employers thought of labour as a commodity, a factor in the profit and loss equation, all notions of mutual obligation and deference were bound to evaporate eventually. 'The good feeling which...used to exist between the Farmer and the Labourer' was sacrificed as the former endeavoured to make a profit 'at the price of justice and liberality to the latter'.[28] Observers noted with dismay and incomprehension the 'general disaffection' and the 'feeling of distrust and animosity' which existed between farmers and labourers such that 'all friendly intercourse' ceased. John Pearse, MP for Devizes, believed that the 'total want of feeling' among farmers for their labourers made 'violent means' inevitable if the latter were to obtain any increase in wages.[29] The process of agricultural improvement increased the social distance between the farmer and the labourer in arable areas to 'an unbridgeable chasm' and it is scarcely surprising that social tension and conflict intensified as a result.[30]

Although Cobbett had warned as early as 1806 that rural England was becoming a society with 'but two classes of men, *masters*, and *abject dependants*', few had wanted to believe him.[31] By 1830, when the 'rural war' which he had predicted finally erupted on a grand scale, it was impossible to ignore the fact that the countryside was deeply divided and that the continued security of the masters was at risk. Conflict in the countryside was far more pervasive than is usually recognised by analyses which are restricted to considerations of 'overt' protest and 'covert' crime.[32] It coloured most aspects of labouring life. The administration of poor relief was probably the principal source of social tension for increasingly it polarised those who controlled relief and those who received it, but conflict was inherent in many aspects of the labour process and the relations of employment. Most obviously, the introduction of threshing machines was an attempt by the farmers to seize control of a particular work process from the labourers and the latter's opposition was an attempt to retain their customary position.[33] The very powerlessness of the labourers created situations in which conflict was almost inevitable. Wage bargaining, for example, was virtually impossible in many villages on the chalk uplands, except in times of crisis, for where large farms were common wages were often 'altogether under the control' of one or two farmers who might employ most of the labour of the parish.[34] The wages for parish employment likewise often depended entirely upon the discretionary power of the overseer.[35] Farmers, landowners and poor law officers regularly used their monopolistic control of relief and employment as disciplinary devices to reward the subservient and punish anyone who dared to contest their authority.[36] In this situation class animosities intensified.

It is likely that agricultural labourers particularly resented the increasing social distance which separated master and man, for it reinforced their utter dependence upon their employers and made explicit their lack of worth. Wiltshire labourers complained to Alexander Somerville that the farmers never spoke to them directly. Instead, they received their instructions from a bailiff, for the 'masters never gives us a chance to speak to them'. On some farms the distance was maintained by severing the manly contact of face to face wage-payment. Farmers, it was claimed, no longer allowed the brutish labourers to enter their houses and paid them through a hole in the wall 'lest they defile the house of a master who gets rich as they get poor'. It was 'enough to drive men mad'.[37] In October 1830, the editor of *The Times* also lamented the fact that 'the national condition for the last half-century' had been to 'make the rich man richer, and the poor man miserably poor', so that old-style relationships had disappeared as the farmer became a gentleman and the labourer 'a brutal slave'. Although *The Times* might maintain that in such circumstances crime was 'the inevitable consequence of desperation', most farmers and landowners had a less generous perception.[38] As possessors of property they were the victims of crimes committed by their social inferiors, by men and women whose lives they expected to control.

One of the most enduring myths about nineteenth century Britain is that the countryside was somehow more peaceful, less violent and less criminal than the urban, industrial environment. Nothing could be further from the truth.[39] The countryside was plagued with crime – the full extent of which we can never know because so much went unreported and unprosecuted – and detection was difficult in a silent, conspiratorial and complicit village community. Arson, animal maiming and property damage, 'the counter-terror of the poor', were common; they were usually acts of vengeance or protest and, therefore, likely evidence of social tension.[40] The picture is less clear for the most common crime of the countryside, the petty theft of produce and livestock by labourers at work.[41] Most petty thefts were a response to poverty, and historians have tended to categorise such offences as 'social' or 'survival' crime because, as Cobbett observed, it was foolish 'to expect morality in a half-starved man'.[42] Petty theft may not have been an explicit protest like property damage but it was the product of social and economic circumstance and the cause of much tension.

The social antagonism associated with endemic rural crime can be detected in the response of its propertied victims. In many parts of southern England farmers and landowners formed themselves into defensive associations to combat crime. The specific purpose of the Aldermaston, Wasing and Padworth Association for the Prosecution of Felons in Berkshire was 'the more effectively to secure the property of the Subscribers' by 'defraying the Expenses of Adverting, Apprehending and Prosecuting' offenders.[43] Rewards were offered for information which led to a conviction. Arson, burglary, robbery and the theft of livestock, as the most serious crimes, naturally attracted the largest inducements, but those offered for minor theft and property damage indicate the variety of rural crime which the propertied sought to deter.[44]

| | |
|---|---:|
| Stealing or damaging any Waggon, Cart, Plough or other Instrument of Husbandry or Stealing any Hay, Fodder, Seeds, Corn or Grain Thrashed or Unthrashed | £2 2s 0d |
| Cutting, Lopping, Topping or breaking down or Stealing any Timber or other Tree or any Wood or Underwood | £2 2s 0d |
| Stealing any Gates, Stiles, Rails, Pales, Posts, Hedges, Cages, Stakes, Cages, Iron Bars, Hurdles or Fences or any Iron Work belonging thereto | £1 1s 0d |
| Stealing any Wheat, Peas, Beans or other Corn from any Field or Inclosed Ground | £2 2s 0d |
| Stealing any Turnips, Carrots, Potatoes or other Roots, Fruits or Vegetables from any Fields or Inclosed Grounds, Orchard Garden or other Place | 10s 6d |

Prosecution societies were a tacit acknowledgement of the vulnerability of property which the mass poverty of the countryside jeopardised. The recognition of this fact even found its way into suggestions for the design and layout of farmsteads. According to Charles Waistell, a designer of farm buildings, one of the highest priorities was the need to keep the labourers under constant surveillance. A farmhouse, therefore, required 'at least one window on the ground floor belonging to a room that is constantly occupied, and the window of the farmer's bedroom should face the yard…[for] stock and servants cannot be too much under the eye of their master'.[45] Waistell's advice acknowledged the fact that in southern England the rural community was irreconcilably divided and that ordinary working men were likely to be driven to crime in order to survive in difficult times.

Of all rural crimes, poaching was the source of the most intense antagonism between rich and poor.[46] By their zealous protection of furred and feathered game the privileged landowners appeared to place pleasure above the survival of many rural families. Hunting game was the most visible symbol of social superiority; it was a privilege reserved to very few who qualified by virtue of their wealth and status. The unqualified, freehold and tenant farmers and the mass of labourers, could not take game even on land they owned. Rabbits, hares and game birds thus belonged not to the person on whose land they were found but rather to 'an entire social class, the English country gentleman'.[47] As rural poverty deepened after 1815 the incidence of poaching increased and so did the social resentments it provoked. The numbers convicted for poaching offences at the Dorset Quarter Sessions increased almost sevenfold between 1814 and 1818.[48] Fewer than twelve people a year in Wiltshire were sentenced under the game laws between 1790 and 1810; by the late 1820s the figure had risen to ninety-two.[49] In April 1823, twenty-two of the seventy-seven people in the Berkshire county Bridewell had been committed for poaching.[50]

Although the statistics for game offences are significant in themselves, they have even greater meaning as an index of the ubiquity of poaching for only a tiny fraction of offenders was ever detected or prosecuted. Prosecution associations, severe penalties, man-traps and spring-guns all failed to reduce the incidence of a crime which was not only a reflection of poverty but also an expression of a conflict of social values. A witness before a Select Committee in 1827 noted that poaching in Hampshire reflected 'the low rate of wages and want of sufficient employment' but added that it was seen as a crime only by the landowners; the labourers 'say God has made the game of the land free, and left it free'.[51] No shame or disgrace attached to poaching for, as John Benett noted, the labourers believed that they had 'a natural right' to the wild creatures.[52] The men who took part in the protests around Kintbury and Hungerford certainly shared this view. They lived near some of the largest game preserves in southern England and they voiced 'not a little indignation…against the severity of the game laws and the frequent commitments' by game-preserving magistrates.[53] Poaching was always a barometer of economic distress, but it was also a potent source of social antagonism and contributed significantly to the growing confrontation between privilege and poverty.

Fear and disillusion undoubtedly shaped the reaction of local and national authorities to the rural disturbances at the end of 1830. Although the benefit of hindsight allows us to see how inappropriate were the punishments meted out, we should not forget how the events of that late autumn appeared to contemporaries. Talk of revolution was in the air. There was, wrote the editor of the *Berkshire Chronicle*, 'a dangerous and Revolutionary spirit abroad' which was 'evident to every observant person'.[54] The forces of law and order were powerless before the massive expression of rural discontent and it is little wonder that farmers, landowners and other propertied residents of the countryside were genuinely fearful about the outcome. Some turned their houses into fortresses. At Moreton House in Dorset, where 'it was judged necessary to block up all the lower windows…as well as the doors', the owners sat up at night and organised patrols in expectation of an attack.[55] The Duke of Buckingham placed cannon at his principal doors, a swivel-gun at each window and armed 100 men of his villagers with cutlasses.[56] Mary Mitford, who lived in a village on the borders of Berkshire and Hampshire, recorded the alarm caused by the labourers' 'day-light marches on the high road, regular and orderly as those of an army…[and] midnight visits to lonely houses, lawless and terrific as the descent of pirates'. The 'preparations for defence…[and] the nightly collecting of arms and armed men within our own dwelling' were no less 'shocking', for they showed that the countryside was in a state of social, civil war.[57] That was certainly how the events of 1830 were long remembered. A generation later Richard Jefferies, an observer of rural affairs, recalled the interior of a Wiltshire farmhouse where 'an old yeomanry sabre' was a reminder of 'the days of the machine-burning – which was like a civil war in the country, and is yet recollected and talked of'.[58]

Mary Mitford's alarm was echoed in the flood of correspondence directed first to Sir Robert Peel and then Viscount Melbourne as successive Home Secretaries. Many of the letters suggested that the civil power was on the point of collapse. The Newbury magistrates acknowledged their inability 'to cope with the danger owing to the formidable and threatening bearing of the Mob' while at Andover the magistrates confessed that there was 'barely a semblance of civil government' within their jurisdiction.[59] The protesting crowds were everywhere scornful of the authorities; at Shaftesbury they assaulted the mayor and some special constables, and in several places prisoners were rescued from lawful custody.[60] Gaols, the most obvious physical manifestation of the power of the state, were considered likely targets. Reading was 'in a state of the greatest excitement' because of a rumour that a crowd was coming to release protesters imprisoned in the gaol. At Abingdon, where the prison was reportedly 'by no means secure', reports of an attack kept the townsfolk on nocturnal alert while 'a general rising' to rescue the prisoners was expected at Warminster.[61] The Town Clerk of Winchester also anticipated an invasion by five or six hundred labourers from Barton Stacey, Bullington and Micheldever 'for the purpose of destroying the Bridewell' at a time when, according to another correspondent, the city was absolutely defenceless, without soldiers or special constables.[62]

The manner in which a society is prepared to use violence is one of the clearest indicators of the character of that society's political life, and in late 1830 it must have seemed as if the authorities were preparing for a bloodier stage of civil conflict.[63] Their actions quite possibly added to the mood of crisis. The initial response of magistrates in most centres across the four counties was to request assistance in the form of troops or arms with which to re-equip the recently demobilised mounted yeomanry. The mayor of Poole thought 'fifty or sixty brace of pistols would be a great acquisition'; eighty sabres and belts were despatched by the Office of Ordnance to arm the defenders of Abingdon and another county magistrate asked the Home

Department for sufficient 'pistols or light carbines to arm about a dozen persons' engaged in nightly patrols.[64] Far more frequent than requests for arms were pleas that soldiers be garrisoned in the country towns. The government at no stage had enough troops to meet all the requests, but the fact that local authorities looked immediately to a military solution reflected the prevailing state of alarm.

Where local yeomanry companies were revived their presence was a confirmation that the forces of landed power and property were prepared to wage a social civil war on the impoverished.[65] A few, wise men recognised the danger of aligning military might with economic self-interest in a war against the hungry and oppressed. The use of military force 'to trample down the elastic resistance to positive suffering' would, it was claimed, bring the country to a 'precipice' for 'when blood is once shed by the soldiery' the character of the protest would be 'entirely changed'.[66] The Earl of Radnor acknowledged that the yeomanry had been very effective in Wiltshire but he warned Melbourne that it had been at the cost of even greater tension between the labourers and their employers.[67] Another Wiltshire gentleman requested the disposition of soldiers noting that without them, 'we must form…into a military band to defend ourselves' and the result would inevitably 'bring on a civil war'. In any event, the die was cast for 'Master must be against servant and servant against Master for the next age'.[68] While few, perhaps, had quite such an apocalyptic vision, many thought that they saw in the apparent collapse of the social order a portent of revolution.

It is often the case that what people believe to be happening is much more significant in determining how they behave than what actually occurs. The Swing disturbances had no coherent revolutionary purpose but in the turmoil of the moment it was easy for those who wanted to detect imminent revolution to do so. In Berkshire the labourers' actions were seen as part of a systematic and 'deliberate attack on property'. The gentry in the north and west of the county, conscious of 'the great danger their property will be exposed to by their leaving their houses', requested that the Special Commission sit at Abingdon to save them a journey to Reading which would leave their estates unguarded.[69] According to the Duke of Buckingham, the magistrates in central Hampshire were 'completely cowed' and his area 'wholly in the hands of the Rebels'.[70] A Dorset landowner claimed to 'have seen decided symptoms of an anxiety for a Revolution that may wipe off all debts'. He had found 'yeomen exciting the notion' that the revolution had actually begun and 'only needed the aid of their Class and of those below them to perfect its completion'.[71] The readiness of farmers to exploit the crisis by linking wage increases with rent and tithe reductions and their widespread reluctance to serve as special constables was especially alarming for it fractured the solidarity of the propertied.[72] And the labourers in Hampshire, J.H. Rickman believed, had discovered 'the power of forcing concession' which they would exercise 'progressively towards the climax of absolute domination'. Those who were 'at the summit of society' were, therefore, 'on the top of a volcano composed of the physical strengths of a pauper population…plentifully surcharged with the sulphur of discontent and of underhand traiterous (sic) excitement'.[73] Many shared Edward Foster's view that the labourers' successes in securing wage increases had provided 'a fatal example…of successful insurrection' and endorsed his call for action to 'strike consternatation into the hearts of the Insurgents…with unwonted terror and severity'.[74]

The language of menace used by protesting crowds probably sounded like a tocsin of revolution. Several weeks before the disturbances began in Wessex *The Times* reported the threats of a speaker at a gathering of labourers in Sussex. This year, he said, 'we will destroy the corn stacks and threshing machines…next year we will have a turn with the parsons and the third we will make war on the statesmen'.[75] At Ashton-Tirrold the labourers declared that they carried bludgeons 'to stand up for our rights and defend ourselves…we mean to tackle you farmers first, and then we'll have at the parsons and bishops'. Thomas Mackrell led the machine breakers at East Garston when they marched behind a red and black banner carried by a labourer who was heard to swear 'be d-d if I don't wish it was a revolution and that all was a fire together', while tricolour flags were displayed at Ramsbury and elsewhere. 'You gentlemen have been living long enough on the good things', William Oakley informed the magistrates during the confrontation in Hungerford Town Hall, 'now is our time and we will have them'.[76] A Hampshire crowd refused to heed a magistrate's advice to be patient shouting that 'we have waited long enough, we'll wait no longer'. The time had come for men 'to demand their rights' and, according to an associate of the Mason brothers, 'things had not yet come to the worst…there would be bloodshed before the end'.[77] At Fawley, where the poor had endured the indignity of being harnessed to the parish cart, they told Lady Cavan that they had been 'oppressed long enough and would bear it no longer'.[78] A similar resolution resounded in protests throughout the four counties and the spectre of revolution must have seemed very close when the following bitter toast was heard in many taverns and beer shops across southern England:

> Ye gods above, send down your love,
> With swords as sharp as sickles,
> To cut the throats of gentlefolks,
> Who rob the poor of victuals.[79]

Although there is little evidence that the labourers' protests were ever co-ordinated beyond the limits of adjacent villages, most magistrates and landowners refused to accept that social upheaval on such a scale was possible without the presence of agents of sedition. In looking to find external causes they showed how removed they were from the real nature of the social crisis which surrounded them; they could not accept that Hodge had any initiative even when driven by despair. Many believed, with Mr

Rigby of Yately Lodge in Hampshire, that the 'honest peasantry' was incapable of using arson as a means of protest; the inspiration, therefore, lay with 'foreign emissaries' or 'wicked conspirators'.[80] Peel's assurance that 'outside instigation' was the cause of the troubles was more comforting than the Duke of Richmond's timely reminder to the Lords that their failure to respond to the petitions of the poor made them seem the enemies of the labouring classes.[81] French Jacobins, Irish Fenians and itinerant incendiaries featured significantly in some of the more lurid and imaginative explanations. The *Berkshire Chronicle* reminded its readers that arson attacks in Normandy were 'the ominous precursor' of the French Revolution and suggested that the fires in England pointed to 'an extensive and systematic conspiracy'.[82] Some concerned citizens believed that sedition was being spread through the Post Office; letters bearing strange initials which were to be called for by strangers alarmed Henry Leeke of Havant, and the Town Clerk of Newport wanted letters traced to their senders in London, the source, he was certain, of the 'attempts to excite Riots and Burnings'.[83] More commonly though, blame was attributed to the followers of radical critics like Cobbett and Hunt. In Berkshire Lord Carnarvon detected the hand of Cobbett, whose papers were 'distributed all over the neighbourhood', while from Dorset a correspondent urged Melbourne to investigate the fact that disturbances seemed to break out within two days of the 'notorious' Hunt's visits to towns and villages in the south-west.[84]

It is almost impossible to know precisely how widely radical ideas circulated in the countryside but it is likely that their influence was more extensive than is generally recognised.[85] Contemporaries certainly believed that radicalism and the stimulus of events in France were significant factors in the disturbances; 'inflammatory papers' and 'seditious publications' caused grave concern, especially since it was reported that the labourers received the news from France 'with delight'.[86] Radicalism took root where people had access to ideas and information, a more egalitarian social environment and opportunities for frequent association.[87] In many villages, local craftsmen provided political education and leadership; the tailors and shoemakers in the villages around Winchester were 'universally politicians' according to a local magistrate.[88] Working-class democrats were everywhere and in the larger 'open' villages, where the influence of the squire and parson was less significant and tradesmen of all sorts more numerous, radical political ideas and religious Dissent flourished.[89] By 1830 a significant portion of the working population had at least a minimal reading ability and the writings of radical journalists like Carlile and Cobbett circulated widely, even among rural labourers.[90] Cobbett's *Political Register*, according to the Attorney General in 1831, had a 'prodigious effect' on working people all over the country, who clubbed together 'in great societies' to buy copies which were read, and read aloud, 'in many places where the poor are in the habit of resorting'.[91] One such society, the significantly named 'Radical and Musical Society' with members in the villages of Wonston, Sutton Scotney, Bullington, Micheldever, Newton Stacey and Barton Stacey, was inextricably bound up with the disturbances in the villages of central Hampshire.[92]

As happened elsewhere in the countryside, the Society drew together craftsmen, small farmers and labourers in the cause of radical reform. Its leader, Enos Diddams, a correspondent of Cobbett, was a shoemaker and among its supporters who were later transported were James Pumphrey, a road surveyor, the Mason brothers, who combined work on their smallholding with gardening and day-labour, a ploughman and several labourers.[93] The Masons regularly read the *Political Register* aloud to a group of twenty to thirty of their fellow villagers at Bullington. In October 1830, before Hampshire was touched by disturbance, the Society organised a petition from the villages of Wonston, Barton Stacey and Bullington which Joseph Mason carried to the King at Brighton. This remarkable document from 'the working and labouring classes' attributed their hunger, 'misery and distress' to the people's lack of representation in a Parliament filled with men 'in whom the people have no confidence'. The 176 petitioners also protested about excessive taxation on the 'necessaries of the poor man's life', government overspending on grants, pensions and sinecures 'wantonly heaped on the...aristocracy', the tithes paid to 'rich men in the church', and the game laws which punished labouring men for taking 'for our own use the wild birds and animals...those things being kept for the support of the rich'.[94]

These village radicals, dismissed by *The Times* as 'Hampshire bumkins', who devoured the words of Cobbett and were prepared to petition the King in the name of the 'sovereign people', organised and directed one of the largest protests in southern England.[95] The reformers held a meeting less than a week before the disturbances around Micheldever began, and there is clear evidence that members of the Society directed the strategy of strikes and machine-breaking. At Sutton Scotney the labourers met at night to hear Joseph Mason read an unsigned letter which he and others recognised as coming from Enos Diddams.[96]

> It said we was all to leave off work; and the Sutton men was to go out and stop the ploughs. They was to send home the horses for the farmers to look after themselves, and was to take the men with them. And they was to go and turn the men out of the barns. And they was all to go and break the 'sheens' as the farmers had got to do the thrashing.

The Society was severely disrupted by the prosecutions after the disturbances, but popular radicalism could not be silenced. Within a year the Winchester National Union was sending delegates into the surrounding villages to remind labourers of their 'political rights' and urging them to 'exert themselves' and 'unite together'.[97] In the villages of Wonston, Sutton Scotney and Barton Stacey, the sphere of the old

'Radical and Musical Society', the political union attracted the support of 'one half of the Labourers and upwards'.[98] The Mason brothers and others who had shown leadership during the protests had done their work well, so well in fact that, like other known radicals and trouble-makers, they would later be singled out for punishment.

Before the persecution could begin, however, the countryside had to be brought to order; a task which the new Whig government pursued with vigour. The 'war', Grey declared a few days after taking office, would be won only if the danger was met promptly and with severity.[99] Melbourne's first actions as Home Secretary were to issue a proclamation offering rewards for information which led to the prosecution of rioters and incendiaries, and a circular letter to magistrates urging them to enrol special constables. A further circular warned the magistrates to resist all the labourers' attempts at intimidation and called on them to defend the rights of property against 'Violence and Menace'.[100] Lord Chancellor Brougham assured the House of Lords that the sword of justice would be 'unsheathed to smite' the rebels 'with a firm and vigorous hand'.[101] The rhetoric displayed a confidence designed to reassure the propertied and stiffen their resistance, for in reality the government had very limited resources at its disposal. To defeat Swing it was forced to rely on the 'traditional and typically English' devices of local levies, special constables and the yeomanry.[102]

Associations for 'mutual defence', which Peel had suggested to the Deputy-Lieutenant of Berkshire, together with the yeomanry, provided the principal means for harrying the labourers across the countryside while small armies of special constables defended towns and villages against invasion.[103] The men of property were mounted and armed, as their opponents were not, and few crowds were able to win a skirmish with such forces. In Hampshire, Wellington, as Lord Lieutenant, encouraged the 'unequivocally combative' response taken by some leading landowners.

> I induced the magistrates to put themselves on horseback, each at the head of his own servants, retainers, grooms, hunters, gamekeepers armed with horsewhips, pistols, fowling pieces and what they could get, and to attack in concert, if necessary, or singly, those mobs, disperse them and take and put in confinement those who could not escape. This was done in a spirited manner in many instances, and it is astonishing how soon the country was tranquillised…by the activity and spirit of gentlemen.[104]

Furthermore, every country house was, Colonel Brotherton noted, 'a strong point' capable of withstanding attack.[105] From their comfortable and often well-defended fortresses the gentry sallied out to break up gatherings and hunt down the leaders of the insurrection. Charles Dundas and Lord Craven led a posse of three hundred horsemen on a charge through Berkshire in pursuit of the Kintbury and Hungerford rioters.[106] Mounted men blocked off all the routes out of Kintbury while Dundas winkled suspected rioters out of the public-houses, cottages, stables and outhouses where they attempted to hide. William Westall was taken at the Lion and others at the Blue Ball. Once Kintbury was secure the regular and irregular cavalry swept through Inkpen, East and West Woodhay and Highclere before returning to Newbury after eight hours in the saddle. It had been, Dundas informed the Home Secretary, a 'good days sport'.[107]

Large numbers of special constables supplemented the mounted forces; around four hundred constables were recruited at Abingdon and three hundred at Hungerford.[108] Throughout Wessex, in most towns and large villages, the residents set up constabulary forces to protect property by forestalling invasion. Townships were divided up and each zone had a patrol under the leadership of a designated individual; the small borough of Bridport, for example, had three hundred and thirty constables in sections of ten.[109] In the event of any disturbance, the section gathered at its leader's house where they were provided with their staves of office before proceeding to the market square to receive directions from the magistrate. The special constables constituted a veritable army; over four thousand special constables were enlisted in Dorset alone, which certainly helped to limit the scale of the upheaval in that county.[110] The citizen forces made the towns secure and the mounted posses were useful in breaking up crowds and arresting individuals, but it is doubtful if they contributed much to the defeat of Swing. In most places the disturbances were self-limiting and once a wage increase had been agreed or some other grievance removed the men went back to work. The labourers were not intent on revolution. They had protested to obtain work not to lose it altogether.[111] But they had frightened the landowners and farmers, they had destroyed the myth of rural paternalism. They had shown how inadequate the forces of coercion were and their protest threatened the government with its 'worst nightmare', simultaneous upheaval in town and country, north and south.[112] To revenge themselves for this assault on their tranquillity, local authorities acted swiftly to round up protesters but it was the government which determined how those unfortunates would be treated.

Special Commissions were set up to try prisoners in the worst affected counties because the government feared that local magistrates, who had authorised wage increases and thus implicitly confirmed the legitimacy of the labourers' cause, might, if left to their own devices, deal too leniently with those before them. Peel had been horrified by the sympathetic and tolerant treatment meted out to protesters in Kent in the early days of the disturbances, and Melbourne was similarly alarmed by the conciliatory attitudes of magistrates in Norfolk. By using Special Commissions the government was able to apply a policy of maximum severity, uncompromised by local considerations, and deliver an unambiguous message that protest and machine-breaking, anywhere in the country, would be dealt with sternly. The Duke of Wellington, who had pressed the idea of a Special Commission on the new government, expressed the hope that it would 'tend to tranquillise' not only his county 'but the Country in general'.[113] One set of commissioners moved through the south-west from Winchester to Salisbury and Dorchester; another met at Reading and Abingdon in Berkshire before proceeding to Aylesbury in Buckinghamshire. In this way the trials of prisoners in the most disturbed counties were underway even as the protests continued in East Anglia, the Midlands and elsewhere. The judges were not impartial adjudicators of legal process; their role was to use the terror of the law to defend the interests of the propertied against the poor. They were well chosen for the task. Sir James Park had no 'particular eminence as a lawyer' and was better known for his 'irritability about trifles' and his extreme Tory prejudices. Sir John Vaughan, a contemporary noted, had 'not the slightest notion of the law' and was famous for his bullying tactics 'in any case in which plain country people were the parties'.[114] The stage was set for a series of spectacular show trials.

The social and political purpose of the Special Commissions was revealed in the formal addresses to the Grand Juries which opened proceedings in each centre and the issues which the judges addressed in their judgements. The Commissioners knew that their remarks would receive great publicity and they delivered a clear message. Firstly, they asserted the values of liberal political economy and raised the ghost of Luddism. Wages could only be set by market forces; 'it was intolerable', declared Baron Vaughan at Winchester, 'that persons should by physical strength compel wages to be raised'. Machinery, moreover, was beneficial; so much was invested in 'this valuable property' across the nation that it was an 'imperative necessity' that the law protecting it be applied 'with severity'.[115] If labourers were allowed to dictate terms and dispense with machinery which they felt injured them 'how could a similar right be denied 'to those who are employed in the fabrication of cloth...or any other article wrought in the various manufactures of the kingdom'?[116] If property was not protected as the keystone of social order, wealth would be destroyed and 'capital and industry transferred to some more peaceful country'.[117]

Secondly, the judges defended the social order; they condemned the 'evil men' and radicals who attempted to undermine it by convincing the lower orders 'that a determination prevails amongst the higher classes to oppress them'. The disturbances had threatened 'that bond of mutual interest and goodwill' which existed to 'unite the higher and lower classes'.[118] From the bench the judges maintained that the landowners had the labourers' best interests at heart, and they delivered homilies on the social responsibilities of those burdened with wealth: it was 'an impudent and base slander...that the upper ranks of society care little for the wants and privations of the poor'. Finally, they warned of the anarchy which would follow if the rural disturbances were not met with the full force of the law. Men of experience knew, said Justice Park at Reading, 'that any compromise obtained by yielding to threats can never be permanent'.[119] The folly of conceding wage increases on the 'first appearance of danger from tumultuous assemblies' suggested to working people that 'every thing may be accomplished by force' so that 'examples of weakness would soon be followed by other acts of violence and still greater demands'.[120] The judges roundly condemned the efforts of labouring people to exercise some control over their lives by the only means they had; protest was 'not to be endured', it could 'never be tolerated'.[121] To save the nation from a 'relapse into the barbarism of savage life' it was 'incumbent on Government to endeavour to stem the torrent'; the remedy lay 'in the law of the land'.[122] If this was done, Justice Park believed, the Commissions would achieve an important objective; they would 'instruct the ignorant and deluded' throughout the country of 'the risks and penalties' involved in protest and machine-breaking.[123] Questions of social justice and distress were irrelevant and not admitted in mitigation for 'the peace and prosperity of the country' required that 'examples should be made of offenders against the law'.[124]

Most of those tried before the Commissions were charged with offences under three Acts of 1827 and 1828.[125] Many were likely to receive a death sentence several times over. The destruction of buildings or 'machinery used in carrying on any trade' by 'persons riotously and tumultuously assembled together to the Disturbance of the Public Peace' was a felony punishable with death. Threshing-machines, to the regret of at least one Hampshire magistrate, were not thought to come under this Act and their destruction was only a transportable offence.[126] Robbery was a capital offence, irrespective of the sum, and demanding property 'with menaces' a felony which could bring transportation for seven years to life. If, in the course of a confrontation, someone was injured, the wounding was a capital offence if a charge of murder could have been laid had death ensued. Furthermore, the penalties under these Acts applied to everyone in a crowd where extortion, violence or destruction occurred, irrespective of their proximity to the event or the unwillingness of their participation. An injury caused by a stone, decreed Baron Vaughan, made 'every person forming part of a riotous assembly...equally guilty as he whose hand may have thrown it'.[127]

The all-encompassing interpretation of these Acts left many labourers exposed to capital charges; few of those transported to New South Wales had not been capitally convicted. One third had risked the noose for their part in the destruction of manufacturing machinery and damage to buildings at foundries and mills in Hungerford, Wilton, Upper Clatford and Fordingbridge, and the attacks on the poorhouses at Selborne and Headley. Most of the remainder were convicted of robbery for behaviour which was virtually indistinguishable from customary, collective begging. It was immaterial how small the amount, how insignificant the property damage, how civil the behaviour or how willing the donation; robbery was a capital offence. John Ford faced death for one shilling, Shadrach Blake for a tea-caddy and Job Waldron for accepting money after the crowd had asked for, and been refused, victuals even though the farmer acknowledged that 'the robbery was not personal'.[128]

The policy of judicial terror was chillingly deliberate; 178 men were sentenced to die in Hampshire, Berkshire and Wiltshire to curtail upheaval in the region and forestall it elsewhere. Eleven were reserved for execution. The remainder had their sentences commuted to transportation. Those who by word or deed had shown themselves to be leaders were marked down for the severest punishment. William Oakley and Alfred Darling who, with William Winterbourne, had been the leaders of the crowd which confronted the magistrates in the Town Hall at Hungerford were reserved for execution although only the last named was hanged. In Hampshire, Henry Eldridge and John Gilmore were reserved for the part they played in the destruction of the manufacturing establishments at Fordingbridge and Upper Clatford, as was Robert Holdaway for his role in the attack on the poorhouses at Headley and Selborne. James Annells too was marked down to die, but for very different reasons. Baron Vaughan 'thought it necessary to make an example of him' not for his part in a robbery of twenty-five shillings but for the implied threat of an arson attack.[129] Many others came perilously close to losing their lives instead of their liberty in the cause of public instruction. According to Baron Vaughan, it was touch and go whether Joseph Arney's life 'ought not to be sacrificed to the offended justice of his country' and James Toomer only narrowly escaped the gallows while disturbances continued which 'almost render it necessary to make further examples'.

The Commissioners were particularly severe on the artisans and craftsmen before them who, they maintained, had no grounds for involving themselves in matters of rural wages and threshing machines. Because such people were often community leaders and sometimes known radicals they seem to have been marked down for special treatment. According to the judge, the offences of Oakley and Darling were the more heinous because they were not agricultural labourers.

> You, William Oakley, I may here observe, were a carpenter, and had no business or pretence to mix yourself up in these transactions; and you, Alfred Darling, being a blacksmith by trade, had no concern in them, and could not have had the shadow of a right to take the part you did.[130]

Thomas Goodfellow and John Aldridge, both blacksmiths, Robert Page a carpenter and Isaac Burton a tailor were particularly condemned by Justice Park; as tradesmen they had no part in the labourers' protest.[131] Richard Pollen, Chairman of the Hampshire Quarter Sessions, directed his colleagues' attention to the presence of 'Taylors, Shoemakers etc.' in the crowds who were 'universally politicians' and recommended that they should be 'selected' for prosecution.[132] According to a farmer who petitioned on his behalf, George Carter was harshly judged because he was a blacksmith by trade and it is likely that Abraham Knight, whose involvement in a machine-breaking was very doubtful, suffered because he was a shoemaker.[133]

The trials also provided local authorities with an opportunity to get rid of those they regarded as notorious troublemakers. The Vicar of Selborne, William Cobbold, wrote to Melbourne in outrage when he learned that a petition was circulating on behalf of Aaron Harding and John Heath. He argued that their sentences of transportation for life should not be remitted because they were 'the most desperate and daring characters' in his parish and 'the terror of the neighbourhood'; if they were ever 'let loose on society again there is no saying what may happen'.[134] As a magistrate, landowner and victim of machine-breaking and assault at Tisbury, John Benett consciously selected 'bad characters' for arrest and trial. He personally wrote out many of the depositions against protesters which he collected from witnesses who were his tenants and probably employees.[135] Political radicals and men with a little education were also singled out for exile. In opening the case against Joseph and Robert Mason, the Attorney-General directed the jury's atttention to 'their superior education and intelligence' which, coupled with the fact that they were not mere labourers, made their crimes far more serious. Robert's efforts to prompt the villagers of Longparish, Hurstborne and Wherwell into petitioning the King, as the meeting at Sutton Scotney had done, were already known to the Home Department.[136] The prosecution endeavoured to link Cobbett with the disturbances in central Hampshire and tried to elicit confessions to that effect from men in Winchester Gaol.[137] Details of the political activity of the members of the Radical and Musical Society caused great amusement in court when Enos Diddams appeared as a character witness for the Masons but his testimony was allowed only because it actually worked against them.[138]

The Crown went to extraordinary lengths to secure a conviction against the Masons. Joseph was acquitted once and Robert twice before they were finally convicted. In Robert's case, all that was proved against him was the fact that he was part of a crowd which demanded five shillings from the Reverend James Joliffe and that he carried a stick. Although he secured an admission from the victim that he had never done a dishonest deed or committed a breach of the peace, and although he argued that he had been pressed to accompany the crowd, it was to no avail. How well the Masons understood the social and political charade which was being played out is revealed in Robert's final defiant remarks. Asked if he had anything to say for himself, he replied

If the learned Counsel who has painted my conduct to you, was present at that place and wore a smock frock instead of a gown, and a straw hat instead of a wig, he would now be standing in this dock instead of being seated where he is.[139]

Even after the trials were concluded the authorities endeavoured to fix a more serious level of responsibility on the Masons for the organisation of the protests around Micheldever. Joseph Carter, the treasurer of the Micheldever crowd, was approached 'times and times' in Winchester Gaol by a clerical visitor who offered him immunity 'if I would only tell what I knowed agin them'. With others he was made to watch the execution of James Cooper and Henry Cook; it was, he said, an attempt 'to frighten us by it to tell all we knowed'. 'Had I told what I knowed, they'd ha' been hung…but I wouldn't split'.[140] The Masons were sentenced to death, later commuted to transportation for life, and it is difficult not to conclude that they were victims of political vengeance.[141]

## REPRESSION

| County | Cases | Guilty | Gaoled | Death | Executed | To be transported |
|---|---|---|---|---|---|---|
| Berks | 162 | 121 | 78 | 27 | 1 | 45 |
| Dorset | 62 | 29 | 15 | 6 | 13 | |
| Hants | 298 | 190 | 68 | 101 | 3 | 117 |
| Wilts | 339 | 200 | 47 | 52 | 1 | 152 |

Complaints about the social injustice of prosecuting labourers for reacting to circumstances they had not created and petitions for leniency poured into Westminster, even from the most seriously affected counties. Petitioning began in Hampshire and Berkshire as soon as the Commissions passed sentence. Within thirty-six hours, 15,000 residents of Reading had signed a plea for the reprieve of those reserved for execution which noted that their offence was 'in the common opinion…not considered capital'.[142] From the far north of England a petition from Newcastle-on-Tyne sought mercy for the 'guilty but deeply oppressed' labourers whose crimes were 'to a profound degree extenuated' by the 'intolerable private sufferings and public wrongs of the class from which they emanate'.[143] 'Why', asked an editorial in *The Times*, 'are the poor, starving, ignorant, misled, labourers to be selected for ruin?'[144] The answer, had one been forthcoming, might have been that an example had to be made of the agricultural labourers which would be clearly understood in the manufacturing regions of the Midlands and the North. When Grey replaced Wellington, he informed the Lords that 'the principle of my reform is to prevent revolution' and the first action of his cabinet was to plan the reconquest of the countryside.[145] Wellington believed that the Special Commissions were a success; at the end of December he noted that the Winchester show trials had 'already worked a good effect' and expressed the hope that their 'consequences will be long felt'.[146] The worst treatment had been handed down in Hampshire, where the first Commission had resolved to set an example, and in Wiltshire where far more death sentences would have been passed had the destruction of threshing-machines been a capital offence. The bald statistics of official vengeance in the table above cannot convey, however, the terror and grief which the sentences provoked.[147]

The executions were resented and the state's victims mourned but there were few of them and their fate had been settled. Far more draconian was the exile of the transported. Whatever the term of years, the sentence was effectively for life as Baron Vaughan told Joseph Watts, 'you will leave this country...never to return'.[148] To the families of these men transportation was a living death and every day 'wives, sisters, mothers, children, beset the gates' of Winchester Gaol with displays of grief which *The Times* correspondent found 'truly heartbreaking'.[149] At Salisbury the vehicle brought to the court to carry the prisoners away was surrounded by women and children desperate for one last glimpse of their menfolk. Weeping and wailing they tried to clasp the hands of their loved ones just once more as they stepped into the cart which was to take them away forever.[150]

## Notes

1   *The Times*, 21/12/1830.
2   E.J. Hobsbawm & G. Rudé, *Captain Swing*, London, 1969, pp. 308-9.
3   G. Rudé, *Protest and Punishment: The Story of the Social and Political Protesters Transported to Australia 1788-1848*, Oxford, 1978, pp. 250-1.
4   W.H. Hudson, *A Shepherds Life*, London, 1981, p. 159.
5   S.H. Palmer, *Police and Protest in England and Ireland 1780-1850*, Cambridge, 1988, p. 386.
6   J. Stevenson, *Popular Disturbances in England 1700-1870*, London, 1979, pp. 232-33; A. Fox, *History and Heritage: The Social Origins of the British Industrial Relations System*, London, 1985, pp. 96-8.
7   Stevenson, op. cit., p. 233.
8   John Doherty's *United Trades Co-operative Journal*, August 1830, cited in P. Hollis (ed), *Class and Conflict in Nineteenth-Century England 1815-1850*, London, 1973, p. 166.
9   N. Gash, *Aristocracy and People 1815-1865*, London, 1979, p. 146.
10  H. Pelling, *A History of British Trade Unionism*, Harmondsworth, 1963, pp. 36-7.
11  Stevenson, op. cit., p. 235.
12  For this paragraph see M. Brock, *The Great Reform Act*, London, 1973, pp. 88-98.
13  A Constitutional Reformer, *History of the Shaftesbury Election*, Shaftesbury, 1830.
14  Petition of the labourers of Sutton Scotney in W. Cobbett, *Two-penny Trash*, No.12, Vol. II, London, July 1832, p.271.
15  *The Journal of Mrs Arbuthnot 1820-1832*, entry for 7 November, in E.A. Smith (ed), *Reform or Revolution: A Diary of Reform in England 1830-32*, Stroud, 1992, p. 24.
16  C.H. Church, *Europe in 1830: Revolution and Political Change*, London, 1983,
17  Brock, op. cit., p. 105.

18  R. Quinault, 'The French Revolution of 1830 and Parliamentary Reform', *History*, Vol. 79, No. 257, 1994, pp. 377-93.

19  R. Wells, 'Social Protest, Class, Conflict and Consciousness in the English Countryside 1700-1880', in M. Reed & R. Wells (Eds.), *Class, Conflict and Protest in the English Countryside 1700-1880*, London, 1990, p. 184.

20  *Annual Register*, London, 1830, p. 21.

21  Brock, op. cit., pp. 106-9.

22  Successively, C.C. Greville, *A Journal of the Reigns of King George IV and King William IV*, entry for 8 November; J.C. Hobhouse, *Recollections*, entry for 4 November; Princess Lieven, 6 November, all in Smith, op. cit., pp. 23-9.

23  Letter of 9 November in ibid., p. 29.

24  H. Newby, *Country Life: A Social History of Rural England*, London, 1987, pp. 45-6; J. P.D. Dunbabin (ed), *Rural Discontent in Nineteenth Century Britain*, London, 1974, p. 14.

25  Georgiana Ellis to Caroline Lascelles, 1 December, in Smith, op. cit., p. 45.

26  E. Richards, 'Captain Swing in the West Midlands', *International Review of Social History*, 19, 1974, p. 86.

27  Hobsbawm & Rudé, op. cit., p. 47; Newby, op. cit., p. 32; Richards, op. cit., p. 87; K. Snell, *Annals of the Labouring Poor: social change and agrarian England 1660-1900*, Cambridge, 1985, pp. 102-3; J.H. Porter, 'The Development of Rural Society', in G.E. Mingay (ed), *The Agrarian History of England and Wales, Vol. VI, 1750-1850*, Cambridge, 1989, pp. 851-2.

28  Parliamentary Papers, *Report of the Royal Commission on the Poor Laws* 1834 (hereafter *RC Poor Laws*, 1834), Vol. XXXIV, pp. 13, 416, 421, 425 (Coleshill, and Burghclere, Fawley, Minstead).

29  PRO, HO 52/6/14.

30  D.R. Mills, 'The quality of Life in Melbourn Cambridgeshire in the Period 1800-50', *International Review of Social History*, 23, 1978, p. 384.

31  Cited in P. Horn, *The Rural World 1780-1850: Social Change in the English Countryside*, London, 1980, p. 53; see too, W. Howitt, *The Rural Life of England*, London, 1838, p. 104; *DWG*, 23/12/1830.

32  M. Reed, 'Social Change and Social Conflict in Nineteenth-Century England: A Comment', in Reed & Wells, op. cit., pp. 100-14.

33  Ibid., p. 106.

34  J. Caird, *English Agriculture in 1850-51*, London, 1852, p. 85.

35  Parliamentary Papers, *Select Committee Report on that Part of the Poor laws Relating to the Employment or Relief of Able-bodied persons from the Poor Rate*, 1828, Vol. IV, p. 4.

36  A. Somerville, *The Whistler at the Plough*, Manchester, 1852, pp. 381, 389, 411.

37  Ibid., p. 385.

38  *The Times*, 30/10/1830.

39  See for example, A.J. Peacock, 'Village radicalism in East Anglia 1800-1850' in Dunbabin, op. cit.; D. Jones, 'Rural Crime and Protest', in G.E. Mingay (ed), *The Victorian Countryside*, Vol. 2, London, 1981; G. Rudé, *Criminal and Victim: Crime and Society in Nineteenth-Century England*, Oxford, 1985; R. Wells, 'The Development of the English Rural Proletariat and Social Protest 1700-1850', in Reed & Wells, op. cit.; J.E. Archer, *'By a flash and a scare': incendiarism, animal maiming and poaching in East Anglia 1815-1870*, Oxford, 1990.

40  Quarter Sessions Calendars of Prisoners 1825-29, Wiltshire Record Office (hereafter WRO), A1/125/52H-55; D. Jones in G.E. Mingay, *A Social History of the English Countryside*, London, 1990, p. 155; Peacock, op. cit., p. 27; Archer, op. cit., pp.67-221; E. Billinge, 'Rural Crime and Protest in Wiltshire 1830-1875', Ph.D. thesis, University of Kent, 1984, pp. 102-3,116-7.

41  Horn, op. cit., p. 182; Wells, 'Social Protest, Class, Conflict and Consciousness', p. 174.

42  W. Cobbett, *Rural Rides*, Harmondsworth, 1967, p. 262; Rudé, *Criminal and Victim*, p. 78; C. Emsley, *Crime and Society in England 1750-1900*, London, 1987, pp. 2-5.

43  Berkshire Record Office (hereafter BRO), D/P 3/28/1; for other examples of prosecution associations in the county see D/ER O5 (Whitchurch, Streatley and Basildon), D/EX 382/1 (Wokingham), D/EX 618/1/1 (Wantage), D/P 61/28/1 (East Hendred). For additional examples see HRO, 44 M 69/ K 2/11, 19, 20, 23 for the associations in Alresford, Herriard, Odiham and Preston Candover andDorset Record Office (hereafter DRO), D/SEY/447 and PE/SPV/OV 5, for those at Sturminster Newton and Stour Provost. See too the Articles of the North Bradley Association for the Prevention of Robberies andThefts and the Protection of Persons and Property, in *Wiltshire Tracts*, Vol. 64, No. 11.

44  Articles of Agreement for the Whitchurch, Streatley and Basildon Association, 1822, BRO, D/ER O5.

45  C. Waistell, *Designs for Agricultural Buildings, Labourers' Cottages and Farm Houses*, 1827 in J. Woodforde, *Farm Buildings*, London, 1983, p. 30. To judge by the frequent reports of nocturnal confrontations between labourers in the yard and farmers in upstairs windows many of the latter followed Waistell's advice.

46  H. Hopkins, *The Long Affray: Poaching Wars 1760-1914*, London, 1986.

47  P.B. Munsche, 'The Game Laws in Wiltshire', in J.S. Cockburn (Ed.), *Crime in England 1550-1800*, London, 1977, pp. 210-11. To qualify for the privilege of shooting game a person was required to own land worth £100 a year, or lease land worth £150 a year, or be the eldest son of a person of higher degree or the

owner of a franchise. 'It required fifty times as much property to kill a partridge – or of course a hare – as to vote for a knight of the shire', Hopkins, op. cit., p. 63.

48    B. Kerr, 'The Dorset Agricultural Labourer 1750-1850', *Proceedings of the Dorset Natural History and Archaeological Society*, Vol. 84, 1962, p. 162.

49    Armstrong, op. cit., p. 72.

50    Hopkins, op. cit., p. 155.

51    Cited in W.A. Armstrong, 'The Position of the Labourer in Rural Society', in Mingay (ed), *Agrarian History* Vol VI, p. 830; J. Arch, *From Ploughtail to Parliament*, London, 1986, pp.159-63.

52    Cited in Billinge, op. cit., p. 115.

53    Public Record Office (hereafter PRO), HO 52/6/27.

54    *Berkshire Chronicle, Winsor Herald* (hereafter *BCWH*),6/11/1830.

55    H.G. Mundy (ed.), *The Journal of Mary Frampton*, London, 1885, p. 363.

56    W.B. Baring to Harriet Baring, Hampshire Record Office (hereafter HRO), 100 M 70/F4.

57    M.R. Mitford, *Our Village: Sketches of Rural Character and Scenery*, Vol. V, London, 1832, pp. 5-7. Posters appeared in towns and villages urging the labourers to resist 'the Traitors who would expose you to all the Horrors of Civil War', WRO, 413/23.

58    Cited in J. Chandler, *Wessex Images*, Stroud, 1990, p. 154.

59    PRO, HO 52/6/7; 52/7/105.

60    PRO, HO 52/7/329, 319; 52/6/95,92.

61    *BCWH*, 27/11/1830; PRO, HO 52/6/97,41,118; 52/11/117.

62    PRO, HO 52/7/5,192; Sir W. Heathcote to Duke of Wellington, HRO, 25 M 61/2/2/2,4.

63    C. Tilly cited in Palmer, op. cit., p.35.

64    PRO, HO 52/7/324; 52/6/74,88.

65    The Yeomanry was a volunteer cavalry force, usually organised in troops of fifty to sixty horsemen, first established in 1794 during the panic that England might be invaded by armies from revolutionary France. It was a force recruited from the men of property who could afford a cavalry horse and all the accoutrements and was generally regarded as a bulwark of conservatism. The Thatcham Volunteers in central Berkshire were established in 1798 but were used chiefly to put down food riots and other local social and economic protests. P. Allen, *History of Thatcham*, Thatcham, 1980, p. 39.

66    *Reading Mercury, Oxford Gazette* (hereafter *RMOG*), 29/11/1830.

67    PRO, HO 52/11/124. The Wiltshire Yeomanry Cavalry was organised in nine troops and consisted of 302 men, PRO, HO 52/11/91. John Benett was second-in-command of the Hindon Troop which was involved in the Pyt

House affray, WRO 413/23. For a partisan account of the activity of the Wiltshire Yeomanry in repressing protest in 1822 and 1830 see H. Graham, *The Annals of the Yeomanry Cavalry of Wiltshire*, Liverpool, 1886, pp. 62-97.

68  PRO, HO 52/11/26.

69  PRO, HO 52/6/54, 137.

70  Duke of Buckingham to Duke of Wellington, HRO, 25 M 61/2/2/9.

71  PRO, HO 52/7/262.

72  PRO, HO 52/7/80, 106, 289, 303; 52/11/50, 132; Billinge, op. cit., pp. 176-8, 198-9.

73  PRO, HO 52/7/99.

74  PRO, HO 52/7/116; 52/11/202; 52/6/145; W. Portal to Duke of Wellington, HRO, 25 M 61/2/2/1.

75  *The Times*, 14/10/1830.

76  Ibid., Ashton-Tirrold, 10/1/1831; East Garston, 8/1/1831; Hungerford, 22/11/1830; Ramsbury, *DWG*, 25/11/1830.

77  Ibid., 30/12/1830; 29/12/1830; 25/12/1830.

78  Ibid., 29/12/1830.

79  I. Anstruther, *The Scandal of the Andover Workhouse*, Gloucester, 1984, p. 18; Wells, 'Social protest, Class, Conflict and Consciousness', p. 186.

80  *RMOG*, 29/11/1830.

81  Hopkins, op. cit., p. 179; *The Times*, 3/11/1830.

82  *BCWH*, 13/11/1830.

83  PRO, HO 52/7/101,168.

84  Hopkins, op. cit., p. 179; PRO, HO 52/7/293. See also T. Assheton Smith to Duke of Wellington, 'that Hunt is concerned I have not the least doubt', HRO, 25 M 61/2/2/34 and Lord Malmesbury to Wellington on the presence of subversive missionary strangers 25 M 61/2/2/49.

85  The generally accepted view is that radicalism 'touched' the Swing disturbances in a few places but that it was 'insignificant' overall; see Hobsbawm & Rudé, op. cit., p. 219, Stevenson, op. cit., pp. 242-3.; R. Foster, *The Politics of Power: Wellington and the Hampshire Gentlemen 1820-52*, Hemel Hempstead, 1990, pp. 70-71. This judgement has been substantially eroded by Wells, 'Social protest, Class, Conflict and Consciousness', pp. 181-98.

86  A. Charlesworth, *Social Protest in a Rural Society: The Spatial Diffusion of the Captain Swing Disturbances 1830-1831*, Norwich, 1979, p. 33; PRO, HO 52/7/314,198; Quinault, op. cit., p. 389; *RC Poor Laws*, 1834, see response to Question 53 pp. 11,17, 23, 27, 28, 29, 139, 142, 411, 423, 424, 428, 433, 566, 572, 574, 575, 578.

87  Charlesworth, op. cit., p. 36.

88  PRO, HO 52/7/27.

89   E.P. Thompson, *The Making of the English Working Class*, Harmondsworth, 1968, p. 201; D. Mills & B. Short, 'Social Change and Social Conflict in Nineteenth-Century England: The Use of the Open-Closed Village Model', in Reed & Wells, op. cit., pp. 95-6; G.E. Mingay, 'Rural War: The Life and Times of Captain Swing' in Mingay (ed), *The Unquiet Countryside*, London, 1989, p.36.

90   J.M. Golby & A.W. Purdue, *The Civilisation of the Crowd: Popular Culture in England 1750-1900*, New York, 1985, p. 129; A. Kussmaul (Ed.), *The Autobiography of Joseph Mayett of Quainton 1783-1839*, Aylesbury, 1986, pp. 70-1; B. Reay, *The Last Rising of the Agricultural Labourers: Rural Life and Protest in Nineteenth-Century England*, Oxford, 1990, pp. 60-4; Wells, 'Social Protest, Class, Conflict and Consciousness', p. 128; but contrast with Mingay, 'Rural War', p. 41.

91   J. Sambrook, *William Cobbett*, London, 1973, pp. 173-4.

92   Charlesworth, op. cit., p. 34 notes the proximity of these villages to the London road which was a significant factor in the spread of protest.

93   Somerville, op. cit., p. 263; it is significant that in letters from NSW Joseph Mason instructed his mother to contact Diddams and he was the first name in a list of those fellow radicals who Robert wished should be shown his letter, see A.M. Colson, 'The Revolt of the Hampshire Agricultural Labourers and its causes 1812-1831', M.A. Thesis, University of London, 1937, pp. 287, 301, where the letters are reproduced. These letters, believed lost for many years, have recently been deposited in HRO, 92M95.

94   Cobbett, *Two-penny Trash*, July, 1832, pp.268-72.

95   *The Times*, 3/1/1831, 25/12/1830; *The Salisbury and Winchester Journal* (hereafter *SWJ*), 6/12/1830 and see Chapter 2.

96   Somerville, op. cit., pp. 262-3.

97   Wells, 'Social Protest, Class, Conflict and Consciousness', p. 189.

98   Col. W. Iremonger to Richard Pollen, 29/10/1832, HRO, 25 M 61/4/3/34.

99   Cobbett, *Political Register*, 27/11/1830

100   WRO, 1553/12; BRO, D/E Pg O1/4.

101   J.L. & B. Hammond, *The Village Labourer 1760-1832*, London, 1920, p. 246.

102   Palmer, op. cit., p. 393.

103   Note on PRO, HO 52/6/11. The Berkshire justices in November 1830 recommended that associations be established in each parish to pay and equip a mounted patrol and that the Yeomanry be reconstituted as special constables. M.D. Neuman, *The Speenhamland county: poverty and the poor laws in Berkshire 1782-1834*, New York, 1982, p. 98.

104   Hopkins, op. cit., pp. 186-7; *SWJ*, 29/11/1830; Foster, op. cit., pp. 74-83.

105   PRO, HO 52/11/119.

106  PRO, HO 52/6/50. *RMOG*, 29/11/1830.

107  PRO, HO 52/6/43.

108  PRO, HO 52/6/64, 95. The Overseers at Earley near Reading prepared for trouble in the parish of Sonning by laying in a stock of seventeen dozen newly painted constable's staves. BRO D/P 113/12/28.

109  PRO, HO 52/7/221; for the Wiltshire plan see WRO. 413/23.

110  *Dorset Country Chronicle, Somersetshire Gazette and General Advertiser* (hereafter *DCC*), 2/12/1830.

111  Dunbabin, op. cit., p. 20.

112  Palmer, op. cit., p. 387; Hobsbawm & Rudé, op. cit., p. 257.

113  Duke of Wellington to Mr Fleming, HRO, 25 M 61/ 2/2/38; for Wellington's pressure for a Special Commision see 25 M 61/2/20, 21, 25.

114  J. Grant, *The Bench and the Bar*, [1837], cited in V.A.C. Gatrell, *The Hanging Tree Execution and the English People 1770-1868*, Oxford, 1994, p. 504.

115  *The Times*, 31/12/1830 (Vaughan - Winchester), 28/12/1830 (Park - Reading), 3/1/1831 (Parke -Salisbury), 12/1/1831 (Alderson - Dorchester).

116  Ibid, 21/12/1830.

117  Ibid., 3/1/1831

118  Ibid., 12/1/1831 (Alderson - Dorchester), 21/12/1830 (Vaughan - Winchester), 3/1/1831 (Parke - Salisbury).

119  Ibid., 28/12/1830.

120  Ibid., 3/1/1831.

121  Ibid., 28/12/1830 (Park - Reading), 21/12/1830 (Vaughan - Winchester).

122  Ibid., 21/12/1830, 28/12/1830, 3/1/1831.

123  Ibid., 28/12/1830.

124  Ibid., 10/1/1831; for examples of trials where evidence of distress was not admitted see 29/12/1830, 4/1/1831, 5/1/1831, 10/1/1831, 5/1/1831; also *BCWH*, 1/1/1831, 8/1/1831.

125  *Public General Statutes*, London, 1827, pp. 253-90; (7-8, Geo. IV Cap. 29, 7-8, Geo. IV Cap. 30, 9, Geo. IV Cap. 31.).

126  PRO, HO 52/7/27.

127  Hammonds, op. cit., p. 249.

128  J. Chambers, *Wiltshire Machine Breakers*, Vol. 2, Letchworth, 1993, p. 219.

129  *The Times*, 31/12/1830.

130  Ibid., 5/1/1831.

131  Ibid., 5/1/1831; *BCWH*, 8/1/1831.

132  PRO, HO 52/7/27.

133  Chambers, *Hampshire*, p. 195, *Wiltshire* Vol. 2, pp. 117-8.

134  Chambers, *Hampshire*, p. 235.

135  WRO, 413/23; M. Dalton, 'The Pyt House Riot and the Tisbury-Tasmania

Connection', Typescript Ms., Wiltshire Local Studies Library.

136 PRO, HO 52/7/237. He even offered to carry the petition to London.

137 Cobbett, *Two-penny Trash*, July, 1832 pp.276-7. For a splendid analysis of Cobbett's links with popular radicalism in this part of Hampshire see I. Dyck, *William Cobbett and Rural Popular Culture*, Cambridge, 1992, pp. 171-78.

138 'There were ten persons present at that meeting. It was a meeting of the lower and middle classes of society to present a petition to the King. It was not a petition to raise wages, to break machinery…It was a petition to his Majesty about the poor. The sovereign people of this meeting determined to send a person up to present their petition to the King. The sovereign people (here laughter was heard) determined to defray the expenses of the man they sent up by a subscription of a penny, a twopence…each. The sovereign people subscribed 17s to carry the man to Brighton (laughter was heard again). He was to go as cheap as he could. He was not to have all the funds of the sovereign people (more laughter)'. *The Times*, 25/12/1830.

139 Slightly different versions exist of this speech see *SWJ*, 3/1/1831; *Hampshire Chronicle and Southampton Courier*, 3/1/1831; Cobbett, *Two-penny Trash*, July 1832, p. 276; *Report of the Proceedings at the Special Commission holden at Winchester, December 20th 1830 and eight following Days*, London, 1831, p. 90.

140 Somerville, op. cit., p. 263; Cobbett's, *Two-penny Trash*, July, 1832. Many of the prisoners assembled to watch the executions wept uncontrollably, at least one fainted and all were angered by the barbarous injustice they witnessed. When they left the yard an epitaph was discovered chalked on a door - 'Murder for Murder - Blood for Blood', Colson, op. cit., p. 211.

141 Nineteen signatories of the petition were indicted for their part in the Swing disturbances.

142 Hobsbawm & Rudé, op. cit., p. 261; *RMOG*, 10/1/1831.

143 PRO, HO 52/7/245.

144 *The Times*, 31/12/1830

145 Quinault, op. cit., p. 392.

146 Duke of Wellington to Sir H. Taylor, HRO, 25 M 61/2/2/58.

147 Table based on Hobsbawm and Rudé, op. cit., pp. 308-9.

148 Chambers, *Wiltshire*, Vol. 2, p. 206.

149 *The Times*, 8/1/1831.

150 Ibid., 10/1/1831.

# PART TWO

# RECONSTRUCTED LIVES

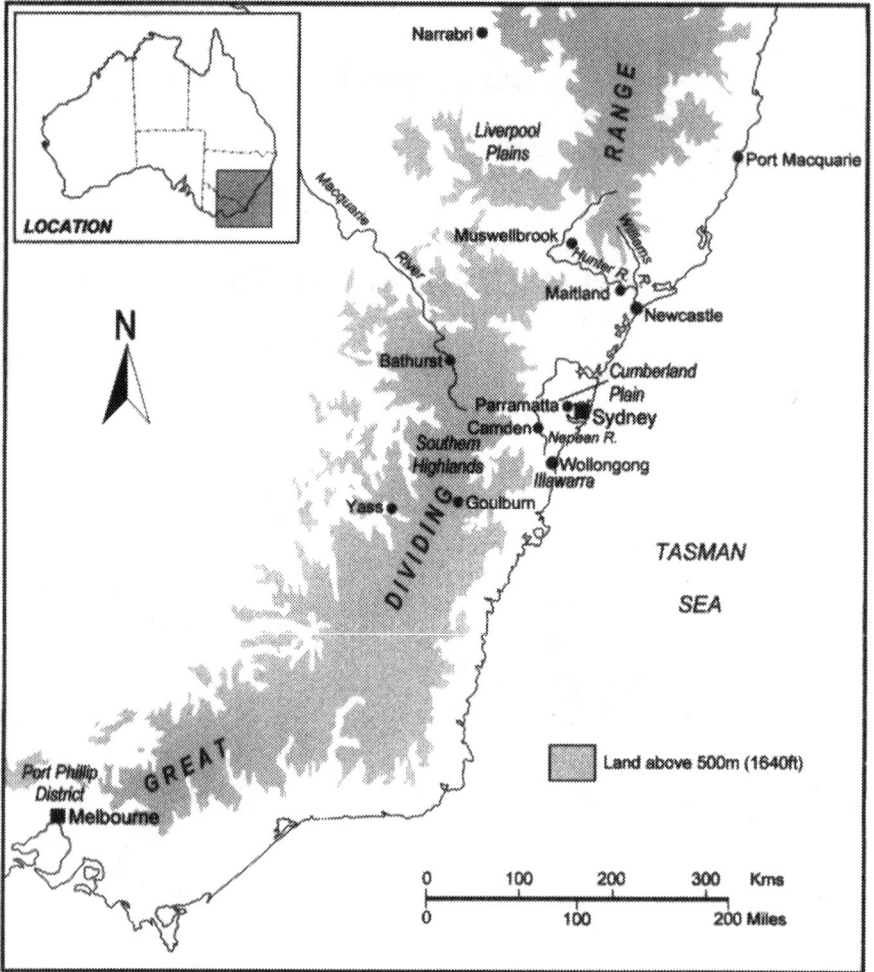

**South-East Australia**

## Chapter 6

# 'FAREWELL! I SHALL NEVER SEE YOU MORE':
# FROM ENGLISH VILLAGE TO AUSTRALIAN BUSH

When Justice Baron Vaughan sentenced a group of protesters to transportation at Salisbury on 27 December 1830, the prisoners' womenfolk 'set up a dreadful shriek of lamentation'. Rushing forward to clasp their loved ones, several cried out, 'Farewell! I shall never see you more'.[1] Similar scenes were played out at the other Special Commissions in Berkshire and Hampshire. When the terrifying melodrama of trial and sentence was finally concluded, all that remained was for the actors to depart and the audience to disperse. The grief of the prisoners and their families reminds us of their tragedies and the great uncertainties which they faced. All understood the meaning of exile; banishment for ever from their native land, from their familiar haunts, from established rhythms of life and from loved ones and friends.

The Salisbury verdict was a double blow for the family of eighteen-year old John Jennings, a freckled-faced whitesmith, whose brother, Charles, had been transported to New South Wales for poaching just over a year before.[2] Jennings' plea from the dock, 'I am but a youth my Lord; pray remember that', did not save him from transportation although the court spared his life because of his 'tender years' and because he might have been 'ill-advised by those who ought to have taught them better.'[3] For these Wiltshire protesters and the others who were transported, the descent from the dock was only the beginning of a long journey which ended for the majority with death in a strange, far-off land.

Of the 138 Wessex men transported to New South Wales, 132 arrived on the *Eleanor*, which reached Sydney on 25 June 1831; two were transported on the *Captain Cook* in August 1832 and the remainder came on the *Planter* in the following October. The arrival of any ship, especially a convict transport, was always a matter of some interest in the colony, but the ships which brought these men to New South Wales were only a small part of a continual pattern of arrivals and departures. In 1831, the *Eleanor* was one of sixteen convict vessels which carried a total of about 2,000 convicts (only 500 of whom were women) to Sydney in that year.[4]

The local press recorded these important shipping movements. The *Sydney Gazette*, announcing the arrival of the *Eleanor*, marked out her convicts as being different when it specified somewhat erroneously that they had all been convicted of machine-breaking. It noted that they were 'mostly robust men' who 'had conducted themselves with uniform decorum during the voyage' and observed that the 'number of useful mechanics' and agricultural labourers would prove an 'acquisition to the colony.' In an obvious attempt to reassure potential employers, the *Gazette* identified the qualities which it believed mattered most for these men to be productive while under sentence and in their subsequent colonial careers.[5] Long before they arrived in New South Wales, the most realistic among the Swing transportees had probably already concluded that they would spend the rest of their days in the colony.

By reconstructing as far as possible the lives of the Swing men in New South Wales, we may open another window through which to view the male convict experience. So much has been written about the mass of male convicts as a whole that more particularised studies are long overdue.[6] Most studies of convictism are based on the abundant sources of the transportation process and shed little light on the way the convicts reconstructed their lives in the colony. Babette Smith has demonstrated the value of going beyond the statistics of the convict indents in relation to female convicts, and it is time to rescue at least some male convicts from the deadening and depersonalising hand of the statistician.[7] The arrest of the Swing protesters, their arraignment, trial and sentencing to transportation began a journey which changed their lives irrevocably. Both literally and metaphorically it was the bridge between their two worlds, their English villages from where they came and the Australian bush where the majority served their sentences and lived out their lives.

By 1830 the prisons in Wessex were better managed and more sanitary places than they had been fifty years previously, though it is doubtful if they were more humane as a result of the changes wrought by the new penology. The cells and corridors were cleaned and disinfected regularly, while routine inspections by visiting magistrates monitored the diet, health and religious welfare of the prisoners. On arrival at Winchester Gaol, for example, a prisoner had a bath and a medical inspection, his clothes were taken away for fumigation and he was issued with a uniform of coarse material. Prison rules included personal hygiene. Men had to shave at least twice a week, wash their face and hands and comb their hair once a day and 'bathe and wash their feet as often as they shall be directed'. A cake of soap, provided on admission, was renewed each Saturday and prisoners put on a clean shirt on Sundays.[8] Similar regulations applied in the other prisons. At Reading, the prisoners received a chaff-filled mattress, a blanket and rough sheet and a jacket, waistcoat and trousers of brown fustian.[9] In the winter of 1830-31, however, the system all but collapsed under the unusually large number of protesters who were confined before and after the Special Commissions.

Most prisons in the four counties were designed to accommodate fewer than one hundred inmates but so many men were arrested during the disturbances that prisoners were crammed into the county gaols, bridewells and houses of correction. As solitary confinement, segregation and silence could not be enforced, it seems likely that the protesters were spared the worst excesses of the scientific penal system. The County Gaol at Reading, for example, constructed to house about one hundred prisoners at most, was swamped by double that number for more than a month, reaching a peak of two hundred and fifty.[10] Despite the removal of female convicts to the adjacent Bridewell to provide more room, cells scarcely suitable for two held six and even seven men, some of whom did not receive either bedding or fresh clothing. Overcrowding combined with a foetid atmosphere at night contributed to health problems. It was impossible to ventilate the building effectively or separate the healthy and the sick and 'accordingly a loathsome disease, commonly called the 'Itch' made its appearance'. Overcrowding also made prisons less secure and gaolers more wary. When it was alleged that the protesters in Reading Gaol planned 'to rise upon the Turnkeys in the chapel during Divine Service' and make their escape, the numbers of men in the chapel were restricted. This restriction deprived the prisoners of some opportunities to leave the very cramped conditions of the cells. In Winchester Gaol, daily services were 'considered inexpedient' while the prison was so full.[11]

We know very little about the time the protesters spent in their various gaols before they were sent to the hulks but it is likely that their only comfort lay in the company and solidarity of their fellow victims. Joined in a common cause, they had already been confined together for some weeks. Their protests, which had been communal and village-centred, often involved ties of blood as well as those of shared experiences. The *Eleanor* indent identifies four sets of brothers, a father and son and a pair of cousins. The presence of relations and fellow villagers who had participated in an unprecedented wave of protest and spoke the same language, probably provided an emotional and physical buffer between the protesters and the common criminals, most of whom came from towns and cities.

The hulks were the next stage in the convict's rite of passage. The majority of the Wessex convicts did not travel far to reach Portsmouth, though travelling in fetters in a wheeled vehicle on English roads was probably very uncomfortable. It also could have its dangers. William Oakley, who led the Kintbury 'mob', having failed to escape from Reading gaol, tried unsuccessfully to get his companions to overturn the enclosed cart in which they were travelling.[12] Perhaps Oakley's fellow prisoners, realised that escape was pointless, perhaps they had lost the will to resist. They had made their protest and their cause was dead.

The majority of the Wessex men who were to sail on the *Eleanor* arrived on board the hulk *York* at Portsmouth between the fifth and the tenth of February 1831.[13] On embarking, they were fitted out with a jacket, waistcoat, breeches, shirt, handkerchief, stockings and shoes. These garments did not mark them out as prisoners and were probably of equal quality to the clothes they usually wore.[14] Moreover, time on the *York* might have helped them to adjust to shipboard life before they experienced the open sea. George Shergold, the elder, of Stapleford, however, would have found the conditions little different from those which he had experienced as a sailor in the service of the British East India company.[15] They may even have been superior. Since the *Eleanor* left Portsmouth on 19 February, none was confined on the hulk for longer than a fortnight. The rapidity with which they were shipped indicates a well-oiled bureaucratic machine, efficient management and, perhaps, the desire of the authorities to send them on their way as quickly as possible.

Having been kept in close confinement in county jails for some weeks, possibly in irons, the men on the *York* probably welcomed the opportunity to do physical labour on shore. That was the lot of all able-bodied convicts on the hulks regardless of the length of their stay. The Tolpuddle martyr George Loveless, for example, arrived on the *York* on a Saturday, went to work on the Monday with the gun wharf party and continued 'in this employment' while he was at Portsmouth.[16] A daily routine regimented the convicts, occupied their time constructively and took them off the hulk during the day. The nature of their tasks varied according to location but at Portsmouth they worked mainly in the dockyards. The prisoners seem not to have found the labour particularly onerous and they actually received some pay for doing it. This work certainly had a great number of advantages over its alternative – spending all day in solitary confinement in a cell picking oakum or some other mindless, repetitive task which drove many insane. Loveless, who understandably had a great sense of grievance, found nothing to complain about in relation to his daily work or his treatment during his time on the *York*. Any mention of the hulks, however, usually arouses a strong emotional response and conjures up images of neglect, horror and brutality based upon nothing but a profound ignorance.

Generally speaking, historians, if they comment on the hulks at all, apart from the usual strictures, seem to regard them as an aberration. The fact that they began as a temporary expedient for two years only and that Lord North himself when first Lord of the Treasury regarded them as an 'experiment' in 1778, has tended to obscure their significance.[17] The Hulks Act in 1776 proposed a radical solution for a pressing problem. Unlike the existing but inadequate system of prisons, the state controlled and financed the hulks. Duncan Campbell, who set them up, was no longer a private contractor but a paid official. A major figure in the transporting of convicts to North America, his role in the establishment and running of the hulks gives a false impression of continuity between transportation to the American colonies and the establishment of the hulks. Most significantly, under the Act the state retained property in the labour of the convict. At the time, opponents of the measure recognised that the Act fundamentally changed the relationship between the state and its people.[18] The reasons for these profound changes are beyond the scope of this book but the Hulks Act instituted a fundamentally different system which represented a dramatic break with the past. The assumptions behind the Act also contributed to the creation of a convict system in New South Wales very different from that of North America.

Contrary to popular belief, the convict or civil hulks were not derelict vessels abandoned as unseaworthy. Hulk is a technical term relating not to the soundness of a vessel but to a ship which was laid up for a variety of reasons and dismasted. The first prison hulks, the *Tayloe* and the *Justitia*, were seaworthy merchant ships which Campbell, an experienced shipping contractor, had been using to transport convicts to the American colonies.[19] While most hulks were merchantmen, some were naval vessels. It made a great deal of sense after the Napoleonic Wars to use them in some way. HMS *Bellerophon* became a prison hulk immediately after she had brought Napoleon to England en route to his exile in 1815. Unless the government deliberately carried him on an unseaworthy vessel, it is reasonable to assume that the *Bellerophon* began its career as a hulk in good condition. The *York*, a superannuated ship of the line, became a prison hulk in 1820.[20] The famous etching of her at anchor at Gosport on the western side of the entrance to Portsmouth Harbour in 1828 shows a still splendid, sturdy vessel but with the incongruity of washing prominently hanging on a line and what appears to be the galley perched on the forecastle between the mast and the bow.[21] By 1831 there were ten vessels at various locations: three each at Portsmouth and Woolwich, and one at Devonport, Sheerness, Chatham and Deptford.[22]

In 1831, the civil hulks held almost 4,000 convicts, all of whom had been sentenced to transportation. As one ex-convict put it, 'the Hulks is transportation'. Those judged to be 'unfit for transportation', about 17 per cent, remained on the hulks and worked at 'less onerous tasks'. Of the others, 'all those for life, for fourteen years', and the 'incorrigible seven years convicts' were 'sent out of the country'. Those who were not transported could 'be selected for pardon' after four years provided there was 'no fault against them.'[23] By the time the Swing protesters were awaiting transportation, life on the hulks had become closely regulated and less arbitrary. Even in the earliest days when conditions on the hulks at Woolwich on the Thames were at their worst, they compared favourably with those on convict ships to the American colonies. Prisoners on the hulks were healthier than those of the same class imprisoned in many other places in England, and especially those in London. They were also better fed, as they had to be in order to do the work which was an important part of their daily routine. Most importantly, the system held out some hope to the prisoners by providing for remissions and pardons.[24]

It is not very difficult to find contrasting contemporary views of life on the hulks even among the convicts themselves. Some present the worst possible picture while others found little to complain about and even seem to have enjoyed the camaraderie and way of life.[25] The most extreme convict criticisms usually came from men who were not the average, illiterate, urban thief. George Loveless, the Tolpuddle martyr, who saw himself as different from the common herd, says almost nothing about the *York,* where he awaited transportation. His horror was reserved for his fellow ship-mates on the voyage who were, for him, 'monsters as I never expected to see, and whose conduct I am not capable of describing'. The ex-convict and convict witnesses before the Select Committee on Secondary Punishments in 1831 and 1832 had few criticisms of any substance about their time on the hulks. Significantly enough, those among them who had experience or knowledge of the new peniten-tiary, Millbank, regarded the hulks as preferable.[26] Lack of water for washing was their main complaint but the general level of cleanliness varied according to the hulk.[27] It is clear, however, that they all liked the companionship, the drinking – illicit spirits more so than the licit small beer – the gaming, smoking, singing, dancing and talking. They had no complaints about the food and could buy goods freely from vendors who came on board. At the end of their evenings, according to A.B. 'we all break up just like a public house shutting up.'[28]

Getting convicts to Australia alive and healthy was an enormous undertaking. It is all too easy to underestimate the success of the British government in achieving the results it did. In this case the figures almost speak for themselves. The overall death rate was 1.8 per cent for roughly 142,000 convicts transported to New South Wales and Van Diemen's Land between 1788 and 1840. At its worst, the mortality rate was an appalling 18.7 per cent for the period from 1788 to 1799. However, more than half these deaths occurred on the disastrous Second and Third Fleets which are so often regarded as the norm instead of the aberration they were. Between 1815 and 1840, when transportation to New South Wales finished and when the number transported was ten times greater than that of the period 1788-1815, the mortality rate was 1.1 per cent. On the convict hulks it was 3.9 per cent for about the same period. These rates were an extraordinary achievement especially in relation to the hulks which retained those convicts who were too sick and too feeble to be trans-ported. Mortality rates on the hulks and the transports fell dramatically after 1814. In this period, no epidemics occurred on any convict ship.

Sound ships with good bottoms were basic to the whole operation and the convict transports established an unequalled record. No convict ship ever foundered in over 400 voyages to New South Wales. An amazing statistic, it proves the quality of the vessels. Equally impressive was the fact that no convict ship was wrecked before 1833, a record which attests to the seamanship of captains and crews. Bateson's claim that 'apart from the Indiamen, the transports were drawn from the very dregs of the merchant marine' is not sustained by his evidence.[29] Although convict transports were usually privately owned merchantmen, the British government kept overall control by chartering through tender and by imposing certain conditions. A naval officer inspected the ships, and the majority of transports had the highest and next best classification. Even vessels in the second class were 'well found' in equipment and 'deemed capable of carrying a dry cargo safely.'[30] After 1819 with the ending of the British East India Company's monopoly, prospects of easier return cargoes might have attracted even better ships as transports.

Payment according to the number of convicts landed was a powerful incentive to keep them alive, but it was not necessarily a guarantee that they would be healthy when they came ashore.[31] As the figures demonstrate, shortcomings were more likely in the period before 1815. The ending of the Napoleonic Wars and the less than satisfactory condition of convicts arriving in New South Wales on three ships in 1814 coincided with the most significant changes of all. These were in relation to the position, responsibilities and powers of the surgeons who received the title and authority of surgeon superintendent. Undoubtedly, both as a result of the end of the war and the nature of the changes, the surgeons after 1815 were a better calibre as well as humane and compassionate in their treatment of prisoners. They were the agents of order responsible for punishment, closer control, greater efficiency and a more structured and supervised shipboard routine with its emphasis upon hygiene and cleanliness. Every berth was numbered; the clothes of each convict bore the number of the berth; each mess had its number stamped on its plates and water kegs.[32]

Each highly structured day began as early as 4.30 a.m. on some ships with the cooks first up on deck. Prisoners washed at sunrise by throwing buckets of water over each other. After ablutions the elected captains of each mess, which usually consisted of six people, fetched the daily rations. On the *Eleanor* that task would have involved at least another twenty-two convicts in addition to the cooks moving about the ship. The prisoners swabbed the deck, brought up their bedding and stowed it naval fashion in rope nets above the rails. After breakfast they cleaned the prisons before they worked at trades, picked oakum or attended classes in reading and writing conducted by a fellow prisoner, perhaps as Robert Mason did on the *Eleanor.* Fixed duties and a daily routine which required convicts to be on deck for four hours a day kept the men busy and organised from 6 a.m. until supper at 4 p.m.[33] Mustered below at sunset, they were then locked in. The nights were theirs to occupy as they pleased. The rules and duties which so effectively filled their day were clearly displayed about the ship. This regularisation was, as Humphery concludes, 'part of a conscious experimentation with techniques of institutional supervision'.[34] Its success in achieving healthy conditions rested largely with the surgeon superintendents for whom order and control were not merely ends in themselves.

Regardless of the evidence, there is a popular reluctance to accept that convict ships were safe and healthy and that the treatment of the prisoners was, almost without exception, humane and enlightened. Bateson, whose study of the convict ships remains the most detailed and comprehensive, allows his middle-class sensibilities to prevail in the face of his own evidence; the 'stench of the prison, crowded with perspiring humanity, was indescribable,…well-nigh unbearable, and the wonder is that so many prisoners survived the experience.'[35] Crowded conditions and the 'stench of the prison' do not in themselves cause infectious diseases. Either convicts, crew and passengers carried diseases on board at the point of embarkation or the crew and passengers picked them up at one of the ports of call. Time spent on a hulk before a voyage obviously provided an opportunity to identify those with infectious diseases and for those who arrived with an infection to develop the clinical signs. Although surgeons were in no position to understand the transmission of infections, they had discovered that isolation could prevent infection spreading but isolation was no easy matter on a ship at sea. Most importantly, the surgeon superintendent had the right to refuse to embark any convict or passenger.

The surgeon superintendent of the *Eleanor*, John Stephenson, returned some convicts to the hulk because the number aboard was 'too great for the prisons'. He also rejected three soldiers with gonorrhoea as 'unfit for the voyage.' Altogether, convicts, crew and the military guard, accompanied by six women and ten children, totalled 205. Of these, 132 convicts embarked at Portsmouth, all Swing protesters, and three more convicts subsequently joined the ship at the Cape of Good Hope. Apart from some minor scalds, bowel complaints, George Shergold's 'dysentery' and Charles Jerrard's pneumonia, the convicts required little medical attention. The surgeon superintendent had far greater worries with the captain, who was unable to pass urine, and with some of the soldiers who came on board with gonorrhoea. Apparently their symptoms were not as obvious as those of the soldiers whom the surgeon had rejected. One of the wives, also infected, miscarried during the voyage. The soldiers, women and children were the ones who presented Stephenson with 'a great number of trifling complaints.' The Swing transportees who made fewer demands and were less trouble seem to have been much healthier. All survived the journey and this result was achieved even though the 'vessel was being laboursome, & shipped such quantities of water that it was frequently necessary even in a fresh breeze, to have the hatches battened down for two to three days together.' As Stephenson observed at the end of the voyage, the 'poverty of matter in the foregoing journal leaves little room for observation, no set of men perhaps under similar circumstances ever suffered less from disease'. The prisoners were able to disembark in 'excellent condition'.[36]

The voyage itself was uneventful. From England to the Cape, the weather was 'very favourable'. For the first part of the next leg to Sydney, it varied 'greatly from gales to light airs with dense fogs', but in general they had 'strong breezes with clear cold weather'. Certainly the time of their departure contributed to their good health as they did not have to endure the worst of the tropical heat. Robert Mason, who, with his brother Joseph, has left us an account of the voyage, was primarily interested in the sea and the activities of the sailors. In writing home after his arrival in the colony, he described how at night as the 'ship dash through the water it sparkle and appear full of stars, some like a cats coat when you rub her in the dark.' A keen observer and full of curiosity, he set a sailors' song to music and did not mind the noise associated with the changing of the watch at night even though his berth was near the sailors' cabin door to which 'one would come perhaps at 12 at night give 3 stamps on deck and hallow with all his might' [37] Robert was sea sick and 'poorly a great while', but Joseph entirely escaped that particular scourge.[38]

At about noon on 25 June 1831, after a relatively slow journey of 136 days, the *Eleanor*'s northward journey along the coast of New South Wales brought into view the 'elegant light-house of white freestone' on South Head.[39] Marking the entrance to Port Jackson to which it had guided ships since 1817, its beacon stood on the cliffs 353 feet above the sea. By law any ship over twenty-five tons required pilotage and so the *Eleanor* ran up the pilot flag. But despite keen competition for the work, a calm had set in and a pilot came on board only at sunset.[40] By that time a 'gentle breeze [had] occasioned a ripple in the water which glittered beneath the beams of the full moon.'[41] It was not until 9 p.m. that she finally cast anchor in Sydney Cove having completed her seven mile journey westward up the harbour. For the obvious reasons of customs, security and quarantine, convict transports remained offshore until colonial officials completed the necessary procedures and paper-work. On arrival the first duty of the surgeon superintendent was to certify that the ship was free from any 'contagious disease' and had not been in any fever port.[42] On anchoring, the captain of the *Eleanor* celebrated the completion of the voyage by firing two cannon, the noise of which 'echoed and re-echoed among the adjacent rocks.' The prisoners for their part had to contain their curiosity until the next day when they were able 'to view the pretty town of Sydney which stands by the side of the hill.'[43] At that point, according to Joseph Mason, all was 'now conjecture and surmise as to our future destiny'; a state of suspense which was to continue for some time.[44]

By 1831 the population of Sydney was approximately 15,000.[45] It is unlikely that the physical appearance or size of Sydney overawed the men of the *Eleanor*. Most towns in southern England expanded rapidly between 1815 and 1830 and so Sydney's half-built appearance would not have seemed strange. In terms of population, Sydney was more like the towns of Wessex than Manchester, Birmingham, Liverpool or Leeds. Sydney's population was similar to that of Reading, about a third larger than Winchester and Salisbury but significantly smaller than Southampton.[46] A garrison and a prison, Sydney was also a market town full of artisans and retailers and a busy port which drew ships and goods from all over the world. The streets often resonated with the bellowing of livestock, the snorting of horses and the cries of street sellers who told the same lies as those in England. A relatively spacious urban environment, Sydney was as intimately dependent on its hinterland as Dorchester, Andover, Hungerford, Trowbridge or any other English market town.

The 'pretty town of Sydney' had become the site of the penal settlement by default. Botany Bay, chosen in 1786, was a shallow bay, south of the actual site proclaimed on 28 January 1788. Much to the dismay of the founding governor, Arthur Phillip, Botany Bay did not live up to the glowing reports of Sir Joseph Banks. Deciding to look elsewhere, Phillip investigated the harbour to the north which Captain James Cook had named Port Jackson and merely passed by in 1770.[47] After a three-day reconnoitre of the harbour by longboat, Phillip chose a cove with the 'best spring of water' where ships could 'anchor so close to the shore that at a very small expense quays may be made.'[48] Originally intending to bestow the rather grand name of Albion, he called his settlement Sydney after Thomas Townshend, Lord Sydney, Secretary of State for the Home Office when the British Government chose Botany Bay for its proposed penal colony.[49]

The physical characteristics of the site itself, its convict origins, the realities of international commerce and private ambitions greatly influenced the layout, form and character of the town. The harbour where Phillip planted his colony was the product of the drowning of three river valleys at the end of the last ice age. Port Jackson has three narrow estuarine arms reaching to the north, north-west and west with few high cliffs along its foreshores. Its characteristic features were low wooded ridges which ran down to the water creating innumerable bays and coves. As can be seen from early drawings and etchings, dense vegetation covered the harbour's shores. The stream from Phillip's 'spring of water', which became known as the Tank Stream after holding tanks had been cut into its sandstone bed during the drought of 1790, bisected a narrow valley along a north-south axis.[50] Early convict and military housing and associated buildings were on the west side of the stream and of Sydney Cove. Government House and the offices of the official establishment were on the east.[51] This physical division between bond and free quickly broke down but the social segregation which it initially represented continued unabated, though in less overt forms. Two sandstone ridges running from the south to the north crowned the heights of the small valley and ran like two fingers out into the waters of Port Jackson, thus creating Sydney Cove. At the time of first settlement, the cove was about a quarter of a mile wide at its entrance and half a mile long. The eastern ridge finished at Bennelong Point where Fort Macquarie stood, guarding the entrance to the cove. The western ridge ended at Dawes Point with its fort, which was actually more decorative than defensive.[52]

By 1831, buildings had long since ringed the western shore of the cove and had begun to creep eastward from the Tank Stream following the high water mark of its estuary. Behind the seaward face of Sydney, the town stretched out to the south for about two miles along and beyond the Tank Stream. Buildings had gradually covered the slope of the western ridge from the shoreline to the peak, disguising much of its original topography. By contrast, the eastern peninsula was still heavily wooded. Windmills on the ridges, the spire of St James and the tower of St Philip's, dominating the skyline of the town, probably caught the eye of newcomers as they first sighted the settlement from the deck of a ship. It is likely that the dominant ridge on the west next held the gaze. This part of the western peninsula had quickly become known as The Rocks, taking its name from the 'bare mass of white sandstone, often rising in successive layers (like the steps of stairs) from the bottom to the top'.[53]

Houses clung higgledy-piggledy to the side of the ridge following the random layers of rocks. The area itself looked like a rookery and its appearance contributed to its long-established reputation as the dangerous haunt of sailors and colonial low life with its cheap lodgings, crowded, noisy pubs and well-patronised brothels.[54] It was here that Joseph Mason was left to his own devices after his master's agent collected him from the barracks. Hungry, thirsty, 'friendless & penniless', an embarrassed Joseph, sick at heart, found himself 'amid strangers of the vilest description'. For a quiet, reflective and god-fearing man, The Rocks was not a very pleasant introduction to life in the colony.[55]

The Rocks' physical characteristics militated against the ordered straight lines and carefully crafted streetscapes so characteristic of the classical revival, Georgian architecture and the town planning of subsequent surveyors. On the crest of the ridge and just below, nature was more forgiving in accommodating the new fashions. Here in the late 1820s and early 1830s the villas of merchants, ships' captains and lawyers began to grace Kent, Princes, Lower Fort and Cumberland Streets. As early as 1821, William Harper, the assistant colonial surveyor, to whom Matthew Triggs of the *Eleanor* was to be assigned, had built an elegant, single storey stone cottage. Justice Dowling's occupation of it in the late 1820s confirmed the exclusiveness of this part of The Rocks. In 1831 a Mr Egan's residence 'situate' in Cumberland Street was being advertised for sale as suitable for 'private individuals and persons generally connected with the Public Departments'.[56] Convenient to the centre of town and to the cove, but beyond the normal hubbub of a busy port, these houses with magnificent views of the harbour were open to cooling breezes in summer. The most dominant building on the ridge was the two-storey military hospital with its wide double verandahs, the inspiration for which had been brought from India and the West Indies.[57]

On the western shore of the cove, the doorstep of The Rocks, were the main shipping facilities. Robert Campbell, who came free to the colony via India, began to establish his commercial empire there in 1803. His wharf reached out across the rocky and sandy rim of the cove to beyond the low water line. Close by were his warehouses, a 'handsome mansion' and gardens 'full of flowers and fruit trees.' By 1831 Campbell's establishment had become a harbour landmark. George Arlett and Daniel

Hancock, both of whom were assigned to members of the Campbell family, would have noticed these splendid buildings and their surroundings from the deck of the *Eleanor*. Between Campbell's property and the southern shore of the cove lay the town house which the flamboyant Captain Piper, Campbell's brother in law, had built before his fall from grace in 1827. Next to it was the small cottage of the ex-convict, John Cadman, the government coxswain, then the naval dockyard and Kings Wharf, behind which stood the impressive three-storied, Commissariat Stores.[58]

As the gaze continued round to the left, it could take in the stone bridge across the Tank Stream and the impressive houses which backed on to it on both sides of the estuary. Some of these buildings partly obscured the solid stone and brick houses and offices of the colonial officials, the commissariat, judge advocate, chaplain and surveyor general. They lay on the south side of the track which Governor Lachlan Macquarie had named Bridge Street in 1810. One of the few crossroads, it ran from west to east and linked the western side of the Tank Stream to the official establishment on the east. Bridge Street gradually climbed up the side of the Tank Stream Valley towards the eastern ridge and finished at Government House. Slightly isolated and set apart, Government House was particularly prominent by virtue of its size, position, extensive gardens and grounds. It was possible from the cove to look across the government domain to the eastern ridge which rose one hundred feet above sea level. The castellated Gothic building which Macquarie intended to be the stables for his new and very grand government house stood out. Further south along the ridge were the barracks for the governor's mounted guard, the colonnaded general hospital and the Hyde Park Barracks.[59]

As the men on the *Eleanor* did not disembark until the 11 July, they had ample opportunity to examine the face of Sydney during their daily exercise on deck. It must have been an irksome delay and the only break in shipboard routine during this time was the colonial muster. On the arrival of a convict transport, the very efficient local bureaucracy began the task of processing the convicts. The Colonial Secretary and his office managed the overall supervision of convicts which the Superintendent of Convicts and his department carried out. The ships themselves brought indents, lists of the names of their prisoners with their crimes and place, date and length of sentence. The use of the term 'indents', an abbreviation of indenture, was a legacy of convict transportation to the American colonies when contractors purchased a convict's term of servitude as a species of property to be sold on arrival in America.

In the Australian convict system, the state maintained property in the convict's services which it could delegate, usually to a master. He or she had the labour of the convict until the convict had served the full sentence, received a ticket of leave or was removed. Although the phrase 'government servant', which was consistently applied to convicts in New South Wales, appears, on the face of it, to be a mere euphemism, its use reflected the legal position of convicts. Even the sentence of life was a maximum of twenty-one years, and although that limitation was probably cold comfort to the convict concerned, the law did not condemn them to servitude for the rest of their natural life. Convicts under sentence could and did marry and their children were free. Despite the rhetoric of contemporaries and later writers, convicts were not slaves; a fact which needs to be established at the very outset.

Convicts in Australia were perhaps the most fully documented individuals in the British Empire. The creation of increasingly detailed records in the colony was part of the evolution and closer regulation of the convict system in New South Wales. As colonial officials faced growing convict numbers and ever expanding frontiers of settlement, keeping track of convicts and being able to identify them with certainty became crucial. At the shipboard muster, clerks recorded each convict's name, age, literacy, religion, marital status, number of children, place of birth, occupation, previous convictions and physical description including moles, scars and tattoos. Weekly lists of absconders were thus able to provide a detailed physical description as well as the name of the ship which had transported the convict to Australia. From 1833, printed indents were circulated to all magistrates.

During the shipboard muster, or at least before they landed, the convicts were supposed to hand over any money in their possession. It was deposited in the convict's name in the Savings Bank. Usually the individual recovered control of it with a ticket-of-leave or certificate of freedom, although there was provision for the convict to have the 'use of it beforehand', dependent upon good conduct.[60] Altogether twenty-one Swing protesters deposited money which ranged in value from one pound to the ten pounds of Aaron Stone, the brickmaker and woodman from Wiltshire. The average amount per man was about £3 8s 0d, the equivalent, more or less, of a labourer's earnings in the colony for three weeks. It was possible for money to be sent through the colonial agent to a convict and deposited for him; one of the two George Clarkes received money in this way. The amounts involved were not large but by comparison with the convicts on the ships immediately before and after the *Eleanor*, about four times as many of her convicts handed over sums of money.[61] It may well be that they were more readily parted from their money than the average convict, but the surgeon superintendent had persuaded them to give him their money at the beginning of the voyage with the assurance that he would return it to them on their arrival.[62] On his first voyage to Australia, Stephenson was obviously unaware of all the colonial requirements. Apart from the fact that administering convict bank accounts involved considerable trouble and record keeping, their existence emphasizes one of the central and important aspects of the convict system. Convicts had rights and these rights were protected. In this case, they had the right to retain the ownership of their money.

Subsequent notations on the indents kept the small biographies of the convicts up to date while they remained under sentence. Compiled in table form, the information became the legal reality for convicts while they served their sentence. The fact that the convicts themselves referred to the indents as 'the books' indicates that they realised their importance in relation to their lives in the colony.[63] At the very least, the record of their sentence and the year of their trial gave them a date when their punishment should finish, provided they did not incur an additional colonial sentence. The question of their marital status was probably the most significant detail for convicts. It was possible for those still under sentence to marry with the permission of the governor and their master. Marriage could result in de facto freedom through assignment to a spouse who was free. If convicts were married or had said they were, that option was usually denied them while they were still under sentence.[64] Such issues were, however, still a long way off as the Swing protesters waited to land.

The first stage of the journey for the men of the *Eleanor* in the colony began with their disembarkation. It was not until Monday 11 July when the *Eleanor* left for Moreton Bay that her convicts came on shore, but during those long days of waiting they had not been completely isolated. Sydney, like any provincial town, was not short on gossip. There was always interaction between bond and free and among the convicts themselves, even before new arrivals had landed. Small boats swarmed around any vessels seeking news of home, selling fruit and vegetables and ferrying any passengers.[65] Taken ashore in small boats which John Nicholson, the Master Attendant, organized, the convicts landed at Kings Wharf on the western side of the cove.[66] At that stage Isaac Manns, a young groom and servant from Andover in Hampshire, could not have realised that Nicholson, a land holder on the Southern Highlands, was to be his master. Male convicts were taken to the Hyde Park Barracks, unlike the women who usually went from the transport to their assigned destination.[67] The half-hour journey on foot to the Barracks gave the men of the *Eleanor* the chance to see some of the town behind its shoreline facade. It was their first opportunity to find their land-legs after more than nineteen weeks on board. They were probably surprised, and no doubt relieved, to discover that they did not make the journey in irons, which they had worn as a matter of course during their daily exercise on deck.[68] On land there was no need and only a court could sentence a convict to irons in the settlement. Once convicts disembarked, they were subject to the laws of the colony and protected by them.

When the men of the *Eleanor* came ashore, the streets would have been busy with people, both free and bond, going about their business. In most cases it was impossible to distinguish between the two groups because their appearance and demeanour were very similar. Only convicts in government gangs wore distinctive dress, with those in iron gangs in an incongruous, bright yellow.[69] Hawkers, calling out their wares and prices as they went, were a common sight in the streets. They shouted, 'Oysters ho! all fat. Fat and good oysters' and 'Fine Banbury cakes and mutton pies, all hot, all piping hot' in a range of accents.[70] Aborigines ranging from the superficially Europeanised to the semi-tribal added further colour. The flotsam and jetsam of this new society, they often appear in contemporary engravings and paintings of the urban scene. Yet neither Robert Mason nor his brother, Joseph, commented upon them or their first impressions and experiences during their journey to the barracks.

The most important consideration for the Masons, and presumably their ship-mates, seems to have been that they were able to wear the clothes with which they had been issued before boarding the transport. It also seems that the clothing was durable and in reasonably good condition at the end of their long voyage. According to Robert, the fact that they were 'permitted to come on shore' in their 'own clothes' was a 'great indulgence and considered an extraordinary thing by the people'.[71] The Masons evidently had expected that they would be wearing garb which marked them out as convicts. Retaining their own garments probably represented an assurance that they had not lost their identity.[72] Convict dress was, in the main, the same as that of ordinary working people and similar to that worn by masters in their daily outdoor work.[73] Although it might seem that the men of the *Eleanor* received favoured treat-ment, the actual explanation is far more mundane. Shortly after the arrival of the *Eleanor,* and before her convicts were landed, a government order decreed that the 'clothing which arrives with the Male Convicts is not to be issued on board as has been the custom heretofore, but will be delivered into the charge of the Storekeeper of Hyde Park Barracks'.[74]

When the Swing men set off from the wharf, they had a short walk to lower George Street. Its idiosyncratic path followed the track which had wound by the tents pitched in the earliest days of settlement to shelter the convicts of the First Fleet. Turning left into George Street they passed, on the eastern side of the street, a row of stone and brick houses, some with balconies and porticos. In one of these an ex-convict publican, Isaac Nichols, had started the first post office. Mary Reiby, another ex-convict, who had taken over and successfully run the family business on the death of her husband in 1811, had built a three-storey stone house next door to Nichols. George Howe, also an ex-convict and owner of the *Sydney Gazette*, had lived and printed the paper in another but by 1831 the office was on the other side of the street. Further on at the corner with Queens Street were the mansion and shipyard of another ex-convict, James Underwood, now the master of Jason Greenway from Berkshire. The corner block of two and a half acres had only recently been subdi-vided. One of the main developers, the exotic *Marchande de Modes* from Paris, Madame Josephine Rens, had built houses and shops for sale and rent.[75] Shortly before the arrival of the *Eleanor*, she had been advertising an 'excellent eight-room house with good shop, fitted with counter, and glass case, also adjoining small cottage'.[76] Already Sydney was in the process of urban renewal and speculation as the value of land on the harbour foreshores rose.

Before the men of the *Eleanor* reached the corner of George and Bridge Streets, they would have noticed the most prominent building on the western side of that part of George Street – the gaol. Built in 1799, it survived until 1841. Apart from the detention of prisoners and debtors, it was also a place of execution. Despite its high surrounding walls, the general populace was able to watch the hangings from vantage points on the heights of The Rocks.[77] Just a short distance past the gaol, if the Swing transportees had glanced to their right as they turned the corner into Bridge Street they would have seen St Philip's Church, an ugly, ill-proportioned, architectural mishmash, whose tower was visible from the cove. Beyond the church to the south-west were the military barracks and parade ground, which occupied fifteen acres. An impressive sight and imposing manifestation of the military presence, these barracks had the distinction of being the largest in the British Empire at that time.[78] Their location, and the lieutenant governor's residence close by, were relics of Phillip's original grand scheme for Church Hill and its environs (a scheme, which, incidentally, did not include a church).

The Government Lumber Yard on the south side of Bridge Street would have attracted the men's attention as they began to move eastward along the road. It was a hive of activity with the forges and workshops of all the main trades where convicts, retained by the government because of their skills, provided most of the workforce. Here, too, boys from the orphanage could learn a trade. It was also the place where the triangles were located for the flogging of convicts whom the courts had so sentenced.[79] As the Swing convicts continued along Bridge Street, they crossed a stone bridge which dated from 1812 and then walked as far as Macquarie Place which fronted on to Bridge Street. Here, before they turned right into Spring Street, they would have seen the three-storey mansion of Simeon Lord, another ex-convict entrepreneur. A legend in his own lifetime, he was one of a handful of ex-convicts, the exceptions rather than the rule, who made a fortune in the colony. It was only a short walk along Spring Street, where they passed the chaplain's house before turning left into Bent Street. As crooked as its name suggests, Macquarie had called it after one of his judge-advocates, Ellis Bent, who had an unfortunate surname for one in his profession. The houses and offices of the colonial administration took up the entire block separating Bent from Bridge Street. The corner of Bent and O'Connell Streets boasted the fine Georgian house which William Cox had built in the 1820s and which the colonial treasurer had subsequently occupied for a short period.[80] Thomas Hicks, who led the crowd in the affray at Brimpton, was destined for Cox's large estate, Clarendon, near Windsor.

The *Eleanor* men may well have refreshed themselves at the nearby fountain in Bent Street before they completed a fairly steep but short climb to Macquarie Street on the eastern ridge. From this vantage point they had a good view of the cove but they were probably more intent upon reaching the barracks, which lay at the southern end of the street. Perhaps, as they got closer to their destination, they paid less attention to their surroundings, but they could scarcely have ignored the general hospital, the largest and most dominant building of all Macquarie's creations. A two-storey central block stretched 130 feet along the east side of Macquarie Street with freestanding buildings on its north and south ends. With simple, harmonious lines, the double colonnaded facades provided the main ornamentation and visual interest. Built by private contractors in return for rum concessions, the buildings, which took six years to construct, were burdened with the name Rum Hospital. Only the detached end structures still stand to remind passers-by of what once was. [81]

Next to the hospital were the Hyde Park Barracks, another of Macquarie's projects. They were the holding place for newly arrived male convicts and for men under punishment who worked in government gangs. Although there was a gaol in George Street, the barracks were the first purpose-built structure for the housing of male convicts. Three storeys of colonial red-brick, the building is an interesting architectural contrast with the hospital. Much more spartan in appearance, the barracks owes more to Queen Anne architecture than the Georgian which so strongly influenced the ex-convict architect, Francis Greenway, who was responsible for the hospital, barracks and St James' church. The latter, which Macquarie intended to be a courthouse, had been converted into a church whose soaring spire does much to disguise its original judicial purpose. Arrival at the barracks marked the end of the first journey of the Swing convicts in the colony and was last time they would be together as a group. The Colonial Secretary's inspection was the final step of the formal requirement relating to the voyage itself. He reported upon the condition of the convicts and recorded any grievances or complaints. After this inspection, the men of the *Eleanor* were separated from the other convicts at the barracks. To Robert Mason's almost palpable relief, they were 'then put into a backyard with orders not to correspond with those who were sent here for CRIMES.'[82] Having already been assigned, they remained there for varying periods of time until their masters arranged their collection and transport to their places of work.

No doubt most waited apprehensively, wondering just what the future would bring, what their master would be like, how they would be treated and whether they would find some kindred spirits with whom to share the burdens of their exile. Robert Hughes, pandering to popular prejudice, has suggested that colonial New South Wales was 'punitive in its conventions' and 'capricious in its workings'. The convicts 'were no better off than slaves'.[83] By following the Swing protesters through assignment and beyond, we shall be able to determine whether their assignment was indeed a lottery, and whether punishment and mere whim governed their lives as convicts and determined their futures as free men.

## Notes

1   *The Times*, 12 January 1831.

2   The information is recorded under John Jennings' listing. *Eleanor*, Indent, Archives Of New South Wales (hereafter AONSW). Charles Jennings, an ostler with a previous conviction, was transported for seven years for poaching.

3   *The Times*, 12 January 1831.

4   C. Bateson, *The Convict Ships*, Sydney, 1974, pp. 350 and 387.

5   *Sydney Gazette and New South Wales Advertiser* (hereafter *Sydney Gazette*), 28 June 1831.

6   See, for example, L.L. Robson, *The Convict Settlers of Australia, An Enquiry into the Origin and Character of the Convicts transported to New South Wales and Van Diemen's Land*, Melbourne, 1965, pp. 146-183; A.G.L. Shaw, *Convicts and the Colonies: A Study of Penal Transportation from Great Britain and Ireland to Australia and other parts of the British Empire*, London, 1966, pp. 184-265; S. Nicholas and P.R. Shergold, 'Convicts as Migrants', S. Nicholas and P.R. Shergold, 'Convicts as Workers' and S. Nicholas and P.R. Shergold, 'A Labour Aristocracy in Chains' in S. Nicholas (ed.) *Convict Workers: Reinterpreting Australia's Past*, Sydney, 1988, pp. 43-61, 62-84 and 98-110.

7   B. Smith, *A Cargo Of Women, Susannah Watson and the Convicts of the Princess Royal*, Sydney, 1988. Despite Smith's pioneering contribution, thus far there has been little evidence of anyone following in her footsteps.

8   Hampshire Record Office (hereafter HRO), Q 13/14/1, Gaol and Bridewell Regulations, 1822.

9   P. Southerton, *Reading Gaol by Reading Town*, Stroud, 1993.

10  Berkshire Record Office (hereafter BRO), Q/SO 14, Quarter Sessions Order Books 1828-31, Report of Surgeon and Gaoler, 18 January 1831.

11  Ibid., 5 April 1831 and Chaplain's Journal, HRO Q 13/2/7.

12  *Reading Mercury*, 7 February 1831. We owe this reference to Norman Fox.

13  These dates come from the record of prisoners received on board the *York* at Portsmouth, compiled by Jill Chambers, *The Hampshire Machine Breakers*, Clifton, 1990, and *The Wiltshire Machine Breakers*, 2 vols, Letchworth, 1993.

14  Parliamentary Papers, *Report from the Select Committee on Secondary Punishments: Together with the Minutes of Evidence, and Appendix of Papers and an Index*, Ordered to be Printed, 1832, in *Crime and Punishment, 1810-1832*, Vol. 1, Irish University Press Parliamentary Papers, Shannon, 1969, A.B., Evidence, 23 February 1832, p. 32 and pp. 45-49, p. 60.

15  *The Times*, 5 January 1831.

16  G. Loveless, *The Victims of Whiggery; being a statement of the persecutions experienced by the Dorchester labourers; their trial banishment, etc. etc. Also reflections upon the present system of transportation, with an account of Van Diemen's Land,*

*its customs, laws, climate, produce and inhabitants*, London, 1837, p. 10.

17   Shaw, op. cit., p. 43.

18   We are indebted to Alan Atkinson of the History Department of the University of New England who first made us aware of the significance of this Act and its implications for the convict system in New South Wales. D. Byrnes, ''Emptying the Hulks', Duncan Campbell and the First Three Fleets to Australia', *The Push from the Bush: A Bulletin of Social History*, No. 24, April 1987, p. 5.

19   Loc. cit.

20   W. Branch Johnson, *The English Prison Hulks*, London and Chichester, 1957, pp. 89 and 96. It is much outdated, with little understanding of the English penal system and ideas current at that time.

21   Reproduced as the frontispiece in ibid.

22   So much for Robert Hughes' sensationalism, which has them 'anchored in files on the grey heaving water, bow to stern'. In fact, Hughes has confused convict hulks with the hulks for prisoners of war, which were far more numerous, in poorer condition and served a completely different purpose. R. Hughes, *The Fatal Shore: A History of the Transportation of Convicts to Australia 1787-1868*, London, 1987, p. 138. Hughes entertains and titillates by presenting all the stereotypes associated with cruelty and degradation. He has a great eye for the sensational but little historical judgement.

23   A.B., and J.H. Capper, Superintendent of the Convict Establishment, Evidence, 23 February 1832 and 21 July 1831, *Select Committee on Secondary Punishments*, p. 32 and pp. 45-49. Capper had a vested interest in presenting the hulks in the best possible light.

24   A. Frost, *Botany Bay Mirages: Illusions of Australia's Convict Beginning*, Melbourne, 1994, pp. 9-41. Even Branch Johnson who tends to accept the 'horrors' of the hulks, concedes improved conditions. See Branch Johnson, op. cit., pp. 98-108, a chapter entitled, 'Advance of a Sort'. See, for example, Hughes, op. cit., pp. 138-143.

25   See, for example, the evidence of A.B., Mannister Worzt, William Brett and Thomas Knight, all of whom had spent time on a hulk. A.B. was free at the time he gave evidence. The other three were still under sentence. *Select Committee on Secondary Punishments*, op. cit., pp. 49-64 and 83-98.

26   William Brett and Thomas Knight, Evidence, 2 and 7 March 1832, ibid., pp. 93 and 97.

27   See, for example, Mannister Wortz and William Brett, Evidence, 7 March 1832, ibid., pp. 49-64 and 83-98.

28   Ibid., p. 57.

29   Bateson, op. cit., p. 86.

30   Ibid., pp. 83, 84, 88 and 89.

31    Shaw, op. cit., p. 111.

32    K. Humphery, 'A New Era of Existence: Convict Transportation and the Authority of the Surgeon in Colonial Australia', *Labour History*, November 1990, pp. 270-271.

33    For the specific details, see Bateson, op. cit., *p.* 80.

34    Humphery, op. cit., pp. 63-65.

35    Bateson, op. cit., p. 72.

36    J. Stephenson, Journal, *Eleanor, 1831*, Adm. 101/23, AONSW, PRO Reel 3194.

37    Robert Mason to his mother, sisters and friends, Sydney, 27 July 1831, in A.M. Colson, 'The Revolt of the Hampshire Agricultural Labourers and its causes, 1812-1831', M.A., University of London, 1937, pp. 289.

38    *Ibid.*, p. 289.

39    P. Cunningham, *Two Years in New South Wales*, D. S. Macmillan (ed.), Sydney, 1966, [1827], p. 27.

40    G. Andrews, *Port Jackson 200, An Affectionate look at Sydney Harbour*, Sydney, 1986, pp. 55-56 and 365. Mason gives the date of arrival as 24 June but Bateson, op. cit., as 25 June.

41    D. Kent and N. Townsend (eds) *Joseph Mason, Assigned Convict 1831-1837: Doomed to the earth's remotest region*, Melbourne 1996., p. 37.

42    James Lawrence, convict ship, *John*, 8 June 1832, Colonial Secretary In Letters, AONSW 4/2145.

43    Robert Mason in Colson, op. cit., p. 291.

44    Kent and Townsend, op. cit., p.38.

45    R. Therry, *Reminiscences of Thirty Years' Residence in New South Wales and Victoria*, Sydney, 1974 [1863], p. 39, gives the figure of 15000. The Statistics in the *Blue Book of New South Wales, 1831*, are those of the 1828 census which gives the total population of Sydney as 10,871.

46    *Parliamentary Papers*, Census of 1831, Vol. XVIII, Winchester 9212, Salisbury 9876, Reading 15595, Southampton 19324, Oxford 20434, Bath 38063 and Bristol 59074.

47    J.H. Watson, 'Origin of Names in Port Jackson', *Royal Australian Historical Society Journal and Proceedings* (hereafter *RAHSJ*), Vol. 4, Part vii, 1917, pp. 361-362.

48    Quoted by ibid., pp. 363-364.

49    Ibid., p. 364, and A. Frost, *Arthur Phillip, 1788-1814, His Voyaging*, Melbourne, 1987, pp. 165-166.

50    J. F. Campbell, 'The Valley of the Tank Stream', *RAHSJ*, Vol. 10, Part ii, 1924, p. 77.

51    S. Fitzgerald and C. Keating, *Millers Point, The Urban Village*, Sydney, 1991, p. 13.

52  Cunningham, op. cit., p. 28.

53  Ibid., p. 29.

54  One of the most quoted and evocative descriptions of this part of Sydney appears in A. Harris, *Settlers and Convicts: Recollections of Sixteen Years' Labour in the Australian Backwoods*, Melbourne, 1964 [1852], pp. 7-8. Harris actually arrived in New South Wales in 1827. Archaeological excavations in 1994 have resulted in some re-thinking about the nature and quality of life in The Rocks. The Bubonic Plague which manifested itself in that part of Sydney and the subsequent rat hunts and clearances have undoubtedly contributed to its poor reputation.

55  Kent and Townsend, op. cit., p. 41.

56  *Sydney Gazette*, 1 February 1831.

57  *Historic Sydney as seen by its Early Artists*, Sydney, 1983, pp. 24-25.

58  Cunningham, op. cit., pp. 29-30.

59  Scott, op. cit., pp. 176-187.

60  Earl Bathurst, Minute 150, 24 October 1828, AONSW 4/990.

61  The details concerning these transactions come from Convicts' Savings Bank cash book, 1824-1848, AONSW, 2/8390, PRO Reel 58.

62  Kent and Townsend, op. cit., pp. 39-40.

63  On this matter, see A. Atkinson, 'Convicts and Courtship' in P. Grimshaw, C. McConville and E. McEwen, (eds) *Families in Colonial Australia*, Sydney, 1985, p. 21.

64  Ibid., pp. 21-22.

65  Cunningham, op. cit., p. 30.

66  Colonial Secretary to John Nicholson, Master Attendant, 9 July 1831, Copies of Letters sent to the Master Attendant, Masters of Ships, the Harbour Master and the Port Master, 18 December 1830 to 29 October 1832, 31/106, AONSW 4/3779, Reel 2862.

67  The details concerning these aspects of convict management are the most difficult to establish. They seem to have been taken for granted and so are usually not commented upon.

68  Bateson, op. cit., p. 74.

69  Commissariat Office to Colonial Secretary, Sydney, 18 May 1832, reported that 'a sufficient supply of yellow clothing for the convicts employed in Iron Gangs has been sent to the several outstations'. Colonial Secretary In Letters, AONSW 4/2143.

70  'A Walk through Sydney', *South Asian Register*, December 1828, pp. 323-324 in F. Crowley (ed.) *A Documentary History of Australia: Colonial Australia, 1788-1840*, Vol. 1, Melbourne, 1980, p. 378; G.A. King, 'Old Sydney - Grave and Gay', *RAHSJ*, Vol., 21, Part v, pp 273-78. Although King's reminiscences begin

in the 1840s, he provides an evocative description of street life in this period which would have changed very little from that of the 1840s.

71   Robert Mason in Colson, op. cit., p. 292.

72   Even today, popular representations of convicts in books, films, re-enactments and the reconstructed Old Sydney Town (Sydney was never called that) near Gosford, north of Sydney, have convicts in clothes marked with arrows. Augustus Earle's famous lithograph, A Government Chain Gang, 1830, depicts a great variety of convict dress and without a set of irons in sight. Only some have clothes with arrows on them but the arrow simply indicated government property. See M. Maynard, *Fashioned from Penury: Dress as Cultural Practice in Colonial Australia*, Melbourne, 1993, pp. 14-24. The branding of the clothes of convicts working in irons was not begun until 1834. Bourke to Spring Rice, 30 January 1834, Government House, Vol. XVII, p. 606.

73   The Chief Justice of New South Wales was taken into custody when travelling to his Muswellbrook estate because his dress was that of an ordinary working man and he was thought to be an absconding convict

74   Colonial Secretary to F.A. Hely, Sydney, 11 August 1831, Copies of Letters sent re Convicts, 21 May 1831 to 7 October 1831, AONSW 4/3671, Reel 2650.

75   See J. Weingarth, 'The Head of Sydney Cove', *RAHSJ*, Vol. 10, Part V, 1924, p.289; M. Maynard, 'Civilian Clothing and Fabric Supplies: The Development of Fashionable Dressing in Sydney, 1790 1830', *Textile History*, 21 (1), 1990, p. 95.

76   *Sydney Gazette*, 1 January 1831.

77   Ibid., p. 11.

78   Ibid., p. 19.

79   Ibid., p. 145.

80   H. Wright, 'Sites of the New South Wales Treasury', *RAHSJ*, Vol., 4, Part v, 1918, p. 279.

81   Scott, op. cit., pp. 176-178.

82   Original emphasis, Robert Mason in Colson, op. cit., p. 292.

83   Hughes, op. cit., p. 157.

## Chapter 7

# A 'JUST AND EQUAL DISTRIBUTION OF THE PRISONERS OF THE CROWN ': THE PROCESS AND PATTERN OF ASSIGNMENT

The men of the *Eleanor* who arrived in New South Wales only a few months before the departure of Governor Darling from the colony, were assigned and distributed according to his regulations. Shortly after he assumed office in 1826 he initiated a reorganisation of assignment. It was a major undertaking made all the more urgent by the fact that, although the numbers being transported had greatly increased, the demand for convicts had outstripped supply. Assignment had become the distinguishing feature of the convict system as it operated in the colony and, as Darling observed, the 'just and equal distribution of the prisoners of the crown' was 'a matter of great importance to the colony'.[1] Assignment has been the most criticised aspect of the convict system as well as the most misunderstood. Historians, usually by counting heads, have tended to concentrate on the big picture to establish trends but the study of a small group of convicts gives a more intimate understanding. In considering the convict experience of the Wessex transportees, we begin with the methods of their allocation and distribution and their places of assignment. Their masters and their experiences in assignment are the subject of the next chapter.

The promptness with which Darling addressed the reorganisation of the bureau-cracy indicates the centrality of convict management to his administration. He recognised that convict labour was inseparable from the granting of land and he devolved these two most significant areas of patronage to his newly created Land Board, thus explicitly establishing the nexus between labour and land. He did not, however, take the next step and tie the assignment of convicts to the amount of land held. Yet, as we shall see, the number of convicts in an establishment usually mirrored the master's acreage. Resident in Sydney, the three members of the Land Board dealt with applications for 'Servants and Labourers' according to Darling's general regu-lations. On the arrival of a transport, the Principal Superintendent of Convicts prepared a number of pre-assignment lists. A list of all convicts with their occupations and a more specialised one of mechanics and skilled tradesmen identified the labour force available. Applications for convicts in the order they were received and a list of masters who already had mechanics shaped the Land Board's ability to meet the demand. Other claims being equal, 'persons of moral character who pay due attention to the conduct of their servants' and 'new settlers' were to receive preferential treatment. The basic principles of allocation were simple but general, leaving room for some flexibility. As far as possible, 'labourers applicable to Husbandry' were 'to be assigned to Settlers in preference to persons residing in the Towns'.[2]

During 1827, the first full year of the Land Board's operation, it was able to assign fewer than half the number of convicts for whom there were applications. Darling, realising that masters were applying for more convicts than they immediately required, directed the Board that applicants could receive a maximum of three convicts 'from any one batch'.[3] The rather broad regulations for the allocation of convicts left both the governor and the board open to charges of favouritism. When applications for convicts outstripped supply and demand for labour was at a premium, the allocation of convicts received closer scrutiny and prompted greater complaint. As the pre-muster lists have not survived it is difficult, if not impossible, to establish the extent and nature of Darling's interference in the allocation of convicts.[4] In the case of the *Eleanor,* however, correspondence about the distribution of the Wessex transportees offers a unique glimpse into the process of assignment.

The unusually long delay between the arrival of the *Eleanor* and the disembarkation of her convicts possibly contributed to the rumour that the Swing protesters were 'to be assigned specially'.[5] After a slow shipboard muster, the prisoners remained aboard until the details of their assignment were completed. When the Board finished its allocations, the list was sent to Darling for approval. On this occasion, he did not simply endorse the Board's distribution as was his usual practice and he seems to have taken a particular interest in the men of the *Eleanor.* His questioning of the Land Board's recommendations and his delay in approving them did not necessarily arise from the special circumstances of the *Eleanor*'s convicts as political prisoners. The publicity surrounding the arrival of this vessel had alerted land holders to the agricultural skills of her convicts, for which there was great demand.

When the Colonial Secretary returned the *Eleanor*'s list to the Board, he added Darling's instruction that no one was to 'receive more than one servant'. The governor, aware of the demand for the Wessex transportees, thus countermanded his regulation of 1827 allowing up to three men to be assigned to any one individual.[6] By 1831, the demand for convicts, especially for agricultural labourers, made multiple assignment of men from one ship impractical and unwise. In relation to the convicts of the *Eleanor,* Darling suggested to the Land Board that special attention be given to three applications for assigned convicts: those of John Kinchela, the recently arrived Attorney General, Roger Therry, Commissioner with the right of private practice in the Court of Requests, and the Reverend Charles Dickinson, chaplain at the Field of Mars.[7] As a newcomer to the colony, Kinchela was entitled to receive preference. In the event, Darling did not impose his will completely. Kinchela and Dickinson each got a convict but Therry did not. By some circumstance William Cox was allotted two men from the *Eleanor* and four families, the McKenzies and Suttors at Bathurst, the Osbornes on the Illawarra and the Shadforths also each received two.

Other letters followed to the Principal Superintendent of Convicts, F.A. Hely. The Colonial Secretary drew Hely's attention to the 'Remarks, alterations etc made on particular names'. Comparing the list of applicants for assigned convicts with the proposed assignment allocation, Darling had focused on three cases. The first was the failure to assign a brick maker from the three on the *Eleanor* to A.K. Mackenzie, a land holder and former banker of Bathurst. The second was that Captain Rossi, the Superintendent of Police in Sydney and a land holder near Goulburn, had not received a blacksmith from among George Carter, Maurice Pope and John Aldridge. The third query concerned the Board's failure to allocate a gardener, possibly William Cheater or one of the Mason brothers, to Thomas Foster of Petersham. The Land Board explained that the Bathurst Bench had recently removed two convicts from Mackenzie for 'improper treatment', but he got his brick maker in William Sims because, despite his proven shortcomings, he had retained his other convicts and was eligible to apply for more. Rossi's application for a tradesman was unsuccessful because 'it was before determined that none of the Mechanics of the Eleanor should be assigned to any officer of the Government.' Though Rossi missed out, Foster did not. The Board approved a convict for Foster if he were 'now first applicant' for a gardener, and he received William Cheater.[8]

The government reserved certain convicts at the allocation stage. Rather than monopolising skilled men in a large public works programme, the bureaucracy was very selective for a number of reasons. Governor Lachlan Macquarie had been criticised for retaining too many skilled convicts in government employ. Following the Bigge Reports in 1822 and 1823 and the growth in demand for convict labour, more skilled men were assigned to private service. Persistent calls for economy from London played their part as well. Distribution to individual masters was crucial for economy and convict control. Masters bore the cost of feeding and clothing convicts and the maintenance of order on their establishments. Only one man from the *Eleanor* was reserved for government service. The Colonial Secretary directed that James Pumphrey, a road surveyor, should be delivered to the Surveyor of Roads where he could be 'most usefully employed'.[9]

It is clear that Darling examined the *Eleanor's* pre-assignment list carefully and exercised some right of review. Convicts were assigned as far as possible in order of application but 'new settlers', such as Kinchela, could receive preferential treatment according to the regulations. It is probable, however, that Kinchela's access to the governor by virtue of his position in the civil establishment did his cause no harm. Alexander Macleay, the Colonial Secretary, also participated in the assignment process.[10] He received at least two direct requests for convicts from the *Eleanor*. One was from Sir John Wylde, formerly Deputy-Judge-Advocate in the colony, with land holdings at Cabramatta. At the time of his petition he was Chief Justice of the Cape of Good Hope, where the *Eleanor* had revictualled. Although he had abandoned his life and wife in New South Wales, he applied to have '3 or 4 of the convicts assigned to my agent...out of the ship Elenor' (*sic*). Macleay's decision, noted in the margin, 'Land Board to assign one', was conveyed to the Board as a directive from the governor.[11] The second request came from David Masier of Surry Hills, who wanted a gardener. His treatment was rather different. Macleay's instruction was, 'Tell him to apply in usual manner'.[12] There were to be no short cuts for Masier and, as it turned out, no assigned convict either.

A rather brazen attempt to bypass all formal channels, including those of petition, received short shrift. John Stephenson, the surgeon on the *Eleanor*, discovered a stranger on deck busily chatting to convicts. A minion of a minor official, he had come on board to choose a convict for Burman Langa, an acquaintance of his master. Stephenson quickly sent him packing and complained about the breach of manners and security to the Colonial Secretary, who sought an explanation, informed the Governor and subsequently conveyed the vice-regal rebuke. Not only had Langa presumed an entitlement to a convict but he had also sent a man on the vessel without official permission. A contrite apology followed.[13] This episode reveals a certain casualness in relation to shipboard security as well as considerable freedom for the men on board and a misunderstanding about rights to assigned convicts.

Considerable care was taken over the process of assignment. The character of the person making the application and his or her record as a master was examined. The office of the Superintendent of Convicts compiled lists of those whose convicts had been removed and who were not to receive any in the future. Access to convict labour had been one of the incentives used to attract free settlers to the colony and the shortage of workers, bond or free, was a perennial complaint. Most of them had irrevocably committed themselves and their families to the colony. They had everything to lose. Lack of convict labour seriously compromised their economic prospects and their futures. The Land Board was in the unenviable position of trying to follow the regulations, satisfy the needs, as opposed to the demands of masters, and protect the interests and rights of convicts.

Darling's method of allocating convicts to masters proved to be too cumbersome for the numbers of convicts flooding into the colony. It was no easy matter to assign convicts equitably and according to the order of the receipt of applications. There was always a backlog of requests. In the case of the *Mermaid*, for example, the Land Board had struggled with eight separate lists of applications compiled over the previous twelve months. Masters, in an attempt to minimise delays, were applying for two or three times the number of convicts they needed to try to maximise their chances of getting some. The overburdened office of the Superintendent of Convicts had reached the stage when it was 'seldom possible to keep the necessary means of reference in an efficient state'. By the time the *Eleanor* arrived, Darling's system had all but broken down. It took sixteen days to complete the procedures and to land her convicts.[14]

A convict's first experience of the system in New South Wales came with his or her placement from the ship, and that usually meant assignment. The management of this point of entry into the system was much criticised. The House of Commons Select Committee on Transportation, the Molesworth Committee, in its report in 1838 complained about inadequate classification according to 'age, character or the nature of the offence'.[15] Free from the classification much favoured by penologists in Britain, convicts had the opportunity of a fresh beginning and their previous record did not determine their fate. It was their occupation which was most important, but as the majority of male convicts were labourers, often with a variety of skills, even occupation was far less significant than it might have been. Nevertheless, Darling charged the Superintendent of Convicts with the task of classifying 'individuals according to their trades'.[16]

Another factor in assignment which cut across the regulation to distribute convicts according to the order of applications, was the policy of placing as many as possible in rural areas to remove them from the temptations and pleasures of Sydney.[17] Most of the Wessex transportees were agricultural workers and craftsmen with varied skills. These were an immediate advantage and increased their value, but masters knew from their own experiences that even the sneak-thieves of London streets and alleyways could accommodate themselves to rural work very quickly.[18] The character of the master was the other variable in the assignment equation. There is no doubt, says John Hirst, that the 'character of the master, his means, the work he gave the convict to do all affected the convict's lot', but whether or not the convict's lot depended solely on the whim of the masters, as contemporaries and later observers have claimed, will be explored in the next chapter.[19]

We do not know at what stage the *Eleanor* convicts discovered the names of their master and their destination. Robert Mason tells us that the 'governor had provided us all with places before we came on shore' but he did not record when he knew who his master was to be and where he would be going. The Swing transportees remained in the yard at the Hyde Park Barracks until their masters or their agents collected them. Some 'were called out within a few hours'. Joseph, assigned to Hannibal Macarthur at Parramatta, left on 15 July, but Robert, who went to Benjamin Sullivan at Raymond Terrace, north of Newcastle, did not leave until 27 August. Parting from each other and their countrymen, those 'men of honest principle', upset them deeply. Both were fortunate enough to travel to their destinations by boat. Although they were a considerable distance from each other, they were soon in contact by letter sharing news of England and of their shipboard companions.[20]

Shortly before the arrival of the *Eleanor*, Darling discontinued the expensive and inefficient practice of constables delivering convicts to their masters regardless of their location. Instead, he made masters responsible for their servants at the 'place of Assignment', Hyde Park Barracks.[21] The larger land holders living in the more remote rural areas, usually had a Sydney residence or agents on the spot who arranged the convict's conveyance to the place of assignment. The Hunter Valley and the Illawarra could be reached by ship but when convicts were assigned to country areas such as Bathurst or the Southern Highlands and Plains, they usually walked unless they begged a ride from a friendly bullocky. Despite the apparently casual nature of the procedure, the system usually worked well and there were few complaints.[22]

After a period of some months' confinement and closely regulated days, the prisoners' lack of close restraint must have seemed very strange and their new circumstances quite bewildering. Joseph Mason's account of his time spent in The Rocks provides some idea of how the new-found freedom affected him. In his particular case it was a baptism of fire, being abandoned in the least respectable part of Sydney outside a public house and being cheated out of what little money he had. Life in rural England had not prepared him for the language and behaviour he encountered, leading him to observe that he 'had not been misinformed when the character of the inhabitants was painted in dark colours'. A man 'whose knowledge of the world was little more than that of a hermit' had been 'suddenly removed to the opposite side of the Globe & placed in another hemisphere 16,000 miles' from his English village.[23] He showed, however, no inclination to run off or even to explore the area. The open prison of New South Wales had its mental walls which proved, in most instances, as effective as those of stone.

Masters with land outside Sydney, and especially beyond the County of Cumberland, wanted workers for agriculture and pastoralism. As their main establishments often had small, self-contained villages, skilled tradesmen, especially blacksmiths and carpenters, were usually in demand. Regardless of the place of assignment, however, masters were able to move their convicts around to suit their particular labour needs and seasonal activities. Consequently, many Swing convicts ended up in areas far removed from those of their original assignment. Charles Bulpitt, for example, assigned to H.C. Sempill in Sydney, appears in the 1837 muster as still with Sempill but at Invermein on the upper Hunter River, 150 miles away from his listed place of assignment. About 20 per cent of the Wessex convicts did not complete their servitude with their first master. Convicts could be returned to the government and re-assigned. Masters also exchanged convicts. When they applied to the Board for consent, there were usually no problems. William Hawkins went from Alexander Chisholm to Jemima Jenkins, to the satisfaction of all parties. It took some months for the police magistrate at Maitland to realise that Captain John Rancland had transferred John Heath 'without authority'. A carpenter, Heath was returned to the government and the masters admonished. The pattern of allocation of the men from the *Eleanor* was directly related to land use within New South Wales. Convicts went to areas where there was a demand for labour and where there were land holders able to support them. Female convicts, in the main, became house servants in the County of Cumberland. Male convicts supplied the bulk of the rural work force irrespective of their occupation on the indent with the exception of some 'mechanics' and educated convicts.[24]

Of the 126 Swing protesters for whom we have identified a master and place of first assignment, 44 were assigned to masters listed on the indent as being in the County of Cumberland. Of these, twenty-one were in the area of Sydney between the harbour and the toll gates at the top of Brickfield Hill. At that time slightly more than half the population lived in the County of Cumberland, with about a third in Sydney. Only four of the Sydney masters did not hold land elsewhere. Jason Greenway, a carter from Berkshire, went to the enormously wealthy ex-convict, entrepreneur and boat builder, James Underwood, whose striking three-storey mansion in George Street the Swing men passed on their way to the Hyde Park Barracks. Henry Elkins, a groom, was assigned to the newly arrived Attorney-General, John Kinchela, on whose behalf Darling had intervened, and James Down went to A. Hill at the Commissariat. James Baker, a miller, who arrived on the *Portland* in 1832, began his servitude in his trade with William Hall.[25] The majority of Swing transportees assigned to Sydney masters were always intended for rural work elsewhere. Apart from the four in Sydney, twenty-two remained in the County of Cumberland, about 20 per cent of the total known assignments.

The County of Cumberland, the oldest and most developed farming area in the colony, was declining in importance by 1830. Agriculture and pastoralism had been confined to the County for about the first thirty years of settlement. Early experiments at Farm Cove in Sydney having been unsuccessful, Governor Phillip had established an agricultural settlement at Rose Hill in 1789 by making small grants to ex-convicts. A different settlement pattern and community developed on the fertile alluvial soils of the Hawkesbury River which, with the Nepean River and South Creek areas, had become the granary of the colony by 1801. After the disastrous floods of 1809, the acting governor, Paterson, granted land to the west and south of Parramatta to encourage settlement at Cabramatta and Minto and further south at Airds and Appin. Most of these were large grants made to already established land holders. The days of small, thirty and forty acre grants to ex-convicts were all but gone, largely because such men were singularly unsuccessful as farmers.[26] All except three of the twenty-two Wessex men assigned to masters in the County of Cumberland outside of Sydney went to land holders. The largest single concentration was at Parramatta where Shadrach Blake, James Cook, Stephen Hatcher, James Manns, Joseph Mason and Henry Toombs, were initially assigned. By 1831, the soils around Parramatta were beginning to show signs of exhaustion but the area had provided the springboard for some of the oldest rural fortunes in New South Wales.

Outside the County of Cumberland, the main areas of rural settlement were the Hunter Valley to the north, the slopes and plains beyond the Blue Mountains to the west and the northern section of the County of Camden, including the Southern Highlands. Maitland, Bathurst and Berrima, their centres, developed as the main towns, with Maitland becoming second only to Sydney.[27] The fact that so many of the *Eleanor* convicts began their colonial careers in the districts beyond the Cumberland Plain was no accident. Their placement followed the demand for agricultural labour and the rural orientation of the colonial economy matched British penal policy after the Bigge Reports. Darling had been instructed 'to limit' convict numbers in Sydney and to separate them 'from the general mass of Population' so that the 'Convict may be placed out of the reach of pleasures which...prevent Transportation from being an object of terror or the means of Reformation'.[28]

Expansion beyond the Cumberland Plain was essential to colonial development and the implementation of Bigge's recommendations. Governor Macquarie had failed to contain settlement within the County of Cumberland because of the pressure for new pasturage. During a serious drought in 1815 he allowed pastoralists to graze stock west of the Blue Mountains on the Bathurst Plains. A few years later the first settlers were able to take up land for farming on the northern side of the Macquarie River. Macquarie's main concern about settlement at Bathurst seems to have been its distance from Sydney, more than 130 miles by Cox's road. It was the gateway to the interior into which, it was feared, absconding convicts might disappear. For these reasons, the Southern Highlands, the so-called 'New Country', fitted in better with his scheme of things and he encouraged settlement there in preference to Bathurst.[29]

The northern parts of the County of Camden and the Southern Highlands were closer to Sydney, more contained than the Bathurst area and more accessible to the exercise of the governor's authority. A retired ship's surgeon, John Throsby, explored the region with Macquarie's encouragement, convinced the governor of its fertility, and received the first land grant there in 1819 as a reward. During the drought of 1815, Macquarie allowed two men to depasture stock in the area and subsequently granted land, mainly to pastoralists already established on the Cumberland Plain. After the building of a road, Macquarie encouraged small settlers with grants of fifty acres intended for agriculture.[30] Although there are obvious similarities in the timing and nature of the early settlement of Bathurst and the Southern Highlands, marked differences in their rural activities, pattern of settlement and population quickly developed.

Permanent settlement on the Hunter lagged slightly behind that of the other two 'new districts' because of the penal settlement at Newcastle, a place of punishment for convicts found guilty of offences within the colony. Land had not been made available there in the hope of locking convicts in and free settlers out. However, even before Macquarie moved the penal settlement further north to Port Macquarie, he had already breached the walls of this outdoor prison. By granting a stock permit to John Howe as a reward for his discovery in 1818 of a land route from Windsor to the Hunter, Macquarie invited settlement there. In that same year he allowed 'tenants at will' to occupy thirty-acre portions at Wallis Plains (Maitland). Most were ex-convict cedar-getters not farmers and were likely to be itinerant rather than settled. In 1821, Macquarie's last year in the colony, he promised a total of more than 400,000 acres, giving great impetus to settlement on the Hunter and elsewhere.[31] The flood gates had opened.

Ninety-five of the Swing convicts for whom we have a first assignment, went to these three 'new districts'. Almost 28 per cent went to the Hunter, just over 25 per cent to the Southern Highlands and about 18 per cent to Bathurst. Although permanent settlement on the Hunter had initially lagged behind that of Bathurst and the Southern Highlands, it quickly overtook the others. By 1830, the Hunter had almost 14 per cent of the colonial population (7,969), Bathurst slightly increased its percentage to just under 6 per cent (3,454) and the Southern Highlands and Plains had risen to over 7 per cent (4,498).[32] Land use, size of holdings, accessibility, demand for convict labour and the land holders' ability to support assigned convicts determined the population of the 'new districts'. The majority of Swing transportees found themselves in areas of small population thinly spread, more so at Bathurst than on the Hunter and Southern Highlands and Plains.

The most striking demographic feature of the 'new districts' was the preponderance of male convicts. In the Bathurst area, they were 63 per cent of the population in 1828 when just under a quarter of the population was free by servitude or pardon. By 1833, male convicts comprised 87 per cent of the Bathurst population. More than half of the population on the Hunter were male convicts still under sentence in 1828. Males who had served their sentences or been pardoned, were a mere 12 per cent. On the Southern Highlands and Plains in 1828, convicts under sentence were almost half the population with convicts free by servitude or pardon about 20 per cent.[33] Again, the proportion of convicts under sentence remained about the same until 1833.

Clusters of Swing convicts occurred within these three main rural areas of assignment. The concentration of these men in, and within, these locations indicates that they were not, as George Rudé claimed, treated as a special case and deliberately 'widely scattered over the colony.'[34] Even if they were not working for the same master, they were often close enough to fellow protesters to have contact with them if they desired. In some instances their masters were neighbours. On the Upper Hunter, both Charles Milson and Charles Bulpitt were at Segenhoe, Milson assigned to the owner, T.P. McQueen, and Bulpitt to McQueen's manager, H.C. Sempill. Adjoining Segenhoe on the south was the grant of Peter McIntyre, the master of Lazarus Lawrence. On the western boundary of Segenhoe was St Heliers, the estate of William Dumaresq to whom George Shergold was assigned. Another *Eleanor* convict, Robert Baker, was with Francis Little who shared a boundary with St Heliers and with Invermein. Its owner, William Dangar, was master of Charles Symes. William Dumaresq shared a boundary with Francis Forbes' Edinglassie where Thomas Lawrence served his sentence. To the south was the estate of George Forbes, Francis' son and manager, and master of William Waving. Henry Eldridge was assigned to J.B. Bettington whose Piercefield adjoined George Forbes' grant. Altogether ten Swing transportees began their servitude around present-day Muswellbrook.

Another seven were assigned to masters close to, or in, Maitland, the head of navigation on the river, about twenty miles inland from Newcastle. By 1833 Maitland had a population of almost 1,100.[35] It was the crossroads of the lower Hunter through which passed tracks to the west, the north-west, north, south and east. Matthew Triggs and George Clarke were on neighbouring estates. Also in the area were William Newman, Joseph Edney, Charles Pain, John Orchard and James Toomer. All except Triggs, a blacksmith, and Pain, a boat builder, were agricultural workers. It was not very long before Pain's master, Alexander McDougall, was running a punt across the river at Maitland.[36] North of Maitland on the Paterson River, a tributary of the Hunter, were John Nash and Joseph Pope, skilled agricultural workers, assigned to neighbouring masters and Joseph Nicholas, a road and pond maker. The Hunter River and its valley clearly defined the region as a single entity, dominated its activities and was the thread which bound it together in a very distinctive way and contributed to a sense of a single community.

Bathurst with its slopes and plains was more open and less dominated and defined by its river, the Macquarie.[37] This part of the colony was further away and more isolated from Sydney than the Hunter and Southern Highlands, being 130 miles to the west. Despite Cox's road, the Blue Mountains were still a formidable barrier because of the very steep grades to the plateau and frequent rain, mists and chilling cold. The distribution of Swing men to Bathurst masters, mirroring the settlement pattern of the area, was more scattered than on the Hunter. Along the Kelso flats on the north side of the Macquarie River were the carter, Job Waldron, carpenter George Hopgood and George Williams, a farm labourer. The most isolated was John Batten, at Cullen Bullen north of Wallarawang where Thomas Neale served his sentence. South-west from Bathurst at Blayney was Henry Shergold, while closer to the town on the Campbell River were Cornelius Bennett and Charles Read. Further west, about seven miles from 'the settlement', were Adam Thorne at Queen Charlottes Pass and on the same road just south of Bathurst was Thomas Radborn. John Bulpitt, a brick-layer and agricultural labourer, was at Mount Pleasant west of Bathurst.

On the north bank of the Macquarie, west of Kelso at various points along the track leading from 'the settlement' to the north-west were George Hopgood and William Oakley. Nearer to Bathurst other Swing convicts were scattered on both sides of the river, including John Jennings, a whitesmith, and John Gilmore, a stable hand and labourer. It is significant that on the indent of the *Eleanor* the master's place of resi-dence is usually not specific for those convicts assigned west of the mountains but appears as merely 'Bathurst'. It is as if the western slopes and plains were still to a large extent a *terra incognita,* a measure of their isolation and their distance from Sydney.

The Southern Highlands, a mere forty miles from Sydney, were not as isolated as Bathurst and were more geographically defined. Communications were better and the road far less precipitous once the Razorback up to the plateau of the Great Dividing Range had been negotiated. On the plateau itself a number of basins with soils enriched by volcanic activities and alluvial deposition determined the pattern of settlement, while the edges of the plateau circumscribed and defined the area.[38] Four Swing men assigned to the County of Camden – George Shergold, Thomas Whately, Joseph Arney and Thomas Mackrell – were near Camden itself, the closest of these early settlements in this area to the County of Cumberland. Just to the south-west of Camden at Stonequarry were James Burgess and John Burroughs. Another four – Aaron Harding, John Shergold, Isaac Manns and Daniel Sims – went further south to Sutton Forest where there was more intensive, small-scale agriculture. All possessed the basic rural skills, mostly those associated with agriculture, but both Arney, a wheelwright, and Mackrell, a shearer, could make hurdles.

Government policy influenced the timing and nature of settlement on the Southern Highlands and Plains. After the discovery on the border of the Counties of Cumberland and Camden of the lost government cattle, released on the arrival of the first fleet, the Cowpastures, as the area became known, was reserved for the now wild cattle. Macquarie subsequently established three cattle stations on the Southern Highlands at Cawdor, The Oaks and Brownlow Hill. When the government herds were removed to Bathurst, those seeking to depasture stock on the Southern Plains still required permission to move their stock through the Cowpastures.[39] The Great Southern Road had reached the peak of the Cookbundoon Range opening the way, in Macquarie's words, 'into very extensive plains or downs to the westward, forming with the river a very rich landscape'.[40] Goulburn, surveyed in 1828, the principal town of the County of Argyle, was 125 miles from Sydney.

Large land holdings held under tickets of occupation and the scattered nature of the best areas within the county determined the demography of the County of Argyle. Six Swing protesters were assigned to land holders on these southern plains. They were Charles Davis and James Romain, both agricultural labourers, Luke Brown, an ostler, and Henry Bunce, a carter and reaper. Daniel Hancock was a man of more varied skills, a papermaker, a reaper and groom, and Abraham House, a carter and agricultural labourer. Unlike those at Bathurst and on the Hunter, they were widely scattered, Brown in the extreme north at Cookbundoon, Bunce in the south at Lake Bathurst, Davis on the Molongolo River near Bungonia to the east of Goulburn, and Hancock on the Limestone Plains to the west. These men would have found little call for their particular skills because grazing not agriculture dominated on the Southern Plains.

The four *Eleanor* men assigned to the Illawarra, George Carter, Isaac Cole, Charles Green and William Carter, went to masters near Wollongong. Squeezed between the sea and the steep escarpment, the Illawarra was included in the County of Camden. The Illawarra, which had access to Sydney by sea, had been a cedar area from the early years of settlement. Population was small and tended to be scattered and migratory with cedar-getters living in temporary shelters before moving on to the next stand of timber.[41] In 1817, within two years of pastoralists first grazing stock there, Macquarie had made large land grants. Subsequently, smaller grants predominated but as the historical demographer, Jeans, points out, 'the details of settlement in Illawarra are obscure'.[42] That obscurity says a great deal about the type of people and their activities in the early years. A place of sub-tropical rainforest, the Illawarra had much in common with the Hunter River. Both, exported red cedar to the Sydney and overseas markets and were very different from the very lightly treed Bathurst area and the County of Argyle.

More than two-thirds of the Wessex convicts were assigned to landholders. They were the largest employers of labour and usually more able to meet the cost of sustaining their convict establishment. Slightly more than half of their masters owned under 3,000 acres. Almost a quarter of the masters fell in the middle range from 5,000 to 10,000 acres of freehold land.[43] This group included James and William Macarthur, masters of Thomas Mackrell, George Shergold and Timothy May. The Macarthur brothers had 6,500 acres each but also the responsibility of running Camden Park. Jemima Jenkins, to whom William Page was assigned and to whom William Hawkins was transferred, was the largest land holder in this middle range with slightly more than 9,000 acres. Only about 10 per cent of the masters of Swing convicts had more than 10,000 acres of freehold land. Those with the largest freehold, 30,000 acres, were Alexander Berry and his partner, Edward Wollstonecraft, the masters of Joseph Watts.

Most of the masters with small holdings farmed on the Cumberland Plain. Those with between one and three thousand acres predominated in the Southern Highlands and on the Hunter while the Swing protesters assigned to Bathurst usually found themselves on estates of two to five thousand acres. The highest agricultural acreages tended either to be close to the borders of the County of Cumberland or very isolated in the County of Argyle. Both agriculture and pastoralism were important in the enterprises of the masters with large acreages. Berry and Wollstonecraft had an enormous 650 acres under cultivation, 1,200 cattle and 200 pigs. At Segenhoe on the Hunter, T. P. McQueen had 225 acres of crops and more than 4,400 sheep. William Cox had 350 acres under cultivation, more than 8,000 cattle and over 5,000 sheep at Bringelly and further inland.[44]

The larger landholders were the colony's major private employers. William Cox, master of Joseph Arney, had 132 workers of whom twenty-seven were free. Richard Brooks, master of John Aldridge, had 116 and John Blaxland, to whom William Lewis was assigned, 113. From the largest to the smallest land owners, the ratio between free and bond workers was approximately five convicts for every one free.[45] Masters with more than 10,000 acres averaged about thirty-five convicts each with the average dropping to about eight per master for those with less than 2,000 acres. The largest landholders could use convict labour productively and profitably. Although their workers could be numerous, counting heads can be misleading.[46] The average acreage per assigned convict provides a more useful comparison. Those masters with between 5,000 and 10,000 acres had the highest ratio of about 390 per convict. Next highest were those with more than 10,000 acres with 325 acres per convict. The ratio successively declined to the lowest acreage per convict of approximately 140 for those masters with less than 1,000 acres. In other words, these masters were more than three times better off than those with the highest acreage. Slightly more than two-thirds of the Swing convicts went to masters of moderate means holding less than 2,000 acres. The size of the work force of each master while related to acreage, depended, too, upon the location, nature of his establishment and, if rural, the mix of agriculture and pastoralism. Obviously agriculture was much more labour intensive than grazing and sheep more intensive than cattle. Cox, Blaxland and Archibald Bell were among those masters with more than one establishment, a situation which increased their labour requirements and demanded greater management skills. Bell with a mere 2,695 acres in 1828 had a work force of 94, almost half of whom were free. Masters relied upon both bond and free labour and an all-convict work force was only likely on smaller establishments.

Cox, Blaxland and Bell had arrived in the early years of the colony. Blaxland, having been promised a substantial land grant and government assistance, came as a free emigrant with capital but Governor Bligh grudgingly allowed him only 1,290 acres. Later, in 1831, Blaxland received an additional 10,000. Bell was an ensign and Cox a lieutenant in the New South Wales Corps. All three successfully established a home-base and principal residence on the Cumberland Plain before expanding into other areas.[47] Their length of time in the colony enabled them to build up their acreage as well as their convict establishment. Cox, Blaxland and Bell exemplify two types of master: the free emigrant with capital and the military man. More than 80 per cent of the masters of the Wessex transportees whose origins we can establish, had come free to the colony. Two-thirds of them arrived in the 1820s, mainly in response to the change in policy which encouraged emigrants with capital by offering free crown grants and labour. Information about these incentives was widely disseminated throughout Britain and Ireland. A Scot, C. L. Browne, master of John Legg, pointed out that he had 'emigrated on the faith of the Printed Regulation issued from the Colonial Office Downing Street in April 1826'. The master of Abraham Knight, Francis Flanagan, a merchant tailor from Cork, claimed familiarity with the 'conditions upon which persons are permitted to hold lands at New South Wales'.[48] The capital of these free emigrants varied. C. L. Browne came with £809 compared with the £1,000 of J. B. Bettington, master of Henry Eldridge, but Francis Flanagan's £2,000 was about average.[49]

Land was an obvious incentive, as was convict labour. Some of the free emigrants with capital, such as the twenty-one year old Browne, were sons of families expanding into, and investing in, the colony. Having been 'brought up in a country situation in Scotland', Browne spent four years as a clerk in a Glasgow Mercantile House preparing for his future. Family connections helped as he came with a letter of recommendation to W. Jeremiah Browne of the Sydney merchant firm, Aspinall and Browne.[50] George Clarke happened to be assigned to that partnership at Bathurst where Jeremiah Browne had amassed 16,000 acres in three years. C. L. Browne, however, went north to Patrick Plains where he started in a modest way with 2,560 acres and eleven workers, intending, apparently, to earn his living from the land. Another Scot with a mercantile background, Thomas Bartie, master of William Adams, arrived in 1831 and only ten days later successfully appeared before the Land Board.[51] Obviously coming well prepared and with capital of £4,000, he intended to follow a rural life after receiving his free grant of 2,560 acres on the Williams River. James Bettington, master of Henry Eldridge, was a partner in the London firm, John Bettington, Sons and Co. Arriving in the colony in 1827, he opened a general chandlery and hardware store in Sydney but made his mark on the Hunter as a sheep breeder.[52] For men with capital from a mercantile or trading background, land offered an opportunity to acquire a status they were unlikely to attain in Britain.

Almost a quarter of the masters of Swing convicts were military men. Most had come with their regiments to New South Wales, long regarded as one of the worst postings of all. Deciding to settle, having established themselves and their families and obtained land, many sold their commissions to raise capital. As ex-army men, regardless of rank, they were eligible for free land grants under certain conditions.

Robert Holdaway's master, John Harris, had been a surgeon in the New South Wales Corps. Subsequently sent to London, he returned to the colony to settle, built upon already established foundations and amassed just under 8,000 acres at Penrith, Parramatta and Bathurst.[53] William Dumaresq, master of George Shergold, 'having retired from the Service for the purpose of Settling in the colony', received a land grant from Darling. Major Edmund Lockyer, to whom Maurice Pope was assigned, received a free grant of 2,560 acres which he located in the County of Argyle. John Bulpitt's master, Lieutenant Colonel Stewart, a deputy governor of New South Wales, lived in retirement at Mount Pleasant, near Bathurst.[54]

The process by which naval men settled in the colony was somewhat different. After the Napoleonic Wars, the Royal Navy was significantly reduced. For Thomas Hawkins, master of Job Waldron, paid-off and a failure in business, New South Wales represented his main hope. The government storekeeper at Bathurst, he also received a free grant of 2,000 acres. With an inheritance from a distant relative he was able to resign his position and concentrate upon his rural enterprise.[55] Isaac Manns was assigned to John Nicholson, an officer on half pay emigrating to be able to live better than he could at home. After he became harbour master – and government positions were much sought after by high and low because they produced an assured income – he received free grants totalling 1,500 acres.[56] T. B. Wilson, an ex-naval surgeon and a surgeon superintendent on convict transports, gained a colonial land grant during his first visit to Australia. Although James New was assigned to him, Wilson did not settle with his family in Australia until 1836. John Osborne, to whom Isaac Cole was assigned, had also been a naval surgeon. Settling first on the Illawarra, he was followed by two of his brothers. One, Henry, a farmer, starting with that advantage, made his mark on the Illawarra where Isaac Cole was transferred to him.[57]

Some Swing convicts went to civil servants and the judiciary, ranging from Francis Forbes, the Chief Justice of New South Wales, to relatively minor public officials. A number of ex-military men obtained government positions. William Cordeaux, George Druitt, William Dumaresq and Thomas Evernden became landholders and masters of Wessex transportees. The unfortunate Charles Davis, who died a month after arrival, was assigned to the Colonial Treasurer, William Balcombe, and Luke Brown was placed with William Aird, an assistant engineer and then a superintendent of public works. Charles Moore, Jacob Turner's first master, lived at Surry Hills, convenient to his work as a clerk in the Supreme Court.[58] This group, except for Balcombe, seems to have acquired free land grants as supplements to its main source of income. Land, for them, would have been an important affirmation of their upward social mobility.

Only a small number of masters of Swing convicts came from outside these groups. The merchant masters, Henry Donnison, W. H. Dutton, John Hosking, R.

W. Loane, J. McLaren and James Underwood all had modest land holdings. The most flamboyant of all, J. B. Montefiore, at one time owned more than 12,000 acres. He brought a fortune with him, made another fortune in the colony and lost it all in the depression of the 1840s.[59] Three clergymen, members of the official establishment, received men from the *Eleanor*. The best known, Samuel Marsden, balanced his roles of pastor and pastoralist most successfully. Women were just as eligible as men to receive assigned convicts. Two widows, both of whom had emigrated with their children to New South Wales, had Swing protesters assigned to them. One, a widowed emigrant with connections, Jemima Pitt, married again in the colony and on the death of her second husband took over the running of his landed estates, controlling at least 9,000 acres.[60] Other masters of Swing convicts had taken a different path in the colony. An ex-convict, James Underwood, master of Jason Greenway became one of the wealthiest men in the colony. Beginning as a shipbuilder, he diversified into distilling and commerce. Samuel Quinton went to the firm of two ex-convicts, Solomon Levey and Daniel Cooper, a company with wide-ranging commercial interests.[61] Wealthy ex-convicts were, however, the exception rather than the rule. Other ex-convict masters, Richard Archibold of Hunters Hill, William Bradbury of Airds and Alex Fraser of Penrith, to whom Joseph Shepherd, James Simonds and Henry James respectively were assigned, were atypical of their class in requiring more labour than their own families could supply.

Economic status determined access to, and maintenance of, assigned convicts. As one would expect, masters were few among the lower levels of society. John Burroughs was assigned to C. M. Edgehill, a storekeeper of Camden and James Baker went to a Sydney miller. Alfred Darling's master, Thomas Inglis, was a Sydney boot-maker only just beginning to move upwards. Joseph Shepherd served his sentence with Richard Achibold. Free by servitude he had gained a free land grant of 1,000 acres at Hunters Hill on the north shore of Sydney Harbour. A dealer and a vict-ualler, he already had two convict labourers and one convict gardener in 1828. As he was married with a family of five, the lack of any household servants and the small number of convicts suggest limited resources. In a number of ways, he was probably fairly typical in class and status of those who had very few assigned convicts.

Six Wessex men went to native-born masters. All were established landowners at the time but they came from both bond and free backgrounds. William Shepherd's master, Hamilton Hume, whose father had come free, was a self-made man gaining land grants as a result of his well-publicised journeys of exploration. William Lee of Bathurst, George Williams' master, was the son of a convict, born at Norfolk Island. As the result of the patronage of William Cox, he initially received a small land grant at Bathurst and benefited from bringing himself to the attention of J. T. Bigge. Gaining more grants and with two changes of surname, he succeeded in leaving his illegitimacy and convict origins behind. Charles Fay served his sentence with William

Charles Wentworth, also born at Norfolk Island of a convict mother but less successful than Lee in concealing his origins. Although the colonial wealth and the Anglo-Irish upper-class connections of Darcy Wentworth gave William Charles an easier path in life, he was not admitted to the highest levels of colonial society to which he aspired. Daniel Sims went to William Hutchinson junior whose ex-convict father gave his son some economic advantage.[62] The masters of Swing protesters covered a wide social and economic spectrum which matched the social structure of the colony. Assignment followed demand and that demand was highest from those who could both usefully employ convicts and afford the cost of their labour regardless of their civil status and social origins.

If 'a just and equal distribution' of convicts was 'of great importance to the Colony', the allocation of skilled men was a matter which was even more crucial. Demand had always greatly exceeded supply especially during the Macquarie period. Unlike the situation in the early 1820s, when land grants were made contingent upon taking some convicts off the government stores, no such incentives were necessary in relation to skilled convicts.[63] Between 1828 and 1833, carpenters were most in demand with 773 applications. Next were blacksmiths with 462 requests for the 270 available. Applications for sawyers and stonemasons were about the same, with about half successful. Those seeking brickmakers and bricklayers had the best chance of all of getting their man.[64]

The frustration involved in trying to obtain artisans is apparent in the saga of A.K. Mackenzie from Bathurst, whom we have met already in relation to the assignment of the Wessex men. At the time of the 1828 Census, Mackenzie had seven convicts, none of whom was a tradesman.[65] During that year he had applied for several but eighteen months later he was still waiting, hoping that 'it will come to…[his] turn by and by'. In 1831 he got his bricklayer, William Sims, from the *Eleanor*. Before that successful outcome, despite Mackenzie's apparent acceptance of the delay, he asked to have a convict whose master had returned him to the government. Attempting to jump the queue, Mackenzie conveniently forgot to mention in his application that the man was a bricklayer, a fact which the Principal Superintendent established very quickly.[66] Mackenzie had to wait his turn.[67]

If the policy of Earl Bathurst, Secretary of State for the Colonies, had prevailed, all artisans would have been assigned to rural areas. Bathurst was prepared to waste their skills by recommending that those who were strong enough should be put to work in the fields.[68] It was extremely unlikely, however, that masters would have used them in that way. Darling, although he shared Bathurst's view that 'mechanics' were profligate and should be saved from the temptations of urban life, successfully argued that assigning them all as a matter of course to the countryside would do more harm than good.[69] It seems, however, as if there may have been some preference given to rural masters, because in 1830 Alexander Macleay, the Colonial Secretary, admonished the Land Board and instructed them that urban masters 'must be attended to in their turn, as well as persons residing in the country.'[70]

The distribution of tradesman followed the same basic principles laid down by Darling for other convicts. The Land Board dealt with applications in the order they were received. The Principal Superintendent of Convicts furnished lists of applicants and their convict artisans in an attempt to ensure that no single master received a disproportionate number of tradesman.[71] However, the lack of any explicit criteria for passing over an applicant who headed the list, laid the Board and, therefore, Darling open to the charge of favouritism. Most of the men of the *Eleanor* were multi-skilled. William Sims, for example, was a bricklayer, plasterer and slater and John Pointer a top sawyer and carpenter. Fifty-five per cent of the Wessex men practised a trade or some alternative to agricultural labour and a rural bias is apparent in their distribution.[72] No tradesmen from that ship went to a Sydney master. Only one third of them were assigned to the Cumberland Plain. Of the rural areas, the Hunter fared very well with almost a quarter and Bathurst with about a fifth. Tradesmen obviously had advantages over their differently skilled fellows. It remains to be seen, however, whether they fared better than the agricultural labourers in assignment, when they had become free, in the marriage market and in their subsequent lives in New South Wales.

The ability of each governor after 1815 was measured by his administration of the convict system. In the case of the Swing protesters, we have been able to follow the process of assignment and distribution in a way which provides an unusually intimate view of the proceedings. We can see that by 1831 the machinery was showing its limitations. Darling's assignment regulations had complicated the process and left him open to attack. On the other hand, they imposed a certain order and efficiency which had been lacking before his arrival in the colony. Apart from his arbitrary removal of assigned convicts from his enemies in 1830, an act which demonstrated his political stupidity and vindictiveness as well as his power, it seems that in the assignment of the men of the *Eleanor* there was a 'just and equal distribution of the Prisoners of the Crown'.[73] It seems, too, that, apart from the artisans, the *Eleanor*'s convicts were allocated randomly according to the order of the applications. It so happened that the greatest demand for labour came from landholders. But the distribution of this particular group of convicts does not support the findings of *Convict Workers* of a deliberate match between the occupation on the indent and the assigned work.[74] It would appear that from 1826, when Darling introduced his changes and until Bourke altered the rules relating to assignment, convicts were assigned according to the applicant's place on the list, except, perhaps, for a few artisans.

The society which the Swing protesters joined was very different from the one they had left behind. The fact that men had been transported in far greater numbers than women had resulted in an enormous imbalance between the sexes. In 1833, the first year after the 1828 Census for which we have official statistics for population, there were three males to every female.[75] This imbalance favoured women, the majority of whom were convict or ex-convict. Those women eligible to marry not only had the opportunity and government encouragement to do so, but they could be selective in their choice of a spouse. On the other hand, three quarters of the men in the colony were destined never to marry. Those who ran last in the marriage stakes were overwhelmingly unskilled ex-convicts – the greatest losers in colonial society.[76]

New South Wales had a rapidly growing population but its atypical population structure remained essentially the same until after 1840. It was dominated by adult males and had proportionately few children. The colony's population, which was 36,598 in 1828, had reached 60,794 by 1833, an increase of almost 40 per cent.[77] By 1836, when a significant number of Swing men had gained conditional pardons or tickets of leave and were thus able to work on their own behalf and make most decisions about their own lives, the population was about 77,000.[78] Despite this rapid increase, mainly the result of immigration, both free and bond, the population was, until the gold rushes in the 1850s, comparatively small. Very little could pass unnoticed by others and in this respect life in the colony was similar to the village life from which the Swing protesters had come.

The distribution of the colonial population was, however, very different from that of England. New South Wales was a highly urbanised society and the concentration of population in the County of Cumberland made administration easier than it otherwise might have been. By 1836 slightly more than half the population was in this county with about a third of the colonial total in Sydney itself. The other eighteen counties fell within a semi-circle with a 125 mile radius centred on Sydney. Each county, except for Cumberland, had about 2 per cent of the population but the Counties of Northumberland, Cook and Camden on the northern, western and southern boundaries of Cumberland had just over 11 per cent of the colonial population.[79] In the remoter counties, where the population was sparse and consisted largely of male convicts still under sentence, the delegation of authority to unpaid magistrates and of control to masters with limited power over their convicts, was a very effective means of supervision. Demography and necessity meant that convicts, especially those in the more isolated areas, enjoyed a surprising amount of freedom.

## Notes

1   Darling to Bathurst, Sydney, 1 May 1826, *Historical Records of Australia* (hereafter *HRA*), Series 1, Vol. XII, p. 252.
2   Enclosure, Darling to Bathurst, Sydney, 1 May 1826, Sydney, ibid., pp. 252-253.
3   Darling to Goderich, 31 December 1827, Sydney, ibid., p. 673.
4   There are numerous references to the deliberate destruction of convict records.

See, for example, Beverley Earnshaw, 'Computerising the Convicts', *History: Magazine of the Royal Australian Historical Society*, No. 37, October 1994, p.6, who asserts that the 'Principal Superintendent of Convict's records have long been destroyed'. Some were. Any serious research in the Colonial Secretary Papers turns up stray examples. Pre-assignment lists, the applications for assigned convicts and the majority of the assignment registers were not part of the collection of convict records deposited at the State Archives. Other substantial records from the office of the principal superintendent have survived and were deposited. See J. Spurway, 'The Growth of Family History in Australia', *The Push: A Journal of Early Australian Social History* (hereafter *The Push*), No. 27, 1989, pp. 74-76, where he discusses the matter but reaches no firm conclusions about what may have been deliberately destroyed.

5     D. Masier to Colonial Secretary, 29 June 1831, Sydney, Col. Sec. In Letters, Archives of New South Wales (hereafter AONSW), 4/2110.

6     Darling to Goderich, Sydney, 31 December 1827, *HRA*, Series 1, Vol. X111, p. 673.

7     Colonial Secretary to the Land Board, 5 July 1831, Copies of Letters Sent re Convicts, 21 May 1831 to 7 October 1831, AONSW 4/3671, Reel 2650.

8     Colonial Secretary to the Principal Superintendent of Convicts, Sydney, 9 July 1831, Colonial Secretary to the Land Board, Sydney, 18 July 1831, and Colonial Secretary to the Principal Superintendent of Convicts, 8 July 1831, Copies of Letters Sent re Convicts, 21 May 1831 to 7 October 1831, AONSW 4/3671, Reel 2650.

9     Colonial Secretary, Copies of Letters Sent re Convicts, 21 May 1831 to 7 October 1831, AONSW 4/3671, Reel 2650. Pumphrey's indent lists him as 29 years old, an underestimation of five years.

10    'Alexander Macleay' in D. Pike (gen. ed.), *Australian Dictionary of Biography*, 2 Vols, Melbourne, 1966, Vol. 2, p. 178.

11    'Sir John Wylde' in ibid., Vol. 2, pp. 627-629. Sir John Wylde to Colonial Secretary, 2 May 1831, Cape of Good Hope, Col. Sec In Letters, AONSW 4/2110. The *Eleanor* would have carried this letter to Sydney. F.C. Harrington to the Land Board, Sydney, Copies of letters Sent Re Convicts, 21 May 1831-7 October 1831, 31/4819, AONSW 4/3650, Reel 2650, p. 147.

12    David Masier to Colonial Secretary, Sydney, 29 June 1831, Col. Sec. In Letters, AONSW 4/2110.

13    James Stephenson to the Colonial Secretary, Port Jackson, 28 June 1831, 31/4879, Burman Langa to Colonial Secretary, 2 July 1834, Sydney, 31/5002 and enclosure, Colonial Secretary to Burman Langa, 12 July 1831, Sydney, 31/30, Col. Sec. In Letters, AONSW, 4/2110

14    The *Eleanor* arrived on 25 June 1831 and the men did not land until 11 July.

T.C. Harrington to J. Nicholson, Master Attendant, Sydney, 9 July 1831, Copies of Letters Sent to the Master Attendant, Masters of Ships, The Harbour Master and the Port Master, 18 December 1830-29 October 1832, AONSW 4/3779, Reel 2862.

15 Parliamentary Papers, *Report Select Committee of the House of Commons on Transportation, 1837-1838, with Minutes of Evidence, Appendix and Index*, 2 vols, Ordered to be printed, 1838, Vol. 2, Report, p. viii. For the circumstances surrounding the establishment of this committee, see J. Ritchie, "Towards Ending an unclean Thing': The Molesworth Committee and the Abolition of Transportation to New South Wales, 1837-1840', *Historical Studies*, Vol. 17, No. 67, October 1976, pp. 144-164. For the bias of the Report, see Norma Townsend, 'The Molesworth Enquiry: Does the Report Fit the Evidence?', *Journal of Australian Studies*, No. 1, July 1977, pp. 33-51.

16 Darling to Bathurst, 1 May 1826, *HRA*, Series 1, Vol. XIII, pp. 251-253.

17 Bathurst to Darling, 24 September 1826, ibid., Vol. XII, p. 585 and Darling to Bathurst, 1 March 1827, ibid., Vol. XIII, p.136.

18 See, N. Townsend, 'Masters and Men and the Myall Creek Massacre', *The Push*, No. 20, April 1985, pp. 4-32. The depositions are to be found in the Muswellbrook Bench Book, AONSW 4/5601, Reel 671.

19 J.B. Hirst, *Convict Society and its enemies: A history of early New South Wales*, Sydney, 1983, p. 69.

20 Robert Mason, 27 July 1831, Joseph Mason, 30 September 1831, in A.M. Colson, 'The Revolt of the Hampshire Agricultural Labourers and its Causes, 1812-1831', M.A.,University of London, 1937, pp. 292,300; D. Kent and N. Townsend (eds) *Joseph Mason, Assigned Convict, 1831-1837: Doomed to the earth's remotest region*, Melbourne, 1996, p. 51.

21 Darling to Goderich, 8 July 1831, *HRA*, Series 1, Vol. XVI, p. 295. This change seems to have involved the formal assignment of the convicts to the Hyde Park Barracks in the first instance, for 'at least a month' and then subsequently to the master named on the indent. See the Musters and Papers, the *Eleanor*, AONSW 2/8257, Reel 2421.

22 Colonial Secretary to Principal Superintendent of Convicts, 3 August 1831, Copies of Letters Sent re Convicts, 21 May to 7 October 1831, AONSW 4/3671, Reel 2560.

23 Kent and Townsend, op. cit., p. 41.

24 Darling to Bathurst, Sydney, 1 May 1826, *HRA*, Series 1, Vol. XII, p. 253.

25 For Baker's assignment, see *Government Gazette*, 1832, p. 224.

26 D.N. Jeans, *An Historical Geography of New South Wales to 1901*, Sydney, 1972, pp. 23-24.

27 T.M. Perry, *Australia's First Frontier: The Spread of Settlement in New South*

*Wales*, Melbourne, 1964, p.109.

28   Bathurst to Darling, 24 September 1826, *HRA*, Series 1, Vol. XII, p. 585.

29   Jeans, op. cit., p. 101.

30   See ibid., pp. 95-103 and Perry, op. cit., pp. 101 and 103.

31   For the most detailed description of settlement on the Hunter, see G. A. Wood, *Dawn in the Valley: The Story of Settlement in the Hunter River Valley to 1833*, Sydney, 1972, pp. 1-29.

32   We have taken these figures and calculated the percentages from the abstract of returns for the 1828 Census, reproduced by M. R. Sainty and K. A. Johnson (eds), *Census of New South Wales*, [November 1828], Sydney, 1985, p. 15, (hereafter *1828 Census*). Our figures for the Hunter include Port Stephens. The Counties of Camden and Argyle took in the Southern Highlands and Plains.

33   *Ibid.; Returns of the Colony, 1822-1857*, (hereafter *Blue Book*), 1833, p. 161.

34   G. Rudé, ''Captain Swing' in New South Wales', *Historical Studies*, Vol. 11, April 1965, p. 473.

35   *Blue Book*, p. 161.

36   Wood, op. cit., pp. 271-272.

37   The identification of places has come from a number of sources. Unfortunately, Bathurst suffers from a dearth of extended scholarly, local studies. See, however, B. Greaves, *The Story of Bathurst*, Sydney, 1964; W. Foster, 'Hartley The Gateway to the West', *Royal Australian Historical Society Journal* (hereafter *RAHSJ*), Vol. XVIII, Part 5, 1932; W.A. Steel, 'The History of Carcoar 1815-1881', ibid., Vol. XVII, Part 4, 1931; W.A. Steel, 'Dunn's Plains, Rockley. Its History and Personalities', ibid., Vol. XXVI, Part 3, 1940; W.D. O'Sullivan, 'Hartley N.S.W', ibid., Vol. II, Part 12, 1907,8 and 9. See, also, *New South Wales Calendar and General Post Office Directory, 1832*, Sydney, 1966 [1831] and W.H. Wells, *A Geographical Dictionary or Gazetteer of the Australian Colonies, 1848*, Sydney, 1970 [1848]. More recently Bathurst has been better served with M. Pearson, 'Seen through Different Eyes: Changing Land Use and Settlement Patterns in the Upper Macquarie River', PhD., Australian National University, Canberra, 1981, and K. Fry, *Beyond the Barrier: Class Formation in a Pastoral Society, Bathurst 1818-1848*, Bathurst, 1993.

38   Perry, op. cit., p. 96. Apart from the work of James Jervis, and J. F. Campbell and A. Atkinson's *Camden: Farm and Village life in Early New South Wales*, Melbourne, 1988, there is little published material on the history of this area.

39   J. Jervis, 'Settlement in the Picton and the Oaks District', *RAHSJ*, Vol. XXVII, Part 4, 1941, pp. 277-278 and Jeans op. cit. p. 103.

40   Loc. cit.

41   K. and T. Henderson, *Early Illawarra: people, houses, life. An Australia 1838 Monograph*, Canberra, 1983, p. 9.

42   Jeans, op. cit., pp. 113-116.

43   It is really only possible to identify with some certainty freehold acreage. By the time the Swing convicts arrived, land owners were illegally squatting on crown land. As it was impossible to prevent illegal use, Bourke introduced a system of pastoral leases. Even the identification of ownership of crown land is difficult and the acreage given is an indication rather than a definite figure.

44   The figures come from the 1828 Census.

45   These figures come from the 1828 Census and information in the applications for free crown grants which sometimes included the number of convicts and free workers. As applications became more formalised with the use of standard forms, more details were required. See, for example, the applications of John Nicholson, master of Isaac Manns, who listed six convicts and two free servants, and Robert Rodd, master of William Primer, with ten convicts and two free servants. Colonial Secretary Letters received re Land, 1826-1860, AONSW 2/7917, 28/3099, Reel 1157 and 2/7961, Reel 1177.

46   The average number of convicts per master for those who owned more than 10000 acres was actually slightly higher but the workers on the estate of Berry and Wollstonecraft have not been listed in the census. Given the extent of their cultivation and number of stock on the Shoalhaven River on the Couth Coast, they must have had a considerable work force there.

47   J. D. Heydon, 'Archibald Bell' in Pike, op. cit., Vol. 1, pp. 78-79, T. H. Irving, 'John Blaxland' in ibid., pp. 117-118 and 'William Cox' in ibid., pp. 258-259.

48   Colonial Secretary Letters received re Land, 1826-1860, AONSW 2/7788, Reel 1081 and 2/7858, Reel 1127.

49   Colonial Secretary Letters received re Land, 1826-1860, AONSW 2/7920, Reel 1086, 2/7800. Reel 1092, and 2/7858, Reel 1127.

50   Colonial Secretary Letters received re Land, 1826-1860, AONSW 2/7920, Reel 1086.

51   Colonial Secretary Letters received re Land, 1826-1860, AONSW, 2/27796, Reel 1088.

52   Wood, op. cit., p. 198.

53   B. F. Fletcher, 'John Harris' in Pike, op. cit., Vol. 1, pp. 519-520; D. R. Hainsworth, *The Sydney Traders: Simeon Lord and his Contemporaries, 1788-1821*, North Melbourne, 1971, pp. 27-29.

54   Darling to Murray, Government House, 27 February 1829, *HRA*, Vol. XIV, p. 669; U. Peasley, 'Edmund Lockyer and the Second British Empire, 1784-1860', M. Litt., University of New England, Armidale, 1990, pp. 71 and 40; 'Edmund Lockyer' in Pike, *op. cit.*, Vol. 2, p. 123. There is no evidence in the correspondence relating to land that Lockyer missed out on an free army grant through a technicality. He was, however, refused permission to purchase crown land while

a serving officer. Colonial Secretary Letters received re Land, AONSW 2/7908 Reel 1155. T. Barker, 'William Stewart', in Pike, op. cit., Vol. 2, pp. 482-483.

55  'Thomas Hawkins' in ibid., pp. 524-525.

56  Enclosure, Darling to Murray, Government House, 21 July 1830, *HRA*, Vol. XVI, pp. 302-30.

57  G. Wilson, 'Thomas Braidwood Wilson' in Pike, op. cit., Vol. 2, p. 612. He is incorrectly recorded on the indent as T. P. Wilson. *Historical Records of the Central Coast of New South Wales, Bench Books and Court Cases: 1826-1874*, Gosford, 1988, p. 87 and P. J. B. Osborne, 'Henry Osborne' in Pike, op. cit., pp. 303-304.

58  Forbes to Darling, 10 January 126, *HRA*, Vol. XII, p. 155. Old Title Land Grants, 14/21, Land Titles Office of New South Wales, Sydney. The 1828 Census records no land and no convicts. See the entry for his stepbrother, R. J. McKay, 'William Henry Moore' in Pike, op. cit., Vol. 2,pp. 256-259.

59  I. Getzler, 'J. B. Montefiore' in ibid., pp.250-251.

60  R. F. Holder, 'Robert Jenkins' in Pike, ibid., pp. 16-17.

61  G. F. Bergman, 'Solomon Levey' in ibid, pp. 110-111; J. W. Davidson, 'Daniel Cooper' in ibid., Vol. 1, pp. 245-246; 'Thomas Shadforth' in ibid., Vol. 2, pp. 435-436.

62  S. H. Hume, 'Hamilton Hume' in Pike, op. cit., Vol. 1, pp.564-565, V. Parsons, 'William Lee' in ibid., Vol. 2, pp. 101-102 and M. Persse, 'William Charles Wentworth' in ibid., pp.582-589.

63  Brisbane to Bathurst, 29 November 1822, *HRA*, Vol. XI, Series 1, p.179.

64  Col. Sec, Special Bundles, Assignment 1834-1836, AONSW, 4/1116.

65  See entries, C753, C2889, C3368, M938, M2163, W2452 and W2453, *1828 Census.*

66  A. K. Mackenzie to Colonial Secretary, Alexander McLeay, 31 March 1830, Principal Superintendent of Convicts, A.H. Healy to Colonial Secretary, 13 April 1830, T. Evernden, Police Magistrate, Bathurst, to the Director of Public Works, 26 May 1831 and A.K. Mackenzie to Colonial Secretary, Bathurst, 4 May 1831, 31/3538 and enclosures, Col. Sec. In Letters, AONSW 4/2106.

67  A.K. Mackenzie, Bathurst, 9 September 1830, to Colonial Secretary, A.H. Healy, 30/6874 and enclosures, AONSW 4/2081.

68  Bathurst to Darling, 1 October 1826, *HRA*, Vol. XII, Series 1, pp. 591-592. Bathurst was determined that all mechanics should be assigned to rural masters because he believed that the majority were going to urban masters and that it was 'the more necessary to guard against that deception, which the Convicts may otherwise endeavour to practice of passing themselves off for Mechanics, in order to prevent their being disposed of amongst those Settlers, who may be established at a distance from any of the Towns.'

69  Darling to Bathurst, 1 March 1827, ibid., Vol. XIII, pp. 135-136.

70  Macleay to the Land Board, 27 November 1830, Col. Sec. Out Letters, AONSW 3670/Reel 2649.

71  Darling to Bathurst, Sydney, 1 May 1826, *HRA*, Series 1, Vol. X II, pp. 252-253.

72  S.G. Foster, 'Convict Assignment in New South Wales in the 1830s', *The Push*, No. 15, April, 1993, pp. 48. S. Nicholas (ed.) *Convict Workers, Reinterpreting Australia's Past*, Sydney, 1988, has organised occupation groups in such a way that they contain a vast number of different occupations and mechanics have not been treated as a single group. L.L. Robson, *The Convict Settlers of Australia: An Enquiry into the origin and character of the Convicts transported to New South Wales and Van Diemen's Land 1787-152*, Melbourne, 1964, p. 190.

73  Shaw, op. cit., p. 233.

74  S. Nicholas and P. R. Shergold, 'Convicts as Workers,' in Nicholas op. cit., p. 82.

75  Calculated from *1828 Census*, p. 15.

76  M.J. Belcher, 'The Child in New South Wales Society: 1820 to 1837', PhD., University of New England, Armidale, 1982, pp. 119-121, provides a comprehensive and detailed demographic study of this period.

77  *1828 Census*, *Blue Book*, p. 168. Belcher, op. cit., p.114.

78  Ibid., p.116.

79  Ibid., p. 125.

# Chapter 8

# 'I HAD TO COOK MY OWN VICTUALS':

# COPING WITH ASSIGNMENT

The Swing protesters arrived in New South Wales at the beginning of the most intense period of transportation when the British government, fearing the 'dangerous classes', made exile more certain and attempted to render the experience 'worse than death'.[1] The arrival of the *Eleanor*'s convicts coincided with the departure of Governor Darling and the coming of his replacement, Sir Richard Bourke, a man of more liberal sentiments and greater compassion. Opposed to transportation, Bourke had accepted the governorship believing that transportation might end and he was intent upon administering the system as humanely as possible.[2] It was a measure of his approach that his enemies in the colony attacked him as the 'convicts' friend'.[3] When Bourke took office, the men of the *Eleanor* had already been assigned according to Darling's bureaucratic process. The management of convicts had become more systematic as a result of Darling's changes implemented by his indefatigable Colonial Secretary, Alexander Macleay. Macleay, who took up his office in 1826 and resigned in 1837, oversaw the convict system in the period of its largest numbers, greatest change and closest regulation.[4]

The changes were timely. In the fifteen years from Darling's arrival in 1826 to the ending of transportation to New South Wales in 1840, almost 45,000 convicts arrived in the colony. During the 1830s about 3,500 convicts landed each year compared with around 2,200 for the decade, 1820 to 1829, and about 600 from 1810 to 1819.[5] Mass transportation only began after 1815 and assignment to private individuals became the convict system's most distinctive feature following the Bigge Reports. By 1838 almost 70 per cent of convicts were privately assigned. Those men not in assignment were receiving additional or secondary punishment for offences in the colony or were in government employ.[6] As few convicts as possible were a charge upon the state.

Although Darling's changes improved convict administration, Bigge had already established the general principles which would underpin the development of the colony and influence convict management.[7] Bigge was appointed in 1818 to investigate the current state of New South Wales, and the operation of the convict system was a central part of his inquiry. The Secretary of State for the Colonies, Bathurst, instructed him that transportation should become 'an object of real terror'. Realising the potential of pastoralism and recognising the shortage of labour, Bigge recommended the granting of land to free settlers with capital. Initially, because demand for convict labour was low, grantees were obliged to maintain a certain number of convicts. Unlike Macquarie, who retained skilled convicts in government service, Bigge recommended that as many convicts as possible be assigned to private individuals. Masters with capital would generate work for convicts as well as providing their keep, lodgings and immediate management. Reconciling 'punishment with profit' was a practical solution to a number of problems.[8] The scheme reduced the expense of the official establishment. It spread convicts over a wider area, decentralising their control and reducing their opportunity for combination against authority. It also removed them from the temptations of urban areas, or at least from where they were more visible when succumbing to them.

The view that assignment was a 'mere lottery' has a long pedigree and has found ready and widespread acceptance. As a means of organising convict society, assignment had too many variables for mechanistically-minded Benthamites who hoped to make punishment an exact science, and for the evangelical, anti-slavery movement transportation was merely another form of slavery.[9] Assignment, the linchpin of the convict system in New South Wales, became the main focus of attack for those in England and the colony who opposed transportation. Their criticisms gave rise to a distorted view of assignment which has been further modified by the filters of Australian nationalism, egalitarian ideals and the desire to see convict ancestors as victims. The convict system has been a favourite target for some Australian historians as part of their broader attack upon British imperialism and the colonial upper class; radical feminists have seen it as an institutionalised form of male oppression and exploitation of women. There were undoubtedly unkind, unjust and unfair masters but there were also those who were the reverse. It is not very difficult to find examples of both but in following the convict lives of the Swing transportees we have an opportunity to see how they adapted to their convict existence, and perhaps shed more light on the working of the convict system.

By 1838, the year which marked the end of servitude for all but seven of 104 Swing transportees who received absolute and conditional pardons, 128 of the original 138 were still in the colony. Several had returned to England and a few had moved to other colonies. Solomon Allen and John Shergold had travelled with their respective masters to Van Diemen's Land about a year after they arrived on the *Eleanor*. By 1836 Abraham Knight, a former shoemaker, was a sufficiently experienced stockman to overland cattle for his employers, Gardiner and Hawdon, to Port

Phillip where he settled.[10] At least seven Swing convicts died while still under sentence. The oldest was Abraham Childs. Originally assigned to Thomas Macquoid in Sydney, he was serving in an iron gang at Bathurst when he died from 'dysentry' in January 1833. A man of his age, 52, who had been an indoor servant, would have found hard labour in an Australian summer very difficult. Another who succumbed to 'dysentry' at Bathurst in 1836 was Adam Thorne. Thirty-two year old Charles Davis died at Liverpool Hospital shortly after his arrival. Robert Cook, who came on the *Captain Cook* in 1833, also died within a year at Goulburn Plains aged 36. Accidents and harsh colonial conditions took their toll. Childs, Thorne and Cook died in the hottest summer months; William Lewis perished in a fire at Newington, the Blaxland's family seat, in January 1832, and Thomas Warwick drowned in 1835 in the Karuah River, which flowed through the Australian Agricultural Company's land north of Newcastle.[11] Water and fire were common causes of death in the colony as new arrivals, in particular, came to terms with a dangerous, unfamiliar physical environment.

Those who died while still under sentence never faced the decisions which accompanied freedom. One option was to return to England. Australian historians, especially the nationalist writers, have never seriously considered that working-class people might have wanted to leave Australia for their homeland. A significant number of ex-convicts, however, left the colony, though it was probably easier for them to do so in the early years of settlement. About a third of the male convicts and a quarter of the females on the First Fleet disappear very quickly from the colonial records. In the period to 1820, possibly a quarter of those who finished their sentence might have left New South Wales. A disparity between the figures relating to convicts and ex-convicts in the 1828 Census suggests an outflow of convicts no longer under sentence, a disparity which had, however, almost halved by 1841.[12] Men probably had some advantage over women by being able to work a passage home but, on the other hand, women were more able to exploit marriage as a means of leaving the colony. In the later period, it seems that fewer may have returned to England as New South Wales became more settled, prosperous and, thus, attractive. Although the fate of forty-seven of the Swing men remains a mystery, only four are known to have gone home permanently. Nevertheless, given the number who vanish without trace after they became free, it is possible that others left New South Wales.[13]

Probably the first was Joseph Mason who spent his time of servitude with Hannibal Macarthur of Parramatta. By 1838 he was in England where he wrote an account of his colonial experiences. His return, 'through the assistance of kind friends', was aided by a subscription taken up by his fellow radicals in Sutton Scotney. As a result, 'after an absence of seven years' he was 'again seated by an English fireside'.[14] By 1841 George Carter had returned to Tangley in Hampshire. Both had absolute pardons enabling them to leave the colony immediately. The

Swing protesters with conditional pardons could not leave the colony, except for New Zealand, until their sentence had expired. Those with a life sentence were effectively exiled for ever, though at least two slipped through the bureaucratic net. John Pointer joined the rush to the Californian goldfields when the authorities found it impossible to check those leaving the country. William Primer returned to his wife and children at Upham in Hampshire where he had been born and married. She, for her part, had begun petitioning to join her husband, with subsequent support from his master, Robert Rodd of Wollombi, within months of his arrival in Australia. William Sims, among the oldest of the Swing transportees and assigned to a young Charles Cowper, later a premier of New South Wales, was also in England by 1851, living with his elderly wife in St Mary Bourne.[15] Sims appears to have waited seven years between receiving his conditional pardon and an absolute pardon in 1844. Both Mason and Primer fathered children on their return. The Primers named the first child born after William's homecoming Walter Sydney, a poignant reminder of the years his father had lost from his English life.[16]

The longer convicts were in the colony before they were free to return to England, the less likely they were to leave. On hearing of his brother's death in 1863, Robert Mason reminisced about their farewell meeting at Raymond Terrace, north of Newcastle; it was the 'last time we shook hands'. Robert, on that day early in 1837, believed that he would follow his brother 'in less than 12 months'. By then, however, Robert had formed an attachment to a woman and, despite 'what lessons of caution' Joseph delivered, 'ultimately all was of no use – nothing could prevent us coming together'. Although Robert visited England in 1865, he found that he did not experience 'that satisfaction in this my return…as I had anticipated. People and their manners seem altogether strange…and I seem like an alien amongst them'. Poor Robert! Had he known of Joseph's death before he finalised his travel arrangements, he would never have gone.[17]

Some realised, or perhaps decided very early in their sentence, that they would remain in the colony, because they applied to have their families brought to New South Wales under a government scheme which provided a free passage. Introduced in 1824, this indulgence was an incentive for good behaviour. From 1830, when regulations tightened, convicts could apply if they had not incurred a colonial punishment and if they had served a specified time in relation to the length of sentence.[18] A mere eight of the Swing transportees seem to have explored this opportunity.[19] George Carter, John Burroughs, Charles Green, Joseph Edney, Thomas Radborn, James Toomer, Laban Stone and Henry Shergold applied to have their families brought to New South Wales.[20] Burroughs and Edney disappeared from the colonial records after 1837 but Shergold fathered a colonial child in 1839. Toomer's fate is unknown but Laban Stone died at Mudgee in 1875.[21] Radborn's wife and family arrived within about eighteen months of his petition in June 1835. Their first colonial child was born in October 1837.[22] Green's wife seems not to have come. The wives of some Swing transportees decided that they could not wait for the return of their husbands or join them in the colony and formed relationships with other men.[23]

A flurry of petitions reflecting an amazing groundswell of feeling and community spirit had accompanied the trial and transportation of the Wessex protesters. Demonstrating an extraordinary political awareness, these petitions were mainly concerned with overturning or gaining a remission of sentence. In calmer times when reason had replaced fear, and in the wake of the outrage over the Tolpuddle Martyrs, petitions undoubtedly contributed to the British government's decision to grant conditional and absolute pardons. Some petitions were prompted by the desire for family reunion. In late 1832 Charlotte, wife of John Pointer, sought free passage to New South Wales but the family did not reach the colony until 1839. Many petitions undoubtedly arose from the initial shock, dismay and fear of a future without a male provider and the emotional support and affection of a husband. Although no wives arrived while their husbands were still under sentence, applications were made and in each case their husband's master supported the petition and offered to accommodate the couple.[24] Few families, however, seem to have been able to turn their requests into reality by making the long journey to Australia.

The class and status of the master largely determined the work convicts did and the way they were managed. The experiences of convicts in small establishments was very different from those in larger enterprises. Championing of the underdog and antagonism towards wealth and position have contributed to the mistaken view that convicts were better off assigned to ex-convicts on the grounds that they were more likely to be sympathetic and treat their assigned servants well.[25] The balance of complaints about masters serious enough to reach the Colonial Secretary, however, was decidedly against ex-convict, small masters. Class could make a difference but not in the way it is generally believed. Working-class masters usually lacked experience in the management of workers. As their resources were often limited and their number of convicts small, these masters were directly involved in the organisation, disposition and disciplining of their convicts. In larger establishments, masters had less direct dealings with their workforce and were in a more removed, supervisory role. This distancing was quite deliberate. The Macarthurs' practice was 'not to give orders to the convicts' themselves.[26] Like other masters they employed superintendents and at least one overseer for each of their establishments. These subordinates dealt directly with the convicts and took them before the bench when necessary. The success of the master's enterprise depended upon the cooperation of convicts as well as the quality of the men chosen to oversee. Larger establishments also allowed for greater specialisation in the workforce and skilled men were generally subject to less close scrutiny. Unlike convicts in small enterprises who might share the same dwelling as the master and his family, those in large establishments lived separately in huts or barracks where they could have quite considerable freedom. They were not locked in but were free to come and go, as they often did. One of the most striking features of Joseph Mason's account of his experiences as a convict is the freedom he enjoyed and the lack of intrusive supervision.

The usual practice of the larger enterprises was to keep the newly arrived male convict at the home property of the master to see how he behaved and then to transfer those who proved reasonably cooperative to more remote establishments. Mason's master, Hannibal Macarthur, informed him that he would work in the garden of the Parramatta house before going 'to a farm…up the country'. On his second day at Vineyard Cottage, a Sunday, Mason '*chose* to stay in his hut in the garden'. One of a number, it held 'from 2 to 6 and sometimes 8' men. The only matter which gave him 'no little uneasiness' was that 'now I had to cook my own vict-uals'.[27] The quantity and variety of convict rations, however, far exceeded what most of the Wessex men had experienced before.[28] Attendance at the Sunday muster at church was compulsory, a requirement which Mason did not mind. After church he and a shipmate were free to explore their immediate surrounds. At Westwood, Macarthur's property on the Nepean, Mason went much further afield walking up to thirty miles to visit shipmates from the *Eleanor*.[29]

Trust was basic to the successful management of convicts. The convict system was based on a reciprocal relationship which provided advantages for both master and man. As men proved to be responsible and reliable so their circumstances improved. James and William Macarthur, like their cousin Hannibal, set their newly arrived convicts to 'hard labour'. When a convict had proved himself by learning the advantages of regular and orderly behaviour, he was rewarded with less onerous tasks and even some responsibility. The famous overlander Joseph Hawdon, employer of Abraham Knight, had a simple formula for successful convict management; 'I feed them well, and I work them well, by which means I have very little trouble in managing them'.[30] The daily labours and living conditions of workers whether free or bond were the same. Under the terms of the Masters and Servants Act, free workers were just as bound for the period of their agreement as their convict counterparts and were brought before the bench for the same sort of misdemeanours as convicts.[31] Both bond and free could take their masters before a magistrate for failing to meet their responsibilities. Free and bond workers lived, worked and socialised together, shared the same diet and experienced similar freedoms and restrictions. Under these circumstances it was not unrealistic, as James Macarthur noted, to act on the principle that 'where a man behaves well…make him forget, if possible, that he is a convict'. The master of Joseph Watts, the crusty conservative laird of Coolangatta Alexander Berry, even gave his overseers 'strict instructions' that they were never to call the men convicts, 'but merely…Government servants or Government men'.[32]

Joseph Mason's work as a convict was in many respects very similar to his labours in Hampshire though rather different in its domestic aspects. While at Vineyard Cottage, he had tended the four-acre garden set aside for the growing of vegetables – cabbages and potatoes.[33] At Westwood, he saw to a much-neglected vegetable garden of an acre, getting it in order and planting a wider variety of vegetables. After that he was put on to 'every kind of odd jobs on the farm', mowing, reaping, harrowing, hoeing and winnowing as well as trussing the hay and loading the dray, all done with a will and without complaint. At Westwood he ate and slept in a kitchen detached from a cottage where a free man and his wife lived.[34] It seems that Mason was very much his own master. He was free to explore up and down the Nepean river, to visit men on adjacent and distant estates and to carry on an extensive correspondence. Attentive to his duties he earned the trust of his overseers and master.

The working day for convicts on the home property of the master was rather different from that of men working up-country. Although there were no regulations governing working hours, most masters followed the pattern for convicts in government service. The day began at dawn and finished at sunset with an hour for breakfast and a midday meal, a routine familiar to most country folk. Convicts came to regard this daily schedule and a certain volume and quality of rations as the norm.[35] Masters also often provided 'extras' to convicts who conformed. These included wages 'to encourage and conciliate' them, additional food and clothing and particularly 'tea, sugar milk, sometimes tobacco'.[36] Tobacco was much prized and a very profitable crop but those growing it had to exercise considerable vigilance to thwart convict efforts to purloin it. When necessary, of course, withholding rewards or indulgences acted as a form of punishment. So common were these incentives that more than one traveller or newcomer to the colony expressed surprise at what Patrick Leslie called the 'lavish indulgences'.[37] The Macarthurs even kept up the practice of task work, common in the early years of settlement. The Macarthurs' convicts were able to work in their own time and were paid in kind or with a credit at the estate store.[38] In such environments convicts often developed a proprietorial pride in their allotted tasks and in the management of the farm, much as they had done at home. Identification with the master's enterprise as well as mutuality and reward were an important part of convict discipline. On one occasion the Macarthurs responded to news of a proposed attack upon Camden Park by a 'group of escapees' by arming the 'best conducted' of their convicts in whom they 'had perfect confidence'.[39]

Few establishments were as grand, well-organized and fully documented as that of the Macarthurs. Such families with a long history in the colony had progressed beyond their fairly basic early colonial homes. As we have seen, the majority of masters of Swing men arrived during and after the 1820s. Lured by land and labour, they initially built modestly. The farm of Robert Rodd, master of William Primer, was fairly typical. In 1834 he had a weatherboard and shingle dwelling with six rooms, 'necessary outhouses', a barn and a piggery worth £300. Some had little more than the 'slab house and huts' of G. T. Graham of Raymond Terrace with whom James West began his sentence. Among the Swing masters of the 1820s, C. L. Browne probably invested most in establishing his farm on the Williams River. The family dwelling was thirty feet long by twenty-three feet wide, some rooms were finished with lath and plaster, and had panelled, cedar doors. The kitchen was detached as was the usual practice. The men lived in barracks of iron-bark slabs. Browne had built a large barn, stables, piggery, cowhouse, tobacco house, slaughter house and an eight-foot square privy, finished with lath and plaster and cedar and pine floor boards. His property, with its extensive orchard, a vinery and vegetable garden, represented an investment of almost £6,000.[40] The range of buildings reflects the great diversity of agricultural activity on a well-organized and productive farm in the fertile Lower Hunter.

The productivity and efficient operation of the larger estates depended on the sensitive deployment, organisation and management of assigned convicts. Vineyard Cottage, the centre of Hannibal Macarthur's activity, had twenty-two of his thirty-three convicts in 1828. Among them were only four labourers but he had built up a fairly specialised workforce which included a butcher, a tailor, a shoemaker and a miller. All larger establishments had a range of tradesmen and artisans. As Vineyard Cottage was the family home, the staff included house servants, a cook and a coachman in addition to the other workers. Westwood was primarily a farming operation but also ran some sheep; it had a dairyman, presumably for cheese-making, a carpenter and a blacksmith. Macarthur was also running sheep on the Goulburn Plains with four workers, three shepherds and a watchman for the folded sheep at night. One held a ticket-of-leave; the others were still under sentence. All were trusted to do their work far from supervision and penal authority. Macarthur also had an overseer at Vineyard Cottage who was free by servitude and acted as a clerk. His workforce of forty-three was fairly modest given that he had more than 3,000 acres cleared, 369 under cultivation, 45 horses, 527 cattle and more than 6,000 sheep.[41]

Convicts themselves came to have certain expectations about the ordering and management of their lives; they understood what was due to them, they knew their rights. Early in 1837, William Primer of the *Eleanor*, who served his sentence with Robert Rodd of Patrick Plains and Wollombi on the Hunter, was a signatory to a petition from Rodd's assigned convicts. In this document they complained that their master had gone to an outstation in New England for his 'usual term of two months...leaving his farm to the protection of the Government men without the residence of a free or ticket of leave overseer'. The signatories were apprehensive about 'the bad dispositions of some uncontrouled fellow servants on the farm'. This curious but revealing little episode says a great deal about master and convict relationships. The signatories recognised a hierarchy of responsibility in their own ranks, and were exceedingly well informed about their master's affairs.[42]

Apart from the right to petition and to lay complaints before the bench, convicts had a variety of stratagems for expressing dissatisfaction.[43] The most damaging was incendiarism, the standard form of covert rural protest in England between the 1830s and 1870s. Greatly facilitated by the invention of the lucifer match, incendiarism was carried to Australia as part of British rural culture. Arson was by no means common but at least two Swing masters were reprimanded by fires. One was John Buckland of the Cowpastures, Charles Green's master, who seems to have got what he deserved in 1833. Responsibility for the fire was never established but the local magistrate, Henry Antill, implied that Buckland was punished for being 'a very severe master'. Antill added that he 'had occasion more than once to reprimand him for striking and kicking his men'. Moreover, Buckland had brought eleven men before the bench in only three months which suggests that he depended more on punishment than persuasion.[44] Masters in extremely isolated areas relied on their ability to manage their convicts without immediate recourse to the police or the bench. That so many were successful in establishing productive working relationships without threats or punishment says a great deal about the masters as well as their convicts. Although the Swing protests of southern England were one manifestation of the ending of the old moral economy, the system of convict assignment owed a great deal to its assumptions. Convicts expected their masters to behave as masters should.[45] Rank could bestow a certain authority which a lower-class master did not automatically possess, but obedience was more successfully obtained by a scrupulous attention to the responsibilities and duties of a master. Deference and respect had to be earned, they could not be instilled by the lash.

Abraham Knight's master, Francis Flanagan, farmed about 170 miles south from Sydney, some distance from the nearest bench at Goulburn. Although he described himself as a merchant, before he took up his free grant at Broulee he worked as a tailor in Sydney. His property was extremely isolated and the first in the area.[46] When he brought convicts before the Goulburn bench for 'insubordination and mutiny', an investigation of his management resulted in five convicts being withdrawn from his service. When Flanagan appealed, the Colonial Secretary upheld the decision blaming the 'general Management of his establishment' for the 'great insubordination and outrage among his men'. Flanagan was also refused any more assigned convicts and threatened with losing the remainder on his farm unless he made 'an immediate and Satisfactory change in the Management of his servants'. Although his defence was that his men had taken advantage of his 'remote situation', he had brought disaster upon himself by giving some of his men barley to brew as an incentive to work harder on building the family house. It appears that Flanagan had no consistent system of rewards because those not included in the bribe broke into the store, consumed the remainder and turned upon those who had been so favoured.[47]

The qualities of individual masters and magistrates quickly became known.[48] Considerable freedom of movement and weekly musters facilitated the free flow of gossip. According to Francis Allman, the police magistrate at Wollongong, the convicts at Henry Osborne's Mount Marshall 'were more dissatisfied than on many other Establishments'. As a consequence, when convicts in road gangs were being re-assigned, Allman had to threaten them to make them go to Osborn. A similar situation arose with John Buckland. A convict, with a 'very good character', preferred to remain in a road party than to be assigned to Buckland.[49] The Swing convicts assigned to these particular masters – John Nash, Abraham Knight, William Carter and Charles Green – kept themselves out of trouble and when they were free to choose, they looked elsewhere for work.

Not all the Swing convicts managed to stay clear of the law. The early compliance of the Wessex protesters was possibly a measure of the demoralisation of these meek and inoffensive men, and perhaps an indication that their masters did not place them under undue scrutiny. It took about twelve months before the first of the Swing men was brought before the bench. Abraham Childs, in an iron gang at Bathurst when he died early in 1833, must have had at least one previous conviction or perhaps he was consistently disobedient. John Legg, also before the bench in 1833, received fifty lashes for 'gross insolence' but thereafter avoided trouble. Henry Eldridge, however, maintained defiance, or even rage, being found guilty of neglect of duty, violent language and absconding. Punished on five occasions, including time in an iron gang, the refusal of his application to marry probably increased his frustration and sense of grievance.[50] Joseph Arney was punished at petty sessions on three occasions for insolence, neglect of duty and repeated absconding. For the third offence he spent twelve months in an iron gang. When free, he was almost immediately transported for life to Norfolk Island for cattle stealing in 1836. A place of secondary punishment, it was the last resort before execution. Not only did he gain a remission, but in 1844, found guilty of robbing a dray, he survived a second term there as well.[51]

Less than ten per cent of all convicts in this period, however, were sentenced to Norfolk Island or a period in an iron gang.[52] In 1833 George Shergold received fifty lashes for absconding. He then avoided trouble for several years until he was sentenced to a hundred lashes for 'neglect of duty', an offence usually involving stock. The Macarthurs returned him to the government. Within a month he was sentenced to six months in an iron gang for 'repeatedly absconding'.[53] James Cook, found guilty of stealing from his master, was punished severely and sent to an iron gang. Although Cook described the episode as a 'misunderstanding...concerning a bullock', it was a breach of trust which colonial magistrates always punished severely.[54] After this incident, Cook made no further appearance in court. Alfred Darling was also sent to an iron gang for 'assault with the intent to commit a rape'. Darling's master, Thomas Inglis, must have entertained doubts about the conviction for Darling was re-assigned to him at the completion of his sentence. Masters often requested that a convict be returned to them after punishment. The difficulty of getting a replacement was an obvious incentive, and masters generally preferred to keep a skilled worker or a convict whose offences were relatively minor.

Isaac Manns, Isaac Cole and George Shergold were all multiple offenders, punished by flogging before they were sent to an iron gang. Cole and Manns did not offend again after they returned to assignment, though Manns received two further floggings while in the iron gang. Within a short time of his second offence, however, he had become an assistant overseer, prosecuting others in the gang before the bench. Whoever appointed him obviously knew a thing or two. Manns finished his sentence without re-offending. Although he had a record of colonial offences he received an absolute pardon in 1836. John Jennings, reprieved from death in England because the Special Commission concluded that he had been led astray, got himself into trouble in the colony by again being a follower. He and another convict, later identified as the ringleader, left Suttor's farm with passes. Returning with spirits, they distributed the alcohol to other convicts. Both received fifty lashes but Suttor took Jennings back. When the pardons were being processed, he was another to slip through the bureaucratic net. Although his colonial conviction should have disqualified him, he received a pardon nonetheless.[55]

After 1832 arbitrary punishments were almost unheard of in the New South Wales convict system as the power of the magistrates was systematically curtailed. Shortly after his arrival, Bourke had introduced a stricter attention to the rights of convicts and the rule of law in his Summary Jurisdiction Act.[56] It defined the maximum punishment for offences and in some instances laid down the precise penalty. Its main provisions limited a magistrate sitting alone to a maximum punishment of fifty lashes. Two magistrates were required for the sentencing of a convict to an iron gang. Only Quarter Sessions could consign a convict to a place of secondary punishment while the death penalty was reserved for the Supreme Court. Local justices and a steadily increasing number of stipendiary magistrates were appointed to supervise the punishment and treatment of convicts in their area. All punishments, including floggings carried out with a standard lash, were recorded in monthly returns from the benches. The annual average strokes for each convict flogged between 1832 and 1837 was less than the maximum of fifty permitted under Bourke's Act.[57] Masters, even if they were magistrates, did not have 'the power of personally inflicting [corporal] punishment' or of consigning a convict to a road and iron gang'.[58] Convicts had more protection under the law than apprentices or British soldiers and sailors of the lower ranks.[59] Early in Bourke's governorship he clearly demonstrated the tenor of his administration by reversing a number of illegal sentences and by severely censuring three Hunter River magistrates.[60] In 1836 he took the almost unprecedented step of not renewing the commissions of five Justices of the Peace 'who were neither useful or ornamental to the magistracy'.[61]

Corporal punishment and places of secondary punishment have loomed disproportionately large in many discussions of convict discipline in New South Wales but most convicts avoided both. On a conservative analysis it would seem that, making allowance for those punished more than once, fewer than one in ten convicts in the colony could have endured the lash.[62] There is no denying the brutality of flogging and the institutional terror of Norfolk Island but the majority of convicts did not endure these punishments, and for those so punished it did not necessarily mean the end of the line. It is a measure of the differences between the convict systems of New South Wales and Van Diemen's Land that over half the Swing protesters transported to the latter were punished for assorted offences but only 9 per cent of the Wessex men in New South Wales. Given that the Swing protesters were comparable groups transported for the same offences and at the same time, the contrast is stark. It underlines the more penal, oppressive nature of Governor Arthur's regime and the closer scrutiny to which convicts were subject on the island compared with the freer environment and beneficial effects of the assignment system in New South Wales. Taken altogether, as convicts the Wessex men remained an essentially respectable 'set of...harmless inoffensive men', they were not brutalised or criminalised by the convict system.[63] The positive aspects of convict discipline have been much neglected by those wishing to present the darkest possible picture of convict society.[64] As we have already seen, convicts in assignment who obeyed instructions and worked conscientiously enjoyed a degree of personal freedom wholly at odds with the popular notion of tyrannical exploitation. The Swing men were, within limits, 'free' to reconstruct their lives; above all they could marry.

Without exception, masters supported applications to wed by giving their men a good character and by agreeing to support their wives. Of course, masters benefited from having a contented convict and gaining the labour of his wife, but the possibility of retaining the couple as free workers after sentence was no doubt significant. The Swing men who wished to have their wives and families brought to Australia had the active support of their masters. After only eighteen months, Robert Lambert of Bathurst presented a very persuasive case on behalf of his assigned convict, Henry Shergold. Pointing out that Shergold had 'conducted himself in such a Manner as induces me to grant his request...to have his wife...join him', Lambert was prepared to employ the whole family and cover their expenses on arrival and for their journey to Bathurst.[65] We can appreciate the anguish of George Carter which prompted him to seek a family reunion. He had received a letter from his wife who was 'employed in breaking stones on the road' informing him that his family was 'dispersed'. When Carter's initial application was unsuccessful, his master, Henry Donnison of

Brisbane Water, took up the cause. Assuming that Carter probably would be assigned to his wife, Donnison admitted that his 'apparent interest' did not lie in his forwarding the application, but moved by compassion he did so nonetheless.[66]

When the news spread that pardons were being issued for the Wessex men, some masters began proceedings on behalf of their convicts. Francis Little of Invermein recommended Robert Baker, describing him as 'one of the best behaved men on my establishment'.[67] Charles Cowper, who learned about the pardons from English newspapers, added his support to William Sims' petition. As Cowper eloquently put it, Sims 'now advanced in years could not receive a greater boon…and has also hopes of again meeting an aged Wife'.[68] Although the state refused to provide passages, Sims returned to England and was re-united with his wife, dying aged 88 in 1862.[69] Most of the Wessex men learned of pardons by other means. John Horton, once isolated in the County of Argyle but subsequently at Liverpool, noted 'several of my Shipmates and accomplices names published in the Government Gazette', but not his own.[70] Distance and isolation did not prevent James Cook, 'a long way in the Interior of this colony', from learning about the pardons.[71] Isaac Cole, having been 'informed by several people that my liberty had been advertised', petitioned for a pardon but was ineligible because of his colonial offences. Rather than give up hope, he stayed out of trouble and redeemed himself two years later, gaining his pardon by assisting in the capture of a bushranger.[72]

The most attainable incentive for male convicts, as opportunities for apprehending bushrangers and other heroics were obviously limited, was a ticket-of-leave. Although convicts were technically still under sentence and could be returned to servitude, a ticket enabled them to work for themselves, though they were not supposed to own property. To be eligible a convict had to spend a specified portion of their sentence in servitude. The minimum period was four years in a seven-year sentence. Almost a quarter of the Swing protesters had the minimum sentence of seven years. Of these, slightly more than 80 per cent had their ticket by 1837. The first, Cornelius Bennett, received his just over five years after his conviction and fourteen of his fellow protesters followed in the same year. Of the seven-year men with tickets, Joseph Tuck spent the longest time in servitude before he got his ticket in early 1838. The minimum period of six years in a fourteen year sentence was not strictly observed. A ticket was issued to Charles Milson as early as 1835 while William Carter had his by January 1836, but most in this group waited until 1837 and 1838. After that the matter of tickets-of-leave for the fourteen-year men and the lifers becomes complicated because the British government began issuing absolute and conditional pardons in 1836.

The ticket-of-leave scheme generally met with approval, though with minor reservations. The Molesworth Committee, comprised of men resolutely opposed to transportation, acknowledged the positive effects of the ticket but identified some 'abuses' in granting them.[73] Although Edward Parry, of the Australian Agricultural Company, considered that the behaviour of ticket-of-leave holders 'was certainly not good by any means', he added the qualification that it was 'difficult…to pass a judgement on the whole body of such men'. Furthermore, he still regarded the ticket as an 'excellent regulation in respect of inducing [a] return to honesty and industry'. James Macarthur believed that ticket-of-leave holders were 'generally a better conducted class than those who have completed their sentence'.[74]

In obtaining tickets-of-leave the Wessex convicts fared exceptionally well. More than 80 per cent of those with seven-year sentences gained a ticket. Their success rate was four times that of all convicts in the colony between 1825 and 1836, a statistic which is a measure of their respectability and law-abiding character. Some convicts found the greater freedoms of the ticket difficult to handle. It was very much like a parole, but after some years of dependence, having tasks allotted to them and shelter, food and clothes supplied, they were thrown on their own resources. Those unable to cope usually looked to the state for relief and the voluntary surrender of a ticket-of-leave and return to assignment was not unknown.[75] A ticket restricted the holder to a particular area where, as men still under sentence, they were required to attend the weekly muster. Failure to comply or any colonial offence could result in the loss of ticket, as James Baker and Henry Elkins learned at the cost of their independence.[76]

Altogether, 126 of the 138 Wessex men (slightly more than 80 per cent) gained tickets-of-leave and pardons.[77] Home Office bungling in the administration of pardons produced a number of anomalies. Joseph Mason received an absolute pardon but that of his brother Robert was only conditional. Instead of returning to England with Joseph, as Robert had intended, he was trapped in a different sort of prison. As the petitions relating to the pardons reveal, the inconsistencies and omissions generated considerable anguish. The local administration had its problems too. Although Governor Gipps granted conditional pardons to all those still in servitude who had unblemished colonial records, some of those who arrived on ships other than the *Eleanor* were forgotten. The two Jacob Wiltshires who came on the *Captain Cook* and the *Planter* petitioned but without success. Job Hatherell of the *Portland* also initially missed out on a pardon. It was not until 1848 that he received a conditional pardon giving him full freedom of movement in the colony. These delays in gaining freedom must have been extremely galling to those with a clean sheet who were overlooked. The local administration, however, conscious of some of the injustices, took the initiative in freeing three men whose pardons had gone missing – Robert Page, William Carter and John Aldridge.

Transportation to New South Wales was abolished in 1840 and, according to the official record, assignment in 1841.[78] It is not altogether clear whether the management of convicts completely reverted to the state with convicts labouring on public works. In 1840 there were almost 61,000 convicts in the colony with more than

22,000 assigned.[79] Those still under sentence at this time have become the forgotten convicts. As colonial society quickly turned its back on the past, convicts disappeared from collective public consciousness. Four Wessex men were still in servitude after 1840. Joseph Arney did not remain on Norfolk Island for the rest of his life but gained a ticket for Goulburn in 1847. James Cook got his in 1841; Henry Eldridge received his for Muswellbrook in 1844. Alfred Darling, the last *Eleanor* man to be pardoned, obtained his freedom in 1845.

It has generally been assumed that assignment was a lottery which often operated inhumanely and erratically to the disadvantage of the convict. We have investigated one particular group and drawn upon their experience of servitude to present a more positive view of assignment and the convict system in general. Much depended, of course, on the attitude and managerial skills of the masters but a comprehensive study of the all the masters of the *Eleanor's* convicts is far beyond the scope of this book. It was in the masters' interests to have a compliant, willing workforce. Their economic success depended upon it and compliance benefited the convicts as well. The relationship between master and man was symbiotic; it was a relationship the rural workers from Wessex well understood.

In material terms, convicts in New South Wales were as well off as most labouring people in Britain. Contemporaries generally endorsed the evidence of Sir Edward Parry to the Molesworth Committee that the 'condition of the convict, as regarded clothing, lodging and feeding; was in many respects very superior to the condition of the lower classes of the agricultural population in this country'.[80] That was cold comfort, however, to the Swing men and their families in England. Although the Swing protesters were not transported to Robert Hughes' *gulag* but to an open prison, and although assignment was far more humane than the prison system of the new penology, the fact of transportation was the most distressing part of their experience. We should not overlook the anguish of that separation.

> For 65 years one woman slept wakefully at nights and moved softly by day listening for footsteps...In 1831 her husband and brother had been transported...she hoped through each hour; and she died in her chair turned towards the East; because she had heard that it was out of the sunrise that travellers from Australia must come.[81]

## Notes

1 Parliamentary Papers, Hay to Phillips, 25 June 1833, Report, Appendix 1, *Select Committee of the House of Commons into Transportation*, 2 vols, ordered to be printed, 1838 (hereafter Molesworth Committee), 25 June, 1833, Appendix 14, Vol. I, pp. 70-71.

2 Bourke's Minute of Instruction, June 1831, Colonial Office 202/37. See L. G.

Young, 'New South Wales under the Administration of Governor Bourke, 1831-1837', M.A., University of Sydney, Sydney, 1951, p. 62.

3   *Sydney Herald*, 8 December 1833.

4   For the details of Macleay's career, see 'Alexander Macleay' in D. Pike (gen. ed.) *Australian Dictionary of Biography, 1788-1850*, 2 vols, Vol. 2, Melbourne, 1966, pp. 177-180.

5   These figures have been calculated from A. G. L. Shaw, *Convicts and the Colonies: A Study of Penal Transportation from Great Britain and Ireland to Australia and other parts of the British Empire*, London, 1966, pp. 363-367. We have used the number of convicts landed in the colony, a figure which is lower than the number sent.

6   S. G. Foster, 'Convict Assignment in New South Wales in the 1830s', *The Push from the Bush: A Bulletin of Social History* (hereafter *The Push*). 15, April 1983, p. 75.

7   For a fairly unsympathetic view of Bigge, see J. M. Bennett, 'John Thomas Bigge' in Pike, op. cit., Vol. 1, pp. 99-101.

8   For the details of the proposals and a more sympathetic assessment, see J. Ritchie, *Punishment and Profit: The Reports of Commissioner John Bigge on the Colonies of New South Wales and Van Diemen's Land, 1822-1823; their origins, nature and significance*, Melbourne, 1970, pp. 222-223.

9   See J. B. Hirst, *Convict Society and its enemies, A history of early New South Wales*, Sydney, 1983, pp. 9-27.

10   Colonial Secretary to John Atkinson, 2 September 1832, Col. Sec. Out Letters, 32/7158, Archives Of New South Wales (hereafter AONSW), 4/3536, Reel 2281, and J. Chambers, *Rebels of the Fields; Robert Mason and the Convicts of the Eleanor*, Letchworth, 1995, pp. 122, 210- 11.

11   Some of these details come from notations on the indent of the *Eleanor*. Apparently not all deaths of convicts under sentence were recorded in the usual way. Some of these deaths were in Births Deaths and Marriages (hereafter BDM), AONSW. Others come from the Convict Death Register, 1828 to 1879, AONSW 4/4549, COD 16. G. Rudé, ''Captain Swing' in New South Wales', *Historical Studies, Australia and New Zealand*, Vol. 11, No. 44, April 1965, p. 475, has Robert Cook incorrectly identified as Albert.

12   A. Atkinson, 'The Pioneers who left Early', *The Push*, No. 29, 1991, pp. 110-115, and Shaw, op. cit., p. 142.

13   It is unlikely that William Francis accompanied Thomas Mitchell, the Surveyor General, to England in 1837 as Francis married in Sydney on 15 February 1838 having applied for permission in January. BDM, 1838, 294, 90 and Applications for the Publication of Banns, Hyde Park, AONSW 4/2391, Reel 734. E.J. Hobsbawm and G. Rudé, *Captain Swing*, London, 1969, p. 275.

14  D. Kent and N. Townsend (eds), *Joseph Mason, Assigned Convict 1831-1837: Doomed to the earth's remotest region*, Melbourne, 1996, p. 29.

15  Chambers, op. cit., p., 272.

16  For the details and names of the pardons, see Colonial Secretary, Special Bundle, Machine Breakers, AONSW, COD 513. For the English details in relation to these men, see Chambers, op. cit., pp. 149, 252 and 222.

17  R. Mason to his daughter, Lydia, Brookfield, 1864, and to his daughter and others, Wokingham, 16 August 1865, Mason Family, Letters, 1857-1865, Mitchell Library (hereafter ML), MSS 2290, Reel 339.

18  Government Notice, 25 February 1830, *New South Wales Government Gazette*. The applications are to be found in Petitions re Convict Families, 1832-1855, AONSW 4/2188, 4/4492 and4/2550, Reels 699 and 700. Some applications from masters of behalf of their convicts appear in the general Colonial Secretary series. For example, Robert Lambert applied on behalf of Henry Shergold for Shergold's wife and family to come to New South Wales 'at the expense of the Crown'. Colonial Secretary to Robert Lambert, 4 September 1832, Sydney, Col. Sec. Copies of Letters Sent to Individuals and Organisations, 1831-1832, 32/6541, AONSW 4/3536, Reel 291.

19  For the colonial applications, see Petitions re Convict Families, 1832 to 1855, AONSW 4/2188, Reel 699 and 4/2550, Reel 700.

20  John Burroughs was assigned to William Panton, Camden, who applied on his behalf in 1834. The Colonial Secretary rejected the application because Burroughs was not 'eligible for indulgence before July '36'. Col. Sec. In Letters, Petitions, AONSW 4/2247, Reel 2199.

21  J. B. Montefiore on behalf of Laban Stone, 16 October 1832, Copies of Letters Sent to Individuals and Organisations, 32/6648, AONSW 4/3536, Reel 2291.

22  George Radborn was baptised on 17 October 1837 at White Rock near Bathurst, BDM, 1837, 1074, 21. Samuel, born 12 December 1839, Cumberland Street, Sydney, BDM, 1840, 229, 61.

23  Chambers, op. cit., pp. 109-110.

24  Harriet Down, Elizabeth Lewis and Fanny, wife of Henry Shergold, petitioned but failed to join their husbands in the colony. See Chambers, op. cit., p. 95. For the Pointers and Radburns, see, also, pp. 241-47.

25  A. Harris, *Settlers and Convicts, Recollections of Sixteen Year's Labour in the Australian Backwoods*, Melbourne, 1964 [1847], pp. 68 and 184.

26  James Macarthur, 1837, quoted by A. Atkinson, *Camden: Farm and Village Life in Early New South Wales*, Melbourne, 1988, p. 25.

27  Kent and Townsend, op. cit., pp. 42-44. Our emphasis.

28  Weekly rations were to be 12 lbs of wheat or 9lbs of seconds flour or 3.5 lbs of maize meal, or 9lbs of wheat or 7 lbs of seconds and 7lbs of beef or mutton, or

4.5 lbs of salt pork and 2 ozs salt, 2 ozs soap. Any additions to these were 'indulgences'. The clothing entitlement per year was 2 frocks or jackets, 3 shirts, 2 pairs of trousers, 3 pairs of shoes, 1 hat or cap and at least one good wool blanket and 1 wool mattress. Assigned Servants, Circular No 31/18, 29 June 1831, Molesworth Committee, Vol. II, Appendix C, No. 41, p. 236.

29 Kent and Townsend, op. cit., pp. 49, 95-96.

30 Joseph Hawdon to his mother, 6 March 1832, Letters 1831 to 1833, ML A1329.

31 Hirst, op. cit., pp.101-103. For example, Thomas Ryan, a hired servant, free by servitude, was brought before the Bathurst Bench for neglect of duty, losing 55 lambs, a loss he could not explain, and also for absconding. Found guilty, he was sentenced to four months at the Bathurst Gaol and forfeited his wages for the year of £ 18 per annum. 24 June 1836, AONSW 2/8325, Reel 595.

32 James Macarthur, Evidence, Molesworth Committee, Vol. I, p. 163, and Alexander Berry, Reminiscences, p. 180, Berry Papers, Vol. 1, ML Uncat. MSS, 315.

33 Kent and Townsend, op. cit., pp. 46-47.

34 Ibid., pp. 57-58.

35 A. Atkinson, 'Four Patterns of Convict Protest', *Labour History*, No 37, November 1979, p. 33.

36 Bourke to Glenelg, 4 December 1837, Molesworth Committee, Vol. 2, Appendix C, No. 4, p. 233.

37 Patrick Leslie to Walter Davidson, 'Davidson's Account', p. 13, ML MSS A2958.

38 A. Atkinson, 'Master and Servant at Camden Park', *The Push*, No. 6, May 1980, pp. 48-49.

39 James Macarthur, Evidence, 23 May 1837, Molesworth Committee, Vol. 1, p. 199.

40 Colonial Secretary Letters received re Land, 1826-1860, Robert Rodd, AONSW 2/7961, Reel 1117, G. T. Graham, AONSW 2/7868, Reel 1133 and C. L Browne, AONSW 2/7813. Reel 1103.

41 The 1828 Census lists Macarthur as having 24,500 acres but this included 15,000 which were not freehold.

42 Petition, 4 February 1837, Col. Sec. In Letters, 37/1325, AONSW 4/2371. and 16 January 1839, Muswellbrook Bench Book, AONSW 4/5601, Reel 671. For a listing of his workers see, the Cross Reference Index under Rodd, 1828 Census and the index of the 1837 Muster.

43 For a discussion of these see Atkinson, 'Four Patterns', pp. 28-51.

44 Principal Superintendent of Convicts to Colonial Secretary 29 July 1833, 33/4874, AONSW 4/2196, Reel 2198, Enclosure, Henry Antill, Stonequarry

to Principal Superintendent of Convict, Superintendent of Convicts, 33/2628, AONSW 4/2194.1, Reel 2196.

45   Atkinson, 'Four Patterns', p. 55.

46   W. A. Bayley, *Behind Broulee: A History of the Central South Coast of New South Wales*, Moruya, 1964, p. 8.

47   Goulburn Bench to Colonial Secretary, 25 July 1833, T. C. Harington to the Land Board, 31 August 1833 and Francis Flanagan to the Colonial Secretary, 27 September, Shannon View, St Vincent, 33/6687 and enclosures, Col. Sec. In Letters, Miscellaneous, AONSW 4/2195.1

48   See Atkinson, 'Four Patterns', pp. 65-69.

49   F. Allman to Colonial Secretary, 1 February 1834, Wollongong, 34/918, Col. Sec. In Letters, AONSW4/2254.3. John Buckland to the Colonial Secretary, Col. Sec. In Letters. 33/5086, AONSW 4/2194.1. Reel 2196.

50   Principal Superintendent's Office, 20 July 1838, AONSW 38/331, Special Bundle, COD 513.

51   The record of punishments at petty sessions is incomplete because of the partial survival of the bench books recording the details. Machine Breakers transported to New South Wales by the ship Eleanor in 1831. Names of the Prisoners who have not been pardoned in consequence of their colonial offences, Colonial Secretary, Special Bundle, Machine Breakers and Principal Superintendent's Office, 18 May 1837, AONSW COD 513. L. Vincent, *Picton Bench Books*, Vol. 2, 1833-1839. Circuit Court, Berrima, 26 March 1844, AONSW 5/3015, Reel 2758.

52   Shaw, op. cit., p. 216.

53   Principal Superintendent of Convicts to the Colonial Secretary, 18 May 1837, Special Bundle, AONSW COD 315.

54   James Cook, Petition, 40/5023, Col. Sec. In Letters, AONSW4/2513, Reel 2245.

55   Bathurst Bench, 29 February 1836, AONSW 2/8325, Reel 595.

56   For the full details of this act, see Bourke to Goderich, 30 October 1832, *Historical Records of Australia, (hereafter HRA)* Series I, Vol. XVI, p. 781.

57   Enclosure, Gipps to Glenelg, 8 November 1838, ibid., Vol. XIX, p. 654.

58   Bourke to Stanley, 15 January 1834, ibid., Vol. XVLL, p. 322

59   Hirst, op. cit., p. 58.

60   Governor's Minutes, 11 June 1832, Despatches from the Governor of New South Wales,1832-1835, ML A1267-13, Colonial Secretary's Office to John Bingle, 28 May 1832, Bingle Papers, 1829-1837, ML A1825 and Bourke to Goderich, 24 August 1832, *HRA*, Series I, Vol. XVI, p. 722.

61   Bourke to his Son, 17 January 1836, Bourke Papers, Vol. VI, ML A1733; Bourke to Glenelg, 28 February 1836, *HRA*, Series1, Vol. IX, p. 325.

62   The flogging returns for the 1830s record the number of punishments as well as the number of lashes and the annual number of convicts in the colony. Allowance has been made for multiple punishments. See Enclosure, Gipps to Glenelg, 8 November 1838, ibid., Series 1, Vol. XIX, p. 654.

63   Robert Mason to his mother, 27 July 1831. A. M. Colson, 'The Revolt of the Hampshire Agricultural Labourers and its Causes, 1812-1831', M.A., University of London, 1937, p. 287.

64   This is not the place to get involved in the debate between John Hirst and David Neal over the very complex question of the extent of freedom in New South Wales. Our position on the nature of convict society is clear from our discussion. See D. Neal, 'Free society, penal colony, slave society, prison?', and J. Hirst, 'None of the above: a reply', *Historical Studies*, Vol. 22, October 1987, No. 89, pp. 497-524. It is probably more useful to talk about freedoms and to identify the diverse understandings of individuals 'of their place in relation to authority in the colony'. See, in particular, P. J. Byrne, ''The public Good': Competing Visions of Freedom in Early Colonial New South Wales', *Labour History* No. 58, May 1990, pp. 76-83.

65   Robert Lambert to Colonial Secretary, 30 August 1832, Col. Sec. In Letters, 32/6541, AONSW 4/360, Reel 2649.

66   Henry Donison, 20 November 1835, Col. Sec. In Letters, 35/9319, AONSW 4/2282.4

67   Francis Little to the Colonial Secretary, 12 May 1837, Prisoners 1, 1840, Col. Sec. In Letters, Convicts 2, 1837, AONSW 4/2352.

68   Enclosure, William Sims' Petition, Col. Sec. In Letter 37/1760, AONSW 4/2375.2.

69   N. Fox, *Berkshire to Botany Bay: The 1830 Labourers' Revolt in Berkshire. Its Causes and Consequences*, Newbury, 1996, pp. 148-149.

70   Prisoners 1, 1837, Petition, Col. Sec. In Letters, 37/8275, AONSW 4/2376.

71   James Cook to Colonial Secretary, Petition, Col. Sec. In Letters, 40/5023, AONSW 4/3670, Reel 2649.

72   Isaac Cole to Colonial Secretary, 25 June 1838, Col. Sec. In Letters, 38/6583, AONSW 4/1120.4

73   Molesworth Committee Report, Vol. 2, Shaw, op. cit., p.231.

74   Sir Edward Parry, Evidence, Molesworth Committee, 26 February 1838, pp. 67-8, James Macarthur, 26 May 1837, pp.217-18.

75   See, for example, Alexander Reid, Petition, 32/3947, Col. Sec. In Letters, AONSW 4/2145. A blacksmith he found it 'impossible to obtain sufficient employment to maintain himself and His wife'.

76   James Baker, ticket of leave, 39/1120, lost and recovered in 1840/1412. Henry Elkins received his ticket for Windsor in July 1835. It was rendered void in

1837/925 but in 1837 he became free by servitude.

77   Our figures differ slightly from those of Rudé. Altogether we identified 104 with pardons. Of these, twenty-two had also received tickets of leave. The total number of tickets of leave was twenty-nine. For Rudé's figures, 'Captain Swing in New South Wales', *Historical Studies*, 7, 1965., p. 477. We have not included those in the list of pardons whom the local authorities identified as having colonial sentences.

78   Shaw, op. cit., pp.288-289.

79   S. G. Foster, 'Convict Assignment in New South Wales in the 1830s,' *The Push*, No. 15, April 1983, p. 75.

80   Sir Edward Parry, Evidence, 2 February 1838, Molesworth Committee, Vol. 2. p. 67.

81   E. P. Thompson, 'Foreword' in R. Palmer (ed) *The Painful Plough: a portrait of the agricultural labourer in the nineteenth century from folk songs and ballads and contemporary accounts*, Cambridge, 1973, p. 5.

# Chapter 9

# 'IT SEEMS SO HARD NEVER TO SEE YOU
# BUT YOU HAVE NEVER BEEN FORGOTTEN':[1]
# COLONIAL MARRIAGE

When Louisa Batten wrote from England in April 1868 to her uncle, John Batten of the *Eleanor*, telling him he had 'never been forgotten', he had been dead for some months. For more than thirty years the Batten family had defied the tyranny of distance and maintained contact with John as he served his sentence and reconstructed his life in a very different land. Central to that life was a long relationship with, and eventual marriage to, another convict, Honorah McCarthy. For many convicts, intimate relationships gave new purpose to traumatically disrupted lives. Marriage, as the only officially acknowledged form of relationship, was also important as an instrument of convict discipline. Although we have a major study of a group of female convicts for whom marriage was an important and defining part of their lives, there is no equivalent work on male convicts.[2] The men of the *Eleanor* present an opportunity to redress the balance and we can gain some insights into their reconstructed lives through the bureaucratic processes involved in marriage and through the women they married.

The options for male convicts under sentence and when free were significantly more limited than those of women. The convict system was created by men for men. It did not cope with female convicts particularly well and administrative difficulties became their window of opportunity. To put a gloss upon Marian Quartly's clever phrase, women were able to bend the bars both of their prison and circumstances.[3] Female convicts under sentence could usually marry without difficulty unless they had declared themselves married upon arrival in the colony. It was almost impossible, however, for male convicts to use marriage as an escape from servitude.[4] As a result of the gender imbalance in the colony, three-quarters were destined to remain unmarried and they have left few traces of their lives in the civil records, except, perhaps, in the record of their death. But those who married entered the historical record and the marriage registers are a scandalously underused resource for exploring the way convicts reconstructed their lives in the colony.

The penal nature of the colony, its inherent legal ambiguities and its position vis-à-vis English law complicated colonial marriage. It was not until 1828 that an English marriage act applied, at least in principle, to New South Wales, although most legal opinion rejected its applicability to the colony. In any case, if the legal validity of any marriage in New South Wales had been subject to challenge, 'the relevant law...would have been that then deemed to be the Common Law of England'.[5] Hardwicke's Marriage Act of 1753, a measure to prevent clandestine marriages, laid down the procedures for marriage but specifically restricted its operation to England.[6] As a consequence of this Act, English civil law took precedence over church law. The colonial administration regulated marriage according to Hardwicke's Act and the subsequent acts of 1822 and 1823, all of which were explicitly restricted to England.[7]

In New South Wales marriage was a matter of policy and expediency. From the earliest days of settlement, the governors encouraged convicts, especially women, to marry. The marriage of any convict in servitude directly involved the state even if one of the spouses was free. The clergy, in addition to their role as pastors of their flocks, became agents of the state in organising and managing the formal procedures involved in seeking permission to marry. The master of an assigned convict was directly concerned also because the marriage could only proceed if he or she agreed to support the couple.[8] The crucial factor in convict marriage was the record of the marital status in the indent. The colonial administration, acting on the information in its records, determined whether or not a couple were eligible to marry.[9]

Almost 40 per cent of the married Swing transportees took another wife in New South Wales. Some remarried in the colony after the death of their English wife but others went ahead regardless. Charles Milson, Aaron Stone, Robert Baker and Daniel Sims, all married in England, claimed to be bachelors in the registration of their marriage in New South Wales. As free men at the time of their colonial marriages, they did not require the governor's permission.[10] By claiming to be bachelors they were, it seems, intent upon deception. Other Wessex men with English wives, Job Hatherell, Levi Brown, Henry Bunce, Charles Green, Gifford North and Charles Coombs, identified themselves as widowers for their colonial marriages. Some who had married in England may have believed that their transportation, as a de facto death, freed them to marry in the colony. This belief had currency in popular culture in Britain. In Wiltshire, Ann, the wife of Gifford North, described herself as a widow to the 1851 census collectors although her husband was still alive and when he married another woman he described himself as a widower.[11]

As a response to the social problems arising from the expansion of the Empire, the British Parliament passed a series of acts dealing with bigamy, the ending of a marriage and remarriage under certain conditions. The first as early as 1603 allowed for remarriage after a period of absence of seven years if one of the partners did not know the 'other to be living within that Time'. Other acts followed, one in 1795 'for rendering more effectual' the act of 1603 and another in 1822, enabling men and women to remarry, provided they signed an affidavit to the effect that their spouse had died. An act in 1828 gave even greater leeway. It allowed for a remarriage if one spouse were 'continually absent...for the Space of Seven Years...and shall not have been known...to be living within that Time'.[12] Under the terms of this statute, the majority of convicts married in Britain were free to remarry in the colony after seven years.

The clergy in New South Wales, whose power and authority in relation to marriage had been seriously compromised, were uneasy about the state's role in, and attitude to, convict marriage. Seeking to clarify the position, the Reverend Samuel Marsden wrote to Elizabeth Fry in the early 1830s asking her to obtain legal advice relating to remarriage in the colony. The response from the Under Secretary of State was unambiguously direct. He suggested that 'the best plan to adopt is not to have any account taken of whether the women are married or not' and he confirmed that 'it is a law...that any woman who has not heard of her husband for seven years may marry again'.[13] In that same year, the Reverend John Keane of Bathurst, for both moral and compassionate reasons, raised the whole issue with the Colonial Secretary after a number of applications for permission to marry had been refused.[14] Asked for a legal opinion, the Attorney General, John Kinchela, responded by indicating that there was some foundation for the belief that people could remarry after seven years under certain circumstances, but he ruled out sworn affidavits because they were 'seldom entitled to belief' in the colony. Aware of the peculiar difficulties for convicts, Kinchela suggested the 'passing of a colonial act before suggested rendering transportation a civil death as concerns marriage'. The Colonial Secretary saw 'no necessity for publishing this opinion'. His usual strategy was to deal with such cases on an ad hoc basis to avoid establishing any precedents, or to prevaricate and ignore the issue as far as possible.[15]

The governors, largely on moral grounds, encouraged formal marriages solemnised by the Church of England but also accepted those of other denominations. This apparent liberality was a practical response to the significant numbers of Irish Catholics in the colony. In 1820 Macquarie sanctioned Catholic marriage between co-religionists though all such marriages in the colony would have been valid under English common law. The fact that the Executive Council subsequently decided that consistent 'with the practice in England...it does not appear to be expedient at present to enforce the injunction of Governor Macquarie' underlines the arbitrary nature of executive power in the colony. At times it was convenient for the state to accept English practice, at others to reject it. The first statutory provision for marriage in the colony occurred only in 1834 when the local legislature recognised Presbyterian and Catholic unions and made that recognition retrospective. The measure was extended to Wesleyan marriages in 1839 and to those of the Baptist and Congregational denominations in 1840.[16]

By the time the Swing men arrived in New South Wales, convict marriages were arranged according to Governor Darling's well-established procedures. It is a measure of his concern about this matter and his bureaucratic mentality that he instituted changes within months of his arrival.[17] As a result, the clergyman calling the banns was responsible for obtaining the requisite details and declarations. When he had gathered all the necessary supporting material, he forwarded the applications to the Colonial Secretary. His office oversaw their processing and returned them to the clergyman who then informed the couple of the decision.[18] This bureaucratic process left some room for manoeuvre on the part of the convict applicants. In the main, however, the state determined the legalities of marriage to suit bureaucratic needs and convict discipline. Although the state promoted morality, its decisions could militate against its moral imperatives by preventing people from marrying. It is clear that clergy were often prepared to turn a blind eye to any 'impediment' to marriage and to take the part of the convict rather than that of the state.[19]

The Swing protesters fared better in the colonial marriage stakes than the generality of male convicts. At least forty-four of the 138 transported to New South Wales contracted a formal marriage, that is about 32 per cent compared to the average for male convicts of about 20 per cent. By 1831, however, the colonial government gave little encouragement to male convicts still under sentence to marry.[20] Altogether twenty men from the *Eleanor* sought the governor's consent. Eight, including three with a ticket-of-leave, applied while still under sentence. Of those eight applicants, six received permission to marry but one of the approved marriages, that of Stephen Hatcher, did not proceed. Two of the successful applicants, Jacob Turner and John Ford, managed to transcend the limitations of their penal status; both married women who had come free to the colony and whose civil status was, therefore, higher than their own.[21]

It was exceptional for a free woman to marry a convict especially one still in servitude and without the advantage of a ticket-of-leave. The authorities discouraged such unions by removing concessions which enabled a man to support his wife. Instead, the woman was required to 'share to some extent her husband's status' in order to serve as a warning to other women who might have contemplated such a marriage.[22] If this warning went unheeded, various accommodations became essential. In most cases the master preferred to keep his assigned convict and gave the necessary assurances to support the wife. When John Ford of the *Eleanor* applied in 1837 for permission to marry Mary Ann Coleman, who had come free, his master, Henry Shadforth, agreed 'to keep both in his service' until John was free or had his ticket of leave. Although Mary Ann was free, she, too, required the consent of her mistress.[23] Governor Bourke had discontinued assignment to a wife in 1833 because the practice had attracted much criticism, although the arrangement had served a useful, humanitarian purpose especially if masters did not co-operate when English wives joined their convict husbands.[24] The instances of free women marrying Swing men in servitude show a bureaucratic flexibility uncommon in the period. During the 1830s official attitudes to mixed unions seem to have hardened, perhaps because such marriages were an administrative nightmare.[25]

When the Swing protesters arrived in New South Wales, almost 53 per cent claimed during their shipboard muster that they were married. As far as the colonial administration was concerned, none of these men could marry, though the state had no means of interdicting any proposed marriage if the intending couple were free. It seems, however, that female convicts may have been more prepared to claim on arrival that they were married even when they were not. Some women may have claimed they were married if they had been in a common-law marriage. Their position was not necessarily a measure of their confusion but a recognition of their understanding of their commitment under common law.[26] Furthermore, it was rumoured among female convicts 'that the maried weman [sic] got their liberty…and the single weman was kept in confinement'.[27] This view reflected a confusion between marital status and the act of marrying in the colony which could advantage women still under sentence.

The main ground for denying consent was that one of the parties had stated on arrival that he or she was married. Levi Brown, who applied in August 1836 for permission to marry Mary Royle, also a convict under sentence, was refused on those grounds. In 1846, as a free man, he made another application. This time his intended was Elizabeth Skinner, a convict with a ticket-of-leave, and the application succeeded. Other Swing men, Henry Bunce, William Legg and Job Hatherell, all of whom were recorded as married in the indent, applied for permission to marry and managed to slip through the bureaucratic net without any trouble. It seems that the clerks of the Principal Superintendent of Convicts did not always check the records fully because 20 per cent of the successful applications involving Swing men should have been refused on the grounds that they had declared themselves married on arrival. As Charles Green discovered, however, there were vigilant clerks. The application of Rose Cunningham, a convict, to marry Green, free by servitude, was refused in 1842 because he had 'stated on arrival he was married…The accompanying letter is considered a fabrication'.[28]

When Rose became free and was not required to seek permission, she married Charles at Appin in 1846. He described himself in the marriage registration as a widower while Rose, a widow, presented herself as a spinster. In this instance, the couple waited four years before marrying. Obviously trying to maximise their chances by avoiding undue official scrutiny, Charles, some months before they married, obtained his certificate of freedom for which he had been eligible since 1837.[29] Similar battles of wits were waged many times by convicts and ex-convicts who often demonstrated great determination to have their way. On Rose's part, it was a considerable sacrifice as she remained in servitude. After all that, she died within two years of the marriage and Green married again in 1851.

Presumably Green's letter, discounted as a 'fabrication', contained a report of the death of his English wife. The Colonial Secretary's office treated these letters with suspicion, quickly eliminating any obvious fabrications such as those with a Sydney postmark. Many with English and Irish postmarks were rejected as well. There was little bureaucratic benefit of the doubt in relation to eligibility to marry. Jane Burroughs, a convict still under sentence, sought the governor's permission to marry Charles Fay, of the *Eleanor*, in 1838. By that time he was free, but permission was refused because he was listed as married in the indent. In his case he quite accurately described himself as a widower in the application for permission to marry.[30] When it was rejected, Fay produced a letter, dated 1833, from his mother-in-law in England informing him that his wife was 'no more in this life' because his failure to write had 'Broke her heart'. Jane Burroughs and Charles Fay married three days after they received the governor's permission, a timing which indicates that the clergyman concerned, as if to assert some control over his own sphere, had begun the reading of the banns before official approval had been given.[31]

In 1839, Daniel Hancock successfully fought the same battle with the full support of a clergyman, the Reverend J. Vincent, and the master to whom he had been assigned. When Hancock's application to marry a convict was rejected, he appealed and produced three letters from his family to prove the death of his English wife. Free by the time of his application, he was able to contact his former master, Robert McKay Campbell, who provided an affidavit to the effect that Hancock had received the letters while assigned to him. Nevertheless, despite the trouble Hancock went to, this marriage did not proceed. Thirteen months later, he married Anne Henley who had come free to the colony with her parents. As the marriage was by licence, for which the couple paid over £4, Daniel must have been doing reasonably well.[32] Some Swing protesters did not marry even though the couple had received permission. George Durman and Sarah Dowling, a convict under sentence, both of the Paterson River in the Hunter Valley, obtained the governor's consent in 1841 but they did not marry. About two years later, Durman and Mary Ayton, also under sentence, sought permission and married at Dungog where they both lived.[33] The successful applications involving a Wessex man were far more likely to result in marriage by comparison with the rate of completion for other colonial applications.

The bureaucratic machine did not always run smoothly and could occasion delays during which ardour may have cooled. Henry Eldridge and Anne Braslin applied for permission to marry when both were still under sentence. Unfortunately, Anne's Irish accent or the recording clerk's inattention at the muster had resulted in her name being recorded as Brisbane. Permission was refused on the grounds that her ship had not carried a convict named Braslin. The Reverend C.P. Wilton appealed on her behalf and although the marriage was finally approved, it did not occur.[34] Neither party subsequently contracted a marriage in New South Wales. About a quarter of the approved applications marriages from Swing protesters did not lead to marriage.

Male convicts and ex-convicts faced enormous difficulties in finding a partner in the colony; generally possessing few skills and little capital they were unattractive as marriage partners.[35] Among most historians that judgment has usually been passed on the female convicts. L.L. Robson in his pioneering work claims that they, 'were not the sort of women to attract men into marriage'. Yet Robson's estimate that 42 per cent of female convicts married in the colony weakens his conclusion. The figure is significantly higher than his estimate for transported men at a mere 8 per cent. Later figures derived from 'adults married, cohabiting, or with children' in 1828 were 58 per cent for women and a mere 14 per cent for men. [36] In assessing the marriage rates for women, we should make allowances for those who were either too old or too young to marry and for those who stated on arrival that they were married. Overall, those women who wanted to marry and were free to do so were in a seller's market.[37]

Most married male convicts probably believed that there was little point in applying for permission to marry while under sentence. The Wessex men, because of their pardons, should have had a good start in the marital stakes. By 1837 more than two-thirds of them were free. Consequently they had some advantages as long as those already married did not wish to marry a convict still under sentence. Although the Swing protesters were reasonably successful in finding wives, it took them on average about sixteen years, almost twice as long as the average for all male convicts in the colony.[38] As unsophisticated countrymen, they may have found female convicts too worldly-wise and intimidating. The women, for their part, may have felt that the Wessex men lacked drive and ambition. Whatever understanding the Swing protesters had of the legal implications of separation from their wives, those with wives in England were more likely to delay marriage in the colony. The married men among them may have clung longer to the hope that they would be re-united with their families. Perhaps they were reluctant to commit themselves to another woman because they saw their English marriage as binding.

At least four of the Swing transportees who married in the colony were in a common-law relationship beforehand. Three married their common-law wife. It has been possible to identify thirteen common-law marriages, about half of which involved men who had wives in Wessex. It is apparent from the high percentage of Swing men who had married in England that they prized legal marriage. In the colony, too, the advantages for married couples had contributed to the development of a culture in which formal marriage was valued. The accumulation of capital, however modest, was another desideratum as far as marriage and inheritance were concerned, but the Swing men generally fared poorly in this respect. The reluctance of parents to identify a common-law relationship points to a considerable change in popular culture since the earliest years of settlement.[39] English wives and children are generally listed on death registrations but not any subsequent colonial liaisons and offspring.

An English marriage seems to have been an impediment for some. Slightly more than half of the Swing protesters in common-law relationships in the colony had married in England. John Aldridge, for example, fathered a child by Ellen Lyons, a currency lass, in 1837. Listed as married in the indent, he stood to lose his ticket if the liaison became known so legal marriage was not an option at that stage. The infant died shortly after birth. The couple had two more children but John and Ellen did not marry until 1848 when, as a free man, John described himself as a bachelor in the marriage registration.[40] The reasons for the delay are not clear but he may have waited until the death of his English wife. In the case of the single Wessex men who cohabited in New South Wales, the main impediment to marriage seems to have been the marital status of their partners some of whom had already married in the colony and lived to regret it.

John Batten, single when transported, fathered children in the 1840s by Honorah (Hanna) McCarthy. By the time of their third child's baptism in 1846, she had become 'Batin formerly McCarthy'. She and John finally married at Penrith in 1852. A servant from Cork, transported in 1831, she married a Thomas Green at Parramatta four years later. Free by 1838, she had a child, registered only under her name, at the Female Factory in 1841. Having left her husband, Thomas Green, but living with another man, she avoided official notice and delayed marriage to John Batten even when legally free. The colonial administration did not keep any systematic records of convict marriages but, in this case, Honorah's marriage to Green was noted on the indent and on her certificate of freedom issued in 1838.[41] She had reason to be wary even though the main concern of officialdom was the marital status of those convicts seeking permission to marry.

The Wessex men, like most convicts, were handicapped by their civil status which restricted their choice of a partner. Almost 60 per cent of those marrying in the colony took a convict or ex-convict wife. The Swing men were least attractive to the native-born. About 30 per cent of the group married women who had come free, usually assisted emigrants or widows whose class, status or children may have diminished their chances of marriage. Nearly half of the Swing protesters' wives were Irish. Just over a third were English and about a quarter were equally divided between the native-born and those from outside Britain. The difficulties the Swing men encountered in finding partners, largely because of their marital status, become strikingly obvious when we look at the average age of the spouses. The women were almost thirty and the men about forty. By comparison, the average age at marriage for all ex-convicts in the 1828 Census was twenty-six for women and thirty-two for men.[42] Almost a quarter of the Wessex men married in their late forties and early fifties. The oldest was George Shergold who wed twenty-seven year old Maria Understat only four years before his death aged sixty-three.[43] The civil structure of the population practically ensured that they would marry a woman who came as a convict. In this period, two-thirds of the women over the age of twelve in New South Wales were or had been convicts. As the national balance between English and Irish female convicts was almost equal, the number of mixed marriages was correspondingly fairly high.[44]

Practicality and pragmatism played a significant role in the determination of female convicts to embrace matrimony as quickly as possible. When assigned, often to do 'all work' in very modest households, they frequently failed to satisfy the mistress of the establishment. Unlike male convicts, they were consistently under very close scrutiny without any buffers between them and their mistress. Male convicts, who were usually answerable to an overseer, commonly had little direct contact with their master. The dynamics of the relationship between the mistress and her household servant were significantly different and were more likely to result in direct conflict between servant and mistress. An additional limitation on female convicts was the fact that they usually worked and slept in the house. Marriage either to a convict or a free man provided some relief. Even if a female convict continued to work as a servant for her master or her husband, she had her own household. Once a female convict married, it was important for her to stay married while still under sentence. If her husband died, she returned to the convict system for re-assignment unless she held a ticket-of-leave. In such circumstances marriage became a very practical business for many women.

Lydia Mills, wife of Robert Mason of the *Eleanor*, was just such a woman. She arrived in the colony on the *Henry Wellesley* in early 1836. From Staffordshire, aged twenty-two and single, she did 'all work' in a tavern and was transported for seven years for 'man robbery'. Tattooed on her upper and lower left arm with the initials, PCLM and PCSLM, she had lost the forefinger on her right hand and the canine tooth on the left side of her upper jaw. Her physical description suggests a hard life and her crime and work that she was a streetwise thief who probably stole from a member of her own class. On arrival, she was assigned to Benjamin Sullivan of Raymond Terrace. The following year, she married James Clarke, a ticket-of-leave holder at Christ Church, Newcastle. Later, with her own ticket, she successfully applied to marry Martin Birkenwood, free by servitude, but the marriage did not take place. A month after that application, November 1841, she and Robert Mason received the governor's permission to marry. The ceremony took place at Dungog in early January 1842 when Lydia described herself as a widow. They settled in the town where she died at the age of forty-six in 1858.[45]

Some degree of design seems to have governed Lydia's marital decisions. In each case her prospective spouse was free of the convict system. Such men had more to offer than an assigned convict. She had met Robert several years previously at Sullivan's, where he, too, had been assigned, and probably lived with him for a while. We do not know why the marriage to Birkenwood did not proceed but presumably Lydia and Robert met again when both were living in Stroud. The apparent practicalities of her arrangements do not necessarily rule out the possibility of affection or even love. More than twenty years later, when Robert wrote to their adopted daughter with news of his brother's death, he reminisced about the last occasion on which he had seen him. According to Robert, Joseph had stayed with him and Lydia for 'nearly a week' in January 1837 and had 'plainly seen' how they 'were attached'. 'What lessons of caution did he give me…ultimately all of no use – nothing could prevent our coming together.'[46] Yet Lydia married James Clarke in February 1837, one month later and did not marry Robert until 1842. Some of the better educated and more respectable among the Wessex men evidently had reservations about marriage to a convict woman.

In many ways Lydia was a typical female convict, sharing a number of characteristics with the other female convicts who married Swing protesters. More than 90 per cent were domestics of one kind or another. Only three were not. Margaret Shea, transported from Cork when she was seventeen, was a market girl, Rose Cunningham was a country servant from County Tyrone, and Elizabeth Skinner, a Devonshire dairy woman. When Margaret married Thomas Whately in 1838, she was only nineteen, young enough to bear a large family, but Rose was forty-six when she became the wife of Charles Green and Elizabeth was fifty-three at the time of her marriage to Levi Brown.[47] Unflattering physical descriptions of these women suggest a hard life. Scars were common. Some had teeth missing. Elizabeth Skinner had 'hairy moles' on her jaw and had lost several front teeth.[48] The majority had been convicted of some form of theft but they were not innocents abroad. Mary Ayton, who married George Durman in 1843, had eleven previous convictions and was still only twenty when transported for highway robbery in 1840. Both her sister and brother had been transported five years earlier. Margaret Shea was transported in 1836 with her sister, Judith, and mother, Honora. All market women, they had been convicted of stealing fowls. While the two girls were first offenders, their mother had three previous convictions.[49]

Marriage to a woman who came free or was born in the colony was usually straightforward but even those who were free could not entirely suit themselves. When John Ford of the *Eleanor* applied for permission to marry Mary Ann Coleman, she required permission from her mistress because the Masters and Servants Act regulated servants in similar ways to the convict system.[50] Single girls who came free to the colony usually became domestic servants with lives like those of their convict counterparts. If they came alone and were under twenty one, they faced the additional problem, as Mary Ann discovered, that they lacked a parent or legal guardian to give the necessary consent. In her case, the fact that she was marrying a convict brought her under the scrutiny of the Colonial Secretary who refused the governor's permission. The clergyman involved in the application intervened without success. Twelve months later, after Ford had received his absolute pardon, the wedding took place in Sydney with a different clergyman and the registration notes that it was with the 'consent of the legal guardian'! [51]

A free woman usually had a certain advantage if only because of her civil status; she did not have the threat of convict discipline hanging over her head. Nor need she fear that the bureaucratic machine could find her out. Free women probably believed that they had greater room to manoeuvre if they wished to leave a marriage and to marry again. Unlike men, it was probably easier for women to cover their tracks because each time a woman married, she changed her name. When cohabiting, she often took the name of her partner which she could easily cast off and revert to her maiden or her marital name. A woman could establish herself in a different community where her previous life and marital status became what she claimed. When children were involved, it was more difficult, but not impossible, for women to create a new personal history for themselves in another marriage or relationship. The need to provide for herself and her children was obviously an important spur to finding another partner.

A case in point was Catherine McCann, a native-born girl with convict parentage who married Abraham House. Born in 1805, she wed Robert Chydd in 1819 and had a child. Within a few years, she was living with a Thomas Smith whose name she assumed and by whom she had at least five children between 1823 and 1834. She probably met House about 1850. Settling in, or near, Yass they married in 1856 with her claiming to be a spinster. Assigned to the County of Argyle, House had held his ticket-of-leave for Goulburn and worked in County King, both convenient to Yass. It was not until 1864, a year before Catherine's own death, that her first husband died. Although one of her Smith daughters had settled near Yass, the only marriage which House, her third husband, identified on her death registration was hers to him, dated erroneously to 1850. Presumably he intended to cover the fact that they had been in a common-law relationship before they married for none of Catherine's children was included. [52]

Catherine, the daughter of convicts, was typical, in terms of social class, of the women who married Swing protesters. As is only to be expected, most of the native-born were children of convicts. Some did their best to disguise their colonial origins and to hide them from their contemporaries but while the colonial population remained relatively small deception was difficult. The great flood of immigrants that washed over Australia with the discovery of gold in the 1850s facilitated the concealment of the convict stain but did not remove it.[53] Ex-convicts survived well into the twentieth century and some children of Swing convicts lived until the early 1950s. Despite attempts to whitewash convicts and to present them as injured innocents, as the Wessex men certainly were, convict forebears still present problems for some people. How much greater must these have been for convicts and their offspring as they confronted the every-day realities and social discrimination of a convict society. Women seem to have been more sensitive about their convict origins than men. Ann Salter, the native-born wife of the Berkshire bricklayer, William Sims, was determined to hide her colonial origins. During her life, she maintained she was born in London, a claim which also appears on the registration of her death. This sensitivity was, perhaps, intended to conceal her first marriage to a convict. With three children from that union she described herself as a widow on her marriage to Sims in 1841.[54] Ann and William who had nine children, both died at Ryde in 1885 where they had spent most of their married life.[55]

About the same proportion of Wessex men who took native-born wives married free immigrants. The majority of these women from the labouring population came to the colony with some form of assistance. [56] Although there was strong opposition both in New South Wales and in England to the shovelling out of paupers, the early period of assisted emigration involved chiefly the impoverished and destitute. Assisted emigration began in 1832, shipping out single Irish and English women selected from charitable institutions and workhouses. Lack of stringency in selection was a major and justified criticism as the promotion and management of the scheme quickly became the domain of ship owners and entrepreneurs. The *Red Rover*, the first ship to arrive in New South Wales carrying single, Irish women, became a byword for immorality. Those despatched under this system between 1832 and 1836, started life in the colony against the odds. They faced suspicion and exploitation, lacking the support and forms of redress available to female convicts. Single, assisted women, not part of a family group, experienced the same prejudices as female convicts from those with little direct contact with working-class women and limited understanding of their mores and behaviour.[57]

In the early years of the bounty scheme, single women were lodged in the government Lumber Yard on their arrival while local ladies' committees sought places for them. In the case of the *Layton*, however, which arrived in 1833, the immigrants, described by Bourke as being of 'very indifferent character', so affronted their would-be benefactors that it proved 'impossible to form a Ladies' Committee for their dispersal'.[58] Unlike female convicts, immigrants could not go direct from the ship to their place of employment. Although the state could not command free women in the manner of convicts, it was expected to bear the responsibility for them when their mistresses found them unsatisfactory. As is well known, Caroline Chisholm did her best to help these women who were vulnerable because they lacked both family support and the protection from the state available to female convicts. However, the state did not abandon them completely. It had developed, as part of the management of convicts, various mechanisms and support systems enabling it to care for destitute women. Elizabeth White, a bounty immigrant, went from the Liverpool Benevolent Institution to the Female Factory for the delivery of her child in 1834 some years before she met and married Isaac Burton.[59]

Criticism of single, female immigrants continued unabated. In an attempt to minimise these problems and to lessen the burden to the state, Governor Bourke in 1835 proposed a more closely regulated bounty system by which private individuals in the colony would bring out emigrants to work for them. Married couples produced higher bounties than single girls, who were required to travel 'under the protection' of a family group, though contractors, in their haste to fill their ships, did not always observe the regulations relating to suitability, ages and safeguards. Bounty immigrants Ann and Eliza Henley, who married Daniel Hancock and Isaac Manns respectively, were more fortunate because they came with their family on the *Fairlie* in 1838. An agricultural family from Brede in Sussex, they settled at Sutton Forest on the Southern Highlands, a well-established farming area. Thomas, the head of the family, was a farmer, his wife and son, farm servants, and the older girls domestics. In other words they had much in common with the Swing protesters and were the type of emigrants the colony wished to attract.[60]

Within two years of the Henleys' arrival, eighteen-year-old Ann had married. Eliza was seventeen when she married three years later.[61] Immigrant girls were just as keen to marry as convict women and probably did so for very similar reasons. Sarah Skelton Comber, who came on the *Layton* in December 1833, married Jacob Turner three months later, he having applied successfully for permission in the previous month. Mary Ann Coleman, of the *James Pattison* and Ellen Keefe (O'Keefe) of the *Duchess of Northumberland*, both married less than two years after their arrival. As we have already seen, lack of permission had delayed Mary Ann's union with John Ford of the *Eleanor*. Ellen first became the wife of John Seward, a ticket-of-leave holder. After she was widowed and left with five children, she married William Cheater of the *Eleanor* within two years of the death of her first husband. The marriage broke down irretrievably. Both were living at different addresses at the time of his death and his estate, with 'goods sworn at £10', went to the solicitor responsible for drawing up his will.[62]

It was no easy matter for male convicts and ex-convicts to find a wife in the colony. In this respect, the Wessex men fared better than the average. The fact that most had valued rural skill seems not to have enhanced their chances in the marriage stakes. Their innocence, lack of drive and general failure to accumulate capital may well have diminished their opportunities. The fact that so many were already married probably delayed their search for a colonial partner. Some Swing protesters married more than once in the colony but about two-thirds of them failed to attain the goal of a wife or partner. When they were successful in finding a partner, or in being chosen as a partner, the Swing transportees usually married a woman who lived and worked close by. These were the women whom they had an opportunity to meet and to associate with on the same footing. The women, for their part, were similar to the Swing protesters in terms of class and status, though fewer of them would have endured the same impoverishment and misery in their own country as the Wessex men. On the other hand, their backgrounds and experiences were so different that these differences may have militated against the Swing transportees. To some extent, their very strengths may have become encumbrances in the colony. When they did marry, their class, their wives, their places of settlement and the trauma of their unjust transportation largely determined their way of life and future as well as that of their children.

## Notes

1    Louisa Batten, to her uncle, John Batten, England, 16 April 1868, held privately.

2    B. Smith, *A Cargo of Women: Susannah Watson and the Convicts of the Princess Royal*, Sydney, 1988.

3    M. Quartly, 'Bending the Bars; Convict Women and the State' in K. Saunders and R. Evans (eds) *Gender Relations in Australia: Domination and Negotiation*, Sydney, 1992, pp. 144-157.

4    A. Atkinson, 'Convict and Courtship' in P. Grimshaw, C. McConville and E. McEwen (eds) *Families in Colonial Australia*, Sydney, 1985, p. 22.

5    For a detailed discussion of these vexed issues, see C. H. Curry, 'The Law of Marriage and Divorce in New South Wales (1788-1850)', *Royal Australian Historical Society Journal* (hereafter *RAHSJ*), Vol. 41, Part 3, 1955, pp. 97-98.

6    Section 18, 'Nothing in this Act contained…shall extend to any marriages solemnised beyond the seas.'

7    3 Geo. IV, C 75, 22 July 1822 and 4 Geo. IV, C 76, 18 July 1823.

8    Colonial Secretary to Marsden, 2 October 1826, Colonial Secretary Out Letters, 21 August to 4 December 1826, Archives Of New South Wales (hereafter AONSW), 4/3631, Reel 2916, p.408. We owe this reference to Alison Vincent.

9    We have encountered more than one case in the Colonial Secretary's correspondence of the state disallowing a marriage and forcing the couple to undergo another ceremony because the governor's permission had not been sought.

10    Charles Milson, bachelor of Segenhoe, free, married Annie Maria Lyons, spinster, of Segenhoe, free, 7 November 1837, banns, consent of friends, Church of England, Maitland, BDM, 1837, 1869, 21. Aaron Stone, bachelor, married Ann Redhead or West, spinster, 6 July 1840, both of Sydney, Scots Church,

Presbyterian, BDM, 1840, 30, 469. Robert Baker, bachelor, married Julia Bargin (Bergen, Berrigan), spinster, 5 September 1842, both of this parish, Church of England, Scone, BDM, 1842, 507, 26. Daniel Sims, bachelor, married Emma Park, spinster, 17 October 1844, bachelor, Scots Church, Presbyterian, BDM, 1844, 1988, 76. For the pardons, see Colonial Secretary, Special Bundle: Machine Breakers, AONSW COD 513.

11    Gifford North lived in a common-law relationship which produced at least one child before he married Maria Gardner. Gifford (junior) was born 29 August and baptised 17 October 1847, Church of England, Windsor, BDM, 1847, 32, 1185, marriage, 16 January 1852, Presbyterian, Scots Church, Sydney, both of Windsor, widower and spinster, BDM, 1852, 282, 81 and death of Gifford North, 28 March 1866, Windsor, AONSW 1866/961. For the English census details, see J. Chambers, *Rebels of the Fields: Robert Mason and the Convicts of the Eleanor*, Letchworth, 1995, especially the entry for Gifford North, pp. 233-234.

12    1 Jacobi I, c. 10 and 11, 1603; 35, Geo 11, 3, c. 67, 19 May 1795, 3 Geo IV, c.75, 1822 and 9 Geo Iv, c. 22, 27 June 1828.

13    Elizabeth Fry to Samuel Marsden, 23 May 1832, quoted by Smith, op. cit., p. 68.

14    The bundle on the matter is incomplete. Keane obviously forwarded letters which he had received, to the Colonial Secretary as part of applications for the publication of banns. The bundle also includes a case from 1837. Col.Sec. In Letters, AONSW 4/2151.2.

15    Marginal comments, Applications for the Publication of Banns, Bathurst, 16 May 1832, Col. Sec. In Letters, AONSW 4/2151.2. J. J. Kinchela to T. C. Harrington, 10 December 1832, Sydney, 13 December 1832 and Schedule No. 21, 11 December 1832, with marginal comments, AONSW 4/2151.2.

16    Lachlan Macquarie to the Rev. Phillip Conolly and John Joseph Therry, Sydney, 14 October 1820. The judgement of Lord Stowell in Dalrymple *v.* Dalrymple, quoted by Currey, op. cit., p. 98. Darling to Bathurst, 6 September 1826, Sydney, Enclosure No. 2, Extract from Minute No. 16 of the Executive Council, 8 July 1826, *Historical Records of Australia* (hereafter *HRA*), Series 1, Vol. XII, pp. 546-547. Currey discusses the legal technicalities of, and changes in, the legal situation. Currey, op. cit., pp. 101 and 104. This important act, which seems to be completely ignored in any discussion of colonial marriage in this period, was 5 Wm IV, c. 2.

17    Circular Letter, Colonial Secretary to Colonial Clergy, 5 April 1826, Col. Sec. Out Letters, 30 March to 26 April 1826, AONSW 4/3528, Reel 2915, p. 147.

18    For our period, there are two sets of official records relating to convict marriage, the Registers of Convicts' Applications to Marry, 20 December 1825 to 26 February 1851, and Applications for the Publication of Banns, 1826 to 1841, which usually provide more information about the couple and include

supporting material and letters. It seems that the files for banns after 1841 have been lost or at least not yet discovered. Both sets of records which were part of the one process, are held by the AONSW.

19 See, for example, Rev. C.P.N. Wilton to Colonial Secretary, Newcastle, 2 November 1836, AONSW 4/2304.1. Wilton appealed successfully on behalf of a convict, who though married in the records, had been previously given permission to marry. That marriage did not eventuate and when he subsequently applied to marry another woman, permission was refused.

20 Atkinson in Grimshaw, op. cit., p. 29.

21 Stephen Hatcher, Applications for the Publication of Banns, 1826 to 1841, Parramatta, AONSW 4/2304.2, Reel 730. Jacob Turner married Sarah Comber Skelton, 27 March 1834, Church of England, St Lawrence, BDM, 1834, 1275, 18. The applications for banns record that she came free on the *Layton* which carried emigrants to the colony in 1833. AONSW 4/2226.3, Reel 726. John Ford 28, *Eleanor*, 1831, bond, life, Mary Ann Coleman, 18, *James Pattison*, 1836, CF, Applications for the Publication of Banns, Narellan, 1837, AONSW 4/2344.1, Reel 732. John Ford of Sydney and Greendale married Mary Ann Coman (Coleman) of the same place, 4 June 1838, Presbyterian, St Andrews, Sydney, BDM, 1838, 3088, 74, and 328. She arrived on the *James Pattison* from Cork on 2 February 1836.

22 Atkinson in Grimshaw, op. cit., p. 24.

23 Applications for the Publication of Banns, 1837, Narellan, AONSW 4/2344.1, Reel 732.

24 For the details concerning the ending of assignment to wives, see Bourke to Stanley, 20 January 1834, Sydney, *HRA*. Series I, Vol. XVII, p. 341, 2 and 3 Wm IV. c.62. Several cases of distress arose from a master's refusal to support a convict's wife. The usual method was to threaten to remove the convict from his master and assign him to his wife. See, for example, Principal Superintendent of Convicts to Colonial Secretary, Sydney, 10 April 1833, Col. Sec. In Letters, 33/203, AONSW 4/2185.

25 Atkinson in Grimshaw, op. cit., pp. 24. See, also, Memorandum, 20 December 1832, Col. Sec. Out Letters, AONSW, 4/2173.

26 On arrival in the colony in 1829, Ann Bates alias Murray stated that she was married to a man who had been transported and named him and his ship. When she subsequently applied for permission to marry another man in the colony, she explained that she had been only living with the man she had named as her husband. He, on the other hand, claimed to be single on arrival and asserted that no such relationship had existed. Applications for the Publication of Banns, Maitland, 1830, AONSW, 4/2018, Reel 3035.

27 Mary Hughs to the Rev. J. E. Keane, 5 June 1832, Col. Sec. In Letters, AONSW 4/21251.2.

28 Applications for the Publication of Banns, Levi Brown and Mary Anne Royle, 9 August 1836, Windsor, AONSW 4/3502.2, Reel 731. He described himself as a widower and she as a widow but both had stated on arrival they were married. Register of Convicts' Applications to Marry, 21 July 1846, p. 127. Levi Brown, described as a widower, married Elizabeth Skinner, widow, 13 August, 1846, Presbyterian, Scots Church, Sydney, BDM,1846, 678, 77. Certificate of Freedom, 46/467, AONSW 4/4404, Reel 1022, and marriage, 31 August 1846, Scots Church, Sydney, BDM, 1846, 302, 32. Henry Bunce, Register of Convicts' Applications to Marry, 7 October 1841, Bungonia, AONSW 4/4513, p. 256. William Legg applied on 28 August 1845. He married Mary Ann (Marion) McKinnon who held a ticket of leave, on 5 October 1845, by Catholic rites at Campbelltown. Register of Convicts' Applications to Marry, 28 August 1845, AONSW Reel 715, marriage, BDM, 1845, 395, 94. Job Hatherell, Register of Convicts' Applications to Marry, Scone, 15 October 1844, AONSW 4/4514, p. 73. He married Honorah, (Norah) Sweeny on 13 November 1844, Scone, Church of England, BDM, 1844, 623, 29. Register of Convicts' Applications to Marry, 29 June 1842, Appin, AONSW 4/4513, p. 110. Marriage of Rose Cunningham and Charles Green, 31 August 1846, Church of England, Campbelltown, BDM, 1846, 302, 31, death of Rose Cunningham, 14 October, Appin, BDM, 1848, 473, 33 and marriage of Charles Green to Elizabeth Henness, 1 May 1851, Church of England, Appin, BDM, 1851, 368, 37.

29 Convicts did not automatically obtain their ticket of freedom but had to collect it themselves. Apart from the fact of having a piece of paper which said they were free and, of course, identified them as having been convicts, a certificate of freedom had little value except if an ex-convict wished to leave the country.

30 Chambers op. cit., p.172.

31 Applications for the Publication of Banns, Jane Burroughs to Charles Fay, 21 March 1833, AONSW 4/2443.5. Marriage, 27 December 1838, Church of England, Lane Cove, BDM, 1838, 1790, 22. It requires a minimum of two weeks to call banns on three successive Sundays.

32 Daniel Hancock, 32, *Eleanor*, FS, Sutton Forest, Margaret Ridding or Redding, 22, *Sir Charles Forbes,* 7 years, B, 28 August 1839,Applications for the Publication of Banns, AONSW 4/2441. The file contains a petition from Daniel Hancock appealing against the rejection of the application and letters from his father dated 30 September 1835 and 2 September 1836, and one from his sister, 16 August 1836. These letters reveal that Hancock had regular contact with various members of his family. Marriage, 11 November 1840, Church of England, Camden, BDM, 1840, 520, 24.

33 Register of Convicts Applications to Marry, 1837 to 1842, AONSW 4/4513, p. 122, 4/4515, p. 247, George Durman, 36, *Eleanor,* life, CP, Sarah Dowling, 22,

*Whitby*, 7, bond, date of permission, 25 August 1841, Paterson. Register of Convicts Applications to Marry, 1842 to 1851, p. 31, George Durman, 39, *Eleanor*, CP, Mary Ayton, 27, bond, *Surrey*, both of Dungog, 1 August 1843. Marriage, Church of England, Dungog, 6 November 1843, BDM, 1843, 511, 27.

34   Applications for the Publication of Banns, Newcastle, 2 November 1836, Enclosures, 36/8076. 36/9670 and 36/10265, Col. Sec. In Letters, AONSW 4/2301, Reel 730.

35   M. Belcher, 'The Child in New South Wales Society: 1820 to 1837', PhD., University of New England, Armidale, 1982, pp. 145-147. In a detailed analysis of the 1828 Census in relation to occupation and marriage, Belcher establishes that 'amongst the more economically advantaged groups there exists a disproportionately large number of married couples.' He concludes that the 'chances of a labourer, that is the great majority of men, getting a wife and having a family appear to be very remote.'

36   Ibid., p. 123. Belcher transcribed all entries on to cards and was able to identify multiple entries and women who were cohabiting more readily. Spouses do not always appear as part of the same family entry. As Belcher points out the number cohabiting in the colony has usually been overestimated. He concludes that it was just under 10 per cent. Ibid., p. 144.

37   Robson, in common with other male historians of his generation, accepted the adverse moral judgments of female convicts by contemporary observers and, therefore, assumed that few female convicts married. See *The Convict Settlers of Australia: An Enquiry into the Origin and Character of the Convicts transported to New South Wales and Van Diemen's Land 1787-1852*, Melbourne, 1965, p. 142. The figures come from pp. 135 and 142, and the percentages have been calculated from pp. 188 and 183.

38   Belcher, op. cit., p.160.

39   The absence of a marriage registration but the baptism of children has been categorised as a common-law relationship. On attitudes to common-law marriages, see Belcher, op. cit., p. 144-145.

40   Ticket of leave 35/665, AONSW 4/4097, Reel, 922, baptism, Julia, born 19 April and baptised 19 April 1837, John and Ellen Aldridge, blacksmith, Church of England, Liverpool, death, Julia, infant, 3 days, 21 April 1837, daughter of a blacksmith, Church of England, Liverpool, BDM, 1837, 891, 21, marriage, bachelor and spinster, both of this parish, 2 October 1848, Denham Court, Church of England, St Marys, BDM, 1837, 2652, 21 and 1848, 164, 33. John Aldridge's death certificate certified by his wife, shows two males deceased but does not list the deceased daughter. One of the cases about which the Reverend J.E. Keane appealed, concerned a ticket of leave man living with a woman who had married thirteen years earlier before transportation. The colonial Secretary

had refused their application for marriage and Keane was concerned that unless they married, she and her three children would 'be all thrown adrift on the world if his ticket be taken.' Enclosure, 1 April 1837, Col. Sec. In Letters, AONSW 4/2151.2

41  Indent, *Hooghly,* 27 September 1831, AONSW, 4/4016, Reel 905. Applications for the Publication of Banns, Thomas Green, 29, *Albion,* 1828, FS, Joanna McCarthy, 26, *Hooghly,* 1831, bond, 1835, Parramatta, AONSW 4/22691.1, Reel 727, marriage, Thomas Green and Anna McCartny, 19 October, 1835, Church of England, Parramatta, BDM, 1835, 1121, certificate of freedom, 38/922, 16 October 1838, AONSW4/4343. Baptism 28 January 1841, born 2 January 1841, Catholic, St Patrick's Parramatta, no father listed, Female Factory, BDM, 1841, 145, 241. Marriage, John Batten and Hanna McCarty, bachelor and spinster, 8 June 1852, Church of England, Penrith, BDM, 1852, 435, 38. Although neither John nor Hanna signed the marriage registration, it is often the case that people known to be literate did not sign. Whether or not they did, could depend on the clergyman and the circumstances. We have found a number of instances when they signed and on other occasions they did not. It is also the case that some listed in the indent as unable to read or write could and did sign their names.

42  Belcher, op. cit., pp. 160 and 162.

43  Death, BDM,1862/1193.

44  These proportions which did not change significantly before 1841, were calculated from the table summaries, M.R. Sainty and K.A. Johnson (eds) *Census of New South Wales, November 1828,* Sydney, 1985, p. 15.

45  Marriage, James Clarke to Lydia Mills, Church of England, BDM, 1837, 1802, 21, Applications for the Publication of Banns, Newcastle and Paterson, AONSW 4/2344.2 and 4/4513, and Registers of Convicts' Applications for Permission to Marry, AONSW, 4/4513, p. 263. Marriage, Robert Mason to Lydia Clarke, Church of England, BDM,1842, 482, 26. There were no baptisms registered for James and Lydia Clarke and it has not been possible to identify a death for James Clarke.

46  Robert Mason, Brookfield, 1864, Mason Family Letters, 1857-1865, ML MSS 2290; D. Kent and N. Townsend (eds), *Joseph Mason, Assigned Convict, 1831-1837: Doomed to the earth's remotest region,* Melbourne, 1996, pp.163-64.

47  Applications for the Publication of Banns, Narellan, 4 June 1837, AONSW 4/2344.1, Reel 732, marriage, Thomas Whatley and Margaret Shea, 2 July 1838, Church of England Narellan, BDM, 1838, 1256, 24, Rose Cunningham, 31 August 1846, Church of England, Campbelltown, BDM, 1846, 302, 31. Levi Brown, 53, *Eleanor,* free, Elizabeth Skinner, 53, *Surrey,* 14 years, TL, 21 July 1846, AONSW F 801, p.127. Elizabeth Skinner and Levi Brown, 3 August 1846, Presbyterian, Scots Church, BDM, 1846, 678, 77.

48  Indent, *Surrey,* 18 July 1840.

49  Marriage, George Durman to Mary Ayton, with consent of governor, Dungog, Church of England, BDM, 1843, 511, 27. Thomas Whately to Margaret Shea, with consent of governor, Church of England, Narellan, Church of England, BDM, 1838, 1883, 22. Indent, *Pyramus* (2), 14 December 1836 and the *Waterloo* (5), 6 September 1836. The three women were tried on the same day for the same offence.

50  Although J.B. Hirst, *Convict society and its enemies; A history of early New South Wales,* Sydney, 1983, pp. 57-58, claims there were peculiarly convict crimes, free workers were brought before the bench for drunkenness, neglect of duty, insolence, drunkenness, absconding and absenting themselves in the same way as convicts. The main difference lay not in the charges but the punishments. See ibid., pp. 101-102 for a discussion of the Masters and Servants Act.

51  Applications for the Publication of Banns, 4 June 1837, Narellan, AONSW 4/2344.1, Reel 732. Marriage, 4 June 1838, Presbyterian, St Andrews, Sydney, BDM, 1838, 3088, 74.

52  Catherine McCann, baptism, Peter and Mary McCann, 21 July 1805, Church of England, St Phillip's, Sydney, BDM, 1805, 1455, 1. Marriage, Catherine McCann and Robert Chydd, 12 November 1819, Church of England, Castlereagh, BDM, 1819, 2447, 3. A child of that marriage, Ann, is listed in the 1822 Muster. Baptisms, Mary Chydd, 16 November 1823, Thomas Smith and Catherine Chydd, Church of England, Castlereagh, BDM, 123, 6364, and Esther Smith, 15 June 1834, Thomas and Catherine Smith, Church of England, St Phillip's, Sydney, BDM, 1834, 264, 18. Ticket of leave for Abraham House 35/759, AONSW 4/ 4099, Reel 923. He is listed in the 1841 Census in County King, 3, Gun Gun Creek, AONSW 4, X951, p.135, R 2223. Death, Catherine House, 7 May 1865, Fish River, BDM, 1865/6525. Death, Robert Chydd, Tamworth, BDM, 1864/5926. Marriage, Abraham House to Catherine Chydd, 5 April 1856, both of Yass, bachelor and spinster, at Yass, Church of England, 1856, 16, 43.

53  One of the most illuminating and succinct discussions of these issues is J. Spurway, 'The Growth of Family History in Australia', *The Push: A Journal of Early Australian Social History,* No. 27, 1989, pp. 74 - 84.

54  Applications for the Publication of Banns, Isaac Mason, 27, *Surrey,* bachelor, 1831, bond, Ann Salter, 19, BC, spinster, 1836, AONSW 4/2303, Reel 729. Marriage, Isaac Mason, bachelor, bond, and Ann Salter, spinster, free, both of this parish, banns, consent of governor, both literate, 31 January 1836, Field of Mars, Church of England, BDM, 1836, 210, 20. Baptisms, BDM, 1838, 732, 22 and 1840, 797, 24. There is no baptism for the third Mason child, William, who died at Goulburn in 1878, BDM, 1878/5992. Death, Isaac Mason, shoemaker, Hunters Hill, 4 August 1841, BDM, 1841, 797, 24. Marriage, William

Sims, bachelor, and Ann Mason, widow, both of this parish, banns, 17 December 1841, Church of England, Parramatta, BDM, 1841, 316, 25. As the informant for the birth of a child, Ann claimed to have been born in London. Clara, 3 May 1862, Ryde, AONSW 1862/13276. Death, Ann Sims, 30 September 1880, Ryde, BDM,1880/10040. George Sims, a son, the informant for the registration, gave Elizabeth, formerly Alexander, as her mother.

55   Deaths, William, BDM, 1880/10002 and Ann, BDM, 1880/10040.

56   The best general discussion of the various schemes still remains R.B. Madgwick, *Immigration into Eastern Australia, 1788-1851*, Sydney, 1969, pp. 89-166.

57   For a discussion of these attitudes, see M. Sturma, 'The Eye of the Beholder: The Stereotype of Female Convicts 1788-1852', *Labour History*, 34, 1978, pp. 3-10. Assisted female immigrants have thus far received little historical attention.

58   Bourke to Stanley, Government House, 21 January 1834, *HRA*, Vol. XVII, p. 346.

59   The matron of the Benevolent Institution to the Colonial Secretary, Col. Sec. In Letters, AONSW 4/2222.3. applications for the Publication of Banns, Isaac Burton, 32, *Eleanor*, 1831, FS, Elizabeth White, 18, *Bussorah Merchant*, CF, 1839, Queanbeyan, AONSW 4/2442.97, Reel 2215.

60   Bourke to Glenelg, Government House, 14 October 1835, *HRA*, Vol. XVIII, pp.161-163. Madgwick, op. cit., pp. 150-151. See above, footnote 47.

61   Marriage, Daniel Hancock married Ann Henley, both of Sutton Forest, 11 November 1840, by licence, both illiterate, Church of England, Camden, BDM, 1840, 520, 24. Samuel and Eliza Henley were witnesses to the marriage. Marriage, Isaac Manns, bachelor, free pardon, married Eliza Henley, spinster, free emigrant, both of this parish, banns, 12 March 1843, Church of England, Camden, 1843, 353, 27. The details of the family come from the listing for the *Fairlie* which arrived on 6 December 1838, AONSW 4/4830, Reel 1290.

62   *Layton. James Pattison*, AONSW, COD, 425B. Ellen is listed as a housemaid aged twenty, *Duchess of Northumberland*, AONSW, COD, 394. For details concerning Mary Ann Coleman, see footnote 63 above. John Seward, 28, *Asia*, 1831, TL, 38/769, Ellen O'Keefe, 23, *Duchess of Northumberland*, 1837 CF, Applications for the Publication of Banns, Sydney, 1839, AONSW 4/2435.91. Marriage, John Seward to Ellen O'Keefe, Sydney, BDM, 1839, 375, 90 and 1839, 84, 130. Death, John Sayward,12 November 1848, shoemaker, Williams River, BDM, 1848, 1031, 33. William Cheater, death, 2 May 1875, West Maitland, RGNSW 75/7326. Probate, Supreme Court of New South Wales, Series 2/ 1553, Reel 3016, Society of Australian, Sydney.

# CHAPTER TEN

# 'ALL NOW CONSIDERED THEMSELVES FREE':

# LIVING, WORKING AND DYING IN

# COLONIAL NEW SOUTH WALES

On 18 March 1863 the body of Thomas Goodall was discovered in Newcastle Harbour. The local newspaper knew enough of his past to identify him as someone 'transported for machinery breaking'. The ploughman, reaper and shearer from Andover had become a farmer owning land on Mosquito Island in the Hunter River near Hexham. Goodall's skills did not particularly distinguish him from the other transportees but he was conspicuously more successful having accumulated substantial capital which the newspaper valued at £1,200.[1] The Swing protesters, with their rural skills and general good character, possessed certain advantages as they set about rebuilding their lives in the colony but their futures mainly depended upon their aspirations and drive and the extent to which they remained prisoners of their English past. Goodall did not marry and there is no evidence of a common-law relationship yet his marital prospects should have been good. A frugal man, he managed to save money while still under sentence and shortly before his pardon had lent £37 to his master.[2] Although he acquired wealth and status as a farmer he failed to find a bride, perhaps because of his temperament. At the time of his death, he was involved in a rancorous dispute with a neighbour who was alleging false imprisonment. Legally in the wrong, Goodall had finally backed down and was in the process of buying off the complainant but at the same time being fairly unrepentant and argumentative.[3]

Goodall was an exception to the anonymity characteristic of the colonial lives of men who did not form a relationship and father children. It has proved impossible to follow forty-seven of the 138 of the Wessex transportees after they became free. All the men in this category remained, as far as we can judge, unattached. It is generally accepted that men without a partner and children moved more freely from place to place and were extremely mobile both within New South Wales and, to a lesser extent, across colonial borders. For Russel Ward these were the bushmen, the true Australians, the ex-convict 'men of the outback', the 'nomad tribe', going from one job to the next.[4] Many of those we cannot trace may have joined this largely invisible tribe, following seasonal work and living their lives alone.

The Wessex men whose lives we can follow divide equally between those remaining in the area of their assignment and those leaving it. Most of those settling in Sydney had been assigned there in the first instance. Jacob Turner, at Surry Hills, became a gardener, as did Daniel Sims. William Sims continued his trade as a bricklayer and mason and, when the heavy work became too much, he also scratched a living as a gardener. Jason Greenway worked as a quarryman but died a labourer, not unexpectedly, of phthisis.[5] Life in Sydney, especially for the working classes, was particularly difficult during the depression of the early 1840s and the skilled suffered along with the semi-skilled and unskilled. The Viccus family, living in Cumberland Street in The Rocks, certainly fell on hard times. Edmund Viccus, a waterman, died a pauper in 1849 in the Benevolent Asylum while his baby son survived him by only a few months.[6] A Select Committee on the Petition from Distressed Mechanics and Labourers in 1843 revealed abject poverty and appalling living conditions in Sydney comparable with the worst of British cities. Although the discovery of gold gave the economy an enormous boost, conditions in the slums of Sydney remained unrelieved with cesspools 'full to capacity', open ditches full of sewage, evil smelling piles of rubbish, factories 'issuing forth immense volumes of smoke', slaughter houses spewing out offal into waterways and destitute families living in one room of a tenement.[7] Despite these conditions, the colony was and remained highly urbanised.

Convicts predominated in country areas where the demand for labour was greatest. When the Wessex men were free, only a few travelled far from their place of servitude. William Adams, assigned to the Williams River, was working on the nearby Paterson by 1837 but died a selector near Narrabri in 1887. A long way from the Hunter, his quest for independence, living on his own land, had involved a considerable journey.[8] The path Adams followed had been well-worn by those leaving the Hunter in search of land as the north-west frontier expanded. Samuel Quinton went south from Sydney ending up at Tumut. Timothy May also moved southwards, travelling in stages, a common pattern for itinerant bush labourers. He was at Cabramatta, then Camden, and died at Coolac near Gundagai. William Oakley, originally at Bathurst, died in Scone which was accessible from Bathurst through Mudgee by a track north-east to Pandora's Pass.[9] Job Waldron, also at Bathurst, could have travelled south-east through the Abercrombies to the Southern Highlands or southwards down the great inland corridor of the western slopes and plains to the Monaro.[10]

Most Swing transportees did not go far by colonial standards and remained where they were when they became free. John Wheeler, originally at Wollombi on the Hunter, had been re-assigned to Thomas Shadforth of Mulgoa, on the Nepean south of Windsor. In 1837 he got his ticket for the district of Windsor and died seven years later in the Sydney Infirmary.[11] Henry Eldridge, having incurred colonial punishments, was re-assigned to Samuel Wright at Merton on the Hunter, and held his ticket-of-leave for that district where he spent the rest of his life.[12] Matthew Triggs remained with the Harpers at Luskintyre just north-west of Maitland, staying in the area until his death in 1853. Well-established and prosperous Maitland, very much a brick-built town, had obvious attractions for Triggs, a bricklayer.[13]

About two-thirds of the Wessex transportees with a partner settled in one particular region. Almost 80 per cent of those remaining in New South Wales lived in agricultural rather than pastoral areas. The man's location when he became free determined the place of permanent settlement for almost 60 per cent of couples. Robert Baker was assigned to the Scone district where he served his sentence, received his ticket-of-leave, married into a local Irish family, the Berrigans, farmed and ran cattle, raised his children and died in 1863. Julia, his wife, surviving him by some twenty years, lived out her days in the village of Scone.[14] Charles Bulpitt and Job Hatherell, both assigned to Invermein on the Hunter, also lived, worked and died in the area.[15] Some moved along the valleys of the Hunter and its tributaries, the Williams and the Paterson. Robert Mason, for example, served his sentence at Raymond Terrace, married in Stroud in 1842 and became a publican in Dungog.[16]

The other main region where Swing men settled took in the Nepean Valley and the Cowpastures on the southern boundary of the County of Cumberland, the Bargo Brush and the Southern Highlands. Even before settlement, the Southern Highlands had gained a reputation for being 'particularly beautiful and rich, resembling a fine extensive pleasure ground in England'.[17] The imagined Englishness of the landscape had its man-made counterpart in the characteristically English houses of the large landholders. The great houses of this part of the colony were built solidly and early in its history, proclaiming their masters' belief in their own permanence and in the future. It was an area, too, in which ex-convicts had successfully established themselves as freeholders and where tenant-farming was widespread. Closeness to Sydney and the Great Southern Road gave farmers and small businessmen distinct advantages. The Wessex transportees would have found more reminders of home in its villages, farming economy and community life than their fellows on the Hunter and the western slopes and plains of Bathurst.

As might have happened in England, familiarity with a particular place and association with a particular employer provided strong reasons for remaining where work was assured. Isaac Manns spent at least forty years on the Southern Highlands moving around within that circumscribed and sparsely populated world. Beginning his married life as a labourer at Browly owned by John Waite, himself an ex-convict,

Manns was a tenant-farmer at Sutton Forest, Berrima, Bong Bong and Mount Broughton.[18] Thomas Whately also began his free working life as a labourer. By 1843, he had become a tenant at Thomas Hassall's Cherith, doing well enough to buy sixty-one acres in 1852.[19] James Burgess became the lock-up keeper at Stonequarry, a position he probably gained through the support of Henry Antill, his former master and the local magistrate. Two years after Burgess had become free, he was a constable, presumably through the patronage of Antill. The Antills' support for Burgess was obviously important in his decision to settle in the area of his assignment. When he twice lost his position as a constable and was reduced to the level of a labourer, they employed him at Jarvisfield where he died as a labourer in 1865.[20] John Ford developed a similar relationship with the Shadforths of Ravenswood, Mulgoa. After a short time as a servant and labourer for George Wentworth on an adjoining property, Ford became a labourer for the Shadforths and a tenant farmer on Ravenswood for at least ten years. On his wife's death, he remarried and the family moved to Camden. When he died, he was a 'rough carpenter' at Narellan.[21]

Further south, the Southern Tablelands of the County of Argyle were very different. Stockholders grazed their herds on 'wide, treeless plains', parts of which 'promised but did not yield good pasturage'. Good land was at a premium and 'rather widely scattered'. Any small settlers were usually landless men who ran a few cattle.[22] There was little here to remind the Wessex transportees of home and less demand for their agricultural skills, although there was usually some farming on the larger pastoral runs. Abraham House, assigned to the County of Argyle, held his ticket for Goulburn and married at Yass, a centre of fine wool growing. During his servitude, he became a shepherd, an occupation he worked at for the rest of his life.[23] Stephen Williams was probably a shepherd while assigned to James Hassall, an important woolgrower, first at Bringelly on the Nepean and then at Yass. While living in Goulburn, Williams married Elizabeth Browning in 1842 but their first child was born later in that same year at Boorowa. As he intended to farm, he stayed in that area even after his wife had left him. Starting in a modest way, Williams bought land and took up a selection while labouring and farming.[24] Henry Bunce also purchased land and subsequently selected. Assigned to E. S. Hall junior at Lake Bathurst in the south of the County of Argyle, where he served his time and where he married, Bunce had settled in Goulburn by 1863 where both he and his wife, Mary Jordan, died.[25]

Goulburn, the first inland city, became a rich agricultural and market centre.[26] Astride a crossroads, it was a gateway south-westwards to Yass, the inland plains and the Riverina or due south to the Limestone Plains and then to the Monaro. Isaac Burton, however, did not follow the usual migratory path. At Yass in 1837, he must have backtracked to some extent on his way to Queanbeyan on the Limestone Plains, near the site of Canberra. As a tailor, he may have been searching for a sufficiently diversified settlement to provide a demand for his skills. It was at Queanbeyan that he met and married Elizabeth White, a free immigrant most probably working as a domestic servant. Their children were born at Queanbeyan, where Isaac and Elizabeth spent their married life. On her death, Isaac moved to be with his son at Wolumla near Bega on the far south coast.[27] Few Wessex transportees chose to remain in this part of the colony when free.

Most Swing men, especially those with families, preferred the settled areas of the colony to the frontier but those in common-law relationships were more inclined to live in the more isolated places. Henry Spicer, originally at Sir John Wylde's Vanderville, south-west of Camden, was working at Yass by 1837. When he and Mary Anne Maloney had their first child in 1844, he was labouring on Robert Campbell's pastoral run, Delegate, on the Snowy River in the Monaro. Aaron Harding went even further than the Spicers when he moved from Sutton Forest to South Australia with his partner, Ellis Sargent. After emigrating in 1838, the Sargent family had settled on the Southern Highlands where four children were born. In 1845, Ellis bore Harding a son. Shortly after the couple departed for South Australia, taking with them the youngest Sargent children. The story did not end happily, for Harding died in 1851 and Ellis and her children had to fend for themselves. Left to support six children, she married again within a year.[28]

Wessex men assigned to Bathurst where sheep stations predominated were, like those in Argyle, less inclined to remain where they were when they became free. Isolation from larger markets was a deterrent to small-scale farming at Bathurst, where land was largely devoted to pastoralism rather than agriculture and, as a result, tenant-farming was rather limited. Moreover, population west of the Blue Mountains had lagged behind that of other regions. With proportionately fewer women, the chances of finding a partner were lower than in other places. Only three protesters assigned to Bathurst married there. Within a year of John Gilmore's wedding to Elizabeth Taylor, in 1839, he had become the superintendent of a farm at Homebush, Sydney. From there, the couple went to Raymond Terrace, near Newcastle. As he became a settler – that is someone with access to land but only marginally above a labourer   the move to Raymond Terrace, where the Gilmores' second child was born, may have been an attempt at independence. Three years later he was in the Clarence River district in northern New South Wales, where he met his second colonial wife, Catherine Slavin. The fate of his first wife and family is a mystery.[29] After spending some time as an overseer on a cattle station, he and Catherine were living in Grafton by 1857 where they jointly ran a public house until his death in 1866.[30] Another Wessex transportee assigned to Bathurst, George Hopgood, also finished his working life as a publican. Having married Ann Hines in Bathurst, he followed his trade as a carpenter until he was at least fifty years old, later moving to Sydney where he was a builder before taking over a public house.[31]

Several Swing men assigned to the Bathurst area later returned with a partner.

John Batten left Cullen Bullen north of Wallerawang shortly after receiving his absolute pardon. After living in a common-law relationship with Honorah McCarthy at Penrith and Goulburn, they married in 1852. Four years later, he purchased land at Breakfast Creek near Rylstone, west of the mountains.[32] Another Bathurst assignee, Thomas Neale, when free, had gone to Penrith at the foot of the Blue Mountains where he met his partner, Mary Ann Hughes.[33] By 1851, the Neale family was in Bathurst. Returning as a carrier to a part of the colony with which he was familiar, he was well placed to benefit from the discovery of gold in the region. Within a few years, Thomas had become an orchardist near Orange in the central west, living there until his death, in 1895, in a house fire which also claimed the life of his wife.[34] John Pound, married Catherine McVicar in 1843 at Thomas Evernden's property, Bartletts, where both were living and working. After they left Evernden, they went further west to the Carcoar district where Pound worked for various landholders and for himself as a tenant-farmer. In 1854 he purchased a country lot on Rocky Bridge Creek, adjoining land owned by his father-in-law.[35] Thomas Radborn, also assigned to Evernden, settled in the Carcoar district with his English wife and children, not very far from the Pounds. Having received a ticket-of-leave in 1835, Radborn had continued working for his former master. When the Radburns' first Australian child was born, he was still with Evernden working at White Rock, south-west of Bathurst. By 1841, the family had travelled further south-wards, about twenty-five miles from Bathurst, to Teapot Swamp where Thomas supported his family as a tenant-farmer and occasional labourer. In 1854 he purchased land at Neville, south of Teapot Swamp and bought another twenty acres within two years. The long journeying of Harriett and Thomas had finally finished. After more than thirty years, with about six years of enforced separation, they had come to rest at a place where they died and were buried.[36]

Small farmers, tenants, freeholders or selectors, usually had a hand-to-mouth exis-tence. While food was plentiful, their diet was poor, typically salted meat, damper and very sweet black tea, much the same as convict rations. Very high consumption of sugar had usually rotted their children's teeth by the time they were twenty. Fruit trees and vegetable gardens were rare and produce, even if they were inclined to buy it, was expensive. They lived as they would have been forced to do in England, very frugally. Depending on the area, most would have started out in bark huts, perhaps progressing to slab dwellings or wattle and daub with shingle roofs.[37] We have some idea of what might have been the ultimate dwelling for small farmers in the period following the gold rush from the house Thomas Whately built at The Oaks in the County of Camden on his sixty-one acres. A house on one's own land probably repre-sented the climactic achievement for that family and for others among the Swing men who became small farmers. Whately's was a small cottage, probably of two rooms with a detached kitchen, its size suggesting modest aspirations. Constructed of sawn weatherboards with a corrugated iron roof, glazed windows and sound chimney it signified a certain permanence, a testament to Whately's endeavours.[38] Within the dwelling itself privacy would have been as limited as in the cottages of agricultural labourers in Southern England. At least seven of the Whatelys' twelve children could have been living with their parents at the one time.

Whately was one of only a handful of Wessex men who purchased land in New South Wales. His sixty-one acres represented a fairly large holding by comparison with other members of the group. Stephen Williams, the largest land owner (as distinct from land holder), held sixty-seven acres freehold. Selling forty acres for £100 in 1871, he selected more land near Young, acquiring 150 acres in all. Large by English standards but small for the colony, Williams' selection scarcely justified the description of him as a squatter on his death in the following year.[39] Henry Bunce, John Pound, Thomas Radborn and John Batten purchased country lots of thirty acres which had a minimum price of £1 per acre. Most acquired their land in the early 1850s.[40] In other words, it took them over twenty years either to accumulate sufficient capital or to accept the idea of landownership. John Batten, in fact, made his first purchase two years after his son. Henry Spicer, a farmer at the time, bought twenty-four acres near Bombala but he failed to get a living from his land and spent his later years as a shepherd on a pastoral run.[41] These modest holdings were primarily intended for cultivation although the acreage probably provided little more than subsistence so that most relied on outside labouring and seasonal work to provide for their families.

Others purchased land for different reasons. Charles Pain, a boat and barge builder assigned to the Hunter, became a draper in Goulburn. He, William Cheater and Robert Mason bought town and village allotments for dwellings and small businesses. Cheater's total of eleven lots at Seaham, near Newcastle, was probably a speculative investment, apparently unsuccessful, because he died as a labourer at West Maitland in 1875.[42] As Robert Mason discovered, real estate could prove to be a burden. After the death of his wife he talked of selling his property and returning to England, estimating the value of his houses at Dungog and nearby Brookfield at between £2,000 and £2,500. When he was finally able to sell the last of them some six years later in 1864, he realised only £350 on buildings he had been unable to maintain. At the time he described himself proudly and modestly in the dealings as a yeoman although the term was more accurately applied to his brother Joseph, who had returned to England and tenant-farming.[43]

Only about 20 per cent of the Wessex transportees became farmers. As less than half of this group owned sufficient land to farm, the others must have been tenant-farmers. Australian historians have generally overlooked tenant-farming and its significance, largely because they could not conceive of its existence in their mythically egalitarian and classless society. Tenant-farming was widespread in the agricultural areas of New South Wales, providing a well regulated and most successful way for farmers, like Robert Baker and Thomas Whately, to get a start, especially on the Hunter, in the Nepean Valley and on the Southern Highlands. By 1861, when free selection began (a form of tenancy in which the state was the lessor), two-thirds of the agriculturalists in New South Wales were tenant-farmers, outnumbering freeholders by almost four to one.[44] Stephen Williams and Henry Bunce took advantage of free selection but they had already secured a base by the purchase of land, and had rural skills. Landless men without agricultural experience who selected in remote areas often condemned their families to hardships and mere subsistence.

Robert Baker became an overseer and then a tenant-farmer on Dartbrook near Scone. He stands out as one of only ten Wessex men who made a will. Although making a will does not necessarily prove material success, Baker and his Australian family had a better life than would have been possible for his English family in Wiltshire. He settled, married and reared his colonial family in the Scone district, his place of assignment. Known locally as a machine-breaker, he prospered, securing two farms on Dartbrook. He left one of these to his son, Robert, and the other to his unmarried daughter, Ann. They and their married sister all received gifts of stock. By comparison with his life in Wiltshire he had fared quite well, leaving an estate worth £100.[45] Before his exile, his family had required poor relief, and he had been removed as a pauper to his home parish.[46] After his death, his son erected a beautifully carved headstone on his father's grave. As local stone was lacking, stone masons rare and monumental work expensive, especially when it came from the yard of Thomas Browne of Maitland, it would have been a costly undertaking. Headstones were not only 'monuments of respect and affection' but also 'symbols of substance'.[47] In this case the substance was that of his son.

Job Hatherell's life in the colony was rather less smooth and comfortable. When Hatherell gained his ticket-of-leave, he worked as a bullocky for William Dumaresq, his master's brother. Commonly travelling between Muswellbrook and Maitland, he made an occasional trip to the Liverpool Plains and New England. His life in Wiltshire would not have prepared him for such distances and he must have learnt the skills of bullock driving while assigned. Teams, however, were expensive to purchase and it is unlikely that he owned his own. Originally at St Heliers near Muswellbrook, he transferred his ticket to Scone where he met and married a widow, Honorah Sweeney, who had seen her first husband, the local lock-up keeper, and her twin baby boys die in the space of a few weeks. Her own death, from a mismanaged delivery, left Hatherell with the surviving Sweeney child.[48] At the time the couple were living at St Heliers. Despite his steady job as a bullocky, they lived in the most wretched poverty without beds, and 'not two chairs nor even one of any kind in the house'.[49] Hatherell was no stranger to poverty; while he was growing up in Wiltshire his father had been regularly on the parish. There was to be no memorial for

Honorah or Job. Buried without a clergyman, Hatherell died as a labourer, the same station in life as his father.[50] Almost half the Swing protesters shared that occupation at the time of their death, the largest, single occupational group among them. Most spent their life in manual toil exactly as they would have done in England.

There is little in the colonial lives of most of these men and their families to distinguish them from other members of their class. The Pointer family, however, was one exception. When John Pointer gained his freedom, he was at Cassilis on the upper Hunter but he settled with his English wife and family at Parramatta. Within ten years he had purchased land at Tempe overlooking Botany Bay. The commercially wealthy had gentrified this area by building substantial villas set in extensive gardens. When they sold up in an attempt to avoid bankruptcy in the 1840s depression, the grounds of these estates were subdivided, creating opportunities for the aspiring. Secure at home, Pointer joined the rush to the Californian goldfields in 1851. A year later, his wife, Charlotte, began selling up at his direction and joined him. It was a move not without some conflict as Charlotte was reluctant to follow. Writing from California, Pointer told her not to 'put any stoar on the place for you will find a better here so no more from you'. Apparently the Californian adventure was successful, for when the couple returned to Australia, he again bought land at Tempe. With property came social status, and within a few years Pointer described himself as a gentleman; that is, someone who did not labour for his living.[51] The Pointers' land dealings and their Californian venture reveal determination and aspirations which allow us to know them a little more intimately. By comparison, the lives of most Wessex transportees were uneventful and did not involve adventure and risk-taking to the same extent. The more ordinary their lives, the less we can usually know about them. The commonplace and everyday leave few traces in the historical record except perhaps for the central events of birth, marriage and death and it is in such records that we find the faint traces of the transported as they formed relationships, raised families and reconstructed their lives as free men.

Altogether, sixty-seven couples were identified in New South Wales. As we have already seen, some men married more than once or had a known relationship with more than one woman. Slightly more than one third seem not to have had children.[52] A high level of fertility and fecundity has generally been assumed for the pre-gold rush period.[53] This assumption has often been accompanied by the belief that women were unable to control their fertility and that working-class people did not or could not exercise restraint in sexual relationships. Most children of the Wessex transportees were born after 1841. A study of the two preceding decades has found an average family size for that period of 5.3 which compares with 4.4 for the Swing families.[54] Smaller families are only to be expected given the high average age of the women marrying the Wessex men. The younger the woman was at marriage, the more children she was likely to bear. Ann Henley was only eighteen when she married Daniel

Hancock. By the time she was thirty, the average age of the protesters' spouses at marriage, she had given birth to seven children, including one set of twins. Altogether, the family numbered fourteen with the last born in 1870 when Ann was forty-eight years old. Despite the number of children, the family was surprisingly mobile. Hancock, a carrier, took them to Adelaide in South Australia where they remained for about three years. After they returned to New South Wales he became a publican at Berrima and the licensee of public houses at Binnalong, Gunning and Forbes. [55]

Wessex transportees fathered at least 154 children in New South Wales before 1856, 90 per cent of whom were baptised.[56] The rate of baptisms was extremely high compared with other available figures for New South Wales and southern England and cannot satisfactorily be explained as a matter of customary ritual.[57] Marriage and burial were regarded as more important ceremonies than baptism, which had few immediate or obvious advantages. The baptism of a child, therefore, can often be more revealing about the attitudes of parents to matters of faith and respectability than the other rites of passage, because baptism involved more than a perfunctory or necessary observance of a religious practice. The average delay of about 30 weeks between birth and baptism does not necessarily indicate indifference but rather the exercise of denominational preference. Couples waited until the clergyman of their choice was available. Although marriages usually occurred on weekdays, almost two-thirds of baptisms of children of Wessex transportees took place on a Sunday. The clergyman may have determined the date of the ceremony but a Sunday baptism made it possible for both parents to attend and emphasizes, perhaps, the importance attached to it. Even couples in common-law relationships sought baptism for at least one child. They were, however, less likely than those legally married to have all their children baptised. Alfred Darling and Elizabeth O'Reilly had only two of their twelve children baptised, and George Arlett and Ann Matthews three of their nine, perhaps because some children died before they could be baptised by a clergyman.[58] Apart from the baptism of twins, the Arletts were the only other Wessex couple to have more than one child baptised at the same time. The isolation of these families in very remote areas, however, may explain this particular circumstance, but obviously parents went to considerable lengths to have their children baptised and regarded baptism as important for each child in its own right.

It has been claimed that the working classes in the colony were very casual about and even antagonistic to religious belief, and that denominational affiliations were often accidental, according to which clergyman happened to be available.[59] However, the occasions when the Wessex men exercised denominational choice suggest that this view is rather overstated. All the men of the *Eleanor* had identified themselves as Protestant on arrival in the colony. Sixty per cent of those who married in New South Wales, chose the rites of the Church of England; almost a quarter married in

Presbyterian ceremonies, 15 per cent in Catholic and less than 2 per cent in Wesleyan. The low figure for Catholic marriage indicates that, in this matter at least, the husband's denominational preference generally prevailed. As slightly more than 40 per cent of the wives of Swing protesters were Irish Catholics, it seems that denominational adherence was weaker among women, traditionally the nurturers of faith. All the Catholic marriages took place in the Catholic strongholds of Sydney and Maitland. In Ireland the lines had been clearly drawn between Catholic and Protestant and mixed marriages were rare, but in New South Wales up to the late 1860s the situation was rather more fluid. When it came to the baptism of children, a slightly different denominational pattern emerges from that of the marriages. Although about 60 per cent were baptised in the Church of England, Catholic baptisms amounted to more than 20 per cent.

Almost two-thirds of parents were consistent in the denomination of the baptism of their children. The denomination of the baptism of the first child tended to hold for the rest, a pattern which gives the lie to the view that children were often baptised by the first clergyman who happened to come along. If parents changed denomination, they remained with the new one for subsequent baptisms. The children involved in these instances usually had an Irish Catholic mother. The shift to Catholicism probably reflects the growth of a Catholic consciousness and a more disciplined denominational community. William, the first born of Honorah McCarthy, was baptised Catholic, as were two subsequent children, but another three were not baptised at all.[60] Although John Gilmore and Catherine Slavin had married in a Presbyterian ceremony, all their children were baptised Catholic, while Gilmore's children by his first wife had been baptised according to the rites of the Church of England.[61]

Changes are not always explicable in terms of the denomination of one of the parents. George Hopgood and Ann Hines were married by a Wesleyan Methodist clergyman in Bathurst, with George declaring that he was a member. Ann, born in the colony with a Protestant father, had been baptised in the Church of England.[62] Wesleyanism was well established in Bathurst, which had its first resident minister in 1836 and its own chapel a year later.[63] However, three of the Hopgood children were baptised Catholic and two were not baptised at all.[64] Subsequently, the children themselves showed little denominational consistency. Although two married by Catholic rites, another married in the Presbyterian Church. Hopgood and one son were buried without a clergyman. The other son, baptised and married in the Catholic Church, was buried according to the rites of the Church of England. When Ann, their mother, remarried, she did so in the Catholic Church.[65] Such inconsistencies might reflect the religious indifference so often attributed to the colonial population or, alternatively, the search for a spiritual home.

Some families never wholly resolved the problem of religious difference. Thomas

Whately married Margaret Shea, an Irish Catholic, in 1838 according to the rites of the Church of England. Although their first child was not baptised, the other five born before 1856 were. The average delay of about forty-four days between their birth and baptism was significantly lower than the overall average for Swing families of thirty weeks. Perhaps the fact that Whately was a long-time tenant of the Reverend Thomas Hassall, who married the couple and baptised their babies, hastened the ceremony and played some part in their denominational choice. Even after the family left Hassall's property, however, the Whatelys continued to baptise their children in the Church of England. Some Whately children later made their own decisions about their religious affiliation by converting to Catholicism as adults and remaining resolutely Catholic. Their mother was buried with Catholic rites in 1897, having survived her husband by sixteen years. A Church of England clergyman conducted Thomas's burial service. The same divide at death occurred in the case of Robert Baker and his wife, Julia Berrigan, at Scone.[66] Their separation in death mirrored the division between Catholic and Protestant, which was so deeply entrenched in colonial society by the late-nineteenth century that religious tolerance had all but disappeared.

Almost eighteen per cent of Swing transportees married in a Presbyterian ceremony. Usually, but not invariably, the marriage registration identified those who were communicants. Levi Brown, Aaron Deadman, Gifford North and Daniel Sims all laid claim to being communicant Presbyterians. Mary Randell, wife of Deadman, and Maria Gardener, who married North, identified themselves similarly. When John Pound married Catherine McVicar in a Presbyterian ceremony in the district of Bathurst, she was a communicant. Her family, Scottish emigrants, continued their firm adherence to Presbyterianism in the colony. Both witnesses to Catherine's marriage were themselves Presbyterians, and all the couple's children were baptised in that denomination. Catherine's denomination prevailed within the Pound family, as was more likely in a strong Presbyterian community like Bathurst with its own minister. Daniel Sims, a declared Presbyterian at the time of his marriage, was the only Swing protester buried according to Presbyterian rites.[67]

The Wessex men and their partners were not passive in matters of faith or lacking religiosity. As the majority lived outside the County of Cumberland, where clergymen of all denominations were readily available, their actions in choosing to baptise their children in a particular denomination speak loudly about religious sensibilities and respectability. The protesters seem to have rejected religious dissent, choosing instead religious conformity and respectability. Their choices are another indication of their essential conservatism and their desire to escape from their turbulent past. Although a significant number settled on the Hunter, where religious dissent was strong and where they might have found it easier to choose that path, they generally favoured the security and respectability of the Church of England.

Although the majority of the Swing men served their sentences in three areas, often on adjoining properties, and although they tended to settle in those same areas, they had little to do with each other once they were free. None of their children inter-married. Wessex transportees were not witnesses to the marriages or burials of their comrades with whom they had suffered so much. The reconstruction of their lives did not include an association with each other. Closing the door as far as possible on their previous life, they clearly desired to leave their convict origins behind. While they 'all...considered themselves free', they were, nevertheless, chained to their English past.[68] Most returned successfully to that obscurity which is the usual fate of working people. Only Robert Mason, that resolute radical, attracted further atten-tion. Active in local politics, he wrote articles for the *Maitland Mercury* and acquired sufficient influence that he believed the local member would lose his seat, if he were only 'to say the word'.[69] Very few shared Mason's interest in politics. When manhood suffrage was introduced into New South Wales in 1858 only Henry Bunce, William Page, Henry Spicer, Gifford North and Jason Greenway exercised their right, although subsequently another sixteen registered to vote in colonial elections.

Most of the Swing transportees seem to have desired nothing more than to put down roots in their new land. Once they married and settled on a patch of ground they rarely moved again. Their lives had a stability and anonymity which mirrored the English experience that had been denied them. Pioneering families in many ways, their children often adopted the attitudes and habits of their parents. For example, of the six members of the Pound family who married, four remained in Carcoar, one was in Bathurst and one in Camperdown in Sydney. Two married their McVicar cousins.[70] The majority of the Pound grandchildren were born in the Carcoar area and adjacent districts. For the children of the Wessex transportees, rural demography usually limited their choice of marriage partners as it had done in the case of their parents. Opportunities to meet and socialise with those outside their own class were especially limited in country areas, with their rigid social hierarchies. Two of Thomas Radborn's English-born daughters married convicts. Both ceremonies took place in the Parish of Carcoar where Radborn had been a labourer and shepherd.[71] The children of Thomas Radborn, like those of the Pounds, were not inclined to move from the place where their parents had settled, where they themselves married and where their babies were born. Equally, it was unusual for children to marry above their father's class. That possibility was more likely to be realised, if at all, in the next generation.

The men of the *Eleanor* were never forgotten by those in Wessex, nor did they forget their loved ones in England. News travelled in both directions. Although the Mason correspondence is unique in its regularity and detail, many families main-tained contact with England. As we have seen, the families of John Batten and Daniel Hancock wrote to them regularly. Literacy on the part of those maintaining ties across the oceans was not absolutely essential, though obviously it made communi-cation easier. The illiterate relied on scribes and messages carried by friends.

Historians have seriously underestimated the closeness of emigrants' ties with home and their ability to stay in touch, largely because their letters are less likely to have survived than those of the upper classes. Charles Milson was exceptionally literate and kept in touch with his English family very easily. When his English-born son, Richard, who was also literate, arrived in Australia in 1857, he knew that his father was at Aberdeen near Muswellbrook.[72] George Nash, a free immigrant, settled near Dungog in the same area as his brother John, a Swing protester. Thomas Shergold and his sister Sarah, siblings of the convicts, George and John Shergold, also came to the colony.[73] Family reconstitutions will continue to forge further links in the chain of emigration as they identify other members of a convict's family coming to Australia, providing a greater understanding of the process and pattern of emigration and of their colonial experiences.

Family reconstitution has allowed us to answer the question of what happened to the majority of the Swing protesters after they had become free. Unlike George Rudé who had 'no certain means of finding out' about their fate in the colony, we have had the advantage of having open access to the registrations of birth deaths and marriages.[74] But what has it revealed? The findings may disappoint those who wish for stories of triumph in their convict forebears. Wishful thinkers might like to imagine that Britain's involuntary exiles triumphed in their new land but substantial material success and upward social mobility were most unusual. A subset of the English working class, the convicts of the *Eleanor*, like most other convicts, merged into the working class of New South Wales. Colonial Australia was no more a working-man's paradise than Victorian Britain; in the colonies it was men, or women, with capital who prospered. One or two of the Swing transportees amassed modest sums which they would probably not have done in England and most enjoyed regular, better-paid work in the labour-hungry colonies than they would have found in Wessex. But it is the sheer ordinariness of their reconstructed lives which speaks to us from the evidential fragments found in the registrations of births, deaths and marriages.

Books, like lives, have a beginning, a middle and an end, and our story of the Swing transportees is almost finished. Their lives in England cruelly disrupted by unjust punishment, they began new ones when transported. Through the bureaucratic machinery which recorded their existence we have examined the process of reconstruction and we find them at the last in the death registrations. Thirteen per cent of the Wessex transportees were, at death, described as tradesmen. Charles Milson, a carpenter, began his free working life in the colony with his ex-master, H. C. Sempill, manager for Thomas Potter McQueen of Segenhoe, just north of Muswellbrook. One of the largest single estates in the Hunter, it was there that Milson met Annie Lyons, his future wife. After McQueen established his private town, Aberdeen, Milson left Segenhoe which had suffered a series of upheavals. He worked as a carpenter around the district but settled for a time in the town where he hoped to purchase an allotment, a hope which remained unrealised.[75] Annie, a midwife, supplemented the family's income but she died in 1865 in an accident on her way to a delivery. Described as having been 'ailing for years', Milson died nine years later living with his English-born son, a bush worker.[76]

A trade did not necessarily advantage the Swing men in the colony when free. Although there would have been considerable demand for the skills of Thomas Goodfellow, a blacksmith, his life finished in complete destitution. When he gained his absolute pardon, he continued to work for his master, James Glennie, of Falbrook, Patrick Plains. Rather than setting up independent forges and being self-employed, blacksmiths generally became employees on large farms and pastoral runs. When Goodfellow married in 1849, he was still at Patrick Plains but working at St Claire where he met his wife, Ann Gannon, a widow. No children were baptised or registered from that marriage. Twenty years later we find him at Anambah near Maitland. In 1881, he died in the Benevolent Asylum in West Maitland.[77]

The circumstances of a death can often be revealing about the life. Goodfellow was not the only Wessex transportee to die in an asylum. Almost ten per cent of those whose deaths are identifiable, ended their days as paupers in these charitable institutions. A similar percentage died in a hospital, although hospitals may also have served as benevolent institutions.[78] Most received some medical care as they neared their end; after 1856, seventy per cent of Swing men who died in New South Wales had professional medical attention in the period leading up to their death. Most died in their place of residence, some when living with a daughter or son. Single men, such as Timothy May and Samuel Quinton, were still labouring when they died at the ages of sixty-nine and seventy-two respectively. Their employer or the undertaker was the informant for the death registrations.

Although 'success' is a wholly relative, highly imprecise and usually irrelevant measure of a human life, it is an idea deeply embedded in colonial and convict studies. The notion is expressed in many ways but underpinning all is the belief that, in spite of much adversity, as convicts or free settlers, the early colonists 'succeeded'. They endured their sufferings, tamed the land, seized the opportunities they could not have in Britain, grew physically bigger and more robustly democratic until they reached the mythic proportions of the Anzacs. In material terms few of the Swing protesters succeeded in New South Wales, but it is unrealistic to have expected otherwise. They had protested in 1830 to obtain a living wage but few envisaged any major change in their circumstances. Their aspirations were modest; they hoped for a life free from destitution. Most would have expected to spend their lives toiling in a familiar environment. Living in New South Wales seems not to have altered their conservatism or increased their ambitions. Some became tenant-farmers, a position which they were unlikely to have achieved in England, but few aspired to own land. Failing to escape their past, their aims generally remained modest. They did not build castles in the air but usually occupied humble, rough-timbered, dwellings on the ground. On the whole, New South Wales was not a land flowing with milk and honey nor a place of remarkable opportunity. The lives of the Wessex protesters were not fundamentally different from what might have awaited them in England, with one major difference – the spectre of hunger did not consistently haunt their door. With that, most would have been content.

## Notes

1   *Newcastle Chronicle*, 21 March 1863.

2   Curator of Intestate Estates, Archives of New South Wales (hereafter AONSW) 6/3566, No. 2426.

3   The circumstances of this dispute are included in matters relating to the settlement of the estate as the person concerned applied for the payment of £50, the equivalent of two years wages for a labourer.

4   R. Ward, *The Australian Legend*, Melbourne, 1958, pp. 73-74, 101.

5   Births, Deaths and Marriages (hereafter BDM); BDM 1835, 473, 19, BDM 1836, 391, 20, BDM 1838, 331, 22, BDM 1840, 368, 24, BDM 1842, 610, 26, BDM 1850, 2318, 55, BDM 1847, 1222, 55. Registration of death, 26 December 1862, died at Paddington, 53 years, Registrar General of New South Wales (hereafter RGNSW) 1862/ 1997. Death, Daniel Sims, 22 May 1885, 76 years, RGNSW, 1885/1075.

6   Death, 24 June 1849, aged 36 years, BDM 1849, 226, 34. Death, infant, 29 October, five months, 1849, BDM 1849, 559, 34. This registration identifies the infant as the son of a pauper.

7   'Report from the Select Committee on the Petition from Distressed Mechanics and Labourers with the Minutes of Evidence', Votes and Proceedings of the New South Wales Legislative Council, 1843, p. 720 and pp. 719-751. A series of articles entitled 'The Sanitary State of Sydney appeared in the *Sydney Morning Herald* from 1 February to 5 April 1851.

8   Free Selection before survey began in 1861 in New South Wales. By paying a small deposit, people could select land within designated areas. The most readily available freehold land was usually isolated. The best land closest to Sydney had been progressively alienated from the earliest days of settlement. William Adams, death, 18 November 1886, describes him as a selector. RGNSW 1886/12166.

9   Samuel Quinton, death, 26 August 1876, RGNSW 1876/10338. Timothy May, death, 28 April 1877, RGNSW 1877/5627. William Oakley, death, township of Scone, 8 June 1846, labourer, aged forty, BDM 1846, 31, 1065.

Ticket-of-Leave Butts, 1827-1875, 37/148, AONSW 4/4109, Reel 926

10  See J. W. McCarty, 'The Inland Corridor', *Australia 1888: A Bicentennial History* No. 5, September 1980, pp. 33-49.

11  John Wheeler, death, Sydney Infirmary, 28 October 1845, labourer, aged 40, BDM 1840, 1762, 24.

12  Application for Permission to Marry, 1836, AONSW 4/2304.1, Reel 730 and Enclosure, Col. Sec. In Letters, 36/9670. Ticket of Leave Butts, 1827-1875, 44/1229, AONSW 4/4188, Reel 952. Death, 23 October 1887, Muswellbrook, RGNSW 1887/9478.

13  Matthew Triggs, death, Maitland Hospital, 30 November 1853, aged 55, brick-layer, BDM 1853, 1920, 39. Maitland Historical Society, *A History of Maitland*, Maitland, 1983, p. 23.

14  Robert Baker acquired the additional name, George, in his colonial life. Ticket-of-Leave Butts, 1827-1875, 37/1649, AONSW 4/4109, Reel 926. Registration of death, 16 October 1863, RGNSW 1863/5856. Julia Baker, death, 21 January 1884, RGNSW 1884/10117. These death certificates record the name as George Robert Baker and Julia Berrigan (variously Bergin, Berrigan, Bargin and Burrigan). Probate Series 1, No. 5829, Society of Australian Genealogists, Sydney, Reel 3009. The Robert Baker who died on the Shoalhaven in 1864 was born in Leeds. RGNSW 1864/5800.

15  Charles Bulpitt, death, 19 October 1854, Cliffdale near Scone, BDM 1854,1686, 41. Job Hatherell, death, 4 February 1867, at Scone, RGNSW, 1867/7801.

16  Marriage to Lydia Clarke, both of Stroud, estate of the Australian Agricultural Company, 1 January 1842, Church of England, BDM 1842, 482, 26. See Robert Mason to Lydia, 7 and 14 December, 1862, Lyndhurst Vale, Brookfield, Mason Family Letters, Mitchell Library (hereafter ML) MSS 2290, Cy Reel 339.

17  L. Macquarie, *Journals of his Tours in New South Wales and Van Diemen's Land, 1810-1822*, 2 Vols., Sydney, 1956, Vol. I, p. 147.

18  The registration of the baptism for the first child gives his occupation as labourer. BDM 1843, 1754, 28. The registrations of the children born before 1856 list him as a farmer. We have been unable to establish that he purchased land in this period. Isaac Manns married Eliza Henley, both of the parish of Camden, 12 March 1843, Church of England, BDM 1843, 353, 27. Their last child, Ernest Edward, was born there in 1867. RGNSW 1867/6560. The registrations of the baptisms of their children, Mary Ann and Henry, give his occupation as tenant. BDM 1843, 1266, 26 and BDM 1846, 1608, 31.

19  In the baptismal registration for Margaret, Thomas was a farmer although he was still at Cherith and was, presumably, still a tenant. BDM 1848, 1433, 33.

No. 3, Spring Rivulet Allotments, 16 October 1852, Old Title Land Grants, 87/221, Land Titles Office of New South Wales, Sydney.

20  James Burgess, Stonequarry, married Jane Dillon, of the parish of Stonequarry (Picton), banns, consent of governor, 30 February 1837, Church of England, BDM 1837, 1698, 21. They were living at Airds when their first child, Thomas, was baptised. BDM, 1837, 933, 21. They were living at Bargo in 1839, BDM, 1839, 1073, 23 but at Stonequarry when the other children were baptised, James, BDM 1841, 1469, 25, John, 1843, 1673, 28, William, 1846, 1609, 31, Henry 1848, 1203, 34 and Alice Sophia, 1851, 1790, 37. His occupation was labourer at the time of the registrations of James and Alice Sophia. For the details concerning his career as a constable, see Benches of Magistrates, Picton (Stonequarry), 1 March 1839, 4 August 1840, 1 October 1840, 20 May 1843 and 20 April 1857. AONSW 4/5627 and 4/5628, Reels 672 and 673. Death, 15 December 1865, Jarvisfield, Picton, aged 56. RGNSW 1865/5618.

21  John Ford, of Sydney and Greendale, married Mary Ann Coleman, of the same place, 4 June 1848, at Sydney, Presbyterian, BDM 1838, 3088, 74. Maria, baptised 21 April 1839, Greendale, servant to George Wentworth, Church of England, BDM 1839, 1041, 23. Marianne, baptised 1 March 1841, Greendale, labourer, Church of England, BDM 1841, 1438, 25. Mary Ann Ford, death, wife of a farmer, Greendale, Church of England, BDM 1855, 1997, 43. Marriage to Mary Little, 14 July 1856, Greendale, RGNSW 1856/1900. Registrations of births, Henry, RGNSW 1857/5730, Charlotte and Emily, RGNSW 1858/6064, Robert RGNSW 1862/6605, Ann, RGNSW 1864/13626, George, RGNSW 1871/ 8665. Ford's death certificate includes two more children. Death of John Ford, 16 January 1875, Narellan, RGNSW 1875/5482.

22  D. Jeans, *An Historical Geography of New South Wales to 1901*, Sydney, 1972, pp. 96, 97 and 108.

23  Ticket-of-Leave Butts, 1827-1875, 35/759, AONSW 4/4099, Reel 923. Abraham House married Catherine Chyd, both of Yass, at Yass, 5 April 1856, Church of England, BDM 1856, 16, 43. Death, 9 February 1877, Chainy Ponds, RGNSW 1877/9664.

24  Elizabeth Emily, born 29 December 1842, Boorowa, BDM 1843, 1593, 27. Spring Flat Creek, County of King, 5 acres and 2 rods, £58.10. 0, 1 November 1851, Old Title Land Grants, 81/193, Land Office of New South Wales, Sydney, Conditional Purchase Register, 64/2137, AONSW 7/2707, Vol. 10. He was listed as a labourer on the baptismal registration of Kezia, BDM, 2161, 37. Information from a descendant, Beryl Hutchinson.

25  28 January 1854, 30 acres, and 3 November 1836, 30 acres, Co. Argyle, Old Title Land Grants, 92/192 and 132/3093, Land Titles Office of New South

Wales, Sydney. At the time of his first selection, he had 140 acres of freehold land. Conditional Purchases which identify the address of the applicant, 62/584, 63/2415, 69/839. 81/181 and 81/191, AONSW 7/2707, Vol. 10 and 7/2735, Vol. 38. Marriage, Henry Bunce and Mary Jordan, 15 November 1841, both of Lake Bathurst, with consent of governor, Bungonia, Church of England, BDM 1841, 883, 25. Mary Bunce (Bence), death, 13 July 1873, Goulburn, RGNSW 1873/4247. Henry Bunce, death, 21 May 1887, Goulburn, RGNSW 1887/5922.

26   W. H. Wells, *A Geographical Dictionary or Gazetteer of the Australian Colonies 1848*, Sydney, 1970 [1847], Sydney, p. 187.

27   Assigned to J. McClaren of Sydney, Isaac held his ticket for the District of Argyle, indicating that he had moved during his servitude. Marriage, both of this parish, BDM, 1840, 554, 24. Elizabeth died in Queanbeyan in 1884. RGNSW 1884/13079. Isaac Burton, death, Wolumla, 20 February 1886, aged 78, tailor, RGNSW 86/2065.

28   Per *Woodbridge*, 15 September 1838, AONSW 4/4780, Reel 2654. Baptisms, BDM 1840, 1313, 34, BDM 1841, 1434, 26, BDM 1842, 1435, 26 and BDM 1843, 1740, 28. The occupation of Thomas, the father, for the first baptism is given as labourer. For subsequent baptisms, he was listed as a farmer. Baptism, Aaron, registered under the names of Aaron and Ellis Harding, born 26 September, baptised 23 November 1845, Sutton Forest, farmer, Church of England, BDM 1845, 1870, 30. We are indebted to Wilbur Besanko and Mrs Hilda Symonds for information on this family. A. Porter, *The History and Family Tree of Thomas Sargent and his Wife Ellis (Alice) Packham and their Descendants in Australia 1789-1979, including the Hardy Family*, Adelaide, 1979.

29   Marriage, both of Bathurst, to Elizabeth Taylor, also known as Eliza Johnson, banns, consent of governor, Bathurst, 16 March 1838, Church of England, BDM 1838, 1904, 22, Henry John Gilmore, born 24 January 1839, baptism, 10 March 1839, abode, Homebush, superintendent of farm, Church of England, BDM 1839, 1904, 22, Richard, baptism, born 27 August 1844, baptised 21 September 1844, abode, Raymond Terrace, settler, Church of England, BDM 1844, 2434, 28 and marriage, both of the Clarence, Sydney, 14 May 1847, Presbyterian, BDM 1847, 47, 78. Baptism, 30 January 1847, born 8 December 1846, Clarence River, Catholic, BDM 1847, 530, 66. Parents are named as John Gilmore and Margaret McFadden in this baptism and also that of John Gilmore, born 24 July 1851, baptised 15 September 1851, Ipswich, Catholic, BDM 1851, 2132, 68.

30   Birth, unnamed female, August 1857, North Grafton, labourer, RGNSW 1857/6988. Deaths, John Gilmore, RGNSW 1866/4349 and Catherine, RGNSW 1868/4159.

31  Marriage to Ann Haynes, both of Bathurst, 13 September 1842, Wesleyan, BDM 1842, 54, 83. When their last child baptised, George, was born at Bathurst 15 October 1848, the family were living in Bathurst and his father's occupation was carpenter. In the marriage registrations of two of his children, he is described as a builder. See, for example, the marriage of George Hopgood to Ellen Barr, 29 August 1872, Sydney, RGNSW 1872/878. Death, George Hopgood, 7 December 1867, King Street, Sydney, RGNSW 1867/2001. Thomas Haines, Census of 1828, H 89. Ann is listed as three years old. Death, Thomas Haines, 7 September 1850, Brucedale, aged 72, labourer, Church of England, BDM 1850, 1307, 36. Ann Hopgood, widow, married Samuel Thomas in a Catholic ceremony in Sydney in 1873. Her occupation is given as innkeeper. RGNSW 1873/1411. We are indebted to Tina Russell for information concerning the Hopgood family. Catherine Gilmore's death certificate lists her as a hotel keeper of Victoria Street Grafton, RGNSW 68/4159.

32  Plan of Thirteen Portions of Land on Breakfast Creek and a Branch known as the Badger Ground in the County of Phillip. Surveyed on General Instructions dated 5 February 1856. P. 64/152, Land Titles Office of New South Wales, Sydney. We are indebted to Bill Batten, Sydney, for a copy.

33  Mary Ann, whose father had been transported from Wiltshire, had come to Australia with her mother and siblings to join him, arriving on the *Burrell* in 1832. We are indebted to Chris Fletcher for these details. They settled at South Creek in the Penrith area. A Mary Ann Hughes, aged 18, spinster, free immigrant, married Alexander Pitcairn, with consent of her father, 17 August 1840 at Penrith. One of the witnesses came from South Creek. BDM 1840, 429, 24.

34  The first two children who grew to adulthood seem not to have been baptised. Charles was the first but four years after his birth at Bathurst where the family was living. Born 19 July 1847, baptised 30 March 1851, Thomas and Mary Ann, carrier, BDM 1847, 2318, 37. Birth, William, 28 May 1857, Kelso, RGNSW 1857/4466. Death, 8 November 1895, Brokenshaft Creek near Orange, farmer, 84 years, RGNSW 1885/13663.

35  Marriage, 22 July 1843, both of Bartletts, married at Bartletts, district of Bathurst, Presbyterian, BDM 1843, 1352, 76. Baptisms, William, parents at Bartletts, father a settler, BDM, 1843, 8531, 45, Elizabeth, parents at Cabula, BDM 1844, 8531, 45, Mary Ann, parents at Cabula, BDM 1846, 1575, 48, Elizabeth, parents at Brownlea, BDM 1844, 470, 47, Christina, parents at Cabula, father a farmer, BDM 1848, 109, 50, Jemima, parents at Rocky Bridge, father a settler, BDM 1850, 162, 51 and Katharine, parents at Coal Hole, father a farmer, BDM 1854, 1117, 52. Another five children were born after 1856. Land Purchase, 21 July 1854, in the County of Georgiana, 'on a branch of Rocky Bridge Creek on the south-east corner of Mr McVicar's purchase', Old

Title Land Grants, 96/199, Land Title Office of New South Wales, Sydney.

36 Old Title Land Grants, 112/1247 to 1249, Land Titles Office of New South Wales, Sydney. Deaths. Thomas Radburn, 17 January 1877, No 1 Swamp (Neville), farmer, and Harriett, 20 October 1870, No 1 Swamp, RGNSW 1877/? and 1870/ 3274.

37 M. Cannon, *Australia in the Victorian Age: Life in the Country*, 3 vols, Vol. 2, West Melbourne, 1978, pp. 25-27.

38 Photograph in J. Chambers, *Rebels of the Fields: Robert Mason and the convicts of the Eleanor*, Letchworth, 1995, p. 291.

39 A descendant, Beryl Hutchinson, provided these details. Death, 12 June 1872, Burrangong Hospital (Young), Church of England. A wardsman, acting 'By Information' was the informant for the registration. RGNSW 72/7434. For the details of the selections, see Conditional Purchase Registers, Vol. 38, 71/1070, 3236 and 4492, AONSW 7/2735.

40 Henry Bunce, 30 acres, 28 January 1854 and another 30 acres, 3 November 1856, John Pound, 30 acres, 21 July 1854, Thomas Radburn, 30 acres, 4 February 1854, John Batten, 30 acres, 13 July 1857 and Henry Spicer 15 September 1854. Old Title Land Grants 92/192, 119/3093, 96/199 and 98/215, Land Titles Office of New South Wales, Sydney.

41 Death, Henry Spicer, 25 October 1868, Boco, Cooma, aged 58, RGNSW 3716, and death, Mary Ann, 13 September 1872, Boco, aged 50 years, RGNSW72/3369.

42 Charles Payne, 1 November 1849 and 22 July 1853, William Cheater, 5 January 1852 and 17 May 1852, William Sims, 30 October 1854, Robert Mason and Henry Spicer, 15 September 1854, Old Title Land Grants, Land Titles Office of New South Wales, 224/37 and 235/96, 253/81 and 254/76. 257/75, and 98/215. Death, 2 May 1875, Horse Shoe Bend, West Maitland, aged 73, Church of England, RGNSW 75/ 7326.

43 1 March 1858, 7 August 1861 and 15 January 1864, Old Title Grants, Land Titles Office of New South Wales, Sydney, 62/72, 74/174 and 88/144. Joseph Mason to Lydia, 13 May 1862, Joseph Mason to Lydia, 31 October 1831 and 13 May 1862, Mason Family, Letters, 1857-1865, ML MSS 2290, CY Reel 339. D. Kent & N. Townsend (eds), *Joseph Mason, Assigned Convict 1831-1837: Doomed to the earth's remotest region*, Melbourne, 1996, pp. 175-177.

44 A. Atkinson, *Camden: Farm and Village Life in Early New South Wales*, Sydney, 1988, p. 68, and see, also, 1861 Census.

45 N. Gray, *St Luke's Church, Scone: A Walk Round the Churchyard*, Scone, 1985, p. 16. Gray does not give her source of information but it is likely to have been descendants. Baker's death certificate records his place of death as Quirindi which was the name of his farm and not the settlement in northern New South

Wales. George Robert Baker, registration of death, 16 October 1863, Church of England, RGNSW 1863/5856. George Robert Baker, will, Supreme Court of New South Wales, Registrar of Probates Series 1/5829, Society of Australian Genealogists, Sydney, Reel 309.

46    WRO 1933/21. Chambers, op. cit., pp. 130-131.

47    Gray, op. cit., pp. 25 and 27.

48    Marriage, Job Hatherell, of this parish, widower, and Norah Sweeney, of this parish, widow, banns, with the consent of the governor, 13 November 1844, Church of England, Scone, BDM 1844, 623, 29. Marriage, Job Hatherell, of this parish, widower, Sarah Gerrard, of this parish, widow, banns, January 1847, Church of England Scone, BDM 21 1847, 32, 513. Deaths, Patrick Sweeny, 1 April 1844, aged 43, Stephen, 21 February 1844, aged nine weeks and three days and Patrick, 1 March 1844, BDM 1844, 992, 29, BDM 1844, 993, 30 and BDM 1844, 994, 30. Honorah's first born was Michael, 19 September 1842, BDM 1842, 2186, 61. Death Honorah, 28 July, St Aubins near Scone, aged 39, Church of England, BDM 1846, 1068, 39.

49    The doctor concerned, Dr Goodwin, wrote a fairly scurrilous account of aspects of life in the town and its leading citizens, including a robust defence of himself against the charge of drunkenness while attending the confinement of Honorah Hatherell. A copy is held by the Scone and Upper Hunter Historical Society.

50    We are indebted to David Hatherell for most of the details concerning Job. Ticket-of -leave passports, 5 January 1842, 4 May 1843, 17 June 1844 and 3 March 1846, AONSW 4/4243, Reels 969, 971, 972, and 975. Job Hatherell, death, 4 February 1867, Scone, Church of England, RGNSW 1867/7801.

51    Charlotte arrived with four children on the *Susan*, 18 March 1839, AONSW 4/4784, Reel 2134, p. 82. Entry no. 650, 1841 Census. As Harriett was acting as his agent in the sale of property, she produced an authorising letter, referred to in the title deeds and agreements, Memorandum of Agreement, 30 May 1851, Book 20, No. 556, Conveyance, 6 March 1852, Book 25, No. 221, Indenture, 29 September 1852, Book 25, No. 244 and Indenture, 21 June 1854, Book 32, No. 864 and Indenture, 2 May 1854, Book 142, No. 79. Old System Titles, Land Titles Office of New South Wales, Sydney. Pointer, *William and Mary*, 27 February 1850, Passenger Lists, Departures and Shipping *Mary Catherine*, Shipping Intelligence, Arrivals, *SMH*, 11 November 1851. It seems that two sons-in law also went to California. We are indebted to Wendy Cowley for these references.

52    Extensive researches of all surnames in all variant spellings and marriages after 1856, lead us to believe that this figure is very accurate though obviously there would have been some still-born babies and some babies who were not registered at all.

53  M. J. Belcher, 'The Child in New South Wales Society: 1820 to 1837', PhD., University of New England, Armidale, 1982, pp. 138-139.

54  Ibid., p. 164.

55  Chambers, op. cit. p. 185. Missing from this listing is Daniel's twin, Ann. The twins were born on 21 April 1847 and baptised 16 May 1847. RGNSW 1847, 1528 and 1529, 32. Births, James, 25 December 1857, BDM 1857/5119, Ann, 14 September 1860, RGNSW 1860/5352, Charlotte, 13 March 1863, RGNSW 1863/9821, Elizabeth Jane, 20 May 1865, RGNSW, 1865/3167, and Rebecca Maria, 20 October 1870, RGNSW 1870/ 19535, Death, Ann, 3 November 1890, RGNSW 1890/14237 and Daniel, 20 March 1890, RGNSW 1890/14182. Daniel's son in law described his occupation as farmer in the registration.

56  The number may have been higher but it is impossible to identify children who were baptised under the maiden name of the mother unless subsequently the father of the child continued a relationship with the mother.

57  N. Townsend, ''A Strange, wild set'? Cedar-cutters on the Macleay, Nambucca and Bellinger Rivers, 1838 to 1848', *Labour History*, No. 55, November 1988, p. 19, A. Atkinson, 'Convicts and Courtship', in P. Grimshaw, C. McConville and E. McEwan (eds), *Families in Colonial Australia*, Sydney, 1985, p. 203. These rates of baptism were 53-56 per cent.

58  Baptisms, Ann Maria Darling, BDM 1853, 2906, 72 and Julia Rose, BDM 1855, 3475, 162. Elizabeth, Jacob and George Arlott, BDM 1847, 842, 843 and 844, 70. In each case the total number of children has been taken from the registration of death. If there is a mistake in the number, it is almost invariably the case that the number is understated rather than overstated. Elizabeth Eleanor Darling, death, 19 December 1865, RGNSW 1865/2461. George Arlott (Artlett), death, 23 January 1879, Gilgandra, RGNSW 1879/5252. In both cases the informant was the spouse and likely, therefore, to know the correct number of offspring.

59  See, A. Grocott, *Convicts, Clergymen and Churches: Attitudes of convicts and ex-convicts towards the churches and clergy in New South Wales from 1788 to 1851.* Melbourne 1980. His study is directed at demonstrating the irreligion of the lower classes especially convicts.

60  William, Anne and Daniel, BDM 1841, 145, BDM 241, 1842, 1817, 61 and BDM 1846,469, 82. Death, John Batten, 20 January 1868, lists two females as deceased. Another son, John, was born in 1844. We are indebted to Bill Batten of Sydney for information.

61  See footnote 29 for the details.

62  Marriage, Ann Hines and George Hopgood, both of Bathurst, 13 September 1842, BDM 1842, 54, 83. Baptism, Anne, Thomas and Maria Haines,

Parramatta, Church of England, BDM 1823, 68491. Thomas Haines, H0089, 1828 Census, is listed as a Protestant. When he died at Bathurst he was buried according to the rites of the Church of England.

63  T. Barker, *A History of Bathurst: The Early Settlement to 1862*, Bathurst, 1992, pp.150-152.

64  Thomas, Mary Jane and George, BDM 1842, 54, 83. BDM 1843, 2454, 162 and BDM 1848, 2296, 65. According to George Hopgood's death certificate, there were five children, two of whom were deceased at the time of his death, 7 December 1867. RGNSW 1867/2001.

65  Mary Jane, marriage to Francis Blair, 17 October 1862, Sydney, RGNSW 1862/798. Thomas John, death, 5 September 1888, Callan Park Asylum, RGNSW 1888/2696, marriage, George Hopgood to Ellen Barr, Sydney, 29 August 1872, RGNSW 1872/878, death, George Hopgood, 11 March 1898, Bondi, RGNSW 1898/3779. Marriage, Ann Hopgood to Samuel Thomas, 25 February 1863, Sydney, Catholic, RGNSW 1873/1411. At the time of this marriage, Ann's age was 49 and her place of birth was given as Ireland. Ann Hopgood and Ann Sims, both colonial born, claimed to have been born overseas.

66  Elizabeth, BDM 1840, 1256, 24, Mary Ann, BDM 1841, 1266, 26, Henry, BDM 1843, 1210, 27, Margaret, BDM 1846, 1608, 31 and Daniel BDM 1848, 1433, 33. Death, Margaret Whately, death, RGNSW ?. Thomas Whately, death, 3 August 1881, The Oaks near Picton, aged 67, RGNSW 1881/5775. We are indebted to Robyne White of Goulburn and Trish Jones of Mudgee for details concerning the Whately family. George Robert Baker, death, 16 October 1863, near Scone, aged 61, Church of England, RGNSW 1863/5856 and Julia Baker, 21 January 1884, Scone, aged 71, Catholic, RGNSW 1884/10117.

67  The children baptised before 1856 were, William, BDM 1843, 8531, 45, Elizabeth, BDM 1844, 8531, 45, Mary Ann, BDM, 1846, 1575, 48, Christina, BDM 1848, 1575, 48, Jemima, BDM 1850, 162, 51 and Katharine Jane, BDM 1854, 1117, 52. Among these were the Pipers, McKenzies, the Campbells, Inneses, Busbys, Rankens and Stewarts. See K. Fry, *Beyond the Barrier. Class Formation in a Pastoral Society, Bathurst 1818-1848*, Bathurst, 1993, pp. 130 and 134-137. Daniel Sims married Emma Park, spinster, both of Sydney, 19 October 1844, Sots Curch, Sydney, BDM 1844, 1988, 76 and Daniel Sims, death, 22 May 1885, RGNSW 1885/8501075.

68  Kent and Townsend, op. cit., p. 165.

69  Robert Mason to his daughter, Lydia, Brookfield, 7 December 1863, Mason Family Letters, 1857-1865, ML MSS 2290, C Y Reel 339.

70  William Pound, born 1843, did not marry. Elizabeth, born 1844, married

Edward Jordan in Carcoar in 1869. RGNSW 69/2014. Mary Ann, born 1846, married Thomas Kent in 1871 in Camperdown. RGNSW 71/1961. Christina, born 1848, married James McVicar in Carcoar in 1869. RGNSW 69/2107. Jemima married Joseph Blandford in Bathurst in 1882. RGNSW82/3530. Katherine, born 1854, seems not to have married. John, born 1856, married Mary Ann Spalding in 1886 in Carcoar. RGNSW 67/4555. Matilda, born 1859, married Alexander McVicar in 1884 in Carcoar. RGNSW 84/4287.

71 Lucy married Thomas Clarke, a convict, 15 April 1839. BDM, 1839, 369, 23. Sarah married Joseph Briggs, 6 March 1846. BDM 1846, 31, 435. He had been transported from Hereford in 1836. Marriage of Anne Marie to William Bell, 16 April 1831, both of Carcoar, BDM 1839, 370, 23. He was so described on the registration of his death, BDM 1844, 811, 29. Occupations given for baptisms of George, born 17 October 1837, and Elizabeth, born 16 July 1844, BDM 1837,1074, 21 and 1844, 2173, 30. Registration of their marriage, BDM 1855, 71, 43.

72 Charles Milson to Colonial Secretary, Muswellbrook, 5 February 1844, Col. Sec. In Letters, 44/16, AONSW. We owe copies of this reference to Laurel Riddler and Kevin Milson. The details of Charles Milson's whereabouts are listed under the relatives column of the indent of the *John and Lucy* which arrived on 6 May 1837. Immigration Agents' immigration Lists, AONSW 4/4793-5, Reel 2138.

73 George Nash, the informant for the registration of the death, is identified as a brother of John Nash, death, 30 June 1869, RGNSW 69/3620. Sarah Shergold (Shiregold) married Thomas Douglas in 1840. Both were witnesses to George Shergold's marriage in 1840. Thomas Shergold married Clarissa or Clara Smith in Sydney in 1838.

74 B. Boissery, *The Treason, Trials, and Transportation to New South Wales of Lower Canadian Rebels after the 1838 Rebellion*, Sydney, 1995, see especially, pp. 284-287. See also, G. Rudé, ''Captain Swing' in New South Wales, *Historical Studies*, No. 11, 1965, p. 479.

75 Marriage, Charles Milson, bachelor of Segenhoe, free, Anne Lyons, Spinster of Segenhoe, chapel, banns, BDM 1837,1869, 21. It has proved impossible to identify Annie's origins but as she was undoubtedly working as a domestic at Segenhoe, it is extremely unlikely that she was a daughter of a merchant as claimed on the registration of her death.

76 Death, 1 July 1865, Overton near Muswellbrook, aged 50, RGNSW 65/4788. Death, Charles Milson, 20 March 1874, RGNSW 1874/3496. Charles died near Toryburn in northern New South Wales at Stoney Batter Run where his son, the informant for the registration, was working and living.

77 Marriage, Thomas Goodfellow to Anne Gannon, both communicants, both of

St Clair, Patrick Plains, 24 September 1849, Singleton, Catholic, BDM 1849, 332, 96. A characteristic of Catholic registration (and Presbyterian) before 1856 is that they lack some of the details commonly recorded by clergy of other denominations. Electoral Roll for ?, 1859 to 1860. Death, Thomas Goodfellow, 14 September 1881. The informant was the matron of the Asylum. She correctly identified his place of birth, how long he had been in the colony and gave his age as 79. She provided no details of parents, occupations or marriage. RGNSW1881/11144.

78   In each case the informant for the death certificate was identified as the employer.

# Appendix I

This appendix identifies the behaviour of the Wessex men transported to New South Wales for their part in the disturbances according to the testimony of observers and trial witnesses.

1. Observed to be part of a crowd
2. Exercised leadership
3. Demanded or received money
5. Carried an implement, weapon or stick
6. Observed destroying machinery
7. Uttered threats by word or letter
8. Threatened personal violence
9. Present in a riot
10. Active in an affray
11. Impressed others into a crowd
12. Carried a flag, blew a horn etc.
13. Active as a negotiator
14. Helped to damage buildings

| | |
|---|---|
| Adams, William | 1, 3, 5. |
| Aldridge, John | 1, 5, 6. |
| Allen, Solomon | 1. 2, 5, 7. |
| Arlett, George | 1, 5, 6, 7. |
| Annells, James | 1, 7. |
| Arney, Joseph | 1, 6, 14. |
| Baker, James | 1, 5. |
| Baker, Robert | 1, 2. |
| Batten, John | 1, 2, 3, 5, 6. |
| Bennett, Cornelius | 1, 2, 6. |
| Blake, Shadrach | 1, 2, 3, 4, 7, 14. |
| Brown, Levi | 1, 2, 3. |
| Brown, Luke | 1, 3, 4, 5, 6, 8, 9, 10. |
| Bulpitt, Charles | 1. |
| Bulpitt, John | 1, 14. |
| Bunce, Henry | 1. |
| Burgess, James | 1, 5, 6, 9, 10. |

| | |
|---|---|
| Burroughs, John | 1, 3, 7. |
| Burton, Isaac | 1, 3. |
| Carter, George | 1. |
| Carter, William | 1.6. |
| Cheater, William | 1, 2, 3, 6. |
| Childs, Abraham | 1, 2. |
| Clarke, George (1) | 1, 3, 4, 5, 7, 14. |
| Clarke, George (2) | 1. |
| Cole, Isaac | 1, 6. |
| Cook, James | 1. |
| Cook, Robert | 1, 5, 7. |
| Coombs, Charles | 1, 6. |
| Darling, Alfred | 1, 5, 14. |
| Davis, Charles | 1, 2, 3, 6, 7, 10, 11, 13. |
| Deadman, Aaron | 1, 6. |
| Down, James | 1, 6. |
| Durman, George | 1, 3. |
| Edney, Joseph | 1, 5, 8, 11. |
| Eldridge, Henry | 1, 5, 6, 14. |
| Elkins, George | 1,6. |
| Elkins, Henry | 1. |
| Fay, Charles | 1, 5, 12, 14. |
| Ford, John | 1, 2, 5, 6, 14. |
| Francis, William | 1, 5, 6. |
| Gilmore, John | 1, 2, 5, 6, 8, 11, 13. |
| Goodall, Thomas | 1, 6. |
| Goodfellow, Thomas | 1, 6. |
| Green, Charles | 1, 4, 12. |
| Greenway, Jason | 3, 7. |
| Hancock, Daniel | 1, 9, 10. |
| Hanson, Thomas | 1, 2, 5, 6, 12. |
| Harding, Aaron | 1, 2, 11, 13. |
| Harris, Edward | 1, 3, 5, 6, 9, 10. |
| Hatcher, Stephen | 1, 2, 6. |
| Hatherell, Job | 7. |
| Hawkins, William | 1, 5, 6. |
| Hayter, Charles | 1, 5, 6. |
| Heath, John | 1, 14. |
| Hibberd, William | 1, 3, 6, 7. |
| Hicks, Thomas | 1, 2, 5, 6, 9, 10. |
| Holdaway, Robert | 1, 2, 3, 13. |
| Hopgood, George | 1, 7. |

| | |
|---|---|
| Horton, Charles | 1. |
| Horton, John | 1. |
| House, Abraham | 1, 6. |
| James, Henry | 1, 2. |
| Jennings, John | 1, 2, 5, 6, 7, 14. |
| Jerrard, Charles | 1, 2, 5. |
| Knight, Abraham | 1. |
| Lawrence, Lazarus | |
| Lawrence, Thomas | 1, 6. |
| Legg, John | 1, 5, 6. |
| Legg, William | 1, 3. |
| Lewis, William | 1. |
| Mackrell, Thomas | 1, 2, 3, 4, 5, 6, 7, 8. |
| Manns, Isaac | 1, 2, 5, 14. |
| Manns, James | 1, 2, 13. |
| Mason, Joseph | 1, 2. |
| Mason, Robert | 1, 5. |
| May, Timothy | 1, 5, 6. |
| Milson, Charles | 1, 2, 3. |
| Myland, George | 1, 6. |
| Nash, John | 1, 5, 6. |
| Neale, Thomas | 1. |
| New, James | 1, 6. |
| Newman, William | 1, 5, 6. |
| Nicholas, Joseph | 1, 5, 14. |
| North, Gifford | 1, 3, 5, 10. |
| Oakley, William | 1, 2, 5, 7, 13. |
| Orchard, John | 1. |
| Page, Robert | 1. |
| Page, William | 1, 3, 5, 7. |
| Pain, Charles | 1, 2, 3, 5, 7. |
| Payne, Daniel | 1. |
| Pointer, John | 1, 2, 3, 7, 13. |
| Pope, Joseph | 1, 2, 3. |
| Pope, Maurice | 1, 2, 3, 4. |
| Pound, John | 1, 4, 6, 7. |
| Primer, William | 1, 5, |
| Pumphrey, James | 1, 2, 3, 13. |
| Quinton, Samuel | 1, 6. |
| Radborn, Thomas | 1. |
| Read, Charles | 1, 2, 6, 7. |
| Reeves, John | 1, 3, 5, 7, 8. |

| | |
|---|---|
| Romain, James | 1, 5, 6. |
| Shepherd, Joseph | 1, 3, 5. |
| Shepherd, William | 1, 2, 4, 13. |
| Shergold, George (1) | 1, 6. |
| Shergold, George (2) | 1, 2, 3, 4, 5, 7. |
| Shergold, Henry | 1, 6. |
| Shergold, John | 1, 3, 4. |
| Simonds, James | 1, 5. |
| Simonds, William | 1. |
| Sims, Daniel | 1, 5, 7. |
| Sims, William (1) | 1, 2, 3, 5, 7, 14. |
| Sims, William (2) | 1, 7, 14. |
| Spicer, Henry | 1. |
| Stanford, William | 1, 5, 7, 14. |
| Stone, Aaron | 1, 2, 3, 12. |
| Stone, Laban | 1, 3. |
| Stroud, William | 1, 2, 3, 7. |
| Symes, Charles | 1, 5, 6. |
| Thorne, Adam | 1, 6. |
| Thorne, James | 1, 5, 6, 11. |
| Toombs, Henry | 1. |
| Toomer, James | 1, 5, 6, 7. |
| Triggs, Matthew | 1, 5, 11, 14. |
| Tuck, Joseph | 1, 5, 6. |
| Turner, Jacob | 1. |
| Viccus, Edmund | 1, 12. |
| Waldron, Job | 1, 2, 3, 4, 13. |
| Warwick, Thomas | 6, |
| Watts, Joseph | 1, 2, 3, 5, 7, 8. |
| Waving, William | 1. |
| West, James | 1. |
| Westall, William | 7. |
| Whately, Thomas | 1, 6. |
| Wheeler, John | 1, 5, 6. |
| Williams, George | 1, 4, 5, 9, 10, 11. |
| Williams,Stephen | 1, 3, 4, 5, 8, 9, 10. |
| Wiltshire, Jacob | 1, 3. |

# Appendix II

This appendix links a transportee to a specific incident in the following manner:
Location of protest; Size of crowd; Date.
Protest action and crowd behaviour.
*Eleanor* convicts involved

BERKSHIRE
1. Waltham St, Lawrence, Binfield; 6; 20-21 Nov.
Agricultural machinery destroyed, food, drink and money levied.
Allen, Horton C., Horton J., Simonds J., Simonds W., Wheeler.

2. Beenham, Aldermaston, Wasing, Brimpton; 150-200; 18-19 Nov.
Agricultural and manufacturing machinery destroyed, food, drink and money levied, affray.
Arlett, Brown, Burgess, Hancock, Harris, Hawkins, Hicks, Nash, Williams G., Williams S.

3. Inkpen, Kintbury, West Woodhay, Hampstead-Marshall, Hungerford, Welford; 200-500; 21-23 Nov.
Agricultural and manufacturing machinery destroyed, food, drink and money levied, wage increase demanded.
Aldridge, Bennett, Burton, Carter, Darling, Goodfellow, Green, Greenway, May, Nicholas, Oakley, Page R., Page W., Radborn, Sims (1), Tuck, Waving, Westall.

4. Ashampstead, Streatley, Basildon; 150; 21-24 Nov.
Agricultural machinery destroyed, food, drink and money levied, wage increase demanded.
Edney, Hanson, Milson, Viccus, West.

5. Eastbury, East Garston, West Shefford; 100-120; 23 Nov.
Agricultural machinery destroyed, food, drink and money levied, assault on special constables.
Mackrell.

HAMPSHIRE
6. Barton Stacey, Micheldever, East Stratton; 20-900; 19 Nov.
Agricultural machinery destroyed, food drink and money levied, wage increase demanded.

Annells, Mason J., Mason R., Pumphrey, Turner.

7. Andover, Upper Clatford; 100-300; 19-20 Nov.
Agricultural and manufacturing machinery destroyed, drink levied, wage increase demanded.
Fay, Gilmore, Goodall, Manns I., Manns J., Shepherd, Stanford.

8. Vernhams Dean; 70-100; 21 Nov.
Agricultural machinery destroyed, food, drink and money levied.
Carter, Cook, Hopgood, Neale, Wiltshire.

9. Worting, Wootton St. Lawrence, Monk Sherborne, Oakley; 150; 22 Nov.
Agricultural machinery destroyed, food, drink and money levied.
Baker, Batten, Bulpitt C., Bulpitt J., Clarke (2), Cook, Pain, Warwick.

10. St. Mary Bourne; 200; 22 Nov.
Money levied, wage increase demanded, forced entry.
Bunce, Sims D., Sims W. (2).

11. Highclere, East Woodhay, Burghclere; 200-300; 23 Nov.
Agricultural machinery destroyed, food, drink and money levied.
Payne, Stroud.

12. Selborne, Headley; 200-1000; 22-23 Nov.
Agricultural machinery destroyed, poorhouses attacked, reduction of tithes and wage increases demanded, food, drink and money levied.
Harding, Heath, Holdaway, James, Triggs.

13. Upham, Corhampton, South Stoneham; 250; 22 Nov.
Agricultural machinery destroyed, reduction of tithes and wage increase demanded, food, drink and money levied.
Childs, Primer.

14. Owlesbury; 100; 23 Nov.
Agricultural machinery destroyed, reduction of tithes and rents and wage increase demanded, food, drink and money levied.
Adams.

15. East Wellow; 100-200; 24 Nov.
Agricultural machinery destroyed, reduction of tithes and wage increase demanded, complaint about poor relief, money levied.
Pointer.

16. Fordingbridge, Rockburn; 200-300; 23 Nov.
Agricultural and manufacturing machinery destroyed, food, drink and money levied.
Arney, Clarke (1), Deadman, Eldridge, Hayter, Newman, Quinton, Read.

WILTSHIRE

17. Hippenscombe, Shalbourne; 300-400; 21-23 Nov.
Agricultural machinery destroyed, food, drink and money levied, buildings threatened.
Blake, Baker.

18. Buttermere; 100; 22 Nov.
Agricultural machinery destroyed, food, drink and money levied.
Waldron.

19. South Savernake, Wootton Rivers; 80; 23 Nov.
Agricultural machinery destroyed, food, drink and money levied.
Pope.

20. Aldbourne, Ramsbury; 400; 23 Nov.
Agricultural machinery destroyed, food, drink and money levied.
Durman, Pound.

21. Wanborough; ?; 23 Nov.
Agricultural machinery destroyed, food, drink and money levied, wage increase demanded.
Lawrence, Orchard, Reeves, Toombs.

22. Liddington, Wroughton; ?; 23 Nov.
Agricultural machinery destroyed, food, drink and money levied.
Watts.

23. Hannington; 25-50; 24 Nov.
Agricultural machinery destroyed, food, drink and money levied.
Legg.

24. Latton; ?; 25 Nov.
Agricultural machinery destroyed.
Knight.

25. Enford, Netheravon; 100; 22 Nov.
Agricultural machinery destroyed, wage increase and improved Poor Law allowances demanded.
Romain.

26. Alton Barnes; 200-300; 23 Nov.
Agricultural machinery destroyed, money levied, wage increase demanded, affray, forced entry.
Davis, North, Stone L.

27. Wilton, Quidhampton; 400-500; 24 Nov.

Manufacturing machinery destroyed.
Cole, Down, Francis, Jennings, Lewis, Shergold G. (1), Shergold H., Whateley.

28. Barford, Burcombe, Dinton; 100-200; 24 Nov.
Agricultural and manufacturing machinery destroyed, money levied.
Ford.

29. Whiteparish; 100-150; 23 Nov.
Agricultural machinery destroyed, money levied.
Stone A.

30. Homington, Combe Bisset; 100; 23-24 Nov.
Agricultural machinery destroyed, food, drink and money levied.
Toomer.

31. Broad Chalke, Ebbesbourne Wake, Fifield; 250; 24 Nov.
Agricultural machinery destroyed, food, drink and money levied.
Brown, Burroughs, Hibberd.

32. Damerham; 60-70; 24 Nov.
Agricultural machinery destroyed, money levied.
Cheater.

33. Stapleford; ?; 24 Nov.
Money levied
Shergold G. (2), Shergold J,

34. Tisbury; 400-500; 25 Nov.
Agricultural machinery destroyed, wage increase demanded, affray.
Jerrard.

DORSET
35. Buckland Newton, Pulham, Woolland; 20-50; 27 Nov.
Agricultural machinery destroyed, money levied.
Coombs, House, Legg, New, Shepherd, Spicer, Symes, Thorne A., Thorne J.

36. Stour Provost, East Stour; 150; 29 Nov.
Agricultural machinery destroyed, wage increase demanded, money levied.
Hatcher.

37. Cann; ?; 30 Nov.
Agricultural machinery destroyed.
Elkins G., Elkins H.

38. Cramborne, Edmonsham, Handley; 300; 23 Nov.
Agricultural machinery destroyed, food, drink and money levied.
Pope.

# BIBLIOGRAPHY

**I. Manuscript Collections**

Archives of New South Wales

Convict Indent, or Muster Roll, for the *Eleanor*, 2/8257.

Surgeon's Journal for the *Eleanor*, Adm. 101/23.

Assignment of Convicts, 1834-36, 4/1116.

Colonial Secretary's Correspondence, 4/1798, 1909, 1910, 2081, 2106, 2110, 2143, 2145, 2151, 2173, 2185, 2222, 2915, 3528.

Copies of Letters Regarding Convicts, 4/3671.

Copies of Letters to the Master Attendant, Masters of Ships, Harbour Master 1830-32, 4/3779.

Convicts' Savings Cash Book 1824-48, 2/8390.

Muswellbrook Bench Book, 4/5601.

Register of Convict Applications to Marry 1825-51, 4/4513, 4514

Applications for the Publication of Banns 1826-41, 4/2018, 2226, 2301, 2303, 2304, 2344, 2435, 2441, 2442, 2443, 2480, 3502.

Registers of Births, Deaths and Marriages.

Certificates of Freedom, 4/4343, 4404.

Applications for Free Passage for Wives and Children of Convicts, 4/4492.

Assisted Immigrants, Board's List, 4/4793.

Tickets-of-Leave, 4/4097, 4099.

Deceased Estate Files, 20/6076, ZO 789.

Census of 1841, 4/X951.

Berkshire Record Office

Account by Joseph Mason of his experiences in NSW, D/EWd Z1.

Clerk of Hungerford Division Papers, including depositions 1830-31, D/E Pg O 1/4, 5.

Notice of sentences passed on Swing rioters 1831, N/D 94/1.

Quarter Sessions Order Books, 1791-95, 1828-31, Q/SO 7, 14.

Miscellaneous papers of the Hendred Association for the Prosecution of Felons 1814-34, D/P 66/28/1.

Miscellaneous accounts of the Wantage Association for the Prosecution of Felons 1827-43, D/EX 618/1/1-11.

Articles of Agreement for the Whitchurch Streatley and Basildon Association for the

Prosecution of Felons 1822, D/ER O5.

Articles of the Wokingham Association for the Detection and Prosecution of Felons 1817-19, D/EX 382/1.

Diary of W. Gibbons, Constable of Cookham Dean 1800-39, D/P 43/10/1.

Farm Diary 1824-34, Wilder Estate Papers, D/EWi E17.

Correspondence of H. Stevens with Overseers of Bradfield 1826-30, D/ESv (M) 96.

Englefield enclosure amendment 1827, Benyon Family Papers, D/EBy E20, D/EBb E15.

R.F. Graham to inhabitants of Newbury on enclosure of common fields, 1842, D/EX 241 Z3.

Return of Certified Places of Worship 1852, T/F 30.

Parish Records

Aldermaston - (Baptisms, Marriages) D/P 3/1/5, 6, (Resolutions of Prosecution Association and instruction to watch patrol) 28/1, 4.

Ardington - (Overseers' Accounts 1778-1805) D/P 7/12/1.

Ashampstead - (Baptisms, Marriages) D/P 8/1/3, 4.

Basildon - (Marriages) D/P 14/1/7.

Bradfield - ( Baptisms, Marriages) D/P 22/1/6, 10.

Chieveley - (Overseers' papers and 'Speen Table' of relief) D/P 34/18/5.

East Garston - (Baptisms, Marriages) D/P 59/1/4, 5.

Hungerford - (Baptisms, Marriages) D/P 71/1/8, 80, (Overseers' Accounts) 12/14, (claims under enclosure award 1811) 28/6.

Inkpen - (Baptisms, Marriages) D/P 76/1/4, 5.

Kintbury - (Baptisms, Marriages) D/P 78/1/5, 12, (Poorhouse Minutes, Vestry Minutes 1816-45) 18/4.

Lambourne - (Baptisms, Marriages) D/P 79/1/6, 15.

Sonning - (Overseers' bills and papers, Earley 1830) D/P 113/12/28.

Streatley - (Baptisms, Marriages) D/P 122/1/2, 6.

Tilehurst - (Vestry Minutes 1824-44) D/P 132/8/3.

Wallingford - (Vestry Minutes 1828-31) D/P 139/8/1.

Waltham St Lawrence - ( Baptisms, Marriages) D/P 141/1/5, 8.


Dorset Record Office

Quarter Sessions Order Books, 1827-36, QSM 1/16.

Dorchester Prison Registers, 1812-38, NG/PR 1 B1, 2.

Clerk of Peace and Chaplain's Reports 1824-56, QS/County Prison 8.

Prison Calendars 1824-31, D1/1095 2.

Diary of Henry Kaines of Manston, farmer, D 391/1.

Colfox Family Papers, D/COL/F 25.

Filliter Family Papers, D/FIL/F 59.

Seymer Family Papers, D/SEY/ 19 (Charge to Grand Jury), 308 (duties of Overseer

1820), 310 (relief scale Sturminster Newton), 311-12 (Circulars to Magistrates), 447 (meeting of volunteers to suppress disturbances).

Notice about sale of Portland Common, D1/OM 28.

Letters to D.O.P. Okeden about riots 1830, D1/OP 1.

C.B. Wollaston to E.B. Portman about Commission to try rioters, Photocopy 470/1.

Methodist Records; Weymouth Circuit Plan 1829-30, NM2 C1/MS 1/1.

Methodist Records; Tolpuddle Circuit Plan 1829-30, NM2 S19/MS 1/1.

Scrapbook of Circuit Plans; Sherborne Circuit 1825-98, NM6 C1/MS 1/2.

Parish Records

Beaminster - (Overseers' Accounts 1820-36) PE/BE/OV 9/1.

Buckland Newton - (Marriages) PE/BCN/RE 3/2, (Overseers' Accounts 1802-43) OV 3, 4.

Charmouth - (Vestry Minutes 1818-59) PE/CMO/VE 2.

East Stour - (Overseers' Accounts 1804-29) PE/EST/OV 1/1.

Edmonsham - (Overseers' Accounts 1804-76) PE/EDM/OV 1/3.

Hazelbury Bryan - (Marriages) PE/HAZ/RE 3/2.

Kimmeridge - (Overseers' Accounts 1795-1836) D/689/1.

Manston - (Vestry Minutes 1819-52) PE/MAN/VE 1.

Mappowder - (Marriages) PE/MPD/RE 3/2.

Poyntington - (Churchwardens' Accounts 1756-1931) PE/POY/CW 2.

Pulham - (Baptisms, Marriages) PE/PUL/RE 2/1, 3/2.

Sandford Orcas - (Churchwardens' Accounts 1789-1947) PE/SDO/CW 2.

Sherborne - (Constable's Papers) PE/SH/CO 2, 3.

Stoke Wake - (Baptisms, Marriages) PE/STW/RE 2/3, 1/4.

Stour Provost - (Overseers' Accounts 1797-1830) PE/SPV/OV 5-7.

Sturminster Newton - (Vestry Minutes 1828-40) PE/SN/VE 1/1, (Workhouse Accounts 1800-33) PC/SN/OV 2/4/1, 2.

Winterborne Whitechurch - (Overseers' Accounts 1791-1828) PE/WWH/OV 1.


Hampshire Record Office

Winchester Special Assizes, Dec. 1830, (Proclamation, Charge to Grand Jury, Calendar of Prisoners, Summary of Sentences) 14 M 50/1-4.

Wellington Lieutenancy Papers, 25 M 61/1/60-61, 2/1-59.

Basingstoke Petty Sessional Division, (Depositions etc. 1830) 10 M 57/O3.

Basingstoke Quarter Sessions, Minute Book 1823-36, 8 M 62/31.

County Gaol and Bridewell: Committee Minute Books, Report on Winchester Gaol 1816-17, Q 13/1/2, Journals (Governor's Journal 1829-37, Chaplain's Journal 1820-43) 2/2, 7, Gaol and Bridewell Rules 1822, 4/1.

Farming diary 1828, J. Eggar of Holybourne, 28 M 82/F3.

Farming diary 1815-67, H.R. Bailey of Broughton, 96 M 88/1.

Cash Book, Hunton and Borough farms Micheldever 1825-66, 5 M 68/4.

Diary of S. Attwood, tailor of Basingstoke 1816-70, 1 M 62/27.

Abuse of Poor Laws in the parish of Selborne (manuscript tract by W. Cobbold), 32 M 66/PO 10.

Ashburton Correspondence, 100 M 70/F1-4.

Bonham-Carter Correspondence, 94 M 72/F 15, 16.

Crompton Family Papers, 12 M 60/81.

Jervoise of Herriard Papers, ( Prosecution Association Papers for Alresford, Herriard, Odiham, Preston Candover) 44 M 69/K 2/11, 19, 20, 23.

Sloane Stanley Family Papers, 10 M 55/353.

Tichborne Family Papers, 37 M 48/11.

Frederick Bowker Scrapbook, W/K5/1.

Scrapbook of cuttings on agricultural topics, 10 M 67/1.

Letters from E.J. White pleading the cause of R. Holdaway, Photocopy 378 from originals in the Kent Record Office U1127/C78/28, 29.

Parish Records

Amport - (Marriages) 43 M 67/PR 4.

Andover – (Baptisms, Marriages) 60 M 67/PR 13, 20.

Basingstoke – (Baptisms, Marriages) 46 M 74/PR 10, 19.

Barton Stacey – (Overseers' Accounts etc. 1808-32) 60 M 70/PO 3-5.

Breamore – (Overseers' Accounts 1819-33) 20 M 83/PO 16, (Settlement Examinations) PO 20/4, (Removal Orders) PO 23/15.

Chilbolton - (Baptisms, Burials) 55 M 70/PR 3.

Cliddesden - (Baptisms, Marriages) 31 M 82/PR 4,7.

East Woodhay - ( Baptisms, Marriages) 27 M 77/PR 7, 8.

East Worldham - (Marriages) 28 M 79/PR 2.

Fawley - ( Vestry Minutes 1819-44) 25 M 60/PV 1.

Fordingbridge - (Baptisms, Marriages) 63 M 92/PR 7, 15, (Overseers' Disbursements 1746-1845) PO 2.

Hambledon - (Vestry Minutes 1824-66) 46 M 69/37.

Headley - (Baptisms, Marriages) PSH/HED/2/2, 3/1, (Papers relating to poor relief) 44 M 69/J8/1, 2.

Herriard - (Vestry Minutes 1830-1915) 86 M 82/PV 1.

Hurstbourne Tarrant - (Baptisms, Marriages) 68 M 79/PR 2, 3.

Longparish - (Baptisms) 54 M 69/PR 6.

Micheldever - (Vestry Minutes 1826-66) 7 M 80/PV 1, ( Overseers papers) 18 M 76/PO 1.

New Alresford - (Marriages) 45 M 83/PR 9.

Preston Candover - (Overseers' Accounts) 49 M 69/PO 3.

Rockbourne - (Highway Accounts) 39 M 68/20.

St Mary Bourne - (Baptisms, Marriages) 96 M 82/PR 3, 6.

Selborne - (Baptisms, Marriages) 32 M 66/PR 7, 12, (Overseers' Accounts 1825-35)

PO 6, 8.

Sherfield English - (Baptisms, Marriages) 90 M 83/PR 4, 7.

Tangley - (Baptisms) 42 M 67/PR 5, (Census return 1831) PW 13, (Lease) PW 14.

Twyford - (Vestry Minutes 1758-1857) 21 M 83/PV 2.

Upham - (Baptisms, Marriages) 74 M 78/PR 4, 6.

Vernham Dean - (Prosecution Association poster) 110 M 70/PG 3.

Wherwell - (Overseers' Accounts 1806-19) 13 M 67/PO 2.

Wonston - (Marriages) 448 P/9.


Mitchell Library [Public Library of New South Wales]
Mason Letters 1852-65, MSS 2290.


Public Record Office
Counties Correspondence 1820-50, (Berkshire) HO 52/6, (Dorset, Hampshire) 52/7, (Wiltshire) 52/11.

Western Circuit Indictment Books (Dorset, Hampshire, Wiltshire), ASSIZES/25.


Wiltshire Record Office
Quarter Sessions: Calendars of Prisoners 1820-29, A1/125/52C-55.

Quarter Sessions: Summary Convictions and Depositions A1/260.

Drafts of Reports on Prisons at Marlborough, Devizes and Salisbury 1824-27, A1/512.

Benett Correspondence and Miscellaneous Papers, 413/23.

Miscellaneous letters about machine-breaking, 1553/12.

Miscellaneous Papers and Documents 1803-34, A1/740.

Diary of Richard Massey, schoolmaster at Shalbourne, 2320/1.

Papers relating to Swing disturbances in Wilts. from the Sotheron-Estcourt Papers, Gloucestershire Record Office 1571/X/60, 63, 64.

Parish Records

Broad Chalke - (Baptisms, Marriages) 1261/3, 4, 7.

Bromham - (Miscellaneous records) 518/21.

Dauntsey- (Baptisms) 1070/6, (Overseers' Accounts 1801-28) 1586/35, 36.

Great Bedwyn - (Baptisms, Marriages) 1836/7, 12.

Hannington - (Baptisms, Marriages) 1819/4, 6, (Overseers' Accounts) 26.

Homington - (Baptisms, Marriages) 2703/1, 2181/2.

Malmesbury - (Baptisms, Marriages) 1589/9, 13.

Market Lavington - (Baptisms, Marriages) 836/6, 8.

Tidcombe - (Baptisms, Marriages) 1933/3, 5, (Overseers' Accounts etc.) 14, 18, 19.

Wanborough - (Baptisms, Marriages) 1788/6, 9.

Whiteparish - (Baptisms, Marriages) 830/5, 7, (Overseers' Accounts) 17.

Wilton - (Baptisms, Marriages) 504/11, 12.

## II. Newspapers and Journals

*The Annual Register*
*Berkshire Chronicle, Windsor Herald, Forest Vale and General Advertiser*
*Bulletin.*
*The Devizes and Wiltshire Gazette.*
*Dorset County Chronicle, Somersetshire Gazette and General Advertiser.*
*Hampshire Advertiser and Royal Yacht Club Gazette.*
*Hampshire Chronicle and Southampton Courier.*
*Reading Mercury, Oxford Gazette and General Advertiser.*
*Political Register.*
*The Salisbury and Winchester Journal.*
*Sydney Gazette and New South Wales Advertiser.*
*The Times.*
*The Western Flying Post, Sherborne and Yeovil Mercury and General Advertiser.*

## III. Parliamentary Papers.

S[elect] C[ommittee] on *Gaols and other Places of Confinement*, P[arliamentary] P[apers], 1819, Vol. VII.

S.C. on *Agricultural Distress*, PP, 1820, Vol. II.

S.C. on *Depressed State of Agriculture*, PP, 1820, Vol. IX.

S.C. First and Second Reports on *Distressed State of Agriculture*, PP, 1821, 1822, Vol. V.

S.C. on *Labourers' Wages*, PP, 1824, Vol. VI.

S.C. on *Emigration* from the United Kingdom, PP, 1826 Vol. IV.

S.C. on Poor Laws Relating to the *Employment or Relief of Able-bodied Persons* from the Poor Rate, PP, 1828, Vol. IV.

*Census of 1831*, PP, 1831, Vol. XVIII.

S.C. on *Secondary Punishments*, PP, 1831, Vol. VII, 1831-32, Vol. VII.

S.C. on *Agriculture*, PP. 1833, Vol. V.

*Report on the Poor Laws*, PP, 1834, Vols. XXX - XXXIV, XXXVII.

S.C. of House of Lords into *State of Gaols and Houses of Correction*, PP, 1835, Vol. IX.

S.C. on *Transportation*, PP, 1837, Vol. II.

*Report on the Sanitary Condition of the Labouring Population*, PP, 1842, Vol. XXVI.

Report of Special Assistant Poor Law Commissioners on the *Employment of Women and Children in Agriculture*, PP, 1843, Vol. XII.

*Census of 1851: Religious Worship*, PP, 1852-3, Vol. LXXXIX.

## IV. Other Printed Primary Sources

*The Agricultural State of the Kingdom in February, March and April 1816*, London, 1816.

*A Calendar of the prisoners in His Majesty's Gaols at Reading and Abingdon at the Midsummer Assizes to be Held at Abingdon, July 1818*, Reading, 1818.

*Rules and regulations for the government of the Common Gaol and House of Correction at Reading*, Reading, 1825.

*Report of the Committee of the Society for the Improvement of Prison Discipline*, Third, Fourth and Seventh Reports, London, 1821, 1822, 1827.

*Report of the Secretary of the Mendicity Society for the Shaftesbury District*. Shaftesbury, 1828.

*Public General Statutes*, London, 1827, 1828.

*The Life and History of Swing, the Kent Rick-burner*, London, 1830.

*A Plain Statement of the Case of the Labourer for the Consideration of the Yeomen and Gentlemen of the Southern Districts of England*, London, 1830.

*An Address to the Men of Hawkhurst (equally applicable to the men of other parishes) on their Riotous Acts and Purposes*, London, 1830.

*An Address to the Labourers on the subject of Destroying Machinery*, London, 1830.

*A Country Rector's Address to his Parishioners° with reference to The Disturbed State of the Times*, London, 1830.

*Machine-breaking and the changes occasioned by it in the Village of Turvey Down. A Tale of the Times*, Oxford, 1830.

*The Charge delivered by the Hon. Mr. Baron Vaughan to the Grand Jury at the Castle of Winchester*, Winchester, 1830.

*A True Account of the Life & Death of Swing, the Rick-burner*, London, n.d.

*Common Prudence: A letter addressed to the Peasantry and Labourers of the County of Wilts. on the Incendiary Practices of Some of their Number*, Sherborne, 1831.

*Report of the Proceedings at the Special Commission holden at Winchester, December 20th 1830, and eight following days*, London, 1831.

*The Charge of the Hon. Mr. Justice J. Parke to the Grand Jury°at Salisbury*, n.p., 1831.

*Blue Books of New South Wales*, 1831, 1833.

*New South Wales Calendar and General Post Office Directory, 1832*, [1831], Sydney, 1966.

*Articles of the North Bradley Association for the Prevention of Robberies and Thefts and the Protection of Persons and Property*, n.p., 1834.

*A narrative of the sufferings of Jas. Loveless, Jas. Bride and Thomas and John Standford, four of the Dorchester labourers*, London, 1838.

*County of Wilts. Fisherton Gaol – Statistics of Crime 1801 to 1850. Compiled by the Governor of the County Gaol*, Salisbury, 1855.

*Historical Records of Australia.*

A Constitutional Reformer, *History of the Shaftesbury Election 1830*, Shaftesbury, 1830.

J. Caird, *English Agriculture in 1850-52*, Manchester, 1852.

J. Clare, *The Shepherd's Calendar*, [1827], Oxford, 1993.

J. Claridge, *General View of the Agriculture of Dorset*, London, 1793.

W. Cobbett, *The Poor Man's Friend or Essays on the Rights and Duties of the Poor*, London, 1829.

W. Cobbett, *Two-Penny Trash*, London, 1830-32.

W. Cobbett, *Rural Rides*, [1830], Harmondsworth, 1967.

P. Cunningham, *Two Years in New South Wales*, [1827], Sydney, 1966.

D. Davies, *The Case of the Labourers in Husbandry*, London, 1795.

T. Davis, *General View of the Agriculture of Wiltshire*, London, 1794. With additional material, 1811.

C. Davy, *The Pious and Happy Labourer or The Religion of the Bible the Poor Man's Best Friend*, London, 1820.

C. Davy, *Cottage Sermons or Short Discourses Addressed to Plain People; Being Principally Designed for the Use of Pious Cottagers and those in Humble Life*, 2 Vols., London, 1827.

A. & W. Driver, *General View of the Agriculture of Hampshire*, London, 1794.

F.M. Eden, *The State of the Poor*, London, 1797.

H. Edwards, *A Collection of Old English Customs*, London, 1842.

E. Feild, *An Address on the State of the Country Read to his Parishioners*, Oxford, 1830.

R. Gourlay, *The Village System: Being a Scheme for the Gradual Abolition of Pauperism and Immediate Employment and provisioning of the People*, Bath, 1817.

Hansard's, *Parliamentary Debates*, Third Series, Vol. 1, Oct.-Dec. 1830, London, 1831.

A.J. Hare, *Memorials of a Quiet Life*, 2 Vols., London, 1874.

A. Harris, *Settlers and convicts: Recollections of Sixteen Years Labour in the Australian Backwoods*, [1852], Melbourne, 1964.

P. Henvill, *A Brief Statement of Facts°in the Treatment of the Poor in the Parish of Damerham South in the County of Wilts.*, Salisbury, 1796.

H. Hodgkinson, *A Sermon preached at the Special Assizes at Reading*, December 27, 1830, Reading, 1831.

W. Hone, *The Every day Book or Everlasting Calendar of Popular Amusements, Sports, Pastimes, Ceremonies, Manners, Customs and Events*, London, 1827.

W. Hone, *The Year Book of Daily Recreation and Information*, London, 1839.

W. Howitt, *The Rural Life of England*, London, 1838.

H. Hunt, *Memoirs of Henry Hunt*, 3 Vols., London, 1820.

W.M. Kinsey, *A Sermon on the Present Times*, Abingdon, [1830]

E. Little, 'The farming of Wiltshire', *Journal of the Royal Agricultural Society*, 5, 1844, pp.161-80.

G. Loveless, *The Victims of Whiggery: a statement of the persecutions experienced by the Dorchester labourers; with a report of their trial.* London, 1837.

L. Macquarie, *Journals of his tours in New South Wales and Van Diemen's Land, 1810-1822*, Sydney, 1956.

W. Marshall, *The Rural Economy of the Southern Counties*, Vol. II, London, 1798.

W. Marshall, *Review and Abstracts of the County Reports to the Board of Agriculture: Western Department*, York, 1818.

W.F. Mavor, *General View of the Agriculture of Berkshire*, London, 1813.

M.R. Mitford, *Our Village*, 5 Vols., London, 1824-32.

J.F. Moor, *The Duty of Submission to civil authority: a sermon preached°at Bradfield,°on occasion of the late disturbances in that neighbourhood*, London, 1830.

H.G. Mundy (ed), *The Journal of Mary Frampton from the year 1779 until the year 1846*, London, 1885.

T.G. Northbrook (ed), *Journals and Correspondence from 1808 to 1852 of Sir Francis Thornhill Baring, afterwards Lord Northbrook*, Winchester, 1905.

D.O.P. Okeden, *A letter to the members in Parliament for Dorsetshire on the subject of poor relief and labourers' wages*, Blandford, 1830.

W. Pearce, *General View of the Agriculture in Berkshire; with observations on the means of its improvement*, London, 1794.

Pigot's, *National Commercial Directory*, Manchester, 1830.

R. Therry, *Reminiscences of Thirty Years Residence in New South Wales and Victoria*, [1863], Sydney, 1974.

A. Somerville, *The Whistler at the Plough*, Manchester, 1852.

W. Stevenson, *General View of the Agriculture of the County of Dorset*, London, 1812.

C. Vancouver, *General View of the Agriculture of Hampshire including the Isle of Wight*, London, 1813.

J. Wade, *History of the Middle and Working Classes*, London, 1833.

H. Wake, *Abuse of Poor Rate!! A Statement of Facts submitted to the Candid and Unprejudiced*, Andover, 1818.

H. Walter, *A Letter to the Rev. H.F. Yeatman, LLB, Acting Magistrate for Dorset and Somerset*, London, 1833.

W.H. Wells, *A Geographical dictionary or Gazetteer of the Australian Colonies, 1848*, [1848], Sydney, 1970.

A. Young, *General Report on Enclosures*, London, 1808.

## V. Books and Chapters in Edited Works

*The Introduction of Primitive Methodism into Berkshire 1829-30: A Jubilee Memorial*, Newbury, 1880.

*Stratton Green Baptist Church*, n.p., n.d.

P. Allen, *History of Thatcham*, Thatcham, 1980.

G. Andrews, *Port Jackson 2000, An Affectionate Look at Sydney Harbour*, Sydney, 1986.

R. Anstis, *Warren James and the Dean Forest Riots: The Disturbances of 1831*, Gloucester, 1986.

I. Anstruther, *The Scandal of the Andover Workhouse*, Gloucester, 1984.

G. Aplin (ed), *A Difficult Infant: Sydney before Macquarie*, Sydney, 1988.

F. Archer, *Grain and Chaff Under the Hill*, Stroud, 1991.

J.E. Archer, *'By a flash and a scare': incendiarism, animal maiming and poaching in East Anglia 1815-1870*, Oxford, 1990.

J.E. Archer, 'The Wells-Charlesworth Debate: A Personal Comment on Arson in Norfolk and Suffolk', in Reed & Wells (eds).

J.E. Archer, 'Poachers abroad' & 'Under cover of night: arson and animal maiming', in Mingay (ed), *Unquiet Countryside*.

A. Armstrong, *Farmworkers in England and Wales: a social and economic history 1770 -1980*, London, 1988.

W.A. Armstrong, 'The countryside', in Thompson (ed), Vol. 1.

W.A. Armstrong, 'Food, Shelter and Self-Help', 'The Position of the Labourer in Rural Society' & 'Rural Population Growth, Systems of Employment and Incomes' in Mingay (ed), *Agrarian History*.

A. Atkinson, 'Taking Possession: Sydney's First Householders', in Aplin (ed).

A. Atkinson, 'Convicts and Courtship', in Grimshaw et al, (eds).

A. Atkinson, *Camden: Farm and Village Life in Early New South Wales*, Melbourne, 1988.

M. Baker, *Folklore and Customs of Rural England*, Newton Abbot, 1974.

W. Barnes, *Selected Poems*, Harmondsworth, 1994.

J.B. Barnsby, *The Standard of Living in England 1700-1900*, Wolverhampton, 1985.

J. Barrell, *The dark side of the landscape: The rural poor in English painting 1730-1840*, Cambridge, 1980.

C. Bateson, *The Convict Ships*, Sydney, 1974.

J.V. Beckett, *The Agricultural Revolution*, Oxford, 1990.

Y-M. Berce (Trans. A Whitmore), *History of Peasant Revolts: The Social Origins of Rebellion in Early Modern France*, Oxford, 1990.

M. Berg, *The Age of Manufactures 1700-1820*, London, 1985.

M. Berg, 'Workers and Machinery in Eighteenth Century England', in Rule (ed).

J.H. Bettey, *Dorset*, Newton Abbot, 1974.

J.H. Bettey, *Wessex from AD 1000*, London, 1986.

J.H. Bettey, *Rural Life in Wessex 1500-1900*, Gloucester, 1987.

W. Boase, *The Folklore of Hampshire and the Isle of Wight*, London, 1976.

G.A. Body, *The administration of the Poorhouse in Dorset 1760-1834 with special reference to Agrarian Distress*, Typescript Ms., 2 Vols., 1967. Dorset Local Studies Library.

L. Bonfield, R. Smith & K. Wrightson (eds), *The World We Have Gained*, Cambridge, 1986.

E. Bradby, *Seend: A Wiltshire Village Past and Present*, Gloucester, 1981.

W. Branch Johnson, *The English Prison Hulks*, London, 1957.

E. Brill, *Life and Tradition on the Cotswolds*, Gloucester, 1990.

J. Brewer & J. Styles (eds), *An Ungovernable People: the English and their law in the 17th and 18th centuries*, London, 1980.

M. Brock, *The Great Reform Act*, London, 1973.

T. Buckland & J. Wood (eds), *Aspects of British Calendar Customs*, Sheffield, 1993.

P. Burke, *Popular culture in Early Modern Europe*, London, 1979.

J. Burnett, *A Social History of Housing*, Newton Abbot, 1978.

J. Burnett, *Plenty and Want: A social history of diet in England from 1815 to the present day*, London, 1979.

J. Burnett, 'Country Diet', in Mingay (ed), *Victorian Countryside*, Vol. II.

B. Bushaway, *By Rite: Custom, Ceremony and Community in England 1700-1880*, London, 1982.

B. Bushaway, 'Bulls, Ballads, Minstrels and Manors: Some Observations on the Defence of Custom in Eighteenth-Century England', in Buckland & Wood (eds).

R.W. Bushaway, 'Rite, Legitimation and Community in Southern England 1700-1850: the Ideology of Custom', in Stapleton (ed).

D. Buxton, *Berkshire of one hundred years ago*, Stroud, 1992.

J. Campbell-Kease, *A History of Hazelbury Bryan*, Hazelbury Bryan, 1983.

W.W. Capes, *Scenes of Rural Life in Hampshire among the Manors of Bramshott*, London, 1901.

M.J. Carter, *Peasants and Poachers: A study in rural disorder in Norfolk*, Woodbridge, 1980.

J.M. Chambers, *Hampshire Machine Breakers: The Story of the 1830 Riots*, Clifton, 1990.

J.M. Chambers, *Wiltshire Machine Breakers*, 2 Vols., Letchworth, 1993.

J.M. Chambers, *Rebels of the Field: Robert Mason and the convicts of the Eleanor*, Letchworth, 1995.

J.H. Chandler (ed), *Wiltshire Dissenters' Meeting House Certificates and Registrations 1689-1852*, Devizes, 1985.

J.H. Chandler, *Wessex Images*, Stroud, 1990.

A. Charlesworth, *Social Protest in a Rural Society: The Spatial Diffusion of the Captain Swing Disturbances 1830-1831*, Norwich, 1979.

A. Charlesworth, *An Atlas of Rural Protest in Britain 1548-1900*, London, 1983.

A. Charlesworth, 'The Development of the English Rural Proletariat and Social Protest 1700-1850: A Comment', in Reed & Wells (eds).

J.A. Chartres, 'Country Trades, Crafts and Professions', in Mingay (ed), *Agrarian*

*History*.

S.G. Checkland, *The rise of industrial society in England 1815-1885*, London, 1964.

S.G. & E.O.A. Checkland (eds), *The Poor Law Report of 1834*, Harmondsworth, 1974.

C. Chenevix Trench, *The Poacher and the Squire: A History of Poaching and Game Preservation in England*, London, 1967.

C.H. Church, *Europe in 1830: Revolution and Political Change*, London, 1983.

L.A. Clarkson, 'The Manufacture of Leather', in Mingay (ed), *Agrarian History*.

J.S. Cockburn (ed), *Crime in England 1550-1800*, London, 1977.

E.J.T. Collins, 'The Coppice and Underwood Trades', in Mingay (ed), *Agrarian History*.

A.C. Cox, *Index to the County Records*, Dorchester, 1938.

E. Crittall (ed), *Victoria History of the County of Wiltshire*, Vol. 4, London, 1959.

B. Croucher, *The Village in the Valley: A History of Ramsbury*, Ramsbury, 1986.

F. Crowley (ed), *A Documentary History of Australia*, Vol. 1, Melbourne, 1980.

H.C. Darby (ed), *New Historical Geography of England after 1600*, Cambridge, 1976.

H.C. Darby, 'The Age of the Improver 1600-1800', in Darby (ed).

M.J. Daunton, 'Housing', in Thompson (ed), Vol. 2.

M.F. Davies, *Life in an English Village: An Economic and Historical Study of the Parish of Corsley in Wiltshire*, London, 1909.

P. Deane, *The First Industrial Revolution*, Cambridge, 1965.

P. Deane & W.A. Cole, *British Economic Growth 1688-1959: Trends and Structure*, Cambridge, 1969.

A. Delves, 'Popular Recreation and Social Conflict in Derby', in Yeo & Yeo (eds).

A. Digby, *Pauper Palaces*, London, 1978.

A. Digby, 'The Rural Poor', in Mingay (ed), *Victorian Countryside*, Vol. II.

P.H. Ditchfield, *Old English Customs*, London, 1896.

P.H. Ditchfield, *Country Folk: A Pleasant Company*, London, 1923.

M. Dixson, *The Real Matilda: Women and Identity in Australia 1788 to 1975*, Ringwood, 1976.

J. & P. Drury, *A Tisbury History*, Tisbury, 1980.

J.P.D. Dunbabin (ed), *Rural Discontent in Nineteenth Century Britain*, London, 1974.

I. Dyck, *William Cobbett and Rural Popular Culture*, Cambridge, 1992.

C. Emsley, *Crime and Society in England 1750-1900*, London, 1987.

A. Ereira, *The People's England*, London, 1981.

E.J. Evans, *The Forging of the Modern State: Early Industrial Britain 1783-1876*, Harlow, 1983.

S. Evans, *Historic Sydney as seen by its Early Artists*, Sydney, 1983.

C. Fisher, *Custom, Work and Market Capitalism: The Forest of Dean Colliers 1788-1888*, London, 1981.

S. Fitzgerald & C. Keating, *Millers Point, The Urban Village*, Sydney, 1991.

B.H. Fletcher, *Ralph Darling: A Governor Maligned*, Melbourne, 1984.

R. Floud, K. Wachter & A. Gregory, *Height, Health and History: Nutritional Status in the United Kingdom 1750-1980*, Cambridge, 1990.

R. Foster, *The Politics of Power: Wellington and the Hampshire Gentlemen 1820-52*, Hemel Hempstead, 1990.

A. Fox, *History and Heritage: The Social Origins of the British Industrial Relations System*, London, 1985.

N. Fox, *Berkshire to Botany Bay*, Newbury, 1996.

A. Frost, *Arthur Phillip, 1788-1814, His Voyaging*, Melbourne, 1987.

A. Frost, *Botany Bay Mirages: Illusions of Australia's Convict Beginning*, Melbourne, 1994.

G.E. Fussell, *The English Rural Labourer*, London, 1949.

I. Gandy, *The Heart of a Village: An Intimate History of Aldbourne*, Bradford-on-Avon, 1975.

N. Gash, *Aristocracy and People 1815-1865*, London, 1979.

V.A.C. Gatrell, *The Hanging Tree: Execution and the English People 1770-1868*, Oxford, 1994.

E. Gauldie, 'Country Homes', in Mingay (ed), *Victorian Countryside*, Vol. II.

R. Gifford, 'Guy Fawkes: Who Celebrated What? A Closer Look at the 5th November in the light of Captain Swing', in Buckland & Wood (eds).

K. Gilbert, *Life in a Hampshire Village: the history of Ashley*, Winchester, 1992.

J.M. Golby & A.W. Purdue, *The Civilisation of the Crowd: Popular Culture in England 1750-1900*, New York, 1985.

D. Grace, 'The Agricultural Engineering Industry', in Mingay (ed), *Agrarian History*.

H. Graham, *The Annals of the Yeomanry Cavalry of Wiltshire*, Liverpool, 1886.

H.D. Graham & T.R. Gurr (eds), *Violence in America: Historical and Comparative Perspectives*, New York, 1969.

B. Greaves, *The Story of Bathurst*, Sydney, 1964.

F.E. Green, *The Tyranny of the Countryside*, London, 1913.

P. Grimshaw, C. McConville & E. McEwen (eds), *Families in Colonial Australia*, Sydney, 1985.

E. Halevy, *A History of the English People in 1815: Book I*, London, 1937.

J.L. & B. Hammond, *The Village Labourer 1760-1832*, London, 1920.

N. Hammond, *Rural Life in the Vale of the White Horse 1780-1914*, Reading, 1974.

A. Harris, 'Changes in the Early Railway Age 1800-1850', in Darby (ed).

J.F.C. Harrison, *The Common People*, London, 1984.

M. Harrison, *Crowds and History: Mass Phenomena in English Towns 1790-1835*, Cambridge, 1988.

N. Harvey, *A History of Farm Buildings in England and Wales*, Newton Abbot, 1984.

D.T. Hawkings, *Criminal Ancestors: A Guide to Historical Criminal Records in England and Wales*, Stroud, 1992.

E.G. Hayden, *Travels Round My Village: a Berkshire book*, London, 1901.

K. & T. Henderson, *Early Illawarra: people, houses, life*, Canberra, 1983.

E. Hicks, 'William Cox', in Pike (ed).

J.B. Hirst, *Convict Society and its Enemies: A history of early New South Wales*, Sydney, 1983.

E.J. Hobsbawm, *Labouring Men*, London, 1964.

E.J. Hobsbawm & G. Rudé, *Captain Swing*, London, 1969.

B.A. Holderness & M. Turner (eds), *Land, Labour and Agriculture 1700-1920: Essays for Gordon Mingay*, London, 1991.

C. Hole, *British Folk Customs*, London, 1976.

P. Hollis (ed), *Class and Conflict in Nineteenth Century England 1815-1850*, London, 1973.

H. Hopkins, *The Long Affray: Poaching Wars 1760-1914*, London, 1986.

P. Horn, *The Rural World 1780-1850: Social Change in the English Countryside*, London, 1980.

P. Horn, *A Georgian Parson and his Village. The Story of David Davies 1742-1819*, Abingdon, 1981.

A. Howkins, *Reshaping Rural England: A Social History 1850-1925*, London, 1991.

A. Howkins, 'The English farm labourer in the nineteenth century: farm, family and community', in Short (ed).

P. Hudson (ed), *Regions and Industries: a perspective on the Industrial Revolution in Britain*, Cambridge, 1989.

W.H. Hudson, *A Shepherds Life*, London, 1981.

R. Hughes, *The Fatal Shore: A History of the Transportation of Convicts to Australia*, London, 1987.

A.L. Humphreys, *The Berkshire Book of Song, Rhyme and Steeple Chime*, London, 1935.

E. Huntley, *Boxford Barleycorn: the story of an English village*, Abingdon, 1970.

J.P. Huzel, 'The Labourer and the Poor Law 1750-1850', in Mingay (ed), *Agrarian History*.

M. Ignatieff, *A Just Measure of Pain: The Penitentiary in the Industrial Revolution 1750-1850*, London, 1978.

D.N. Jeans, *An Historical Geography of New South Wales to 1901*, Sydney, 1972.

R. Jefferies, *The Hills and the Vale*, London, 1909.

R. Jefferies, *Field and Hedgerow*, [1889], London, 1948.

R. Jefferies, *Field and Farm: Essays now first collected, with some found MSS*, London, 1957.

R. Jefferies, *The Amateur Poacher*, [1879], Rhyl, 1973.

R. Jefferies, *The Toilers of the Field*, [1880], London, 1981.

R. Jefferies, *Hodge and his Masters,* [1880], Stroud, 1992.

B. Jones (ed), *The Poems of William Barnes,* Vol. I, London, 1962.

D. Jones, *Before Rebecca: Popular Protest in Wales 1793-1835,* London, 1973.

D. Jones, 'Rural Crime and Protest', in Mingay (ed), *Victorian Countryside,* Vol. II.

E.L. Jones, *The Development of English Agriculture 1815-1873,* London, 1968.

E.L. Jones, *Agriculture and the Industrial Revolution,* Oxford, 1974.

I Jones, *The Stalbridge Inheritance 1780-1854,* Dorchester, 1993.

H.B. Kendall, *The Origin and History of the Primitive Methodist Church,* 2 Vols., London, nd.

D. Kent & N. Townsend, *Joseph Mason, Assigned Convict 1831-1837: Doomed to the earth's remotest region,* Melbourne, 1996.

B. Kerr, *Bound to the Soil: A Social History of Dorset 1750-1918,* London, 1968.

M. Kitch, 'Population movement and migration in pre-industrial England', in Short (ed).

J. Knott, *Popular Opposition to the 1834 Poor Law,* London, 1986.

A. Kussmaul, *Servants in Husbandry in Early Modern England,* Cambridge, 1981.

A, Kussmaul (ed), *The Autobiography of Joseph Mayett of Quainton 1783-1839,* Aylesbury, 1986.

E.H. Lane Poole, *Damerham and Martin: A Study in Local History,* Tisbury, 1976.

B. Machin, *Rural Housing: An Historical Approach,* London, 1994.

R.B. Madgwick, *Immigration into Eastern Australia 1788-1851,* Sydney, 1969.

R.W. Malcolmson, *Popular Recreations in English Society,* Cambridge, 1973.

R.W. Malcolmson, 'Leisure', in Mingay (ed), *Victorian Countryside,* Vol. II.

R.W. Malcolmson, 'A set of ungovernable people': the Kingswood colliers in the eighteenth century', in Brewer & Styles (eds).

J. DeL. Mann, *The Cloth Industry in the West of England,* Oxford, 1971.

J.E. Mann, *Hampshire Customs, Curiosities and Country Lore,* Southampton, 1994.

J.D. Marshall, *The Old Poor Law 1795-1834,* Basingstoke, 1985.

E.W. Martin, *The Secret People: English Village Life After 1750,* London, 1954.

G. Martin (ed), *The Founding of Australia: The Argument about Australia's Origins,* Sydney, 1988.

D. Mills, 'Peasants and Conflict in Nineteenth-Century Rural England: A Comment on Two Recent Articles', in Reed & Wells (eds).

D. Mills & B. Short, 'Social Change and Social Conflict in Nineteenth-Century England: The Use of the Open-Closed Village Model', in Reed & Wells (eds).

W. Minchinton (ed), *Agricultural Improvement: Medieval and Modern,* Exeter, 1981.

G.E. Mingay (ed), *The Victorian Countryside,* 2 Vols., London, 1981.

G.E. Mingay (ed), *The Unquiet Countryside,* London, 1989.

G.E. Mingay (ed), *The Agrarian History of England and Wales, Vol. VI, 1750-1850,* Cambridge, 1989.

G.E. Mingay, *A Social History of the English Countryside,* London, 1990.

G.E. Mingay, 'Rural war: the life and times of Captain Swing', in Mingay (ed), *Unquiet Countryside.*

B.R. Mitchell & P. Deane, *Abstract of British Historical Statistics,* Cambridge, 1971.

B.R. Mitchell, *European Historical Statistics 1750-1975,* New York, 1980.

B.R. Mitchell, *British Historical Statistics,* Cambridge, 1988.

P.B. Munsche, 'The Game Laws in Wiltshire', in Cockburn (ed).

B. Nairn, 'Hannibal Macarthur', in Pike (ed).

J.M. Neeson, *Commoners: Common Right, Enclosure and Social Change in England 1700 -1820,* Cambridge, 1993.

M.D. Neuman, *The Speenhamland county; poverty and the poor laws in Berkshire 1782 -1834,* New York, 1982.

H. Newby, *The Deferential Worker: A Study of Farm Workers in East Anglia,* London, 1977.

H. Newby, *Country Life: A Social History of Rural England,* London, 1987.

S. Nicholas (ed), *Convict Workers: Reinterpreting Australia's Past,* Sydney, 1988.

S. Nicholas & P.R. Shergold, 'Convicts as Migrants', 'Convicts as Workers', 'A Labour Aristocracy in Chains', in Nicholas (ed).

I.H. Nicholson, *Shipping Arrivals and Departures 1826-40,* Canberra, 1977.

J. Obelkevich, 'Religion', in Thompson (ed), Vol. 3.

D. Oddy & D. Miller, *The Making of the Modern British Diet,* London, 1976.

D.J. Oddy, 'Food, drink and nutrition', in Thompson (ed), Vol. 2.

W.H. Oldham (ed), *Britain's Convicts to the Colonies,* Sydney, 1990.

D. Oxley, 'Female Convicts', in Nicholas (ed).

G.W. Oxley, *Poor Relief in England and Wales 1601-1834,* Newton Abbot, 1974.

G. Padden (ed), *Tolpuddle: An historical account through the eyes of George Loveless,* London, 1984.

W. Page & P.H. Ditchfield (eds), *Victoria History of the County of Berkshire,* Vol. 2, London, 1907.

W. Page (ed), *Victoria History of the County of Dorset,* Vol. 2, London, 1908.

W. Page (ed), *Victoria History of the County of Hampshire,* Vol. 5, London, 1912.

S.H. Palmer, *Police and Protest in England and Ireland 1780-1850,* Cambridge, 1988.

E.A. Payne, *The Baptists of Berkshire through three centuries,* London, 1951.

A.J. Peacock, *Bread or Blood: A Study of the Agrarian Riots in East Anglia in 1816,* London, 1965.

A.J. Peacock, 'Village radicalism in East Anglia 1800-1850', in Dunbabin (ed).

H. Pelling, *A History of British Trade Unionism,* Harmondsworth, 1963.

H. Perkin, *The Origins of Modern English Society,* London, 1969.

T.M. Perry, *Australia's First Frontier: The Spread of Settlement in New South Wales,* Melbourne, 1964.

H. Phelps Brown & S.V. Hopkins, *A Perspective of Wages and Prices,* London, 1981.

D. Philips, *Crime and Authority in Victorian England,* London, 1977.

D. Phillips, *Berkshire: A County History,* Newbury, 1993.

C. Phythian-Adams, 'Rural Culture', in Mingay (ed), *Victorian Countryside,* Vol. II.

D. Pike (ed), *Australian Dictionary of Biography,* Melbourne, 1966

E.R. Pillow, *Two Centuries of Winchester Methodism,* Winchester, 1985.

J.H. Porter, 'Crime in the countryside 1600-1800', in Mingay (ed), *Unquiet Countryside.*

J.H. Porter, 'The Development of Rural Society', in Mingay (ed), *Agrarian History.*

J.R. Poynter, *Society and Pauperism: English Ideas on Poor Relief 1795-1834,* Melbourne, 1969.

H.C. Prince, 'The Changing Rural Landscape 1750-1850', in Mingay (ed), *Agrarian History.*

H. Proudfoot, 'Fixing the Settlement upon a savage shore: Planning and Building', in Aplin (ed).

M. Quartly, 'Bending the Bars: Convict Women and the State', in Saunders & Evans (eds).

A. Randall, *Before the Luddites: Custom community and machinery in the English woollen industry 1776-1809,* Cambridge, 1991.

A. Randall, 'The Industrial Moral Economy of the Gloucestershire Weavers in the Eighteenth Century', in Rule (ed).

A. Randall, 'Work, Culture and Resistance to Machinery in the West of England Woollen Industry', in Hudson (ed).

B. Reay, *The Last Rising of the Agricultural Labourers: Rural Life and Protest in Nineteenth Century England,* Oxford, 1990.

M. Reed, 'Class and Conflict in Rural England: Some Reflections on a Debate', in Reed & Wells (eds).

M. Reed, 'Social Change and Social Conflict in Nineteenth-Century England: A Comment', in Reed & Wells (eds).

M. Reed & R. Wells (eds), *Class, Conflict and Protest in the English Countryside 1700-1880,* London, 1990.

D.A. Reid, 'Interpreting the Festival Calendar: Wakes and Fairs as Carnivals', in Storch (ed).

T.L. Richardson, 'Agricultural labourers' standards of living in Kent 1790-1840', in Oddy & Miller (eds).

T.L. Richardson, 'Agricultural Labourers' Wages and the Cost of Living in Essex 1790-1840: A Contribution to the Standard of Living Debate', in Holderness & Turner (eds).

L.L. Robson, *The Convict Settlers of Australia,* Melbourne, 1965.

K.H. Rogers & J.H. Chandler, *Early Trade Directories of Wiltshire,* Trowbridge, 1992.

L.T.C. Rolt, *Waterloo Ironworks, A History of Taskers of Andover 1809-1968,* Newton Abbot, 1969.

M.E. Rose, *The English Poor Law 1780-1930,* Newton Abbot, 1971.

S. Roud & P. Marsh, *Mumming Plays in Hampshire,* np., 1980.

G. Rudé, *The Crowd in History,* New York, 1964.

G. Rudé, *Paris and London in the 18th Century: Studies in Popular Protest,* London, 1970.

G. Rudé, *Protest and Punishment: The Story of the Social and Political Prisoners transported to Australia 1788-1868,* Oxford, 1978.

G. Rudé, *Criminal and Victim: Crime and Society in Nineteenth-Century England,* Oxford, 1985.

J. Rule, *The Labouring Classes in Early Industrial England 1750-1850,* London, 1986,

J. Rule (ed), *British Trade Unionism 1750-1850: The Formative Years,* Harlow, 1988.

J. Rule, 'Regional variations of food consumption amongst agricultural labourers', in Minchinton (ed).

L.S., *Untravelled Berkshire,* London, 1909.

M.R. Sainty & K.A. Johnson (eds), *Census of New South Wales: November 1828,* Sydney, 1985.

H.R. Salt, *Gleanings from forgotten fields: the story of the Berks. Baptist Association 1652-1907,* Reading, 1907.

J. Sambrook, *William Cobbett,* London, 1973.

K. Saunders & R. Evans (eds), *Gender Relations in Australia: Domination and Negotiation,* Sydney, 1992.

G. Scott, *Sydney's Highways of History,* Melbourne, 1958.

A.G.L. Shaw, *Convicts and the Colonies: A Study of Penal Transportation fron Great Britain and Ireland to Australia and other parts of the British Empire,* London, 1966.

B. Short (ed), *The English Rural Community: Image and Analysis,* Cambridge, 1992.

P.M. Slocombe, *Wiltshire Farmhouses and Cottages 1500-1850,* Devizes, 1988.

B. Smith, *A Cargo of Women, Susannah Watson and the Convicts of the Princess Royal,* Sydney, 1988.

E.A. Smith (ed), *Reform or Revolution: A Diary of Reform in England 1830-32,* Stroud, 1992.

J.O. Smith, *One Monday in November: The Story of the Selborne and Headley Workhouse Riots of 1830,* Bordon, 1993.

K. Snell, *Annals of the Labouring Poor: social change and agrarian England 1660-1900,* Cambridge, 1985.

P. Southerton, *The Story of a Prison,* Reading, 1975.

P. Southerton, *Reading Gaol by Reading Town,* Stroud, 1993.

G. Spater, *William Cobbett: The Poor Man's Friend,* Vol. 2, Cambridge, 1982.

B. Stapleton (ed), *Conflict and Community in Southern England,* Stroud, 1992.

J. Stevenson, *Popular Disturbances in England 1700-1870,* London, 1979.

J. Stevenson, 'Bread or Blood', in Mingay (ed), *Unquiet Countryside.*

R.D. Storch (ed), *Popular Culture and Custom in Nineteenth Century England,* London, 1982.

R.D. Storch, 'Please to Remember the Fifth of November: Conflict Solidarity and Public Order in Southern England 1815-1900', 'Persistence and Change in Nineteenth Century Popular Culture' in Storch (ed).

E.J. Stowe, *Crafts of the Countryside,* London, 1948.

J.M. Stratton, *Agricultural Records AD 220-1968,* London, 1969.

S.B. Stribling, *History of the Wilts. and East Somerset Congregational Union 1797-1897,* Westbury, 1897.

W.H. Summers, *History of the Congregational churches in the Berks., South Oxon., and South Bucks. Association,* Newbury, 1905.

H. Sykes, *Once a Year: Some Traditional British Customs,* London, 1977.

W.E. Tate, *The Parish Chest: A Study of the Records of Parochial Administration in England,* Cambridge, 1969.

G. Taylor, *The Problem of Poverty 1660-1874,* London, 1969.

J. Taylor, *Memories of Old Berkshire,* Newbury, 1957.

E.P. Thompson, *The Making of the English Working Class,* Harmondsworth, 1968.

E.P. Thompson, *Customs in Common,* London, 1991.

F.M.L. Thompson (ed), *The Cambridge Social History of Britain 1750-1950,* 3 Vols., Cambridge, 1990.

C. Tilly, *Popular Contention in Great Britain, 1758-1834,* Cambridge Mass., 1995

C. Tilly, 'Collective Violence in European Perspective', in Graham & Gurr (eds).

M.E. Turner, *English Parliamentary Enclosure: Its Historical Geography and Economic History,* Folkestone, 1980.

V. Turner, *The Ritual Process: Structure and Anti-Structure,* London, 1969.

W. Turner, *Riot: The Story of the Lancashire Loombreakers of 1826,* Preston, 1992.

J.S. Udal, *Dorsetshire Folk-lore,* Hertford, 1922.

D. Underdown, *Fire from Heaven: Life in an English Town in the Seventeenth Century,* London, 1992.

A. Verey, S. Sampson, A. French & S. Frost, *The Berkshire Yeomanry: 200 Years of Yeoman Service,* Stroud, 1994.

B. Watkin, *A History of Wiltshire,* Chichester, 1989.

M.B. Weinstock, *Old Dorset,* Newton Abbot, 1967.

R. Wells, 'The Development of the English Rural Proletariat and Social Protest 1700-1850', 'Social Conflict and Protest in the English Countryside in the Early Nineteenth Century: A Rejoinder', 'Social Protest, Class, Conflict and Consciousness in the English Countryside 1700-1880', in Reed & Wells (eds).

R. Wells, 'Popular Protest and Social Crime: the Evidence of Criminal Gangs in Southern England 1790-1860', in Stapleton (ed).

R. Whitlock, *The Folklore of Wiltshire,* London, 1976.

R. Whitlock, *A Calendar of Country Customs,* London, 1978.

R. Whitlock, *A Victorian Village*, London, 1990.

A. Williams, *A Wiltshire Village*, London, 1912.

A. Williams, *Villages of the White Horse*, London, 1913.

C. Williams, *Basildon: An Illustrated History of a Thameside Parish*, Reading, 1994.

J. Woodforde, *Farm Buildings*, London, 1983.

A.R. Wright & T.E. Lones, *British Calendar Customs*, 3 Vols., London 1936-40.

D.G. Wright, *Popular Radicalism: The Working-Class Experience 1780-1880*, London, 1988.

E.A. Wrigley, 'Men on the Land and Men in the Countryside: employment in agriculture in early nineteenth-century England', in Bonfield, Smith & Wrightson (eds).

E. & S. Yeo, *Popular Culture and Class Conflict, 1590-1914*, Brighton, 1983.

## VI Articles.

'Thomas Hilliker', *Wiltshire and Somerset Courier*, Jan. 1964, pp. 22-3,30.

'A Very English Rising', *Times Literary Supplement*, 11 Sept. 1969, pp. 989-92.

A. Atkinson, 'Sunshine from Frost', *The Push from the Bush: A Bulletin of Social History*, 26, 1988, pp. 9-23.

A. Atkinson, 'The First Plans for Governing New South Wales, 1786-87', *Australian Historical Studies*, 24, 1990, pp. 22-40.

J. Barber, 'The Agricultural Riots of 1830', *Eastleigh Local History Society Occasional Paper*,16, 1986.

D.A. Baugh, 'The cost of poor relief in south-east England 1790-1834', *Economic History Review*, 28, 1975, pp. 50-68.

M. Blaug, 'The myth of the Old Poor law and the Making of the New', *Journal of Economic History*, 23, 1963, pp. 151-84.

M. Blaug, 'The poor law report re-examined', *Journal of Economic History*, 24, 1964, pp.224-45.

A. Booth, 'Food riots in North-West England 1790-1801', *Past and Present*, 77, 1977, pp. 84-107.

G.R. Boyer, 'The Old Poor Law and the Agricultural Labour Market in Southern England: An Empirical Analysis', *Journal of Economic History*, 46, 1986, pp. 113-35.

D. Byrnes, 'Emptying the Hulks, Duncan Campbell and the First Three Fleets to Australia', *The Push from the Bush: A Bulletin of Social History*, 24, 1987, pp. 2-24.

J.F. Campbell, 'The Valley of the Tank Stream', *Royal Australian Historical Society Journal and Proceedings*, 10, 1924, pp. 63-102.

F.A. Carrington, 'On Certain Wiltshire Customs', *Wiltshire Archaeological and Natural History Magazine*, 1, 1854, pp. 68-91.

E.J.T. Collins, 'Harvest Technology and Labour Supply in Britain 1790-1870', *Economic History Review,* 22, 1969, pp. 453-73.

C.H. Curry, 'The Law of Marriage and Divorce in New South Wales 1788-1850', *Royal Australian Historical Society Journal and Proceedings,* 41, 1955, pp. 97-114.

T. Davison, 'Plough rituals in England and Scotland', *Agricultural History Review,* 7, 1959, pp. 27-37.

P. Dunkley, 'Paternalism, the Magistracy and Poor Relief in England 1795-1834', *International Review of Social History,* 24, 1979, pp. 371-97.

B. Dyster, 'A Series of Reversals: Male Convicts in New South Wales 1820-21', *The Push from the Bush: A Bulletin of Social History,* 25, 1987, pp. 18-36.

B. Earnshaw, 'Computerising the Convicts', *History: Magazine of the Royal Australian Historical Society,* 37, 1994, pp. 6-7.

A.R. Ekirch, 'Great Britain's Secret Convict Trade to America 1783-84', *Historical Review,* 89, 1984, pp. 1285-91.

E.J. Evans, 'Some reasons for the growth of English rural anti-clericalism', *Past and Present,* 66, 1975, pp. 84-104.

S.G. Foster, 'Convict Assignment in New South Wales in the 1830s', *The Push from the Bush: A Bulletin of Social History,* 15, 1983, pp. 35-80.

W. Foster, 'Hartley, The Gateway to the West', *Royal Australian Historical Society Journal and Proceedings,* 18, 1932, pp. 207-45.

N.E. Fox, 'The spread of the threshing machine in central southern England', *Agricultural History Review,* 26, 1978, pp. 26-8.

N. Gash, 'Rural Unemployment 1815-34', *Economic History Review,* 6, 1935, pp. 90-3.

F. Gilmour, 'A Mummers' Play from Limpley Stoke', *Wiltshire Archaeological and Natural History Magazine,* 83, 1990, pp. 155-62.

E. Goffman, 'Symbols of Class Status', *British Journal of Sociology,* 2, 1951, pp. 294-304.

A.G. Harfield, 'Captain William Wyndham of the Hindon Troop Royal Wiltshire Yeomanry', *Journal of the Society for Army Historical Research,* 42, 1963, pp. 27-35.

E. Hawkins, 'Journey from Sydney to Bathurst in 1822', *Royal Australian Historical Society Journal and Proceedings,* 9, 1923, pp. 177-97

G. Hendy-Pooley, 'Early History of Bathurst and its Surroundings, 1, 1905, pp. 230-36.

P.R.A. Hinde, H.R. Davies & D.M. Kirby, 'Hampshire Village Populations in the Nineteenth Century', *Southern History,* 15, 1993, pp. 140-61.

E.J. Hobsbawm, 'Economic fluctuations and some social movements since 1800', *Economic History Review,* 5, 1952, pp. 1-25.

S. Horrell & J. Humphries, 'Old questions, new data: Families' living standards in the Industrial Revolution', *Journal of Economic History,* 52, 1992, pp. 849-80.

K. Humphery, 'A New Era of Existence: Convict Transportation and the Authority of the Surgeon in Colonial Australia', *Labour History,* 1990, pp. 59-72.

E.H. Hunt & F.W. Botham, 'Wages in Britain during the Industrial Revolution', *Economic History Review,* 40, 1987, pp. 380-99.

J.P. Huzel, 'Malthus, the Poor Law and Population in Early Nineteenth Century England', *Economic History Review,* 22, 1969, pp. 430-52.

J.P. Huzel, 'The Demographic Impact of the Old Poor Law: More Reflections on Malthus', *Economic History Review,* 33, 1980, 367-81.

K.S. Inglis, 'Patterns of religious worship in 1851', *Journal of Ecclesiastical History,* 2, 1960, pp. 74-86.

M. Ingram, 'Ridings, rough music and the reform of popular culture in early modern England', *Past and Present,* 105, 1984, pp. 79-113.

J. Jervis, 'Settlement in the Picton and the Oaks District', *Royal Australian Historical Society Journal and Proceedings,* 27, 1941, pp. 276-300.

E.L. Jones, 'Eighteenth century changes in Hampshire chalkland farming', *Agricultural History Review,* 8, 1960, pp. 5-19.

E.L. Jones, 'The Agricultural Labour Market in England 1793-1872', *Economic History Review,* 17, 1965, pp. 322-38.

D. Kent, 'Decorative Bodies: The Significance of Convicts' Tattoos', *Journal of Australian Studies,* No. 53, 1997, pp.78-88.

D. Kent & N. Townsend, 'Deborah Oxley's 'Female Convicts': An Accurate View of Working-Class Women?', *Labour History,* 65, 1993, pp. 179-99.

D. Kent & N. Townsend, 'The Men of the *Eleanor,* 1831: A Case Study of the Hulks and the Voyage to New South Wales', *The Great Circle: Journal of the Australian Association for Maritime History,* 17, 1995, pp. 109-118.

D. Kent & N. Townsend, 'Some Aspects of Colonial Marriage: a Case Study of the Swing Protesters', *Labour History,* 74, 1998, pp. 40-53.

B. Kerr, 'The Dorset Agricultural Labourer 1750-1850', *Proceedings of the Dorset Natural History and Archaeological Society,* 84, 1962, pp. 158-77.

G.A. King, 'Old Sydney - Grave and Gay', *Royal Australian Historical Society Journal and Proceedings,* 21, 1935, pp. 269-287.

P.H. Lindert & J.G. Williamson, 'English Workers' Living Standards during the Industrial Revolution: A New Look', *Economic History Review,* 36, 1983, pp. 1-25.

S. Macdonald, 'The progress of the early threshing machine', *Agricultural History Review,* 23, 1, 1975, pp. 63-77.

S. Macdonald, 'Further Progress with the Early Threshing Machines: A Rejoinder', *Agricultural History Review,* 26, 1, 1978, pp. 29-32.

P. Mandler, 'The Making of the New Poor Law *Redivivus*', *Past and Present,* 117, 1987, pp. 131-57.

P. Mandler, 'Tories and Paupers: Christian Political Economy and the Making of the

New Poor Law', *The Historical Journal,* 33, 1, 1990, pp. 81-103.

H.C. March, 'Dorset Folklore Collected in 1897', *Folklore,* 10, 1898, pp. 478-89, 11, 1899, pp. 107-112.

M. Maynard, 'Civilian Clothing and Fabric Supplies: The Development of Fashionable Dressing in Sydney 1790-1830', *Textile History,* 21, 1990, pp. 87-100.

J. McDonald & R. Schlomowitz, 'Mortality on Convict Voyages to Australia 1788-1868', *Social Science History,* 13, 1989, pp. 285-313.

D. Mills, 'The Quality of Life in Melbourn, Cambridgeshire, in the Period 1800-50', *International Review of Social History,* 23, 1978, pp. 382-404.

J. Mokyr, 'Is there still life in the pessimist case? Consumption during the Industrial Revolution 1790-1850', *Journal of Economic History,* 48, 1988, pp. 69-92.

J.M. Neeson, 'The Opponents of Enclosure in Eighteenth-Century Northamptonshire', *Past and Present,* 105, 1984, pp. 114-39.

M.D. Neuman, 'A Suggestion Regarding the Origin of the Speenhamland Plan', *English Historical Review,* 84, 1969, pp. 317-22.

S. Nicholas & R. Steckel, 'Heights and living standards of English workers during the early years of industrialisation 1770-1815', *Journal of Economic History,* 51, 1991, pp. 937-57.

W.D. O'Sullivan, 'Hartley N.S.W.', *Royal Australian Historical Society Journal and Proceedings,* 1907-9, pp. 299-307.

W.H.P. Okeden, 'The agricultural riots in Dorset in 1830', *Proceedings of the Dorset Natural History and Archaeological Society,* 52, 1930, pp. 75-95.

T. Packwood, 'The Labourers' Revolt', *Mortimer Local History Group,* 1980, pp. 17-20.

J. Philipp, 'Traditional Historical Narrative and Action-oriented (or Ethnographic) History', *Historical Studies,* 20, 1983, pp. 339-52.

S. Piggott, 'Berkshire mummers' plays and other folklore', *Folklore,* 39, 3, 1928, pp. 271-81.

R. Quinault, 'The French Revolution of 1830 and Parliamentary Reform', *History,* 79, 257, 1994, pp. 377-93.

A. Randall, 'The Shearmen and the Wiltshire Outrages of 1802. Trade Unionism and Industrial Violence', *Social History,* 8, 1982, pp. 283-304.

A. Randall, 'Industrial Conflict and Economic Change: The Regional Context of the Industrial Revolution', *Southern History,* 13, 1992, pp. 74-92.

E. Richards, 'Captain Swing in the West Midlands', *International Review of Social History,* 19, 1974, pp. 86-99.

J. Ritchie, 'Towards Ending an Unclean Thing: The Molesworth Committee and the Abolition of Transportation to New South Wales, 1837-1840', *Historical Studies,* 17, 1976, pp. 144-64.

T. Roach, 'The Riots of 1830', *Hampshire Notes and Queries,* 8, 1893, pp. 97-8.

P. Robinson, 'Royal Justice and Folk Justice: Conflict Arising over a Skimmington at Pitterne in 1857', *Wiltshire Archaeological and Natural History Magazine*, 83, 1990, pp. 147-54.

G. Rudé, 'Captain Swing in New South Wales', *Historical Studies*, 11, 1965, pp. 467-80.

J. Rule, 'Social crime in the rural south in the eighteenth and early nineteenth centuries', *Southern History*, 1, 1979, pp. 135-53.

'S', 'The Swing Riots', *Hampshire Notes and Queries*, 3, 1887, pp. 46-8.

R.S. Schofield, 'Dimensions of Illiteracy 1750-1850', *Explorations in Economic History*, 10, 1973, pp. 437-54.

J.S. Sharland, 'The Labourers' Revolt in West Berkshire', *Berkshire Committee Bulletin*, 2, 1953, pp. 9-15.

K.D. Snell, 'Agricultural seasonal unemployment, the standard of living and womens' work in the south and east 1690-1860', *Economic History Review*, 34, 1981, pp. 407-37.

J. Spurway, 'The Growth of Family History in Australia', *The Push: A Journal of Early Australian Social History*, 27, 1989, pp. 53-111.

W.A. Steel, 'The History of Carcoar', *Royal Australian Historical Society Journal and Proceedings*, 17, 1931, pp. 239-88.

W.A. Steel, 'The First Land Grant Beyond the Blue Mountains', *Royal Australian Historical Society Journal and Proceedings*, 29, 1938, pp. 313-18.

W.A. Steel, 'Dunn's Plains, Rockley. Its History and Personalities', *Royal Australian Historical Society Journal and Proceedings*, 26, 1940, pp. 197-234.

M. Sturma, 'Eye of the Beholder: The Stereotype of Women Convicts 1788-1852', *Labour History*, 34, 1978, pp. 3-10.

W.E. Tate,'A Handlist of Wiltshire Enclosure Acts and Awards', *Wiltshire Archaeological and Natural History Magazine*, 51, 1945-47, pp. 127-73.

E.P. Thompson, 'The Moral Economy of the English Crowd in the Eighteenth Century', *Past and Present*, 50, 1971, pp. 76-136.

N. Townsend, 'The Molesworth Enquiry: Does the Report Fit the Evidence?', *Journal of Australian Studies*, 1, 1977, pp. 33-51.

N. Townsend, 'Masters and Men and the Myall Creek Massacre', *The Push from the Bush: A Bulletin of Social History*, 20, 1985, pp. 4-32.

M. Turner, 'Economic Protest in Rural Society: Opposition to Parliamentary Enclosure in Buckinghamshire', *Southern History*, 10, 1988, pp. 94-128.

J.A. Vickers, 'Early Methodism in South-East Hampshire', *Portsmouth Archives Review*, 4, 1979-80, pp. 25-43.

J.H. Watson, 'Origin of Names in Port Jackson', *Royal Australian Historical Society Journal and Proceedings*, 4, 1918, pp. 361-68.

J. Weingarth, 'The Head of Sydney Cove', *Royal Australian Historical Society Journal and Proceedings*, 10, 1924, pp. 287-300.

R. Wells, 'Popular Protest and Social Crime: The Evidence of Criminal Gangs in Rural Southern England 1790-1860', *Southern History*, 13, 1991, pp. 32-81.

R. Wells, 'Migration, the Law and Parochial Policy in Eighteenth and Early Nineteenth Century England', *Southern History*, 15, 1993, pp. 86-139.

G.A. Wood, 'Convicts', *Royal Australian Historical Society Journal*, 8, 4, 1922, pp. 177-208.

J.C. Woodiwiss, 'Captain Swing in Hampshire', *Hampshire Review*, 17, 1953, pp. 72-5.

H. Wright, 'Sites of the New South Wales Treasury', *Royal Australian Historical Society Journal and Proceedings*, 4, 1918, pp. 279-283.

## VII. Theses.

M.J. Belcher, 'The Child in New South Wales Society 1820-1837', Ph.D., University of New England, 1982.

E. Billinge, 'Rural Crime and Protest in Wiltshire 1830-1875', Ph.D., University of Kent, 1984.

A.M. Colson, 'The Revolt of the Hampshire Agricultural Labourers and its causes 1812-1831', M.A., University of London, 1937.

J.L. Gayler, 'The Relief of the Poor in Tilehurst 1770-1850', Oxford Certificate in Local History, 1983.

M.D. Neuman, 'Aspects of Poverty and Poor Law Administration in Berkshire 1782-1834', Ph.D., University of California, 1967.

D. Parton, 'Faces from a Crowd: The Men of the *Marquis of Wellington* 1815', M.Litt., University of New England, 1993.

D.S. Stafford, 'A Gilbert Act Parish: the Relief and Treatment of the Poor in Hungerford Berks. 1783-1834', M.Phil., University of Reading, 1983.

J.K. White, 'A Master and his Men: A Different Perspective on the Revd. Samuel Marsden in N.S.W., 1794-1851', M. Litt., University of New England, 1994.

# Index of people and places